www.wadsworth.com

wadsworth.com is the World Wide Web site for Wadsworth and is your direct source to dozens of online resources.

At *wadsworth.com* you can find out about supplements, demonstration software, and student resources. You can also send e-mail to many of our authors and preview new publications and exciting new technologies.

wadsworth.com
Changing the way the world learns®

FROM THE WADSWORTH SERIES IN SPEECH COMMUNICATION

The Challenge of Effective Speaking

The Challenge of

Effective Speaking

Eleventh Edition

Rudolph F. Verderber

University of Cincinnati

Wadsworth
Thomson Learning

Australia • Canada • Denmark • Japan • Mexico • New Zealand • Philippines • Puerto Rico
Singapore • South Africa • Spain • United Kingdom • United States

Executive Editor: Deirdre Cavanaugh
Development Editor: Maryanne Koschier
Associate Development Editor: Megan Gilbert
Editorial Assistant: Dory Schaeffer
Executive Marketing Manager: Stacey Purviance
Marketing Assistant: Kenneth Baird
Project Editor: Cathy Linberg
Print Buyer: Barbara Britton
Permissions Editor: Susan Walters

Production Service: Cecile Joyner/The Cooper Company
Photo Researcher: Terri Wright
Copy Editor: Margaret C. Tropp
Action Steps Illustrator: Peter Coates Illustration
Compositor: Progressive Publishing Alternatives
Text and Cover Designer: Cloyce Wall
Cover Image: Peter Coates Illustration
Cover Printer: Phoenix Color
Printer/Binder: World Color Book Services, Taunton

Printed in the United States of America
1 2 3 4 5 6 7 03 02 01 00 99

**Library of Congress
Cataloging-in-Publication Data**
Verderber, Rudolph F.
    The challenge of effective speaking/Rudolph F. Verderber.
        p.   cm.
    Includes bibliographical references and index.
    ISBN 0-534-56250-7
    1. Public speaking.   I. Title.
PN4121.V4 2000
99-20915
808.5'1—dc21

Annotated Instructor's Edition ISBN 0-534-56251-5

For more information, contact

**Wadsworth/Thomson Learning
10 Davis Drive
Belmont, CA 94002-3098
USA
www.wadsworth.com**

International Headquarters
Thomson Learning
290 Harbor Drive, 2nd Floor
Stamford, CT 06902-7477
USA

UK/Europe/Middle East
Thomson Learning
Berkshire House
168-173 High Holborn
London WC1V 7AA
United Kingdom

Asia
Thomson Learning
60 Albert Street #15-01
Albert Complex
Singapore 189969

Canada
Nelson/Thomson Learning
1120 Birchmount Road
Scarborough, Ontario M1K 5G4
Canada

brief contents

contents

Chapter 6　Organizing and Outlining the Speech Body   96

Chapter 7　Organizing and Outlining Introductions and Conclusions   118

Part Three ■ Informative and Persuasive Speaking

Chapter 12   Principles and Practices of Informative Speaking   224

Chapter 13   Principles of Persuasive Speaking   254

Chapter 16   Leading Problem-Solving Groups   324

preface

Students of the 21st century are challenged by the diversity of media available to them in preparing for and giving speeches and the diversity of audience needs and interests. With this edition, I have not only updated examples, theory, and references but also offer the students a variety of new materials that will help them more quickly become competent communicators in today's world.

This new edition offers more guidance in technology and also shows the students how to work systematically through the necessary steps of speech preparation. Overall, this 11th edition is designed to capitalize on the teaching methodology that has made *The Challenge of Effective Speaking* a leader in its field. I firmly believe that students who apply themselves to learning the material in this book will be able to give the very best speeches possible. Highlights of the new edition include:

- **Expanded Coverage of Technology.** Greatly expanded and updated coverage of technology throughout the text helps meet the needs of the students of the 21st century. Students are given practical information on utilizing electronic resources, as well as evaluating on-line material. In addition, the text provides specific guidelines for creating computer-generated visual aids.

- **Speeches for Today's Students.** The text is replete with new sample speeches as well as topic suggestions that reflect contemporary issues and concerns.

- **Enhanced Skill Development.** The new edition further extends the strong coverage of skills of earlier editions with even more chapter-by-chapter practical advice on gaining speech skills. For example, in many chapters key steps in the speech preparation process are illustrated with specific examples that help walk the student through the process. Also, exercises and activities throughout give students practical experience in honing skills.

- **More on Outlining.** Because beginning students find outlines to be key learning tools, there are now two chapters on the organizing and outlining process, and more outline samples in the text.

- **Complete Update.** In addition to including contemporary examples throughout that students can relate to, as well as the latest in technology, the book's scholarship has been updated throughout.

New and Enhanced Features

Building on features that received high praise in previous editions, I have developed the following features to further enhance the learning experience.

- **On-line Exercises.** Exercises throughout the text enhance students' mastery of the Internet and help illustrate key points in the chapters. These exercises are facilitated by InfoTrac College Edition, an on-line database that students can access via passwords provided with the text.

- **Technology Tips.** This marginal feature provides useful tips for making the most of on-line resources, as well as practical information and insights into technologies ranging from computer software to cellular phones. Topics include using search engines to fine-tune a speech topic (Chapter 4) and analyzing persuasive messages on television (Chapter 13).

- **Focus on Skills.** These exercises are designed to help students hone their skills in each phase of the speech-preparation process. Through various activities that range from self-recording, observing, reflecting, editing sample material, and writing responses to specific questions, students gain increased mastery of public speaking skills. Activities include brainstorming (Chapter 4), preparing notecards (Chapter 5), writing thesis statements (Chapter 6), and using specific, concrete, and precise language (Chapter 10).

- **Speech Evaluation and Audience Analysis Checklists.** Over nine detailed feedback checklists provide a framework for students to evaluate their own and others' speech skills as well as their speech setting and their audience. The speech evaluation checklists are customized for the various types of speeches covered in the text, including expository, process or demonstration, motivation, and refutation.

- **Reflect on Ethics.** These features outline ethical challenges and require students to think critically in sorting through a variety of ethical dilemmas faced by speakers. Topics include using controversial visual aids (Chapter 9), plagiarism and outlining (Chapter 6), and appropriate citation of sources (Chapter 12).

- **Glossary.** Key terms in the margins provide students with a quick reference to important terms of each chapter. There is also a complete glossary at the end of the book.

- **Sample Speeches and Outlines for Analysis.** Eleven sample speeches (nine student and two professional) are included in the text itself, and numerous additional professional speeches are referred to and accessible via InfoTrac College Edition. Each of the student speeches is preceded by a full sentence outline, accompanied by annotations from the author and in select cases, followed by questions for speech analysis.

Highlights of Changes in Sections and Chapters

The text has retained the basic organization of previous editions. However, some material has been streamlined, and other material completely revised. To sum up the changes by section:

Part One, Orientation: This three-chapter introduction, giving students a solid base for making a first speech and listening to the speeches of their classmates, has been revised throughout.

Part Two, Principles: The primary changes in Part Two provide a more complete and cohesive approach to preparing speeches that are adapted to specific audiences. These eight chapters develop the seven steps of an effective speech plan, and, by the end of Part Two, students are well prepared to give their first major speech. However, since growing class size may demand that graded speeches be delivered prior to a class completing all chapters in Part

Two, we offer Chapter 2, Preparing Your First Speech and Coping with Nervousness, which offers an overview of the speechmaking process. The Annotated Instructor's Edition provides guidance for faculty on where and how to integrate earlier speech assignments. Chapter Two in the Student Workbook supports this coverage by including activities that assist students in early speech preparation and delivery.

Part Three, Informative and Persuasive Speaking: This section has been streamlined to three chapters to help students focus on the most critical elements and tools for developing effective informative speeches, develop reasoning skills, and apply reasoning skills to prepare effective persuasive speeches.

Part Four, Adapting to Other Occasions and Formats: These two chapters have been revised to incorporate the text's new pedagogical features.

Although the entire book has been updated and revised throughout, the following chapters have been revised most extensively:

- **Chapter 1, Introduction to Public Speaking,** gives greater emphasis to the empowerment of effective speaking skills and also includes coverage of the challenges of speaking to diverse audiences, an expanded section on ethical responsibilities, and a new section on critical thinking.

- **Chapter 2, Preparing Your First Speech and Coping with Nervousness,** has a totally revised section on preparing the first speech, culminating in an outline of the seven action steps of speech preparation. It contains more specific guidelines for students on how to reduce their speech apprehension.

- **Chapter 3, Listening Critically,** now focuses more sharply on listening to and analyzing speeches. Moreover, there is a new section on how students can offer motivational feedback on speeches to their peers.

- **Chapter 4, Selecting a Topic, Analyzing the Audience and Setting, and Determining Your Speech Goal,** takes students through topic selection, analysis of audience and setting, and writing a speech goal with a more detailed, step-by-step procedure including a checklist on analyzing speech setting and audience.

- **Chapter 5, Researching Your Speech in the Information Age,** has been totally revised. The chapter now features the use of on-line resources as well as traditional ones in helping students find sources for their speeches. The reader sees how three of the author's students find material by using different sources, with special emphasis on a hands-on approach to accessing information electronically through the school library's database and on the Internet.

- **Chapter 6, Organizing and Outlining the Speech Body,** is the first of two completely revised and expanded chapters on organization and outlining. This chapter has a revised section on *Outlining Main Points* that leads the student through the process step by step, and the section on *Selecting and Outlining Supporting Material* has also been revised.

- **Chapter 7, Organizing and Outlining Introductions and Conclusions,** features revised and expanded sections on the *Introduction* and the *Conclusion*, and it has a new section on *Readying Notes for the Practice Speech*.

- **Chapter 8, Adapting to Audiences,** is a unique chapter in the field and uniformly praised by reviewers of this edition. This chapter illustrates the adaptation process by giving an example of how a student goes about preparing his own speech.

- **Chapter 9, Visual Aids,** has been totally revised. In addition to new material on types of visual aids—including software graphics—the chapter now has sections on *Making Visual Aid Choices* and *Designing Visual Aids*, with summary do's and don't's for students.

- **Chapter 12, Principles and Practices of Informative Speaking,** has been rewritten to focus on several essential principles and now features three types of informative speeches that are most widely used in basic courses: expository, process or demonstration, and speech of extended definition.

- **Chapter 14, Practicing Persuasive Speaking Skills,** has been revised so that the material on reasoning is now easier to understand.

New Resources for Students

With this edition, I feel we have achieved the most outstanding array of supplements ever to assist in making this course as meaningful and effective as possible. All of these student resources are new to this edition. Please contact your local Wadsworth representative for an examination copy, contact our Academic Resource Center at 1-800-423-0563, or visit us at http://communication.wadsworth.com/

- **InfoTrac College Edition.** A fully searchable, on-line database provides students access to complete articles from over 600 scholarly and popular periodicals, updated daily, and dating back four years. This database allows students to expand their knowledge of media issues with contemporary articles from all the major media. A four-month subscription to InfoTrac College Edition is included in the purchase price of this new text, and exercises for using InfoTrac are integrated into each chapter of the new edition. Look for the InfoTrac College Edition logo to signal the InfoTrac College Edition feature.

- **InfoTrac College Edition Student Workbook for Communication,** written by Nancy Rost Goulden of Kansas State University, can be bundled with the text and features extensive individual and group activities that utilize InfoTrac College Edition. The workbook also includes guidelines for students on maximizing this resource.

- **Verderber Web Tutor from Wadsworth/Thomson Learning.** Harnessing the power of the Internet to deliver public speaking aids that support various learning styles, Web Tutor is a web-based learning companion to this text. Features include presentation of chapter objectives and lessons; flashcards with audio, still images, and video; exercises that can be downloaded, completed, and returned to the instructor; discussion topics integrated within the chapter; on-line review questions and tutorials; links to real-world locations for timely information; real-time chat; calendar of syllabus information; e-mail connections (using existing e-mail accounts); and an announcement board. For a demonstration of this product featuring one of Wadsworth's psychology texts, please visit the web site www.itped.com, or go directly to the Web Tutor demonstration at www.ilearntoday.com. This state-of-the-art class management and study tool is available bundled with the text, as a stand-alone, or via on-line subscription.

- **Student Workbook.** New for this edition, this print study guide complements and expands students' understanding of the book. It includes a summary of each chapter, multiple copies of speech evaluation forms included in the text, a research journal, outlining activities and worksheets, and Internet activities. This resource can be bundled with the text or sold separately.

- **A Guide to the Basic Course for ESL Students.** This saleable item can be bundled with the text and is designed to assist the non-native speaker. It features Frequently Asked Questions (FAQs), helpful URLs, and strategies for accent management and overcoming speech apprehension.

New and Proven Resources for Teachers

- **Annotated Instructor's Edition,** written by Judy Santacaterina of Northern Illinois University—with assistance from Christopher J. Miller on technology—couples the student text with extensive marginal annotations for the instructor to create an invaluable resource. Significantly enhanced for this new edition, this is a key resource for the first time teacher, the adjunct, and the experienced. Marginal annotations include additional teaching strategies; class activities including short public speaking assignments; discussion topics; cross references; helpful URLs; and suggestions for strategic integration of our leading supplements program.

- **Instructor's Resource Manual** includes instructional strategies, sample syllabi, suggested grading criteria, chapter summaries, answers to the text's Focus on Skills activities, chapter-specific activities, possible answers to the InfoTrac College Edition activities included in the text, multiple speech evaluation checklists, and a testbank.

- **Multimedia Presentation and Lecture Tool** is text-specific software designed to work with the PowerPoint presentation program and is available on cross-platform CD-ROM.

- **Thomson Learning Testing Tools™** contains test creation and grading for essay, multiple-choice, true/false, fill-in, and matching questions, available in cross-platform (Win/Mac), with flexible delivery via print, diskette, LAN, WAN, or Internet. Instructors have the ability to scramble questions, test and grade on-line, and create multiple versions of a test. The program also features rejoinders to incorrect answers. If a student clicks on an incorrect answer, a tutor box appears to guide the student to the text page references for the correct answer and additional study.

- **The Teaching Assistant's Guide to the Basic Course.** This guidebook is designed for the new Communication teacher or for those who want to refresh their approach. Based on leading communication-teacher training programs, the guide covers general teaching and course-management topics, as well as specific strategies for communication instruction, such as providing effective feedback on performance, managing sensitive class discussions, and conducting mock interviews. This guide is available free to adopters of the text and as a saleable item to other interested parties.

- **Transparency Acetates** for customers who prefer acetates to electronic transparencies. This packet of 35 two-color acetate transparencies is available from the previous edition.

- **CNN Videos** help stimulate class discussions. The series of CNN videos, with video segments keyed to material in the text, is available to qualifying adopters. Ask your Wadsworth/Thomson Learning representative for more information. *CNN Today: Public Speaking Volume I* includes Clinton's "apology" speech, a speech from the Dali Lama, and Queen Elizabeth II's address on the death of Princess Diana.

- **Wadsworth Video Library** is a resource of over 30 videos, including "Oral Critiques of Student Speeches," "Public Speaking: Knowing Your Audience," and "Effective Speeches."

How to Use InfoTrac College Edition

InfoTrac College Edition is a fully searchable on-line university library containing full-length articles from more than 600 well-known magazines, scholarly publications, professional association pamphlets, and encyclopedias.

To access IntoTrac College Edition, simply log on to www.infotrac-college.com/wadsworth. Enter your account ID number, which came with a copy of your text, and begin your search. If you did not receive a password, please contact your local Wadsworth representative or call our Academic Resource Center at 1-800-423-0563. You can use InfoTrac College Edition to search in three ways:

- **Subject Guide.** Subject Guide pages display every indexed topic in which the word you typed in the search box appears, as well as the number of references indexed under each topic. This lets you see exactly what matches your search before you view the citations and enables you to choose a single aspect or topic.

- **Keywords.** Entering one or more keywords will give you the broadest range of citations. Literally any citation that includes your word or words in the title and/or abstract will appear. This is helpful if you have a very specific search word, but less helpful than the Subject Guide if your topic word is broad.

- **PowerTrac.** PowerTrac lets you create complex search expressions that combine different search methods, such as author and topic, or find articles from a particular publication and issue date.

Search Tips

1. Be as specific as possible with search words, so you get citations that are useful to you.

2. If you don't get a lot of matches, try different words. For instance, many articles use "public speaking" as the Subject Guide, but many other articles using "communication" as the subject might also be useful in speech preparation.

3. After you open up an article, use the Link feature to get a list of related articles and topics.

4. When your search results are too broad, use the Limit Search button. This button will allow you to limit the search, for instance, to within a specified range of dates, making your material more timely.

5. Please don't wait until the last minute to do your research with InfoTrac! As with any other library system, it takes time to get to know InfoTrac and the many ways it can help you do research.

Acknowledgments

Although I am responsible for what appears in this book, the content reflects the thoughts of a great many people. I gratefully acknowledge the students who contributed speeches and outlines to this edition. I also thank the many instructors who offered feedback and insights gained through their use of the tenth edition. And my special thanks goes to those who prepared detailed reviews of the previous edition as well as the final draft manuscript of this edition:

Brent Adrian, Central Community College; Barbara Blackstone, Slippery Rock University; Trish Borosky, Trident Tech University; Jerry Elam, Broward Community College; Ernest Ettlich, Southern Oregon University; Gwin Faulconer-Lippert, Oklahoma City College; Kay Garrett, Southern Missouri State University; Darla Germeroth, University of Scranton; Carmen Hunt, El Camino College; Mary G. Jarzabek, Louisiana State University; Peter Marston, California State University—Northridge; Molly Mayhead, Western Oregon University; Susan J. Pawela, The Art Institute of Fort Lauderdale; Jean Perry, Glendale College; Susana Powell, City University of New York: Borough of Manhattan Community College; Jeffrey L. Rinkel, Chattanooga State University; Judy Santacaterina, Northern Illinois University; Amy Slagell, Iowa State University; and James L. Wolford, Joliet Junior College of Fine Arts.

In addition, I appreciate the special assistance of Molly Mayhead of Western Oregon University and James L. Wolford of Joliet Junior College in gathering sample speeches from their students. Thanks also to Judy Santacaterina for creating a completely revised and updated *Annotated Instructor's Edition*, and to Chris Miller, a graduate student at Northern Illinois University, for supplying the URLs included in the Annotated Instructor's Edition; to Mary G. Jarzabek for creating a completely revised and updated Instructor's Manual, Testing Tools, and for creating the Multimedia Presentation and Lecture tool; to Constance M. Ruzich of Robert Morris College for authoring the new student workbook; and finally to Nancy Goulden of Kansas State University, who authored the previous edition's *Instructor's Manual* and *Annotated Instructor's Edition* and for this edition produced the invaluable *InfoTrac College Edition Student Workbook for Communication*.

I would also like to express my gratitude to Deirdre Cavanaugh, executive editor; Cathy Linberg, project editor; Megan Gilbert, associate development editor; and Dory Schaeffer, editorial assistant; as well as all of the other people at Wadsworth Publishing who were involved in this project; and to Cecile Joyner of The Cooper Company who oversaw the production of this book. I would also like to give special thanks to Maryanne Koschier, whose close reading of the manuscript and many suggestions pushed me to an even higher standard. Finally, I want to express appreciation to my wife, Kathleen Verderber, for her contributions and invaluable help in discussing content and pedagogy for this edition.

I am also grateful to those who contributed invaluable information on the public speaking course and on their teaching needs by responding to a detailed survey from Wadsworth Publishing:

Brent Adrian
    Central Community
    College
Frank J. Albert
    Community College of Beaver
    County

Carol Allen
    Northern Illinois University
Sandy Alspach
    Ferris State University
Bob Alto
    Mendocino College

Lorin Arnold
    Rowan University
Richard H. Arthur
    Slippery Rock University
Bronwyn Asplund
    Franklin Pierce College

Nick Backus
   Washburn University
Lynn Badertscher
   Fresno City College
Cynthia L. Bahti
   Orange Coast College
Kimberly D. Barnett Gibson
   St. Mary's University
Carol Barnum
   Southern Polytechnic State
   University
Kimberly Batty-Herbert
   Clovis Community College
Linda Baughman
   Allegheny College
Christopher Beck
   Baptist Bible College
Lillian L. Beeson
   University of Pittsburgh—
   Greensburg
Rose M. Beilman
   Pratt Community College
Elizabeth Bell
   University of Southern Florida
Kristina Bendikas
   Bay Path College
Hope E. Bennin
   Prestonsburg Community
   College
Jim Benson
   Norfolk Technical Community
   College
Marcia Berry
   Azusa Pacific University
Mary Elizabeth Bezanson
   University of Minnesota—Morris
Rodger Biles
   Emporia State University
Andrew C. Billings
   Indiana University
Barbara Blackstone
   Slippery Rock University
Pamela S. Bledsoe
   Surry Community College
Vincent L. Bloom
   California State University—Fresno
Dale L. Bluman
   Shippensburg University
Gael Boardman
   Champlain College
Robert Bookwalter
   Marshall University

Chris Bragg
   College of Southern Idaho
Jeffrey D. Brant
   North Dakota State University
Joseph Bridges
   Malone College
Ken Broda-Bahm
   Towson University
Alan Brown
   University of West Alabama
Esther T. Brown
   Mesa Community College
Earnest Burnett, Jr.
   Alvin Community College
Nicholas Burnett
   California State University—
   Sacramento
M. Lee Buxton
   Bellevue Community College
Andrea Campbell
   State University of New York—
   Delhi
Cheri Campbell
   Keene State College
Donna B. Canfield
   Howard Community College
Joyce Carey
   Normandale Community College
Diane W. Carlin
   Villanova University
Rick Casper
   Dawson Community College
Jimmy E. Cato
   College of Alameda
Ken Chase
   Wheaton College
David Cheshier
   Georgia State University
Anita P. Chirco
   Keuka College
Susan Christensen
   Butte College
Robert A. Christian
   Glendale Community College
Victoria Christie
   Rocky Mountain College
Bonnie Clark
   St. Petersburg Junior College
Loralee Clark
   College of William and Mary
Norman Clark
   Appalachian State University

Donna Clevinger
   Blue Mountain College
Robert A. Cocetti
   University of Nebraska—Kearney
Helen Cogan
   Western Texas College
Edwin Cohen
   University of San Francisco
Frank Colbourn
   Pace University
Teresa Collard
   University of Tennessee—Martin
Sabrina Collins
   Angelina College
Celeste Condit
   University of Georgia—Athens
Diane Conrad
   Riverside Community College
Sr. Germaine Corbin
   University of the Incarnate Word
Terri Cornwell
   Hollins University
Kristin Gatto-Correia
   San Francisco State University
Stanley Crane
   Hartnell Community College
G. Dawn Craner
   Boise State University
Charla A. Crump
   Clarendon College
Lisa Cuklanz
   Boston College
Robert S. Curdiff
   Clearwater Christian College
Mary Albert Darling
   Spring Arbor College
E. K. Daufin
   Alabama State University
Quinton D. Davis
   University of Texas—San Antonio
Karen Lane DeRosa
   Miami University of Ohio
Susan Dittmer
   Missouri Valley College
David Dollar
   Southwest Missouri State
   University
Carol Z. Dolphin
   University of Wisconsin—
   Waukesha
Brian Dose
   Martin Luther College

Walter E. Doyle
Tidewater Community College
Douglas Duke
University of Central Oklahoma
James Duncan
Toccoa Falls College
Helen Dunlap
Corning Community College
Nannetta Durnell
Florida Atlantic University
Betty Jo Durst
Mississippi State University
Karen L. Durst
University of Nebraska
Evangeline East
Solana College
Martha J. Einerson
University of Idaho
Jerry W. Elam
Broward Community College
Susan Redding Emel
Baker University
Helen Emmitt
Virginia Military Institute
Ernest E. Ettlich
Southern Oregon University
Deanna L. Fassett
Southern Illinois University
Joan E. Feague
Baker College
Amanda Feller
Portland State University
Brooke Ferdinand
Northwestern Nazarene College
Katie Fields
Guilford Technical Community
College
Eric Fife
College of Charleston
Raymond L. Fischer
University of North Dakota
Wade Fisher
Centralia College
Carmen C. Fletcher
New York University
James J. Floyd
Central Missouri State
University
Karen A. Foss
University of New Mexico
Anne Fox
College of Charleston

Kathy Fox
Butler University
Dorothy L. Franzone
Texas Southern University
Peter Frecknall
George Washington University
David Fregoe
State University of New York—
Potsdam
Mary Frost
Santa Rosa Junior College
H. W. Fulmer
Georgia Southern University
David C. Gaer
Southeast Community College
Lawrence Galizio
Portland Community College
James D. Gallagher
New Mexico State University—
Alamogordo
Al Gallegos
University of the Incarnate Word
Fred Garbowitz
Grand Rapids Community
College
Lawrence Garfinkel
Long Island University
Robert A. Garner
Central Texas College
Kay Garrett
Southern Missouri State
University—West Plains
Darla Germeroth
University of Scranton
Joseph Giordano
University of Wisconsin—Eau
Claire
Robert J. Glenn
Owensboro Community College
Julie S. Gowin
North Dakota State University
Amanda Granrud
University of North Carolina—
Chapel Hill
Lon Green
Ferris State University
Anne Grissom
Mountain View College
Alyce Grover
Somerset Community College
Jim Grubbs
Simpson College

Angela Grupas
St. Louis Community College—
Meramec
Sherrie Guerrero
San Bernadino Valley College
Douglas Gaerte
Houghton College
Lowell Habel
Orange Coast College
Dan Hahn
New York University
Jill Hall
Jefferson Community College
Reeze Lalonde Hanson
Haskell Indian Nations University
Dale Hardy-Short
Northern Arizona University
Diane Harney
Pacific Lutheran University
Alan C. Harris
California State University—
Northridge
Mike Harsh
Hagerstown Community College
Fran Hassencahl
Old Dominion University
Catherine M. Hastings
Susquehanna University
Sally O. Hastings
Western Kentucky University
Martha J. Haun
University of Houston
Nancy Hayward
Indiana University of
Pennsylvania
Robert L. Heinemann
Messiah College
Joyce Henry
Ursinus College
Jay Hillis
Bevill State Community College
Sandra Hochel
University of South Carolina—
Aiken
William T. Hope
Jefferson Community College
David D. Hudson
Golden West College
Tom Huebner
William Cavey College
Carlton W. Hughes
Southeast Community College

L. Paul Husselbee
Lamar University
Susan Huxman
Wichita State University
Carolyn Inmon
Mt. San Antonio College
Tom Isbell
Central Arizona College
Kirsten Isgro
State University of New York
Joel Iverson
North Dakota State University
D. K. Ivy
Texas A&M University—Corpus
Christi
Mary G. Jarzabek
Louisiana State University—
Shreveport
Timothy C. Jenkins
Alice Lloyd College
Patricia Jenkinson
California State University—
Sacramento
Chris Jennings
Tidewater Community
College
Douglas Jernigan
Southwestern College of
Christian Ministries
E. Claire Jerry
MacMurray College
Willie J. Johnson
Normandale Community
College
Nanette Johnson-Curiskis
Gustavus Adolphus College
Shirley G. Jones
Salt Lake Community College
Douglas Kaya
Leeward Community College
Chris Kennedy
Western Wyoming Community
College
Howard Kingkade
University of South Carolina
Bradford Kinney
Wilkes University
Katherine Kinnick
Kennesaw State University
Amber E. Kinser
East Tennessee State University
Harold J. Kinzer
Utah State University

Michael Kleeberg
Ivy Technical State College
Richard Koepsell
Erie Community College
Linda K. Kopp
Western Illinois University
Charles Korn
Northern Virginia Community
College
Mary Kaye Krum
Florence-Darlington Technical
College
Marcia Kuehl
Western Iowa Technical
Community College
William Kushner
Rowan University
Jim A. Kuypers
Dartmouth College
Linda Larson
Mesa Community College
Pamela H. Lau
Lancaster Bible College
Chris M. Leland
Huntington College
Maria Len-Rios
Georgia Southern University
L. Lofthouse
Wesley College
Don Love
Eastern New Mexico University
Kara Lowe
Pratt Community College
John Luecke
University of Wisconsin—
Whitewater
Christopher Lynch
Kean University
David E. Majewski
Richard Blond College
Joanna Malchano
Trident Technical College
Kathy Malone
New Mexico Union College
Mary Y. Mandeville
Ohio State University
Eric Marlow
Weber State University
Peter Marston
California State University—
Northridge
Ben Martin
Santa Monica College

Ginger K. Martin
Guilford Technical Community
College
Shelia Martin
Erie Community College
Melanie Mason
University of Nebraska—Kearney
Molly Mayhead
Western Oregon University
Michael Mbabuike
Hostos Community College
April McClure
Adams State College
Ray McCormick
Azusa Pacific University
Earl E. McDowell
University of Minnesota
John McGrath
Trinity University
Catherine McNamara
Santa Monica College
James B. McOmber
Valdosta State University
Allen Merriam
Missouri So. State College
Kevin Merritt
Louisiana Technical University
Cathy S. Mester
Pennsylvania State University—Erie
John L. Meyer
State University of New York—
Plattsburgh
Shellie M. Michael
Volunteer State Community
College
John Morello
Mary Washington Community
College
Barry Morris
Pace University
Betty Zane Morris
Shorter College
Eric Morris
Southwest Missouri State
University
Timothy P. Mottet
Austin College
Star Muir
George Mason University
Kenneth Mulzac
Oakwood College
Bill Murphy
Riverside Community College

Bill Neher
　Butler University
Jeffrey Nelson
　Kent State University—Trumball Campus
Mark D. Nelson
　University of Alabama
Thomas Nelson
　Elon College
Christine North
　Jamestown College
Dorotha Norton
　University of Tennessee—Martin
Richard O'Dor
　Duke University
Clark Olson
　Arizona State University
John Olson
　Everett Community College
Susan Opt
　University of Houston—Victoria
Brent M. Ottaway
　St. Francis College
Lori S. Owen
　Henry Ford Community College
Kerry Owens
　Northeast Louisiana University
Patricia Pace
　Georgia Southern University
James M. Pannier
　University of Wisconsin—Barron County Center
Wendy H. Papa
　Ohio University
Ward Patterson
　Cincinnati Bible College
Jean Perry
　Glendale Community College
Rob Pocock
　Hope College
James B. Porter
　Indiana University—Northwest
Laurinda W. Porter
　St. Cloud State University
Paul E. Prill
　Lipscomb University
Tom Puckett
　Eastern Washington University
Randall Pugh
　Montana State University— Billings
Richard Pyatt
　Pace University

Alan Ragains
　Windward Community College
Bill Rambin
　Northeast Louisiana University
Melanie J. Reese
　Boise State University
Melanie Reti-Ross
　Malone College
Chris Reynolds
　Otterbein College
Larry Reynolds
　Johnson County Community College
Susan Richardson
　Prince George's Community College
Craig Rickett
　Spokane Falls Community College
Patricia Rockwell
　University of Southern Louisiana
Rita Rosenthal
　Stonehill College
Liliana Castaneda Rossmann
　California State University— San Marcos
Gail V. Rowden
　Metropolitan Community College
Michael Rowley
　Huntington College
Jody Roy
　Ripon College
Halford Ross Ryan
　Washington and Lee University
Karyn Rybacki
　Northern Michigan University
Andrew Sacks
　DeVry Institute of Technology
Joseph J. Saggio
　American Indian College
Joanna Schultz
　Adrian College
Ann M. Scroogie
　Santa Fe Community College
Nelda Sellers
　Marion Military Institute
Deanna Sellnow
　North Dakota State University
Joan Semonella
　Riverside Community College
Benjamin Sevitch
　Central Connecticut State University
Gail Shadwell
　Elgin Community College

Gale Sharpe
　San Jocinto College
Ned A. Shearer
　Western Illinois University
Stephen M. Shehan
　Adrian College
Sheida Shirvani
　Ohio University—Zanesville
Kara Shultz
　Bloomsburg University
George Sibley
　Western State College
Suzie Sims-Fletcher
　Emerson College
John I. Sisco
　Southwest Missouri State University
Amy R. Slagell
　Iowa State University
Donna Smith
　Ferris State University
Michael Smith
　LaSalle University
Sarah Snider
　Cleveland State Community College
Matthew J. Sobnosky
　College of William and Mary
Denise Sperruzza
　Southern Illinois University— Edwardsville
Jane Staab
　Wheelock College
Alison E. Stafford
　University of Mississippi
Linda Loomis Steck
　Indiana University—South Bend
David Steinberg
　University of Miami
Marlane Steinwart
　Valparaiso University
Gary M. Stephens
　Mesa Community College
Carla Stevens
　St. Ambrose University
Debra Stevens
　University of Montana
Edwin Stieve
　Nova Southeastern University
Russell Stockard
　California Lutheran University
Mark Stoda
　Arizona State University

Ron Stotyn
  Georgia Southern University
Bennett Strange
  Louisiana College
Glynis Holm Strause
  Coastal Bend College
Harry Strine
  Bloomsburg University
Mahla Strohmaier
  University of Alaska
Gary Sullivan
  Wagner College
Cecelia Taylor
  University of Scranton
Amy Thieme
  Eastern Kentucky University
Stephanie Thomson
  Xavier University
Carrie Thornton
  Western Kentucky University
Katherine S. Thweatt
  West Virginia University
Gloria Totten
  Portland State University
Regis Tucci
  Mississippi Valley State
University
Esin C. Turk
  Mississippi Valley State
University
Anita J. Turpin
  Roanoke College
Barbara J. Valenzuela
  Thiel College
Charles D. Veenstra
  Dordt College
Jeremy Vegter
  Maranatha Baptist Bible College
Jim Verhoye
  Century College
Donna R. Vocate
  Arkansas Technical University
David Waite
  Butler University

David Walker
  Buena Vista University
David Walker
  Middle Tennessee State
  University
Donald J. Wallace
  Brewton-Parker College
Dennis Waller
  Northwest Nazarene College
A. Ward
  Trinity Christian College
Mike Wartman
  Normandale Community
College
Ron Wastyn
  St. Ambrose University
Willis M. Watt
  Manhattan Christian College
Charles G. Waugh
  University of Maine—
Augusta
V. A. Waxwood
  University of Pittsburgh—
  Greensburg
Linda Webster
  University of Arkansas—
  Monticello
Ron Weekes
  Ricks College
Mark Weinberg
  University of Wisconsin—Rock
  County Center
M. Weiss
  State University of New York—
  Stony Brook
Lena Hegi Welch
  Trevecca Nazarene University
Kathy Werking
  Eastern Kentucky University
Deborah Wertanen
  University of Minnesota
Clifford E. Wexler
  Columbia-Green Community
  College

Gretchen Wheeler
  Casper College
Toni S. Whitfield
  University of West Florida
Margaret L. Wick
  Ohio State University—Newark
Kathie Wilcox
  Lewis and Clark State College
R. G. Wilke
  Villanova University
Beth Willetts
  Ocean Community College
Arthur William
  Olivet College
Melvin G. Williams
  American International College
Joe Willis
  Odessa College
L. Keith Williamson
  Wichita State University
Richard Wiseman
  California State University—
  Fullerton
Richard Wolff
  Dowling College
Debra L. Worthington
  University of Central Arkansas
Marianne Worthington
  Cumberland College
David R. Wright
  Clarion University
Janis Wright
  Santa Rosa Junior College
Vicky Wuertz
  Florida Southern College
Elizabeth Wynia
  Sisseton-Wahpeton Community
  College
Niki Young
  Louisiana State University
Frank L. Zink
  Ivy Technical State College
Anthony J. Zupancic
  Notre Dame College

The Challenge of Effective Speaking

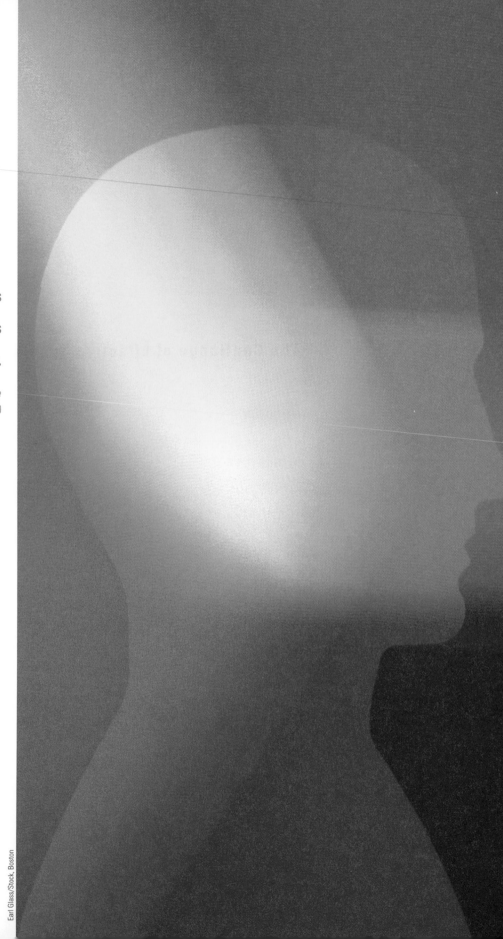

**All the great speakers
were bad speakers
at first.**

Ralph Waldo Emerson, "Power," *The
Conduct of Life* ,1860

Introduction to Public Speaking

Marquez was talking with Bill and Glenna about the movie they had seen. When Bill asked him what he thought of it, Marquez paused for a moment and then cited two reasons why he thought the movie failed to portray characters realistically.

As Heather and Gavin were eating dinner, Heather tried to explain to Gavin why she was upset with the attention he was paying to Susan.

At the monthly meeting of Women's Issues, Nancy Bauer talked with the group about how women can gain strength by being willing to voice their experiences in the work world.

Tom Simmons, candidate for Council, was invited to speak at the University Forum. When he was introduced, he presented his views on the role of government in education.

n all four of the chapter opening situations, we recognize that one person is taking time to present his or her ideas to others. As you read these short descriptions, you were likely to think that the first two sounded like "conversation," whereas the last two were "public speaking."

Yet in each of the four situations, one person has a clearly determined goal in mind—and that goal is to get one or more other people to understand, believe, or act in a particular way. So, all four have some similarities.

Now you might be thinking, "But in the last two, Tom and Nancy knew that they were expected to speak to a group—they prepared ahead, and then gave a speech." True. But isn't it likely that Heather tried to prepare ahead as well? She may well have been thinking about Gavin's attentiveness to Susan for a long time. She may have spent time mulling over what she could say to Gavin, how she could say it, and when would be the best time to say it. The situation may not be one that looks like public speaking, yet Heather's remarks to Gavin are likely to be a product of many public speaking skills. And even Marquez took a moment to organize his thoughts before he responded.

The point? Not only are you likely to be involved in a variety of situations where you will be "giving a formal speech," but you are also likely to be involved in far more "conversational" situations where you will be more effective if you apply public speaking skills in order to meet a particular goal. Thus, instead of thinking about whether what we are engaged in should be called public speaking or conversation, we should think about the skills we have to use to communicate effectively. In short, study of public speaking skills will help you present ideas more clearly and more persuasively in any setting.

In this chapter, we will consider the importance of public speaking, public speaking as an audience-centered communication activity, public speaking and diversity, public speaking and critical thinking, public speaking and ethics, and public speaking as a learned activity.

Public Speaking Is Empowerment

What caused you to register for this course? Perhaps you're here because the course is required, or perhaps a friend or a teacher recommended it, or perhaps you were curious. Whatever the motivation, I believe that before the term is over you'll be thankful that you are here. Why? Mostly because skill at public speaking is a form of empowerment.

First, public speaking is a form of empowerment because mastery of public speaking skills enables you to communicate even complex information in a way that *all* members of an audience can understand. And I think we can all attest to the fact that clear explanation is not always easy. For instance, we've all had teachers whom we've described as "talking over our heads." They understood the material, but they were unable to find ways to make it clear to their listeners.

Second, public speaking is a form of empowerment because mastery of public speaking skills enables you to influence people's attitudes and behavior. It's one thing to know how to solve a problem or to know why people should act accordingly, and quite another to be able to persuade people to believe and act on those decisions. Think of the times in just the past few days that you've tried to influence people. Perhaps you've tried to get a classmate to share your view on immigration policy; perhaps you've tried to persuade your parents to let you use the family car or to bring a friend to dinner; or, an old favorite, perhaps you've tried to get a professor to give you an extension on a project or to change a grade on an assignment. In short, effective public speakers are good at influencing people's attitudes and behavior.

Third, public speaking is a form of empowerment because mastery of public speaking skills will help you in your search for a job. For instance, in a 1989 landmark study, Dan Curtis, Jerry Winsor, and Ronald Stephens asked personnel managers to list the factors that are most important in helping graduating students obtain employment. The top three factors listed by those who responded were oral communication, listening ability, and enthusiasm.[1] In a more recent study, the National Association of Colleges and Employers found that employers still list ability to communicate effectively first.[2]

Fourth, public speaking is a form of empowerment because mastery of public speaking skills is necessary to help you achieve positions of leadership. Speaking effectively is essential in a working environment where you present oral reports and proposals, respond to questions, and train coworkers. Although we tend to think it is our technical expertise alone that is vital to making our mark in our jobs, the reality is that a reputation for effective speaking is likely to be important in being promoted to jobs with greater responsibility. So, whether it is in informing and persuading more effectively, getting a job, or gaining a more responsible position, effective speaking is important.

Public Speaking Is Audience Centered

More than 2000 years ago, Aristotle observed that "the audience is the end and object of a speech." That is, a speaker's words are irrelevant if there are no people to whom the words are directed. A speaker prepares and then delivers a speech with the express intention of achieving a specific goal with an audience of one or more people who have the freedom to accept or reject that goal. Thus, a speech only has meaning insofar as people listen and understand it. Breaking this audience-centered activity down, a speech involves a speaker, a message (the speech), a channel, an audience, a context, noise, and audience feedback.

The Speaker

The speaker is the source or the originator of the communication message. What a speaker talks about and the language used to express those ideas depend on the experiences that have formed that speaker's ideas, feelings, and mood. For instance, a woman from Mothers Against Drunk Driving (MADD) may be driven to carry the message of the organization because the loss of her daughter in a head-on crash involved a drunk driver. Likewise, a man may be motivated to share his beliefs about the importance of community involvement because of the changes in lives he's seen as a result of the intervention of people who cared.

The Speech

A speech contains a **message,** ideas and feelings, that will be presented to the audience through words, sound, and actions symbols that are selected and organized by the speaker and interpreted by members of the audience. The process of transforming ideas and feelings into words, sounds, and actions that make

message *ideas and feelings presented to an audience through words, sound, and actions symbols that are selected and organized by the speaker and interpreted by members of the audience*

encoding *the process of transforming ideas and feelings into words, sounds, and actions*

decoding *the process of transforming messages back into ideas and feelings*

sense is called **encoding;** the process of transforming messages back into ideas and feelings is called **decoding.** Thus, you might communicate your ideas about the plight of children by saying, "Throughout the world, large numbers of children are starving." By listening to what you have said, members of your audience will understand you to be saying, "In all countries, significant numbers of young boys and girls are not getting enough food to sustain a healthy life."

You have been communicating for so long that you probably do not think consciously about either encoding or decoding processes. Nevertheless, these encoding and decoding processes do occur. If your verbal and nonverbal messages are clear and meaningful and/or if the members of your audience are able to share the meanings you are intending, then your speech will be effective.

Since speech messages are likely to be complex, they need to be organized into sections in a certain order for people to grasp the overall meaning more easily. You probably remember times when you could follow another person's message so much more easily because it had a goal, clear main points, and a conclusion that summarized the message.

Because the processes of encoding and decoding messages are at the heart of public speaking and listening to speeches, many of the skills detailed in this book are directed toward improving how you form your messages so that your communication effectiveness is increased.

The Channel

channel *both the route traveled by the message and the means of transportation*

The **channel** is both the route traveled by the message and the means of transportation. Spoken words are carried by sound waves; facial expressions, gestures, and movement are carried by light waves.

In addition, public speaking may occur in person or be delivered over radio or television. Use of radio or television to broadcast a speech introduces different variables that the speaker must understand and adapt to.

The Audience

As we have said, your entire reason for speaking is to gain a specific response from your audience. Suppose you want your audience to understand and perhaps do something about the problem of starving children. Whether you are able to get the desired response depends on your audience's interest in hearing you out, its understanding of what you are saying, and its attitude toward what you have said. If you haven't worked to stimulate your audience's interest in the plight of starving children, or if you haven't presented the information in ways that the audience can understand, or if you haven't been able to get the audience to care about the problem, then you have very little chance of achieving your goal.

The Context

context *the interrelated conditions of communication*

physical setting *the location, time of day, light, temperature, distance between communicators, and seating arrangements*

The interrelated conditions of communication make up the **context.** Think of context as a fabric that combines many strands of fiber. Each strand alters the nature of that fiber. Likewise, a communication context also combines many "strands" or aspects.

One aspect of context that affects your communication is **physical setting**—the location, time of day, light, temperature, distance between communicators, and seating arrangements. For instance, a room where the speaker's

Dennis Brack/Black Star/PNI

Although many people think of speeches as formal affairs, speechmaking skills are relevant to many kinds of communication settings.

P. Cantor/SuperStock

Bob Daemmrich/Stock, Boston

stand is on a stage apart from the audience provides a different context from a room where you can stand on the same level and get close to your audience.

A second aspect of context that affects your communication is **historical setting,** comprised of previous communication episodes. For instance, if you say, "When I explained the nature of the problem at our last meeting," a listener who missed that explanation will have no idea what you mean when you refer to that first speech.

A third aspect of context that affects communication is **psychological setting**—the manner in which people perceive both themselves and those with whom they communicate. For example, suppose that you are feeling pressured because paperwork is piling up. If at the start of your speech you sound out-of-sorts, one person might simply perceive you as unusually cranky that day while another might see you as a mean person.

Noise

Noise often limits the audience's ability to interpret, understand, or respond to messages. **Noise** is any stimulus that gets in the way of sharing meaning. Much of your success as a speaker depends on how you cope with external, internal, and semantic noises.

External noises are the sights, sounds, and other stimuli that draw people's attention away from the intended meaning. For instance, during your presentation on immigration policies, your audience's attention may be drawn to the sound of a bell ringing or the air-conditioning system revving up. The bell and air conditioner sounds are external noise. External noise does not have to be sound, however. Perhaps during your speech people's eyes are drawn to a particularly attractive individual who has arrived late. Such visual distraction is also external noise.

Internal noises are the thoughts and feelings that interfere with meaning. Have you ever found yourself daydreaming during a speech? Perhaps you let your thoughts wander to the good time you had at a party the night before or to the argument you had with a friend that morning. If you have tuned out the speaker's words and tuned in a daydream or a past conversation, then you have created internal noise. Of course, the same thing can happen to your audience when you are the speaker.

Semantic noises are alternate meanings aroused by a speaker's symbols. Suppose you say in your speech that many companies are liberal—meaning generous—to immigrants. If audience members associate the word *liberal* with a political philosophy, they will probably miss your meaning. Because meaning depends on personal experience, others may at times decode a word or phrase differently from the way it was intended. When this happens, semantic noise is interfering with the attempt to communicate.

Feedback

As you speak, members of your audience are likely to respond verbally and/or nonverbally to your messages. These responses, called **feedback,** help you assess whether your audience is paying attention, understands what you are saying, and/or concurs with your message. If the verbal or nonverbal responses indicate that your message was not received, was received incorrectly, or was misinterpreted, you can send the message again, perhaps in a different way, so that your intended meaning is the same as the meaning your audience receives.

historical setting *previous communication episodes*

psychological setting *the manner in which people perceive both themselves and those with whom they communicate*

noise *any stimulus that gets in the way of sharing meaning*

external noises *the sights, sounds, and other stimuli that draw people's attention away from intended meaning*

internal noises *the thoughts and feelings that interfere with meaning*

semantic noises *alternate meanings aroused by a speaker's symbols*

feedback *verbal and/or nonverbal responses to messages*

Different kinds of public speaking situations provide for different amounts of feedback. A speech given on television brings zero feedback, because the speaker is unaware of the audience's response.

The value of in-person speeches over televised speeches is that in-person speeches enable the speaker to monitor nonverbal feedback. If you say, "It's the responsibility of citizens to help those who are unable to help themselves," facial expressions may indicate whether the audience agrees. If many people knit their brows, frown, or shake their head, then you need to discuss the idea more fully. The better you become at reading feedback, the better you will be able to adapt to audience needs.

Some in-person speeches occur in a setting that is informal enough for people to ask questions. Direct interaction between speaker and audience represents the highest level of feedback, but such free flow does not occur in most speech settings.

Model of Public Speaking as Communication

Let us summarize these communication variables of public speaking in a visual form. Figure 1.1 illustrates the communication process in terms of a one-to-one relationship—that is, one speaker to one receiver. In the speaker's mind is

FIGURE 1.1 **A model of communication between two individuals**

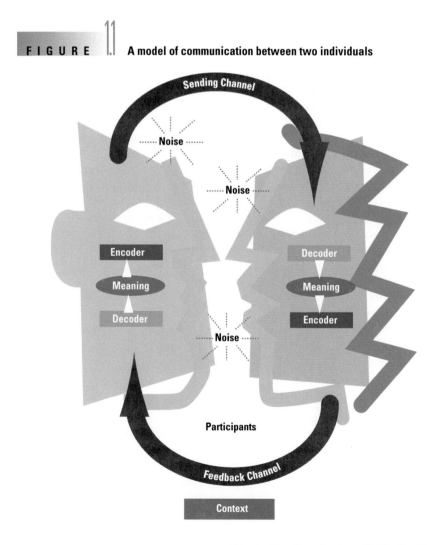

a thought or a feeling that the person means to share. The nature of that thought or feeling is created, shaped, and affected by the speaker's total field of experience, including such specific factors as values, attitudes, beliefs, knowledge, culture, gender, environment, experiences, occupation, and interests. To communicate, the speaker must select words and actions and transmit them via sending channels—in this case, sound (speech) and light (nonverbal behavior).

   Remember that the message consists of words, sounds, and actions that the audience interprets. How audience members interpret a message is affected by *their* total field of experience—that is, by all the same factors that shape the sender's unique experience. On interpreting the message, the receiver sends verbal and nonverbal reactions back to the speaker through the feedback channels. The speaker interprets the feedback in order to understand the response he or she is getting from the receiver.

   The area around the speaker and the receiver represents the physical, historical, and psychological context. During the entire transaction, external, internal, and semantic noise may be occurring at various points that affect the ability of sender and receiver to share meanings.

   In a public speaking situation, all these elements of communication operate simultaneously—and differently—for everyone present. As a result, public speaking is especially complex. While some people focus on the speaker's message, others may be distracted by noise—whether external (the hum of the air conditioning), internal (preoccupation with personal matters), or semantic (a reaction to the speaker's choice of words). Furthermore, all the participants bring their unique perspectives to the communication transaction. Less skillful communicators are oblivious to such factors and plunge ahead regardless of whether they are being understood or even heard. Skillful communicators attend to verbal and nonverbal feedback and adapt their words and nonverbal behavior until they are confident that their listeners have received the meanings they intend to share.

Public Speaking Challenges Speakers to Consider Audience Diversity

diversity *differences between and among people*

Diversity—differences between and among people—affects nearly every aspect of the communication process we have just discussed. We'd like to think that if we all speak the English language, then just using the right words guarantees that everyone will understand what we say. But whether we understand each other depends as much on who we are as it does on the words we use. We are part of a multicultural nation—in fact, we may be the most diverse nation on earth. Although many people try to emphasize racial, gender, and cultural disharmony, there is no other nation in the world with such large populations of diverse people who make their way into all walks of life. Throughout our history, we've experienced huge migrations from different parts of the world. Today, the greatest changes in our population are occurring as a result of migration from Latin America and Asia. At the beginning of the 21st century, the populations of Hispanic and Asian Americans has risen to more than 12 percent and 4 percent, respectively. Combined with the approximately 13 percent African Americans, the total population of minorities is more than 30 percent.[3] Within the next 20 years, this figure is likely to rise to a total of more than 40 percent.

Of course, your own corner of the country may reflect very different ratios. Various cities in the United States have far different percentages of African American, Hispanic, and Asian populations. For instance, in Los Angeles, a city of some 3.5 million, more than 1 million people (29%) are Hispanic; in San Francisco, a city of 750,000, more than 250,000 (39%) are Asian; and in several midwestern cities, such as Cincinnati and St. Louis, 40 percent or more of the population is African American.[4] In contrast, many rural areas and even many states are 90 percent or more European American.[5] At the American Youth Foundation Leadership Conference held in Shelby, Michigan each year, many students coming from these areas report going through their entire school life without seeing anything but white faces.

Certainly the most widely discussed aspect of diversity is cultural. **Culture** may be defined as "'systems of knowledge' shared by a relatively large group of people."[6] It includes a system of shared beliefs, values, symbols, and behaviors. Peter Andersen, a well-respected intercultural communication scholar, goes so far as to say that "culture and communication are inseparable."[7]

culture *systems of knowledge shared by a relatively large group of people*

Junebug Clark/Photo Researchers

Diversity in our country is also represented by differences among people based on gender, age, physical characteristics, and sexual orientation.

Within any large culture there are likely to be other cultures operating at the same time. For instance, within the United States, every business is likely to have its own culture that affects how it operates. Although we may speak of student, medical, and business cultures, to name a few, culture is more frequently used to refer to racial and ethnic groups. For instance, the United States is a country with a large European American culture, but it also encompasses many other cultures, including African American, Hispanic American, Asian American, Native American, Appalachian, and others. Moreover, not all African American, Asian American, or Hispanic people are of one culture. In this text, then, we will just say that within the dominant culture of the United States many other cultures exist.

Our goal is to help you communicate with your audience, whether the majority of that audience shares your culture or is markedly different from you.

But diversity is not just seen in culture. People also differ on other dimensions, such as gender, age, physical characteristics, and sexual orientation. Any failure to take those differences into account when we speak is significant in determining how effectively we communicate.

In many places in this text, we'll confront issues of diversity. Since effective public speaking is audience oriented, you will need to understand and adapt to your audience whether you find that most of the people in the audience are much *like you* or totally *different from you*.

Public Speaking Develops Critical Thinking

When you say something like, "I'd like to figure out a way to make this seem clearer," or "I'd like to be able to convince my husband to take care of the kids while I finish my degree at night," or "Dawn's plan for raising the money just doesn't sound right to me," you are referring to your need for **critical thinking**—an analytical and evaluative process using logic or reasoning to present information in a way that is likely to provide understanding, change a belief, or uncover problems in another person's informative or persuasive message. For instance, in the first statement you are looking for means of clarification; in the second, you are taking the initiative—you must provide a logical approach to be effective; in the third, you are responding—you must be able to analyze what Dawn has said in order to uncover any potential weaknesses. In each case, you need to engage in critical thinking.

critical thinking *an analytical and evaluative process using logic or reasoning to present information in a way that is likely to provide understanding, change a belief, or uncover problems in another person's informative or persuasive message*

Study of public speaking allows you not only to learn aspects of critical thinking, but also to apply them in your own speeches. As you prepare speeches, you will formulate goals, define concepts, ask questions, gather data, organize information, analyze information, put ideas together, and evaluate your own and others' arguments and information. All of these develop critical thinking.

Throughout this book, we will be providing advice to help you improve your critical thinking and opportunities for you to test your critical thinking ability.

Public Speaking Carries Ethical Responsibilities

Whether we call up the words of the Greek philosopher Plato ("The first goal of the speaker is to know the truth"), the Roman educator Quintilian ("The true orator is a good person speaking well"), or such contemporary figures as James McCroskey ("If the communicator seeks to improve the well-being of his audience through his act of communication, he is committing a moral act"), the entire history of rhetoric is infused with the sense of ethical responsibility.

Ethical issues, according to Richard Johannesen, a noted communication scholar in the field of ethics, focus "on degrees of rightness and wrongness in human behavior."[8] Although what is considered ethical is to some extent a personal matter, we still expect society to uphold certain standards that can help us with our personal value judgments. A concern of many is an apparent erosion in moral and ethical standards, especially of teenagers.[9] Families, schools, and religion all share the responsibility of helping individuals develop ethical standards that can be applied to specific situations. As Carl Wellman, a noted philosopher, has pointed out, a person cannot choose and act rationally without some explicit or implicit ethical system.[10] Although an ethical theory does not tell us what to do in any given situation, it does tell us what to consider in making our decisions. It directs our attention to the reasons that determine the rightness or wrongness of any act.

ethical issues *focus on degrees of rightness and wrongness in human behavior*

Christopher Morris/Black Star/PNI

A person cannot choose and act rationally without some explicit or implicit ethical system. Jimmy Carter has always been praised for his ethical standards.

Anyone discovered engaging in what a group believes to be immoral behavior is likely to be admonished by that society or group through social means. Your personal ethic is based on your belief and acceptance of what is considered moral by the communities or groups with which you most closely identify. So, when you behave ethically, you voluntarily act in a manner that complies with expected behavior. Why do people internalize morals and develop a personal ethic? Because most of us regard ourselves as accountable for our conduct, and even, to some extent, for our attitudes and character, and blame ourselves when we fall short of these ideal principles.[11]

When we communicate, we cannot avoid making choices with ethical implications. To understand how our ethical standards influence our communication, we must recognize the ethical principles guiding our behavior. At various places in this text, we will discuss a variety of ethical principles for public speaking. Some of these principles are drawn from what is commonly accepted to be ethical behavior in the United States of America. Some of them come from what experts tell us will lead to trust and promote healthy relationships with our audience. As we discuss ethics, we will note where standards differ across cultures and between men and women and how these difference lead to alternative ethics.

The following guidelines are fundamental to developing ethical public speaking.

1. Tell the truth. Of all the guidelines, this one may be the most important. An audience that consents to listen to you is extending you its trust and expects that you will be honest. If during your speech people believe you are lying to them, or if they later learn that you have lied, they will reject you and your ideas. But telling the truth means more than avoiding deliberate, outright lies. If you are not sure whether information is true, don't use it until you have verified it. Ignorance is seldom accepted as an excuse.

2. Keep your information in perspective. Many people get so excited about their information that they exaggerate its importance. Although a little exaggeration might be accepted as a normal product of human nature, when the exaggeration is perceived as distortion, most people will consider it the same as lying. For instance, suppose you discover that capital punishment has lowered the murder rate in a few states, but in many other states the statistics are inconclusive. If, in your speech, you assert that statistics show that murder rates are lower in states with capital punishment, you would be distorting the evidence. Because the line between some exaggeration and gross exaggeration or distortion is often difficult to distinguish, most people see any exaggeration as unethical.

3. Resist personal attacks against those who oppose your ideas. There seems to be an almost universal agreement that name-calling and other irrelevant personal attacks are detrimental to a speaker's trustworthiness. Responsible listeners recognize that such tactics do not contribute to the speaker's argument and represent an abuse of the privileged status the speaker enjoys.

4. Give the source for all damning information. Where ideas originate is often as important as the ideas themselves, especially when a statement is damning. If you are going to discuss wrongdoing by individuals or organizations, or condemn an idea by relying on the words or ideas of others, provide the sources of your information and arguments. Moreover, since the mention of wrongdoing brings communication to the edge of what is legally defined as slander, speakers should be aware of the legal as well as ethical pitfalls of making damning statements without proof.

5. Fully credit sources of quotations and paraphrases. When people are "under the gun," there's a temptation to use parts of other people's work without citation. But doing so, even in small amounts, is a form of plagiarism. **Plagiarism** means to steal and pass off the ideas and words of another as one's own, or to use a created production without crediting the source. In addition to being unethical, plagiarism in many contexts is also illegal and can lead to the paying of damages.

If you use the exact words of another person, you must indicate that you are quoting directly. For instance, if I used the definition of ethical issues given at the start of this section in a speech, I would say, "According to Richard Johannesen, in his book *Ethics in Human Communication*, ethical issues focus on, and I quote, 'degrees of rightness and wrongness in human behavior.'"

Throughout this book, we will stress the importance of working with a number of different sources of information in order to find out what is "general knowledge," information that can be used without citing a source. In contrast, information that is derived from a single source should be credited.

Most colleges and universities have specific rules and penalties for plagiarizing. These penalties range from failing an assignment, to failing a course, to expulsion from the school.

We will consider more specific ethical questions as we discuss topic selection, audience analysis, selection and use of supporting information, construction and use of visual aids, speech language, delivery, reasoning, use of emotional appeals, establishing credibility, and refutation.

Public Speaking Is a Learned Activity

Brian Spitzberg, whose specialty is communication **competence**, defines it as the impression that communication behavior is appropriate and effective.[12] Applying this definition to public speaking, you will be deemed competent if your speeches are appropriate for the situation and effective in achieving their goals.

What should be of the greatest comfort to you is that public speaking is a learned activity.[13] Our goal is to help you develop public speaking competence: the knowledge of what makes for good public speaking, and the skill to put that knowledge into practice.

The teaching style of this textbook recognizes that none of us learns all there is to know about a subject at once on a first reading. Learning public speaking skills is much like learning a sport. For instance, to learn an effective tennis or golf swing, you first have to understand the basics. You have to know what the components of a good swing are. But even after you have the cognitive knowledge, you don't automatically develop a good swing that works every time. Whether it be golf or tennis, you have to practice. And you have to check to make sure that you are practicing good habits and not bad habits. Even professional golfers find that their swings are off at times. As a result, even professionals like Ben Crenshaw and Tiger Woods work with a coach to help them get their swings back in the groove. So, look at it this way: If even professional athletes must practice skills correctly and get coaching when their swings go wrong, isn't it logical that beginning public speakers need to do the same?

In this text, we use the learning principle of repetition applied to the study of the action steps of speech preparation. In the next chapter of this section, you will be introduced to the action steps. Then, in Part Two, you'll see those action steps expanded to cover preparation for all types of speeches. Finally in Parts Three and Four, you'll see those action steps applied specifically to informative and persuasive speaking, and to other formats and contexts. Each repetition of the steps will function as a new layer of information, so that when you finish this text, you will have a solid speech foundation.

Throughout Part Two, you'll be encouraged to complete Focus on Skills exercises that will take you through the entire process of preparation and practice for your first speech. Completing a series of exercises in order to give a speech might seem overwhelming—why not just do the speech? The point is that each of these exercises is keyed to a specific aspect of the seven action steps. You may say to yourself, "I can skip one or two or more of these," but if you do, it means that you are not forcing yourself to practice what you've studied cognitively. And just as we've already said, what's good for a professional is good for a beginner. When you have finished Chapter 11 and the recommended exercises, you'll be entirely prepared to present your first major speech.

Summary

Public speaking is important to success in nearly every walk of life. Speeches—oral presentations that are usually given without interruption—occur at formal occasions where an audience has assembled expressly to listen, in less formal employment contexts, and during our informal daily conversations.

Public speaking is a kind of communication transaction that involves a speaker giving a prepared speech to an audience through both oral and visual symbols in a specific context. The audience, the speech's end and object, gives verbal or nonverbal feedback that tells the speaker whether the message of the speech was understood or whether some kind of noise interfered with understanding.

Public speaking challenges speakers to consider audience diversity—differences between and among people—that affect nearly every aspect of the communication process. The most widely discussed aspect of diversity is culture, which includes a system of shared beliefs, values, symbols, and behaviors.

Public speaking develops critical thinking—an analytical and evaluative process using logic or reasoning to present information in a way that is likely to provide understanding, change a belief, or uncover problems in another person's informative or persuasive message.

In addition, public speaking carries ethical responsibilities, which focus on degrees of rightness and wrongness in human behavior. Although an ethical theory does not tell us what to do in any given situation, it does tell us what to consider in making our decisions. It directs our attention to the reasons that determine the rightness or wrongness of any act. To understand how our ethical standards influence our communication, we must recognize the ethical principles guiding our behavior.

Ethical public speaking guidelines include telling the truth, keeping information in perspective, resisting personal attacks against those who oppose your ideas, giving the source for all damning information, and fully crediting sources of quotations or paraphrases in order to avoid being guilty of plagiarism (passing off the words or ideas of another as one's own).

Public speaking is a learned activity. During this course, you have the opportunity to learn how to develop public speaking competence: the knowledge of what makes for good public speaking, and the skill to put that knowledge into practice.

Courage is resistance to fear, mastery of fear, not absence of fear.

Mark Twain, *Pudd'nhead Wilson,*
1894

Preparing Your First Speech and Coping with Nervousness

As Prof. Montrose finished explaining the goal of the course, he announced that during the next class period everyone would present a short, personal experience, icebreaker speech. "I'd like you to give a 2- to 3-minute speech. The goal of the assignment is to familiarize you with the steps of speech preparation and the value of considering and using personal experiences in future major speeches."

Andy's first reaction was panic. But as Prof. Montrose briefly explained the basic steps of preparation and gave some tips for coping with nervousness, Andy thought, "I know there's a logic to the steps of a talk and a blueprint to follow—I think I can do this!"

n this course, you may have already been given such an assignment. Why? The best way to cope with the nervousness that all speakers experience is to get on your feet in front of the class as soon as possible. Whether or not you have been given such an assignment, this chapter gives initial guidance in preparing a speech. As you read the chapter, regardless of how you feel now, I think you'll agree with Andy: "I think I can do this!"

Depending on the specific goals of your course, the number of students in your class, and the number and length of assigned speeches, your "icebreaker" might be a short self-introduction, a narrative speech in which you relate a personal experience, or a short speech about a topic with which you have a great deal of personal experience.

In the first part of this chapter, we preview the action steps of effective speech preparation that will be discussed in full in Part Two. In the second part of the chapter, we examine methods of coping with speech nervousness. Although the chapter is directed toward helping you present a personal experience (sometimes called a narrative speech), the steps introduced here are essentially the same for any speech.

An Effective Speech Plan

Whether you are an account agent selling an advertising campaign to Procter and Gamble, a coach trying to motivate your team in its game with your arch-rival, or a student giving a speech in class, to have the greatest chance for success you need to have a speech plan—a strategy for achieving your goal.

An effective speech plan for most speeches is based on the answers to the following questions:

1. What is my goal in this speech?
2. Where can I find the kind of information that I need to achieve this goal?
3. How can I organize and outline this information in a way that is most likely to help me achieve my goal?
4. How can I best adapt my speech to my audience?
5. How can I create visual aids that will dramatize my information?
6. What can I focus on in practicing the language of my speech?
7. What can I focus on in practicing the delivery of my speech?

In the next part of this book, we will answer these seven questions more fully. For now, we want to give the most basic of answers that will help you with an "icebreaker" speech.

Goal

speech goal *what you want your listeners to know, believe, or do*

1. What is my goal in this speech?   Your **speech goal** is a statement of what you want your audience to know, believe, or do. To arrive at such a goal, you begin by selecting a topic. Regardless of whether you are a renowned speaker or are preparing your very first speech, the advice for determining what to speak about is the same: Select a topic that you know something about and that is important to you.

Andy Gilgoff (whose speech outline and speech appear near the end of this chapter in Figures 2.2 and 2.3) was instructed to speak on a personal experience. He considered several experiences that he thought were humorous and that the class would enjoy hearing about. For his topic, he finally chose "the locker story," an embarrassing experience at the local gym when he thought his clothes had been stolen from his locker.

Because a speech is designed to be given to an audience in a particular setting, before you get very far in your planning you need to think about your specific audience so that you can predict their level of interest in the topic, their ability to understand the content of the speech, and their attitude toward you and your topic. You base these predictions on information you gather about your audience, including gender, culture, average age, education level, occupation, income level, and group affiliation. As you study these factors, you can assess the kinds of material the audience is likely to respond to. Although in real life your audiences will vary considerably on each of these characteristics, for this opening assignment you can assume that much of your audience will share many of your characteristics.

The setting can also be an important consideration. Ordinarily the relevant issues are the size of the audience, when the speech will be given, where the speech will be given, the facilities necessary to give the speech, the time limit for the speech, and the specific assignment. Again, since you will be speaking in the same classroom all term, you can determine any peculiarities of the room that you need to take into consideration. Most important for this first speech are the size of the audience and your time limit.

Andy Gilgoff thought that his class would relate to his experience because most students have had fears of forgetting their locker number, forgetting the lock combination, or losing valuables.

He also knew that the speech would be for an audience of about twenty classmates, that the assignment was a narrative speech, and that his time limit was 3 minutes.

Once you have a topic and have analyzed the audience and setting, you can phrase your speech goal. Every speech has a general and a specific goal that the speaker intends to achieve. For most of your in-class speeches, your general goal is likely to be determined by the assignment. You will probably be giving either an informative speech, where you want your audience to understand information, or a persuasive speech, where you want your audience to believe something or act in a particular way. For an icebreaker speech, your goal is likely to be to have the audience enjoy your personal experience.

Your specific goal articulates exactly what you want your audience to understand, believe, or do. For instance, for an informative speech, Glen, a member of the basketball team might phrase his goal, "I want my audience to understand how to shoot a jump shot." Ling, a student who was born in China, might phrase her goal, "I want the audience to have an appreciation of Chinese culture." For this narrative assignment, your goal is likely to be phrased something like Andy's.

Since Andy's assignment was a narrative speech, his general goal was to have the audience enjoy his experience. Specifically, Andy wanted the audience to laugh at his realization that his clothes had not been taken.

Speech Material

2. Where can I find the kind of information that I need to achieve this goal? For most speeches, you want factual information from research sources that you access manually and electronically. But regardless of the speech, you also want to use some of your own humorous, exciting, or interesting experiences. This is why it is so important to select a topic you already know something about—so that you have experiences you can draw from to make the speech more meaningful. For instance, Glen, who is on the basketball team, will be able to give a better speech on shooting jump shots than a person with no basketball experience who has learned about shooting jump shots from reading and interviewing others. Why? Because shooting jump shots is a major part of his experience. Likewise, Ling, the young woman born in China, will be able to give a better speech on Chinese culture than someone who has not had the direct experience that she's had.

For your major class assignments, you may draw material from your own knowledge and experiences, observations, interviews, surveys, and research. For an icebreaker speech, your information will often be drawn primarily from your own experience.

For his personal experience narrative, Andy needed only to reconstruct the details of his gym experience.

If you are called upon to give a personal experience narrative speech, you'll want to build your speech around the following elements of a narrative:

A narrative usually has a point to it—a climax to which the details build. Think carefully about the point of your story.

A narrative is developed with supporting details that give background to and embellish the story so that the point has maximum effect. Try to select and develop details that heighten the impact.

A narrative often includes dialogue. A story is more enjoyable to audience members when they hear it unfold through dialogue.

A narrative is often humorous. Although not all narratives are funny, most have elements of humor. If what happened can be made funny, the humor will hold attention and help establish a bond between speaker and audience.

Organization

3. How can I organize and outline this information in a way that is most likely to help me achieve my goal? Any well-organized speech has a beginning, a middle, and an end. Because it is difficult to work on an introduction until the content of a speech is determined, it often works best to start organizing the body of the speech before considering the introduction or the conclusion. Throughout the process, you will want to work in outline form. Although your inclination may be to sit down and "write out" the speech as it comes to mind, as you read through the following chapters, you'll see how speeches are likely to be better organized and better developed when you work in an outline mode.

You'll want to begin by wording main points carefully, following an organizational pattern that clearly communicates the material. Two of the most common organizational patterns are chronological and topical (later we'll consider several types of organization that you may want to use in your informative and persuasive speeches). **Chronological** means following an order that moves from first to last. So, if your personal experience speech is about an event that happened to you, you are likely to organize the speech with main points that show what happened first, what happened second, and what happened last. In some circumstances, you may find that your speech is best presented topically.

chronological *following an order that moves from first to last*

Topical means following an order of headings. For instance, Ling might have an experience that is interpreted one way by her Chinese parents and totally differently by her American classmates. So, to contrast the two interpretations, she elects to talk about the experience under two headings.

topical *following an order of headings*

Because most personal experiences give events as they happened, they are usually presented chronologically. For instance, Andy Gilgoff arranged his personal experience by talking about what happened first, second, and third.

After you have outlined the body of the speech, you can outline your introduction and conclusion. At the least, you want an introduction that both gets attention and leads into the body of the speech. Because there are never any guarantees that your audience is ready to pay full attention to the speech, find a way to start the speech that focuses attention on your topic. In a short first speech, you might begin by asking a question or making a humorous or startling statement.

Andy Gilgoff began his speech with a humorous statement: "A while back, I joined a local gym with the express purpose of taking up weightlifting in hopes that someday people would have difficulty in telling me and Arnold Schwarzenegger apart."

For most speeches, you will want a conclusion that reminds the audience of what you have said and that hits home in such a way that the audience will remember your words. A narrative speech, however, often ends with a conclusion drawn from the climax. For instance, as you read Andy's speech on p. 33, you'll see that for sake of dramatic effect, he ends with the climax itself. Whereas a major speech has a clearly delineated introduction, body, and conclusion, a narrative is a single, unified story.

When you think you are done, go back over the outline to make sure that the parts are relevant to your goal. For any speech you give, it is important to outline the speech on paper to help you test the logic and clarity of your proposed organization. A complete outline includes key parts of the introduction, the main points, major subpoints of the body and key support, section transitions, and key parts of the conclusion.

When you have finished your outline for your personal experience speech, the structure should look like this:

Topic:

Introduction: (beginning—your opening sentence)

Story: (the body or middle of the speech)

Climax: (end of the speech)

Although some experienced speakers are able to develop a mental outline, most of us need to see on paper what we are planning to do. If the parts of the speech flow logically from one to the next, then the audience should be able to follow your speech.

Andy Gilgoff's outline for his narrative speech is shown in Figure 2.2 on p. 32. Notice that his outline is quite short. An outline usually contains less than one-third the words of the actual speech (see Andy's speech, Figure 2.3 on p. 33). This gives Andy a chance to fill out the speech differently each time he practices it.

Even though an outline for a narrative speech does not include all of the parts you'll be using in major speeches, it does illustrate the specific goal, the three parts of the speech, and the symbols used to designate main points and subpoints.

Audience Adaptation

adaptation *relating a speech to audience interests and needs*

4. How can I best adapt my speech to my audience? Once you have a reasonably well organized speech, you begin the task of adapting that speech to your specific audience. **Adaptation** means relating to audience interests and needs verbally, visually, and vocally. Although an effective speaker considers audience needs at all stages of the preparation process, issues of adaptation become especially important once the basic structure of the speech is established.

Especially for a first speech, the easiest way to adapt to your audience is to create common ground with the audience by using personal pronouns (such as *I*, *we*, *you*, and *our*) and asking rhetorical questions (questions that you don't really expect the audience to answer). For instance, you might begin your speech by saying, "I'm sure we've all had experiences that we'd just as soon forget. . ." or "Do you remember what it was like when you. . .?" Later in the text, we'll discuss other ways of personalizing information. As you gain skill, you'll find that you are able to talk about your information in ways that tell audiences that you are thinking about *them* as you are speaking.

Andy used personal pronouns and other means of creating common ground in telling his personal experience.

Visual Aids

5. How can I create visual aids that will dramatize my information? Even for a very short speech, you may decide to create a visual aid that will help clarify, emphasize, or dramatize the verbal information. Audiences are

Visual aids clarify, emphasize, and often dramatize.

Pedrick/The Image Works

likely to understand and retain information better when they have received that information through more than one sense. By using objects, models, charts, pictorial representations, projections, and computer graphics in creative ways, effective speakers are able to maximize the effect of their high-quality information.

Although visual aids are less likely to be used in a short narrative speech like Andy Gilgoff's, professional speakers are likely to make effective use of visual aids in their major informative and persuasive presentations.

Language

6. What can I focus on in practicing the language of my speech? Ideas are communicated to the audience through verbal and nonverbal means, so choose the wording of main points and supporting materials carefully. If you have not thought carefully about how best to phrase your key ideas, you run the risk of missing a major opportunity for communicating your ideas effectively. In practice sessions, work on clarity, vividness, emphasis, and appropriateness of language.

In his narrative speech, Andy Gilgoff tried to be as specific as possible in relating the details so that the audience would have a clear and vivid mental picture of the events.

Delivery

7. What can I focus on in practicing the delivery of my speech? Although a speech is comprised of words, how effective you will be is largely a matter of how well you use your voice and gestures in delivering your speech. You will want to present the speech enthusiastically, with vocal variety and emphasis, using good eye contact (looking at members of the audience while you are speaking). Later, we will spend considerable time discussing how to achieve these goals. For now, as you prepare for your first speech, just imagine how you look and sound when you're telling a friend about something that has happened to you. You probably look right at the person while you talk; because you're excited, your voice probably shows the excitement; and because you are thinking actively, your face and hands probably reinforce your feelings.

Very few people can present speeches effectively without considerable practice. The goal is to practice your speech until you can deliver it extemporaneously within the time limit. Under no circumstances should you try to memorize the speech. Throughout this text, we emphasize **extemporaneous speaking**—giving a speech that is researched, outlined, and practiced until the ideas of the speech are firmly in mind, but varying the wording from practice to practice and in the actual delivery. By keeping your mind on the main points of the sequence, you will be able to lengthen or shorten the story by including or deleting details of the experience.

The number of times you need to practice a speech will vary from situation to situation. When a speech contains ideas that you are not familiar with, you may have to practice it many times before your delivery is effective or before you can deliver it comfortably within the time limit. On the other hand, when the ideas are familiar to you, you may be able to achieve your delivery goals with very few practices. Although your narrative material is likely to be easily recalled, you may need to practice it several times to reduce the anxiety that many novice speakers feel.

extemporaneous speaking *giving a speech that is researched, outlined, and practiced until the ideas of the speech are firmly in mind, but varying the wording from practice to practice and in the actual delivery*

Dave Schaefer/Jeroboam

Practicing the speech means standing up in a setting that approximates that of the actual speech and presenting the speech aloud.

To practice, find a place where you have room to stand up and picture people sitting in front of you. If you can practice in an empty classroom, great. But you can get a sense of the situation by practicing in your dorm or bedroom. If you have an audio tape recorder, go ahead and record your practice session. When you're ready, go through the entire speech once. Don't stop. If you mess up, don't worry about it—just get through it. When you've finished, listen to the tape or go back over the speech mentally. Look at your outline. Decide what you need to do differently. Then go through it a second time right away. If you're still not happy with the outcome, go through the speech another time or two later—perhaps just before you go to bed.

Andy Gilgoff practiced his speech several times before the day he was assigned to speak. In his speech, Andy spoke enthusiastically while maintaining good eye contact with the class.

The outline that follows and Figure 2.1 summarize the action steps of an effective speech plan that evolve from answers to the seven questions. These steps will be discussed in detail in the eight chapters that make up Part Two of this book.

I.   Determine a specific speech goal that is adapted to your audience. (Chapter 4)

    A. Select a topic from a subject area you know something about and that is important to you.

    B. Analyze your audience.

    C. Analyze your setting.

one

Determine a Goal

two

Gather Information

three

Organize Information

four

Develop a Strategy

five

Create Visual Aids

six

Practice Wording

seven

Practice Delivery

D. Articulate your goal by determining the response that you want from your audience.

II. Discover, gather, and evaluate information you can use in your speech. (Chapter 5)

   A. Survey sources manually and electronically that are most likely to yield quality information.

   B. Record information that is relevant to your specific speech goal on note cards.

III. Organize, outline, and develop your material in a way that is best suited to your particular audience. (Chapters 6 and 7)

   A. Write a thesis statement that indicates the specifics of the speech goal.

   B. Outline main points as complete sentences that are clear, parallel, and meaningful.

   C. Order the main points following an organizational pattern that meets audience needs.

   D. Create section transitions to serve as guideposts.

   E. Create an introduction that gets attention, sets the tone, creates goodwill, builds your credibility, and leads into the body of the speech.

F.   Create a conclusion that both summarizes the material and leaves the speech on a high note.

G.   Review and complete the speech outline.

H.   Prepare speaker notes from the outline.

IV. Develop a strategy for adapting material to your specific speech audience. (Chapter 8)

A.   Establish common ground.

B.   Adapt to audience level of interest.

C.   Adapt to audience level of understanding.

D.   Adapt to audience attitude toward you.

E.   Adapt to audience attitude toward your topic.

V.   Create visual aids to clarify, emphasize, and dramatize verbal information. (Chapter 9)

VI. Practice the speech until the wording is clear, vivid, emphatic, and appropriate. (Chapter 10)

VII. Practice the speech until the delivery is enthusiastic, vocally expressive, fluent, spontaneous, and direct. (Chapter 11)

A.   Use voice and bodily action to develop a conversational quality.

B.   Rehearse the speech until you can deliver it extemporaneously within the time limit.

Coping with Nervousness

By far the most asked question about speaking is, "What can I do about nervousness?" In fact, nearly everyone reports nervousness about speaking, and we can all learn to cope with that nervousness. Whether we call it **nervousness,** stage fright, speech fright, shyness, reticence, speech apprehension, or some other term, the feeling is essentially the same: a fear or anxiety about public speaking interaction.

Although we may feel some degree of nervousness in any situation, the majority of us notice it most in public speaking. Some of this nervousness is **cognitive**—that is, we think about how nervous we're likely to be. Much of the nervousness is **behavioral**—that is, we physically display characteristics. For instance, we may experience stomach cramps, sweaty palms, dry mouth, and the use of such filler expressions as "um," "like," and "you know." People may avoid speaking in public altogether or, if they absolutely must speak, speak for the shortest time possible.

To help cope with this nervousness, keep in mind that fear is not an either-or matter—it is a matter of degree. Most of us fall somewhere between the two extremes of no nervousness at all and total fear. The point is that nervousness about speaking in public is *normal.*

Many of us believe that we would be better off if we could be totally free from nervousness. But Gerald Phillips found from years of study that nervousness is not necessarily negative. He noted that "learning proceeds best when the organism is in a state of tension."[1] In fact, it helps to be a little nervous to do your best: If you are lackadaisical about giving a speech, you probably will not do a good job.

nervousness   *a state of fear or anxiety about public speaking interaction*

cognitive nervousness   *thinking about how nervous you're likely to be*

behavioral nervousness   *physically displaying characteristics of nervousness*

Because at least some tension is constructive, the goal is not to eliminate nervousness, but to learn how to cope with it. Phillips cites results of studies that followed groups of students with speaker nervousness. He found that nearly all of them still experienced tension, but almost all of them had learned to cope with the nervousness. Phillips goes on to say that "apparently they had learned to manage the tension; they no longer saw it as an impairment, and they went ahead with what they had to do."[2]

So, we can conclude that nearly everyone who speaks in public, whether for the first or the fiftieth time, experiences some nervousness. Now let's look at some points to consider as you prepare your first speech.

1. Despite nervousness, you can make it through your speech. Very few people are so bothered by nervousness that they are unable to function. You may not enjoy the "flutters" you experience, but you can still deliver an effective speech. In the years I've been teaching, I've heard thousands of student speeches. In all of that time, I've only had two students who were unable to give the speech. Some others forgot some of what they planned to say, and some strayed from their planned speech, but they all finished. Moreover, some students who reported being scared stiff actually gave excellent speeches.

Experience teaches us that some people who are nervous about speaking do find that the nervousness hurts their performance. But we have enough cases of famous performers who confessed nervousness but still performed at high levels that we have to conclude that nervousness itself does not necessarily hurt performance. Barbra Streisand and Abraham Lincoln both confessed to great nervousness before facing an audience, yet in neither case was their performance hampered by the nervousness.

2. Listeners are not as likely to recognize your fear as you might think. The thought that audiences will notice an inexperienced speaker's fear often increases that fear. But the fact is that audience members are seldom

Arthur Grace/Stock, Boston

Although most speakers confess to nervousness at the prospect of giving an important speech, outward signs of distress are greatly lessened when the speaker is well prepared and has practiced beforehand.

aware of how nervous a person is. For instance, a classic study found that even speech instructors greatly underrate the amount of stage fright they believe a person has.[3]

3. The better prepared you are, the better you will cope with nervousness. Many people show extreme nervousness because either they are not well prepared or they think they are not well prepared. According to Gerald Phillips, a positive approach to coping with nervousness is "(1) learn how to try, (2) try, and (3) have some success."[4] This entire textbook is devoted to helping you become well prepared for your speeches so that you will have more successful efforts. As you learn to recognize when you are truly prepared, you will find yourself paying less attention to your nervousness. Moreover, when you are truly prepared, you're better able to convince yourself that you can do a good job. A study by Kathleen Ellis reinforces previous research findings that "students' self-perceived public speaking competency is indeed an important predictor of their public speaking anxiety."[5]

4. The more experience you get in speaking, the better you can cope with nervousness. Beginners experience some fear because they do not have experience speaking in public. As you give speeches, and see improvement in those speeches, you will gain confidence and worry less about any nervousness you might experience. Research on the impact of basic courses on communication apprehension has shown that experience in a public speaking course can reduce students' communication apprehension scores.[6]

5. Experienced speakers learn to channel their nervousness. As mentioned before, the nervousness you feel is, in controlled amounts, good for you. It takes a certain amount of nervousness to do your best. What you want is for your nervousness to dissipate once you begin your speech. Just as soccer players are likely to report that the nervousness disappears once they engage in play, so too should speakers find nervousness disappearing once they begin to talk.

Specific Behaviors

The following are some specific behaviors that speakers can use to control nervousness. Coping with nervousness begins during the preparation process and extends to the time the speaker actually begins the speech.

1. Pick a topic you are comfortable with. An unsatisfactory topic lays the groundwork for a psychological mind-set that almost guarantees nervousness at the time of the speech. By the same token, having a topic you know about and that is important to you lays the groundwork for a satisfying speech experience.

2. Take time to prepare fully and practice, practice, practice. If you back yourself into a corner and must find material, organize it, write an outline, and practice the speech all in an hour or two, you almost guarantee failure and destroy your confidence. On the other hand, if you do a little work each day for a week before the assignment, you will experience considerably less pressure and increased confidence. In Chapter 11, we'll discuss a complete timetable for preparing major speech assignments.

Experience in preparation and the length and difficulty of the speech will affect your schedule. For instance, experienced speakers often begin research a month before the date they are to give the speech; they then reserve an entire week for rehearsal and revision.

Giving yourself enough time to prepare fully includes sufficient time for rehearsal. Practice your first speech at least two or three times. Your goal is to build habits that will control your behavior during the speech itself. If our national love affair with big-time athletics has taught us anything, it is that careful preparation enables athletes (or speakers) to meet and overcome adversity. Among relatively equal opponents, the winning team is the one that is mentally and physically prepared for the contest. When an athlete says, "I'm going into this competition as well prepared as I can possibly be," he or she is more likely to do well. For example, Michael Jordan's mental concentration and winning attitude is what helps him make the winning basket in so many games! In this regard, speechmaking is like athletics. If you assure yourself that you have carefully prepared and practiced your speech, you will do the kind of job of which you can be proud.

3. Try to schedule your speech at a time that is psychologically best for you. When speeches are being scheduled, you may be able to choose the time. Are you better off "getting it over with"—that is, being the first person to speak that day? If so, volunteer to go first. But regardless of when you speak, do not spend time thinking about yourself or your speech. At the moment the class begins, you have done all you can do to be prepared. Focus your mind on the other speeches and become involved with what each speaker is saying. Then when your turn comes, you will be as relaxed as possible.

4. Control your food and beverages. Don't eat a big meal right before speaking—you may get a stomachache or feel overly loggy. Avoid stimulants like caffeine and sugar—they can get you too revved up. Also avoid drinking milk—milk and milk products can produce a mucus that can affect your voice negatively. The best thing to drink before a speech is water. If you experience dry mouth, try sucking on a mint shortly before you speak.

5. Visualize successful speaking experiences. Visualization is a technique for reducing nervousness that involves developing a mental strategy and picturing yourself implementing that strategy successfully. How many times have you said to yourself, "Well, if I had been in that situation, I would have . . ."? Such statements are a form of visualization. Joe Ayres and Theodore S. Hopf, two scholars who have conducted extensive research on visualization, have found that if people can visualize themselves going through an entire process, they have a much better chance of succeeding when they are in the situation.[7]

Visualization has been used as a major means of improving sports skills. One example is a study of players trying to improve their foul-shooting percentages. Players were divided into three groups. One group never practiced, another group practiced, and a third group visualized practicing. As we would expect, those who practiced improved far more than those who didn't. What seems amazing is that those who only visualized practicing improved almost as much as those who practiced.[8] Imagine what happens when you visualize and practice as well!

By visualizing speechmaking, not only do people seem to lower their general apprehension, but also they report fewer negative thoughts when they actually speak.[9] Successful visualization begins during practice periods. See yourself calm, smiling as you approach the podium. Remind yourself that you have good ideas, that you are well prepared, and that your audience wants to hear

INFOTRAC COLLEGE EDITION

Visualization

Visualization has been recognized as a means of improving performance in many areas, most specifically in athletics. Using InfoTrac College Edition, do a search using the word "visualization" and click on Subject Guide. You'll find many recent sources covering many different areas. Look for "Do Try This at Home" in *Women's Sports and Fitness,* May 1997, and "The Mind of a Champion," *Natural Health,* Jan–Feb 1997. Look specifically for suggested procedures for using visualization.

visualization *a technique for reducing nervousness that involves developing a mental strategy and picturing yourself implementing that strategy successfully*

Speakers, like athletes, are likely to be especially nervous before they begin. But, also like athletes, their anxiety diminishes when they are able to focus less on their feelings and more on what they are doing.

Bob Daemmrich/Stock, Boston

what you have to say. See the audience nodding approvingly as you speak. See them applauding as you finish.

6. Give yourself positive affirmations before you approach the stand. For instance, you might say to yourself, "I'm excited about having the opportunity to share this information with the class," or "I've done my best to get ready, and now I'm ready to speak." Such statements help put you in a positive frame of mind. Although these statements are not magic, they get you thinking on the right track.

If you find yourself engaging in negative self-talk instead, confront your negative statements with positive ones. For example:

If you find yourself saying, "I'm scared," intervene and say, "No, I'm excited."

If you find yourself saying, "Oh, I'm going to forget," say, "I've got note cards. If I do forget, I'll pause, look at my notes, and go on."

If you find yourself saying, "I'm a lousy speaker—what am I doing here?" say, "I'm doing the best I can do for today—and that's okay."

7. Pause for a few seconds before you begin. When you reach the stand, stop a few seconds before you start to speak, and smile at your audience. Take a couple of deep breaths while you make eye contact with the audience;

that may help get your breathing in order. Try to move about a little during the first few sentences; sometimes a few gestures or a step one way or another is enough to break some of the tension.

Persistent Nervousness

When is speaker nervousness a real problem? When it becomes debilitating—when the fear is so great that a person is unable to go through with giving a speech. Recent research has shown that a small number of students are adversely affected by their feelings about speaking. Unfortunately, many of those students respond by dropping the course. But that is not an answer to speech anxiety. In all areas of life, people have to give speeches—they have to get up before peers, people from other organizations, customers, and others to explain their ideas. Although it is never too late to get help, a college speech course is the best time to start working on coping with speech nervousness. Even if your fears prove to be more perception than reality, it's important to take the time to get help.

To start, see your professor outside class and talk with him or her about what you are experiencing. Your professor should be able to offer ideas for people you can see or programs you can attend. As Virginia Richmond and James McCroskey have shown as a result of years of research in communication apprehension, some people do have a need for special programs.[10]

One of the most popular programs is **systematic desensitization,** in which people learn procedures for deep muscular relaxation so that they can visualize participating in a series of communication situations while in a state of deep relaxation.[11] Since "relaxing" is easier said than done, such programs focus on teaching relaxation procedures. The process involves consciously tensing and then relaxing muscle groups in order to learn to recognize the difference between the two states. Then, while in a relaxed state, you imagine yourself in successively more stressful situations—for example, thinking about, preparing for, and finally giving a speech. The ultimate goal is to have people experience calm relaxation as they see themselves giving a speech—and then to transfer that calm feeling to the actual speaking event. Calmness on command—and it works.

systematic desensitization *a form of treatment for reducing nervousness that involves using relaxation techniques while exposing people to the stimulus they fear*

Another program is **cognitive restructuring,** in which people are encouraged to identify irrational beliefs they have about communication. These beliefs are then attacked logically in an attempt to demonstrate to those individuals that they should change their way of thinking.[12] Cognitive restructuring not only helps people identify the illogical beliefs they hold but also provides individualized instruction in formulating more appropriate beliefs. Over time, people can condition themselves to overcome their fears and take a more positive approach to their communication. Many communities offer this type of program.

cognitive restructuring *a form of treatment for reducing nervousness that helps people to identify the illogical beliefs they hold and provides individualized instruction in formulating more appropriate beliefs*

Keep in mind that there are very few speech students who have been so hurt by fear that they can't deliver a speech. The purpose of a speech course is to help you learn and develop the skills that will allow you to achieve even when you feel extremely anxious.

Summary

Preparing a speech involves answering the following seven questions: (1) What is my goal in this speech? (2) Where can I find the kind of information that I

Preparing a Personal Experience Speech

Prepare a 2- to 3-minute personal experience (narrative) speech. Think about experiences you have had that were humorous, suspenseful, or dramatic, and select one that you think your audience would enjoy hearing about.

Figure 2.2 illustrates the kind of outline that is suitable for a short, narrative speech. Figure 2.3 is an example of a student speech that was given to meet this assignment.

need to achieve this goal? (3) How can I organize and outline this information in a way that is most likely to help me achieve my goal? (4) How can I best adapt my speech to my audience? (5) How can I create visual aids that will dramatize my information? (6) What can I focus on in practicing the language of my speech? (7) What can I focus on in practicing the delivery of my speech?

All speakers feel nervous as they approach their first speech. Public speaking nervousness may be cognitive (in the mind) or behavioral (physically displayed). Rather than being an either-or matter, nervousness is a matter of degree.

Because at least some tension is constructive, our goal is not to get rid of nervousness but to learn how to cope with it. Because nearly everyone who speaks in public experiences some nervousness, we need to be aware of several realities. Despite nervousness, you can make it through your speech; moreover, listeners are not nearly as likely to recognize your fear as you might think. In addition, the more experience you get in speaking and the better prepared you

F I G U R E *2.2* **Personal experience speech outline**

Narrative Speech

Specific Goal: I want my audience to laugh at my realization that my clothes had not been taken.

Introduction
   I. I had joined a local gym so that one day I could look like Arnold Schwarzenegger.

Body
   I. I returned to my locker from my usual bone-crushing workout.
      A. The lock was ajar.
      B. My clothes, wallet, and keys were gone.
   II. I raced to the clerk's cage to report the robbery.
      A. I described what had happened.
      B. I pleaded for the attendant to call the police.
   III. I returned to my locker to wait for the police.
      A. To my amazement the lock was back on the locker.
      B. When I opened the door my clothes were there.
      C. I had looked in the wrong locker!

Conclusion
   I. Totally embarrassed, I envisioned being man enough to admit my mistake.
   II. Instead, I said to myself, "I think I'll just go out the back door."

A while back, I joined a local gym with the express purpose of taking up weight lifting in hopes that someday people would have difficulty in telling me and Arnold Schwarzenegger apart. One day, when I had returned to my locker after my usual bone-crushing workout, I noticed that my lock was through the handle of my locker, not through the hole at the bottom that locks the locker. "Dumbhead," I said to myself, "that's a sure way of ending up in trouble." And sure enough, when I opened the locker my worst fears were confirmed—my wallet was gone, my keys were gone, and my pants were gone. I was outraged. I couldn't even drive myself home. I went running out of the locker room and up to the clerk who worked at the desk. I started yelling at him, "Call the police—I've been robbed."

"What happened?" he asked.

"I've been robbed!" I repeated.

"Are you sure?" he asked.

"Of course I'm sure," I said. "I looked in my locker and my clothes are gone!"

"Okay," he said. "I'll call the police."

Because I knew it would take a while for the police to come, I thought that maybe if I went back to the scene of the crime I could find some evidence—perhaps the thief had dropped part of my clothing, or maybe a credit card had fallen from my wallet. So I approached the locker the second time and did a double take when I noticed that now the lock was through the hole at the bottom of the handle as it should have been. "Great," I said. "Now that everything is gone I remembered to put the lock back on right." So I unlocked the locker, opened the door—and found my pants, my wallet, and my keys. A slow red burn of embarrassment began to form. I had looked in the wrong locker—one that was one row behind.

What could I do? "No problem," I said to myself. "I'm a man, right? I can take it, right? I can swallow my pride, look directly at the clerk, and announce 'I've made an error. I'm sorry you had to call the police. In fact, I'll even make the call myself and apologize directly to the police.'"

I took several firm strides back toward the desk, full of resolve and feeling very proud of my manly behavior. Then I stopped and said to myself, "Nah, I'll just go out the back door."

are, the better you will cope with nervousness. In fact, experienced speakers learn to channel their nervousness in ways that help them to do their best.

Even though nervousness is normal, you can use several specific behaviors to help control it. (1) Pick a topic you are comfortable with. (2) Take time to prepare fully and practice, practice, practice. (3) Try to schedule your speech at a time that is psychologically best for you. (4) Control your food and beverages. (5) Visualize successful speaking experiences. (6) Give yourself positive affirmations before you approach the stand. (7) Pause for a few seconds before you begin.

If nervousness is truly detrimental to your performance, see your professor outside class and talk with him or her about what you are experiencing. Your professor should be able to offer ideas for people you can see or programs you can attend.

A good listener tries to understand thoroughly what the other person is saying.

Kenneth A. Wells, *Guide to Good Leadership*

Listening Critically

As Prof. Norton finished her point on means of evaluating social legislation, she said, "Let me remind you that the primary criterion is the value to the general public at large, not the profit people can make from exploiting the legislation."

As Ben, Shawna, and Tim were walking from the class, Ben said, "I was glad to hear that Norton recognized the importance of making profit from social legislation."

"That wasn't her point," said Shawna. "She said that the emphasis is on the value to the general public."

"I'm sure she emphasized profitability. Tim, what do you think she said?"

"Man, I don't even know what you're talking about. I was thinking about my math test this afternoon."

oes the chapter opening conversation ring any bells with you? Have you had times when you'd swear that you heard right when you didn't? If your answer is "Not me," then we congratulate you, for this example illustrates the most common listening problems among people—missing what was said, hearing it but misunderstanding, and/or not listening or not remembering.

Now that we've previewed the action steps in preparing a speech and considered coping with nervousness, we switch our emphasis from speaking to listening—specifically, listening critically to speeches. **Listening**—"the process of receiving, attending to, and assigning meaning to aural and visual stimuli"[1]—is a necessary skill in public speaking. First, we listen far more than we speak. In most professional settings, from 41 to 60 percent or more of our communication time is spent listening.[2] In this course, if you are scheduled for five speeches, everyone in a class of 15 will speak five times, but will hear 70 other speeches! Moreover, many of us are not as good at it as we need to be. For instance, after hearing a 10-minute oral presentation, the average listener hears, comprehends, and retains only about 50 percent of the message. After 48 hours, most listeners can remember only about 25 percent of what they heard.[3]

So, we can see that most of us need to learn to be better listeners. Equally important, becoming a better listener has several benefits for you in this course.

1. Better listening helps us become better speakers. By listening effectively to the 50 to 100 speeches you will hear this term, you will be able to determine how and why various speech methods and techniques work. As a result, you may decide which methods and techniques you should try in your own speeches. You can also hear and see in action the kinds of mistakes to avoid. In addition, by understanding your audience's decoding process and the potential roadblocks to their attending to your speech, you can organize your talk to overcome your listeners' obstacles to active listening.

2. Better listening helps us to become better speech critics. As you learn to listen critically for the ways in which speakers use or misuse the fundamental principles of public speaking, you can provide much better constructive criticism for fellow speakers.

3. Better listening results in our learning more about a great number of subjects. Think of this reason as a bonus: By listening carefully to the many speeches in a public speaking course, you will supplement your education, for the speeches are likely to be on topics from a broad spectrum of knowledge.

In this chapter, we consider the nature and importance of attending to speeches, understanding and retaining speech information, and critically analyzing the effectiveness of the speech. In other chapters, we will address the importance of the speaker's getting and keeping audience members' attention so that they can be more effective listeners.

listening the process of receiving, attending to, and assigning meaning to aural and visual stimuli

Attending to the Speech

attending the perceptual process of selecting specific stimuli from the countless stimuli reaching the senses

Attending is the perceptual process of selecting specific stimuli from the countless stimuli reaching the senses. In other words, attending is really paying attention to what the speaker is saying regardless of extraneous interferences.

Poor listeners have difficulty exercising control over what they attend to, often letting their mind drift to thoughts totally unassociated with the speech.

Remember Tim's response to the question of which interpretation was more on target? "I don't even know what you're talking about—I was thinking about my math test this afternoon." Consider your own experiences listening to speeches, such as your professors' class lectures. Aren't there times that you daydream about something else? Likewise, aren't there times when the speaker's mannerisms, such as throat clearing or pacing, distract you?

Listening to speeches places a special listening burden on us for several reasons. Speeches are relatively uninterrupted, one-way communication. Because we do not have the option of interjecting comments, it is easier for us to let our attention drift, often to the point that we may not hear some of what the speaker is saying. Because there are so many interferences to listening, it's useful to train ourselves to attend to what is being said more effectively.

Let's consider four techniques for consciously focusing attention.

1. Get physically and mentally ready to listen. Suppose that a few minutes after class begins your professor says, "In the next two minutes, I'm going to cover some material that is especially important—in fact, I can guarantee that it will be on the test." How would you behave? If you are a good listener, you are likely to sit upright in your chair, lean slightly forward, and cease any extraneous physical movement. All of these are physical signs of being ready to listen. You may also look directly at the professor—when eye contact is not maintained, at least some information is lost.[4]

Mentally, you are likely to direct all of your attention to what the professor is saying, attempting to block out the miscellaneous thoughts constantly passing through your mind. Recall that when people are talking with you, their ideas and feelings compete with the internal noise created by whatever's on your mind at the moment—a basketball game, a calculus test, a date you're excited about, a movie you've just seen. And what you're thinking about may be more pleasant to attend to than what someone is saying to you. Attending to these competing thoughts and feelings is one of the leading causes of poor listening.

Bob Daemmrich/Stock, Boston

Which of these people are listening attentively? Which aren't? How can you tell?

2. Hear the speaker out regardless of your thoughts or feelings. Far too often, we let a person's mannerisms and words "turn us off." For instance, we may become annoyed when a speaker mutters, stammers, or talks in a monotone. Likewise, we may let a speaker's language or ideas turn us off. If you find yourself upset by a speaker's ideas on gay rights, welfare fraud, political correctness, or any controversial topic, instead of tuning out or getting ready to fight, work that much harder to listen objectively so that you can understand the speaker's position before you respond.

3. Adjust to the listening goals of the situation. When you are listening to a speaker for pleasure, you can afford to listen without much intensity. Unfortunately, many people approach all speech situations as if they were listening to pass time. But in public forums as well as in class, your goal is to understand and retain information or to listen critically to be able to evaluate what speakers say and how they say it. In the remainder of this chapter, we consider guidelines for adjusting your listening to meet the demands of these goals.

4. Identify the benefits of attending to the speaker's words. At times we do this almost automatically, especially when the speaker makes a point of stating the benefits. For instance, your professor's saying, "Pay attention to this explanation—I'll tell you right now, it will be the basis for one of the major test questions," is almost guaranteed to boost your listening efficiency. But you can provide your own motivation. As you listen, ask yourself how you might use the specific information in the near future. For instance, you may be able to use the information in a discussion with your friends, or to help you solve problems, or to understand how to profit. Identifying benefits may motivate you to apply each of the three previous behaviors even more regularly.

Understanding and Retaining Speech Information

understanding   *the ability to decode a message by correctly assigning a meaning to it*

retaining   *storing information in memory and using techniques that will help you identify and recall that information*

active listening behaviors   *specific behaviors that turn a speech into a kind of dialogue*

The second aspect of listening to speeches is to understand and retain what the speaker is saying. **Understanding** is the ability to decode a message by correctly assigning a meaning to it. **Retaining** is using techniques that will help you identify and recall information that you have stored. Both understanding and retaining are facilitated by the use of active listening behaviors. Whereas passive listening behaviors involve just letting the words come and go, **active listening behaviors** are specific behaviors—determining organization, asking questions, silently paraphrasing, attending to nonverbal cues, and taking notes—that help you turn a speech into a kind of dialogue.

Understanding depends on the ability to make sense out of both verbal and nonverbal messages. The larger your own vocabulary, the more likely you are able to understand speakers' content, however erudite their speeches may be; the more you are in tune with a speaker's sound of voice, facial expression, and gestures, the more likely you are to understand the speaker's intentions.

But just understanding is not enough. Good listening also requires us to engage in activities that will help us store information in memory so that later we can talk about the speaker's message and be able to analyze the speaker's effectiveness. To help you both understand better and retain more, let's consider five active listening behaviors.

1. Determine the speaker's organization. Determining the organization helps listeners establish a framework for the information. In any extended message, the speaker is likely to have an overall organizational pattern for the information that includes a goal, key ideas (or main points) to develop the goal, and details to explain or support the main points. Effective listeners mentally outline the organization so that when the speech is over they can cite the goal, main points, and some of the key details.

For instance, during a PTA meeting, Gloria Minton, a teacher, speaks on the topic of teenage harassment. As she talks, she mentions information related to why students harass others, what can be done in schools to deter such harassment, and what can be done at home to help students understand the problem of harassment. In her talk, she includes information she's gained from her experiences at the school and information that she's learned in workshops that relates to each of these points. When Gloria finishes speaking, her listeners will understand that Gloria wants to help parents understand the need to deal with student harassment (her goal), the nature of the problem and what can be done at school and at home to alleviate it (her main points), and the material she has provided to explain or support each point.

Sometimes, people organize their speeches so that it is easy to identify their goal, key points, and details. At other times, however, we must work to be sure that we have a grasp of the organization. You can sort out the purpose, key points, and details of a complex message, and thus increase your understanding of the message, by mentally outlining the message. Asking "What am I supposed to know/do because I listened to this?" will allow you to determine purpose. Asking "What are the categories of information?" and "Why should I do/think this?" will enable you to identify key points. Asking "What's the support?" will enable you to identify the details.

2. Ask yourself questions. Asking yourself questions, as we have seen, helps you identify key aspects of the speech. Asking yourself questions also

Bob Daemmrich/Stock, Boston

People who are active listeners mentally question to anticipate information and silently paraphrase key information that they have heard.

helps you to determine whether enough information was presented. For instance, if a person says, "Swimming is an activity that provides exercise for almost every muscle," active listeners might inwardly question "How?" and then pay attention to the supporting material offered or request it if the speaker does not supply it.

3. Silently paraphrase key information. Silent paraphrases help listeners understand material. A **paraphrase** is not just a repetition; rather, it is a statement in your own words of the meaning you have assigned to a message. After you have listened to a message, you should be able to summarize your understanding. For example, after a person has spent a few minutes explaining the relationship between ingredients and amounts in recipes and the way a mixture is achieved, you can say to yourself, "In other words, how the mixture is put together may be more important than the ingredients used." If you cannot paraphrase a message, either the message was not well encoded or you were not listening carefully enough.

4. Attend to nonverbal cues. Listeners interpret messages more accurately when they observe the nonverbal behaviors accompanying the words, for meaning may be shown as much by the nonverbals as by the spoken words. So, whether you are listening to a politician explaining her stance on deficit reduction or the director of parking explaining the system of priorities for obtaining parking passes to the new parking garage, you must pay attention to tone of voice, facial expression, and gestures. For instance, the director of parking might tell a freshman that he stands a good chance of getting a parking sticker for the garage, but the sound of the person's voice may suggest that the chances are not really that good.

5. Take good notes. Although note taking would be inappropriate in most casual interpersonal encounters, it is perhaps the most important method of improving retention of ideas presented in speeches. Not only does note taking provide a written record that you can go back to, but also by taking notes you take a more active role in the listening process.[5] In short, when you are listening to complex information, take notes.

paraphrase *a statement in your own words of the meaning you have assigned to a message*

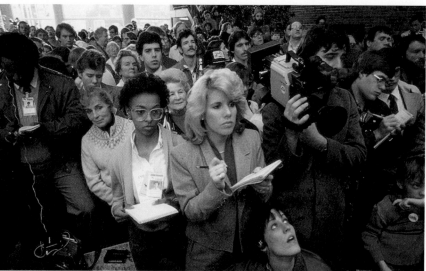

Arthur Grace/Stock, Boston

Just as there are many kinds of speeches, there are many situations in which good listening and note-taking skills will serve you well.

Listening Test

Have a friend assume the role of a coworker on your first day in an office job and read the following information to you once, at a normal rate of speech. As the friend reads the instructions, take notes. Then give yourself the test that follows but without referring to your notes. Then repeat the quiz, this time using your notes. How much did your score improve? Finally, compare your notes to the outline shown in Figure 3.1.

Although the temptation is great to read this item to yourself, try not to. You will miss both the enjoyment and the value of the exercise if you do. Don't look at the answers on page 42 until you have completed the exercise.

****

"Since you are new to the job, I'd like to fill you in on a few details. The boss probably told you that typing and distribution of mail were your most important duties. Well, they may be, but let me tell you, answering the phone is going to take most of your time. Now about the typing. Goodwin will give the most, but much of what he gives you may have nothing to do with the department—I'd be careful about spending all my time doing his private work. Mason doesn't give much, but you'd better get it right—she's really a stickler. I've always asked to have tests at least two days in advance. Bernstein is always dropping stuff on the desk at the last minute.

The mail situation sounds tricky, but you'll get used to it. Mail comes twice a day—at 10 A.M. and at 2 P.M. You've got to take the mail that's been left on the desk to Charles Hall for pickup. If you really have some rush stuff, take it right to the campus post office in Harper Hall. It's a little longer walk, but for really rush stuff, it's better. When you pick up at McDaniel Hall, sort it. You'll have to make sure that only mail for the people up here gets delivered here. If there is any that doesn't belong here, bundle it back up and mark it for return to the campus post office.

Now, about your breaks. You get 10 minutes in the morning, 45 minutes at noon, and 15 minutes in the afternoon. If you're smart, you'll leave before the 10:30 classes let out. That's usually a pretty crush time. Three of the teachers are supposed to have office hours then, and if they don't keep them, the students will be on your back. If you take your lunch at 11:45, you'll be back before the main crew goes.

Oh, one more thing. You are supposed to call Jeno at 8:15 every morning to wake him. If you forget, he gets very upset. Well, good luck. (348 wds)
****

With Notes	Without Notes	
____	____	**1.** Where are you to take the mail that does not belong here?
____	____	**2.** How often does mail come?
____	____	**3.** When should you be back from lunch?
____	____	**4.** What is Bernstein's problem with work?
____	____	**5.** Who gives the most work?
____	____	**6.** What's the problem with Goodwin's request to do work?
____	____	**7.** What are your main jobs, according to the boss?
____	____	**8.** Where are you to take outgoing mail?
____	____	**9.** Where is the post office?
____	____	**10.** How many minutes do you get for your morning break?
____	____	**11.** What is the preferred time to take your lunch?
____	____	**12.** Who are you supposed to give a wake-up call?

FIGURE 3.1 Sample notes for listening test

Duties
  Typing and distribution of mail most important
  Answering phone takes most time
Typing
  Goodwin will give most
    Question spending time on his private work
  Mason not give much
    Get it right—she's really a stickler
  Ask for tests 2 days in advance
    Or get stuck by Bernstein at last minute
Mail
  10 and 2
  Take the mail on the desk to Charles Hall
  Take rush stuff to the campus post in Harper Hall
  Sort mail you pick up at McDaniel Hall—bundle what
  doesn't belong and mark it for return to the campus post office

Breaks
  10 minutes morning—take before 10:30
  40 minutes noon—take at 11:45
Extra
  Call Jeno 8:15   (112 words)

What constitutes good notes varies by situation. Good notes may consist of a brief list of main points, key ideas, or governing points plus a few of the most significant details. Or good notes may be a short summary of the entire concept presented in the complete speech (a type of paraphrase). For lengthy and rather detailed information, however, good notes often consist of a brief outline of the speech, including the overall idea, the main points of the message, and key developmental material. A formal outline helps to create a structure for the information you want to retain and distinguishes among main points, subpoints, and illustrative material. Good notes are not necessarily long; in fact, many speeches can be reduced to short notes in outline form.

Ideally, good notes will look something like the speaker's outline.

analyzing speeches *determining the quality of the speech material—how truthful, authentic, or believable you judge the information to be—and the speaker's skill in communicating content, organization, language, visual aids, and delivery*

determining effectiveness *evaluating the extent to which a speaker has achieved his or her specific goal*

Analyzing Speeches and Determining Their Effectiveness

Analyzing speeches involves determining the quality of the speech material—how truthful, authentic, or believable you judge the information to be—and the speaker's skill in communicating content, organization, language, visual aids, and delivery. **Determining effectiveness** focuses on the extent to which the speaker has achieved his or her specific goal. For instance, when a person tries to explain the effects of a certain drug or tries to convince you to vote for a particular candidate for office, you will want to listen critically to these messages to determine how sound were their explanations and support and how effective they were in getting you to understand or to believe.

In the next two parts of the book, we will be providing information that will help you analyze the various speeches you will be hearing (and preparing) throughout this course.

Bases of Evaluation

From a pedagogical standpoint, the analysis of speeches not only provides the speaker with an analysis of where the speech went right and where it went wrong, but also gives you, the critic, insight into methods that you will want to incorporate or avoid in presenting your own speeches.

As we have said, a speech can be evaluated on at least two bases: how well the speaker has met specific criteria of effective speaking, and the speaker's overall effectiveness in meeting his or her goal.

The second of these, determining the overall effectiveness of a speech, turns out to be a difficult task. On the surface, a speech is effective when it is successful—that is, when it (1) achieves its specific goal or (2) brings the audience significantly closer to that goal. By this criterion, for example, if a speech helps an audience understand the steps of imposition, composition, and printing that are fundamental to the process of magazine production, or if a speech convinces an audience that Congress should pass stricter handgun-control laws, then the speech is considered a success.

Of course, the problem any critic faces is that in most situations there is no objective way to measure the audience's degree of understanding or conviction. Moreover, even if such a measurement could be achieved, the critic still could not be sure whether the audience's understanding or conviction resulted directly from the speech or from other factors.

Specific Criteria for Evaluating Speeches

Because overall effectiveness is so complex, most critics base their evaluation on how well the speaker has met specific criteria of effective speaking. The critical assumption is that if a speech has good content and is well organized, well worded, and well delivered, then it is more likely to achieve its goal.

The Speech Evaluation Checklist on p. 44 contains questions that can be adapted to evaluate any speech. Such a checklist is appropriate for at least two speech situations. The first is when your goal is to provide feedback to a classmate on all aspects of a speech. The second is when you are asked to critique a speech outside the classroom setting. Regardless of the speech you hear, your answers to the questions will provide the basis for a good analysis of the speech.

For a truly comprehensive analysis, however, the speech checklist must relate to the specific type of speech and its specific goal. Within each of the general categories of content, organization, language, and delivery, different questions may apply to different types of speeches. For instance, the evaluation of an informative demonstration speech must consider the visual aids used in the demonstration; the evaluation of a persuasion speech of conviction must consider the reasons and evidence that were used to support the proposition. Accordingly, for all of the speech assignments in this text, where we analyze

SPEECH EVALUATION checklist

Check items that were accomplished effectively.

Content

_____ **1.** Was the goal of the speech clear?

_____ **2.** Did the speaker have high-quality information?

_____ **3.** Did the speaker use a variety of kinds of developmental material?

_____ **4.** Were visual aids appropriate and well used?

_____ **5.** Did the speaker establish common ground and adapt the content to the audience's interests, knowledge, and attitudes?

Organization

_____ **6.** Did the introduction gain attention and goodwill, set the tone, build credibility, and lead into the speech?

_____ **7.** Were the main points complete sentences that were clear, parallel, and meaningful?

_____ **8.** Did transitions lead smoothly from one point to another?

_____ **9.** Did the conclusion tie the speech together?

Language

_____ **10.** Was the language clear?

_____ **11.** Was the language vivid?

_____ **12.** Was the language emphatic?

_____ **13.** Was the language appropriate?

Delivery

_____ **14.** Did the speaker sound enthusiastic?

_____ **15.** Did the speaker show sufficient vocal expressiveness?

_____ **16.** Was the presentation spontaneous?

_____ **17.** Was the presentation fluent?

_____ **18.** Did the speaker look at the audience?

_____ **19.** Were the pronunciation and articulation acceptable?

_____ **20.** Did the speaker have good posture?

_____ **21.** Did the speaker have sufficient poise?

Based on these criteria," evaluate the speech as (check one):
_____ excellent, _____ good, _____ satisfactory, _____ fair, _____ poor.

different types of speech skills, we'll present specific critique checklists that focus on the features emphasized in those particular assignments as well as on the questions that apply to all speeches.

The Importance of Feedback

Although it's important for you to know what to look for in a speech, it is also important for you to know how to give meaningful feedback in class. The goal of feedback is to praise good speech behaviors and to help speakers improve

Michael Newman/Photo Edit

Critical listeners don't accept a speaker's argument until they've heard supporting information and examined its relevance to the claim.

areas of weakness. You might also think of feedback as not just for the speakers, but also for those who will be speaking. For what is said in one class sets the standards for behavior in the next.

For each round of speeches, the professor is likely to state primary criteria—the most important elements for consideration in that particular type of speech. For instance, in the first round, the primary criteria might well be quality of delivery and overall organization. A useful procedure, then, is first to identify what was done well on these criteria and later to talk about what could be done to make speeches even better.

It is especially important to begin with positive feedback. When our behaviors are praised, we are more likely to continue to do well in those areas. So, if for a round of speeches a primary criterion is good delivery, you'll want to identify who did a particularly good job of showing enthusiasm or looking at members of the class during the speech. Make your comments as specific as you can. For instance, "I particularly liked Mary's vocal expressiveness. She did an excellent job in varying pitch and emphasizing key words."

After giving praise, it's a good idea to then ask the question, "Regardless of how good speeches were, what were some things that speakers could have done to make their speeches even better?" This phrasing suggests that even an "A" speech might have been improved in some small way. It also gets away from emphasizing how badly something was done. For instance, someone might say, "Although Mary's organization was very good, she could have improved our understanding of main points by stating each of them in a complete sentence." This phrasing is specific and constructive—much better than say, "I didn't really get Mary's main points."

In a short session of oral feedback, the class is able to see areas in which speakers did especially well and areas where improvement is possible. And, as we said, those speaking next will know the standards they have to meet.

Table 3.1 summarizes how good listeners and poor listeners deal with the three aspects of critical listening: attending, understanding/retaining, and critically analyzing.

TABLE 3.1 **A summary of the three aspects of critical listening**

	Good Listeners	Bad Listeners
Attending to the Speech	Attend to important information	May not hear what a person is saying
	Ready themselves physically and mentally	Fidget in their chairs, look out the window, and let their minds wander
	Listen objectively regardless of emotional involvement	Visibly react to emotional language
	Listen differently depending on the situation	Listen the same way regardless of the type of material
Understanding/Retaining Speech Information	Assign appropriate meaning to what is said	Hear what is said, but either are unable to understand or assign a different meaning to the words
	Seek out apparent purpose, main points, and supporting information	Ignore the way information is organized
	Take good notes	Rely on memory alone
	Ask questions to get information	Seldom or never ask questions
	Paraphrase to solidify understanding	Seldom or never paraphrase
	Seek out subtle meanings based on nonverbal cues	Ignore nonverbal cues
Analyzing Speeches	Analyze on the basis of specific criteria that are relevant to the type of speech	Rely on how they react to the speech in general
	Give useful, specific positive feedback	Give overall evaluations without mentioning specifics
	Consider one or two skills that could have been used better	Focus on negative aspects without showing what could have been done better

Summary

Listening is the process of receiving, attending to, and assigning meaning to aural and visual stimuli. Listening is an active process that includes attending, understanding/retaining, and critical analysis. Reasons for studying critical listening are to become better speakers, to become better speech critics, and, as a bonus, to learn more about many topics.

Attending (hearing) effectiveness is sharpened by getting ready to listen, hearing the speaker out regardless of your thoughts or feelings, and adjusting attention to the listening goals of different situations.

Understanding/retaining is enhanced by determining the speaker's organization, taking good notes, asking rhetorical questions, silently paraphrasing, and paying attention to nonverbal cues.

Critical analysis is the process of both determining how truthful, authentic, or believable you judge a speaker's information to be and determining how effective the speaker is in meeting his or her goal. Because overall effectiveness is so complex, most critics base their evaluation on how well the speaker has met specific criteria related to the type of speech that has been given.

As they were returning from a rally at the University Field House in which candidates for the two Congressional districts that surrounded the University spoke, Nikita asked Lance what he thought of the speech given by Steve Chabot, the Republican candidate for office in the 1st district.

"Chabot, he's just like any Republican; he's going to make sure that big business is all right."

"I didn't hear him talking about big business. I thought he was talking about the importance of limiting the amount of federal government intrusion in state matters."

"Sure, that's what he said, but we know what he really meant."

"I asked you what you thought of the speech. What ideas did he present that turned you off?"

"Listen, you don't really have to listen to any Republican speaking. Everyone knows that Republicans are for big business and only Democrats are going to watch out for people like us."

1. Is Lance's failure to listen critically an ethical issue? If so, why?

2. If Lance really were listening critically, what should he be discussing with Nikita?

The secret of success is constancy to purpose.

Benjamin Disraeli, June 24, 1870

Selecting a Topic, Analyzing the Audience and Setting, and Determining Your Speech Goal

Donna Montez is a marine biologist. See knows that her audience wants to hear her talk about marine biology. But she doesn't know what aspect of the topic she should focus on.

Ben Petrocelli is running for office. For the speech he will give to a group of people living in the West End, he knows that his goal is to say something that will motivate these constituents to vote for him.

Dan Wong has been invited to speak to an assembly at his old inner-city high school. He thinks that he may have a lot to say to these students coming up behind him, but most of all, he wants them to understand the qualities a person needs to do well in college.

Ayanna Cartland is taking a public speaking class. Her first speech is scheduled two weeks from tomorrow, but as of today, she doesn't have the foggiest idea what she's going to talk about.

ny of these chapter opening situations seem familiar? These are just examples of where we might stand with the clarity of our goal when we start our preparation for an assigned speech. Although you may be as far along as Donna or Ben in knowing what you want to achieve in your speech, in this chapter we'll assume that for your classroom speech your situation is more like Ayanna's.

In preparing any speech, the first action step is to determine a specific speech goal that is adapted to your audience and setting. In this chapter, we consider the four major aspects of completing this action step: selecting a topic from a subject area that is important to you and that you know something about, analyzing your audience, considering the speech setting, and articulating the specific response that you want from your audience. Although each issue in the process is discussed separately, they do overlap and are sometimes accomplished in a different order.

Selecting a Topic from a Subject Area

In real-life settings, people are invited to give speeches because of their expertise on a particular subject. But even when an organization requests a speech on a particular subject, selecting the topic is often in the hands of the speaker. What is the difference between subject and topic? A **subject** is a broad area of knowledge, such as the stock market, cognitive psychology, baseball, or the Middle East. A **topic** is some specific aspect of a subject. Thus, an authority on the subject of the stock market might be prepared to speak on such diverse topics as the nature of the New York Stock Exchange, NASDAQ, investment strategies, or bull versus bear markets.

The goal of this section is to help you identify suitable subject areas and then select potential specific topics from those subject areas.

subject *a broad area of knowledge, such as the stock market, cognitive psychology, baseball, or the Middle East*

topic *some specific aspect of a subject*

Identifying Subjects

When you are asked (or required) to give a speech, use the same criteria for identifying subjects as those used by professional speakers. Start by identifying subject areas that (1) are important to you and (2) you know something about,

A C T I O N   S T E P   O N E

Determine a Goal

Determine a specific speech goal that is adapted to your audience.

A. Select a topic from a subject area you know something about and that is important to you.

B. Analyze your audience.

C. Analyze your setting.

D. Articulate your goal by determining the response that you want from your audience.

and then select suitable topics within those areas. Just as Bill Gates draws many of his topics from the subjects of computers and computer programming, Gloria Steinem draws from the subject of feminism, and Jesse Jackson draws from the subject of social and political issues, you should draw your topics from subjects that you know something about and that are important to you.

Subjects that meet these criteria probably include such things as your vocation (major, prospective profession, or current job), your hobbies or leisure activities, and special interests (social, economic, educational, or political concerns). Thus, if retailing is your actual or prospective vocation, tennis is your favorite activity, and problems of illiteracy, substance abuse, and toxic and nontoxic waste are your special concerns, then these are subject areas from which you could draw topics.

Let's consider Ayanna, whom you met at the beginning of this chapter. She is the firstborn child of an African American family and has come to college from her home in Hamilton, Ohio, a small town north of Cincinnati. Ayanna is the first member of her family to go to college. Her parents both work to support their three children. In high school Ayanna loved dramatics and was on the debate team. She thinks she might like to be a lawyer or politician, and her tentative major is history. So as Ayanna began to think about subject areas, she selected history (her college major), dramatics (a hobby), and welfare reform (a personal concern or issue).

At this point, it is tempting to think, "Why not just talk on something I know an audience wants to hear?" The reason for avoiding this temptation is that an audience chooses to listen to a speaker *because* of perceived expertise or insight on a particular subject. When even professional speakers believe that they can talk about anything, they find it very easy to get in "over their heads."

Of course, over time you can become an expert in a particular subject area, and occasionally you may be asked to speak on subjects that are less familiar to you, but to begin with it's a good idea to speak about those subject areas in which you have already spent considerable time developing expertise and insight.

Obviously, speakers do need to be sensitive to their audience and setting. As we will see, information about audience and setting helps shape speech goals and determine the kinds of information used in speeches.

Table 4.1 contains subjects that students in two classes at the University of Cincinnati listed under major or vocational interest, hobby or activity, and issue or concern.

Brainstorming for Topics

To generate a list of specific topics from the subject areas you have identified, you can use a form of **brainstorming**—an uncritical, nonevaluative process of generating associated ideas. Under the subject of tennis, for example, you might list players, equipment, oversize rackets, balls, shoes, serves, drop shots, volleys, forehands, backhands, lobs, net play, two-handed backhand stroke, Wimbledon, U.S. Open, grass, clay, concrete, scoring, rules. Notice in this list that some of the items seem to be categories and other items seem to be specific. As you're going through the process, don't worry about whether there is any order to your items. The goal of this exercise is to amass ideas. Later, when you make a choice, you might decide that you want to focus on a category rather than an item. For instance, you may decide that you want to compare

brainstorming *an uncritical, nonevaluative process of generating associated ideas*

TABLE 4.1 Student subject lists

Major or Vocational Interest	Hobby or Activity	Issue or Concern
communication	soccer	crime
disc jockey	weightlifting	governmental ethics
marketing	music	environment
public relations	travel	media impact on society
elementary teaching	photography	censorship
sales	mountain biking	same-sex marriage
reporting	hiking	taxes
hotel management	volleyball	presidential politics
motherhood	advertising	cloning
fashion design	genealogy	global warming
law	backpacking	child abuse
human resources	horseback riding	road rage
computer programming	sailing	illiteracy
nurse	swimming	effects of smoking
doctor	magic	women's rights
politics	gambling	abortion

TECHNOLOGY tips

After you have identified a subject area for your speech, you can use the electronic databases or the Internet to help you as you brainstorm for topic ideas. Try this technique. Using the Internet, go to a search engine such as Yahoo!, Lycos, or Infoseek, and enter the keyword for your subject. As you read through the citations that your search identifies, note words that are related to your subject and add those to your brainstorming list.

tennis surfaces, in which case you'll talk about grass, clay, and concrete. When you start with a subject area of expertise and interest, you often can list 20, 30, or even more related topics.

To brainstorm for topics, divide a sheet of paper into three columns. Label column 1 Major or Vocation, column 2 Hobby or Activity, and column 3 Personal Concerns (Issues). Work for at least a few minutes on one column. Then

FOCUS ON skills

Brainstorming for Topics

The goal of this practice is to help you select a topic for your first speech.

Divide a sheet of paper into three columns. Label column 1 with your major or vocation, such as Art History; label column 2 with a hobby or an activity, such as Chess; and label column 3 with a concern or an issue, such as Water Pollution.

Working on one column at a time, brainstorm a list of at least 20 related topics for each column. (See below.)

Check one topic in each column that has special meaning to you or that seems particularly appropriate for your classroom audience. Then select one of these three topics for your first speech.

Hobby: Magic

tricks	Houdini	secrets	card tricks
paraphernalia	Copperfield	vanishing	animals
staging	training	trapdoors	dexterity
sleight of hand	Magic Castle	rigging	
displacement	vocabulary	costs	
magicians	dangers	staging	

begin a second column. Although you may not finish all three columns in one sitting, try to list at least 20 items in each column before you begin evaluating them. When the list under each column is complete, read the entries and check the topic that strikes you as particularly important or that might be of special interest to your audience.

Brainstorming allows you to take advantage of the basic commonsense principle that just as it is easier to select a correct answer to a multiple-choice question than to think of the answer to the same question without the choices, so too it is easier to select a topic from a list than to come up with a topic out of the blue. Instead of asking, "What should I talk about?" ask yourself, "What is the topic under each subject heading that is most compelling to me?"

Analyzing the Audience

Speeches are given for a particular audience. No matter what your specific topic, how you go about discussing that topic depends to a large extent on the nature of your audience. Consequently, early in your preparation process, you need to analyze your prospective audience to lay the groundwork for audience adaptation.

Audience analysis is the study of the specific audience for your speech. **Audience adaptation** is the active process of relating your speech material directly to your specific audience. Audience analysis includes (1) gathering essential audience demographic data in order to determine in what ways a majority of audience members are alike and (2) making predictions of audience level of interest in, knowledge of, and attitudes toward you and your topic. The results of this analysis can guide you in determining your goal and in developing strategies for selecting supporting material, organizing the material, and presenting your speech in ways that adapt to your specific audience.

audience analysis   *the study of the specific audience for a speech*

audience adaptation   *the active process of relating your speech material directly to your specific audience*

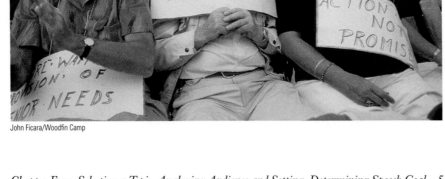

John Ficara/Woodfin Camp

Effective speakers can use audience age as a particularly good predictor of their interests, knowledge, and attitudes.

For instance, suppose that Manuel Sanchez, who plays on the varsity tennis team, is scheduled to give two speeches—one to a group of elementary school children and one to the Community Social Society. Manuel would consider specific characteristics of his two audiences (audience analysis) to determine an audience profile. Then, during his preparation period, he would think of ways of communicating to each of these markedly different audiences (audience adaptation). At this stage of preparation, we focus on the audience analysis. Then, throughout the remainder of the preparation process, we use what we have learned in order to consider various means of relating to our specific audience (audience adaptation).

Kinds of Audience Data Needed

Let's first consider what kinds of audience data you need for your speech; then we'll consider ways in which you can get that information.

Since all audiences are different, sometimes in subtle ways, the goal of audience analysis is to find out in what ways they are alike and in what ways they differ. By finding out how the members of a particular audience are alike, you'll have a basis for selecting information that will resonate with large segments of the audience. By finding out how the members of a particular audience are different from each other and from *you*, you can use that information to determine what you will have to do to adapt to them.

Most of us find it easy to talk with people who are like ourselves. For instance, college men of roughly the same age and background have enough in common that they find ways to talk with each other rather easily. On the other hand, a college man who is giving a speech to a group of adult businesswomen cannot assume that he can relate to them as easily. So, given the reality that even your classroom audience is likely to contain some or many people who have different backgrounds and experiences, you must be willing to think about similarities and differences as you gather information, organize, and fill out the structure of your speech. By drawing a profile of your specific audience, you have the data to make intelligent decisions about how you need to proceed with your speech.

The specific categories in which you need accurate audience data are age, education, gender, occupation, income, culture, geographic uniqueness, and group affiliation.

Age   What is the average age of your audience, and what is the age range?

Education   Do audience members have high school, college, or postcollege education, or are their education levels mixed?

Gender   Will your audience be primarily male, primarily female, or fairly well balanced?

Occupation   Does the majority of your audience share a single occupation, such as nursing, banking, drill-press operating, teaching, or sales?

Income   Is the average income level of your audience high, low, or average?

Culture   Is your audience alike ethnically—that is, mostly of the same race, religion, or nationality?

Geographic Uniqueness Are audience members from the same state, city, or neighborhood?

Group Affiliation Do the majority of audience members belong to the same social or fraternal group?

Then you use the audience profile to make predictions about how that audience might look at your speech topic and goal. For instance, an audience of young boys of low-income families from the inner city differs markedly from an audience of adult men and women who all attend the same church.

Ways of Gathering Audience Data

Now that we have considered the kinds of audience data you need to help you predict how an audience will receive your speech, let's consider the three ways you can gather that information.

1. Assemble data you have observed or solicited. If you are in some way associated with your audience (as you are with your classroom audience), you can get much of the significant data about them from personal observation and from a simple survey. For instance, from being in class for even a couple of sessions, you will have a good idea of class members' approximate age, the ratio of men to women, and their racial makeup. As you listen to them talk, you will learn more about their interest in, knowledge of, and attitudes about many issues. Moreover, you have an opportunity to survey their ideas specifically.

2. Question the person who scheduled your speech. When you are invited to speak, ask your contact person to supply as much of the data listed above as possible. Even if the information is not as specific as you would like, it will still be useful.

3. Make intelligent guesses about audience demographics. If you can't get information in any other way, you will have to make informed guesses based on such indirect information as the general makeup of the people who live in a specific community or the kinds of people who are likely to attend a speech on your topic.

Using Data to Predict Audience Reactions

The next step in audience analysis is to use the data you've collected to predict the audience's potential interest in, knowledge of, and attitudes toward you and your topic. These predictions form a basis for the development of your speech strategy, which we will consider in greater detail in Chapter 8 as we discuss means of constructing a strategic plan of audience adaptation.

Audience Interest Your first goal is to predict how interested the audience is likely to be in your topic. For instance, suppose that one student is planning to talk about rock and roll music and another student is planning to talk about classical music. Because of the nature of a typical classroom audience, we might predict that the class is more likely to show immediate interest in rock and roll than in classical music. This does not mean that the speech on classical music is doomed. All it means is that the one speaking on classical music recognizes that initial interest might be lower. This person will have to think of ways of beginning the speech that will spark interest. How this is done we will consider later.

Audience Understanding   Your second goal is to predict whether the audience has sufficient background to understand your information. For instance, continuing with the two speeches on types of music, since the audience is going to be more familiar with rock and roll, both speakers have potential pitfalls they must consider. The rock and roll speaker must recognize that the audience may already know quite a lot about traditional rock and roll. Thus, this audience is going to have the background to understand the speech, but will be looking for more depth. The classical speaker must recognize that since the audience is likely to know less about classical music, he or she will have to define terms carefully and relate material to audience experience. Again, how this is done we will consider later.

Audience Attitude toward You as Speaker   Your third goal is to predict your audience's attitude toward you. Your success in informing or persuading an audience is likely to depend on whether it perceives you as a **credible** source of information—that is, whether the audience perceives you as having knowledge and expertise, being trustworthy, and having an engaging personality.

credible   *being seen by an audience as having knowledge and expertise, being trustworthy, and having an engaging personality*

   1. Having knowledge and expertise includes your qualifications or capability, or what is referred to as your "track record." Is there any information to suggest that your audience will accept you as an authority on your topic? If you answer yes, what makes you think so? For instance, Manuel Sanchez can predict that his audience is likely to accept his knowledge and expertise once he lets them know that he is the top-seeded player on the varsity tennis team. Similarly, when Michael Jordan talks with audiences about basketball, Colin Powell talks with audiences about military strategy, and Madeline Albright talks with audiences about diplomacy, they can predict that their audiences will recognize their knowledge and expertise.

   If, on the other hand, your knowledge and expertise are not readily apparent, you will predict that your audience will not automatically recognize your knowledge and expertise. Then you will have to consider strategies for building your credibility in the speech.

   2. Being trustworthy refers both to a person's character (honesty, dependability, moral strength) and apparent motives (reasons for giving a speech on this topic). Is there any information to suggest that your audience will see you as having character and good motives? If you answer yes, what makes you think so? In your case, especially for your first speech, the audience is likely to have little to go on. Thus, in your speech, you will have to be careful not to say or do anything that would cause the audience to question your motives.

   Trustworthiness is very important to a speaker, for if the audience doubts a speaker's character or motives, the speech is likely to fall on deaf ears. Thus, in a speech on the effects of tobacco, an audience is more likely to believe a physiologist than a tobacco company executive.

   3. Having an engaging personality refers to a person's likability—a judgment that is often based on first impressions. Is there any information to suggest that your audience will find you likable? If you answer yes, what makes you think so? For instance, audiences often look favorably on speakers who show enthusiasm, seem to be warm and friendly, have a ready smile, and seem to really care about the audience. Because perception of personality weighs so much in determining a person's credibility, we'll focus on the elements of effective delivery in Chapter 11.

Audience Attitude toward Your Topic   Your final goal is to predict your audience's attitude toward your topic. Audience attitudes are usually expressed by opinions that may be distributed along a continuum from highly favorable to hostile. Even though any given audience may have one or a few individuals' opinions at nearly every point of the distribution, in most audiences opinions will tend to cluster at a particular point on the continuum. Using data from your audience analysis, you can make reasonably accurate estimates of audience attitude. Is there any information to suggest that your audience will have a favorable attitude toward listening to a speech on your topic? If you answer yes, what makes you think so? For instance, skilled workers are likely to look at minimum wage proposals differently than are business executives; many men will look at women's rights proposals differently than will most women; a meeting of the local Right to Life chapter will look at abortion differently than will a meeting of NOW (National Organization for Women). The more data you have about your audience and the more experience you have in analyzing audiences, the better are your chances of accurately judging audience attitudes.

Surveying Students to Test Predictions

At times, you may find it worthwhile to survey your classroom audience to test or to validate your predictions. A **survey,** often in the form of a questionnaire, is a means of gathering information directly from people. Surveys may be conducted orally or in writing. Whatever your topic, you can obtain useful information through a survey. The four kinds of questions most likely to be used in a survey are called two-sided, multiple-choice, scaled, and open-ended.

survey   *means of gathering information directly from people, often using a questionnaire*

1. Two-sided questions call for a yes/no or true/false response. These questions are used most frequently to get easily sorted answers. For a survey on television violence, you might consider a two-sided phrasing such as

Do you believe that prime-time television programming contains too much violence? _____ Yes _____ No

Although two-sided questions do not offer people the opportunity to express their degree of agreement or disagreement, you do get a quick count of opinion, and such surveys are easy to conduct orally.

2. Multiple-choice questions give respondents alternatives. For a survey of student television viewing, you might phrase the following question:

For the following question, check the choice that is most accurate.
   I watch television

_____ 0 to 5 hours a week

_____ 5 to 10 hours a week

_____ 10 to 15 hours a week

_____ 15 to 20 hours a week

_____ more than 20 hours a week

3. Scaled questions allow a range of responses to a statement. Scaled responses are particularly good for measuring the strength of a person's attitudes toward a subject. If you decided to use scaled questions regarding television violence, for the statement "Prime-time television programming contains too

FOCUS ON skills

Analyzing Your Audience

The goal of this exercise is to help you determine the nature of your speech audience and record your predictions about their response to your prospective speech topic.

1. Copy or duplicate the audience analysis checklist below. Next to the second heading, Predictions, write the topic you plan to use for your first speech.

2. Fill in the checklist, including both data about your classroom audience and predictions about their reaction to your topic.

3. Save the results. You will use the data from this checklist to help you in determining a strategy for adapting to your audience.

Data

AUDIENCE ANALYSIS checklist

1. The audience education level is ___ high school ___ college ___ postcollege.

2. The age range is from ___ to ___ . The average age is about ___ .

3. The audience is approximately ___ percent male and ___ percent female.

4. My estimate of the income level of the audience is ___ below average ___ average ___ above average.

5. The audience is basically ___ the same race ___ a mixture of races.

6. The audience is basically ___ the same religion ___ a mixture of religions.

7. The audience is basically ___ the same nationality ___ a mixture of nationalities.

8. The audience is basically from ___ the same state ___ the same city ___ the same neighborhood ___ different areas.

Predictions

1. Audience interest in this topic is likely to be ___ high ___ moderate ___ low.

2. Audience understanding of the topic will be ___ great ___ moderate ___ little.

3. Audience attitude toward me as speaker is likely to be ___ positive ___ neutral ___ negative.

4. Audience attitude toward my topic will be ___ positive ___ neutral ___ negative.

much violence," you might want to give each person a range of choices. The following example measures a range of audience attitudes.

Circle the answer that best represents your opinion:

I believe that prime-time television programming contains too much violence.

Strongly agree / Agree somewhat / Don't know / Disagree somewhat / Strongly disagree

You could, of course, include more than one question.

Bob Daemmrich/Stock, Boston

Effective speakers adapt to the requirements of different settings. The size of the audience, the physical setting, the purpose of the speech, and the audience's expectations are just some of the factors to take into account when planning a speech.

Tom Bean/AllStock/PNI

4. Open-ended questions encourage statements of opinion. These questions produce the greatest amount of depth, but because of the likelihood of a wide variety of responses, they are the most difficult to process. For your survey on television violence, you might ask this open-ended question:

> If you were to write a letter to the FCC about whether there is too much violence on prime-time television, what would you recommend?

After you give the survey, you need to process the results. If the survey indicates a clear-cut trend, then use the results of the poll to help make a point in your speech. If the poll is inconclusive, then it's wise to avoid making too much of the results.

Considering the Setting

setting *the location and occasion for a speech*

Considering the **setting**—the location and occasion for the speech—provides a speaker with guidelines for both meeting audience expectations and determining the tone of the speech. Since your class meets regularly at the same time under the same conditions, your consideration of setting is not much of a challenge. But as you give speeches under other conditions, you'll find that time spent considering the setting could be very important. For instance, consider this scenario. You are representing your college at a nearby corporation's Career Day. You are one of the presenters at the afternoon forum on "Why My College Provides an Excellent Educational Opportunity." All you know is that there are four other presenters and that the talks will be given somewhere at the corporate site next Wednesday afternoon. What facts about the setting do you need to know?

1. How large will the audience be? If you are anticipating a small audience (perhaps up to 50 people or so), you can gear yourself for an informal setting in which you are close to all listeners. With a small audience, you can talk in a normal voice and feel free to move about. In contrast, if you anticipate a large audience, in addition to needing a microphone, you probably will want to make your presentation more formal.

2. When will the speech be given? The time of day can affect how the speech is received. If a speech is scheduled after a meal, for instance, the audience might be lethargic, mellow, or even on the verge of sleep. As a result, it helps to insert more "attention getters"—examples, illustrations, and stories—to counter potential lapses of attention.

3. Where in the program does the speech occur? If you are the featured speaker, you have an obvious advantage: You are the focal point of audience attention. In the classroom, however, and at some rallies, hearings, and other events, there are many speeches, and your place on the schedule may affect how you are received. For example, speaking first or last can make a difference. If you go first, you may need to "warm up" the listeners and be prepared to meet the distraction of a few audience members strolling in late; if you speak last, you must counter the tendency of the audience to be weary from listening to several speeches.

4. What is the time limit for the speech? The amount of time you have to speak greatly affects the scope of your speech and how you develop it. Keep in mind that the time limit for classroom speeches is quite short. People often get overly ambitious as to what they can accomplish in a short speech. "Three Major Causes of Environmental Degradation" can be presented in five minutes, but "A History of Human Impact on the Environment" cannot.

But problems with time limits are not peculiar to classroom speeches. Any speech setting includes actual or implied time limits. For example, a Sunday sermon is usually limited to about 20 minutes; a keynote speech for a convention may be limited to 30 minutes; a political campaign speech may be limited to 45 minutes or an hour.

5. What are the expectations for the speech? Every occasion provides some special expectations. For classroom speeches, one of the major expectations is meeting the assignment. Whether the speech assignment is defined by purpose (to inform or to persuade), by type (expository or descriptive), or by subject (book analysis or current event), your goal should reflect the nature of that assignment.

Meeting expectations is equally important for speeches outside the classroom. At an Episcopalian Sunday service, for example, the congregation expects the minister's sermon to have a religious theme; at a campaign rally, listeners expect a speech on political issues; at a social dinner event, the audience often expects a lighthearted and entertaining talk.

6. Where will the speech be given? The room in which you are scheduled to speak also affects your presentation. If you are fortunate, your classroom will be large enough to seat the class comfortably. But classrooms vary in size, lighting, seating arrangements, and the like. A room that is long and narrow creates different problems for a speaker than one that is short and wide. In a long, narrow room, for instance, the speaker's voice must be louder to reach the back row, but eye contact can be limited to a narrower range. Likewise, in a dimly lit room, try to get the lights turned up, especially if you are planning to use visual aids. Investigating the environment for the speech helps you to meet the demands of the situation.

Since outside the school setting speakers often encounter even greater variations in rooms, you'll want to have specific information about seating capacity, shape, number of rows, lighting, whether there is a speaking stage or platform, distance between speaker and first row, and so on, before you make final speech plans. If possible, visit the place and see it for yourself.

7. What facilities are necessary to give the speech? For some speeches, you may need a microphone, a chalkboard, or an overhead or slide projector and screen, or a hookup for your laptop computer. In most instances, speakers have some kind of speaking stand, but it's wise not to count on it. If the person who has invited you to speak has any control over the setting, be sure to explain what you need. But always have alternative plans in case what you have asked for is unavailable. It's frustrating to plan a computer PowerPoint presentation, for example, and then discover that there's no place to plug in the computer!

Considering the Setting

The goal of this exercise is to help you determine the nature of your speech setting.

1. Copy or duplicate the setting checklist below.
2. Answer the questions about the setting for your first speech.
3. Save the results. You will use the data from this checklist to help you in determining strategies for adapting to your audience.

Setting Checklist

1. How large will the audience be? _____
2. When will the speech be given? _____
3. Where in the program does the speech occur? _____
4. What is the time limit for the speech? _____
5. What are the expectations for the speech? _____
6. Where will the speech be given? _____
7. What facilities are necessary to give the speech? _____

Writing the Speech Goal

Once you have chosen your topic and analyzed the audience and setting for your speech, you continue the preparation process by identifying the general goal you are hoping to achieve and then writing a specific speech goal. For instance, even though Julia is planning to talk to the class about illiteracy, she still needs to determine what she wants to achieve in her speech.

General Goal

general goal *the type of speech you are intending to give—entertaining, informing, or persuading*

The **general goal** is the type of speech you are intending to give. Most speeches can be classified under one of three major headings: entertaining, informing, or persuading. Because speech is a complex act that may affect an audience in different ways, these headings are useful only to show that in any public speaking act, one overriding general goal is likely to predominate. Consider the following examples.

Jay Leno's opening monologue on *The Tonight Show* is a speech that may give some information and may even contain some intended or unintended persuasive message, but his general goal is to entertain his audience.

A history professor's lecture on the events leading to the Gulf War may use humor to gain and hold attention, and the discussion of events may affect the class's attitudes about war, but the professor's primary goal is to explain those events so that the class understands them.

Political candidates may amuse us with their anecdotes about life in politics and may give us some information that clarifies aspects of key political issues, but their general goal is to persuade us to vote for them.

Although some public speakers give speeches solely for the purpose of entertaining, in this text we focus attention on informative and persuasive speeches — the kinds of speeches most of us give in our daily lives, and the kinds that you are likely to be assigned in this course.

Specific Goal

The **specific goal,** or specific purpose, is a single statement that specifies the exact response the speaker wants from the audience. For a speech on the topic "Evaluating Diamonds," the goal could be stated as "I would like the audience to understand the four major criteria for evaluating a diamond." For a speech on "Supporting the United Way," the goal could be stated as "I would like the audience to donate money to the United Way." In the first example, the goal is informative: The speaker wants the audience to understand the criteria. In the second example, the goal is persuasive: The speaker wants the audience to donate money. Figure 4.1 gives further examples of specific goals that clearly state how each speaker wants the audience to react to a specific topic.

specific goal *a complete sentence that specifies the exact response the speaker wants from the audience*

Now let us consider a step-by-step procedure for completing the specific speech goal.

1. Write a first draft of your speech goal that includes the infinitive phrase that articulates the response you want from your audience. Suppose Julia begins her first draft on the topic of illiteracy by writing,

> I want my audience to understand illiteracy.

She has now indicated that she recognizes that her goal is to have the audience *understand* something. So she now has the start of an informative speech goal. Suppose instead she had started,

> I want to explain illiteracy.

Although it appears to be a reasonable goal, it puts the emphasis on the speaker rather than on the audience's response. Make sure that the goal begins with an expression of desired audience response.

2. Revise your first draft until you have written a complete sentence that specifies the nature of the audience response. The draft, "I want my audience to understand illiteracy," is a good start, but "understand illiteracy" is not clear. Exactly "what" about illiteracy is it that Julia wants her audience to understand? As Julia works with the wording, she amends it to read,

FIGURE 4.1 **Specific speech goals**

Entertainment Goals
I would like my audience to be amused by my portrayal of an over-the-hill football player.
I would like my audience to laugh at my experience as a waiter.

Informative Goals
I would like my audience to understand the major techniques graphologists use to analyze handwriting.
I would like my audience to understand the three basic forms of mystery stories.

Persuasive Goals
I would like my audience to believe that drug testing by business and industry should be prohibited.
I would like my audience to join Amnesty International.

I would like the audience to understand three aspects of the problem of illiteracy.

This draft is a complete-sentence statement of her speech goal. Notice that it includes the desired response, "to understand three aspects of illiteracy." Now the question becomes, does the phrase "understand three aspects of illiteracy" fully capture what she will be talking about? Is she concerned with illiteracy in general? Or perhaps about illiteracy in a specific situation? As Julie thinks about it, she sees that what she really wants to focus on is how illiteracy hurts people who are trying to function well at work. With this in mind, she revises the goal by writing,

I would like the audience to understand three aspects of the problem of illiteracy *in the workplace.*

Now she has limited the goal not only in number of aspects but also by situation.

3. Make sure that the goal contains only one idea. Suppose Julia had written,

I would like the audience to understand three aspects of the problem of illiteracy in the workplace and to prove how it is detrimental to both industry and the individual.

This draft includes two distinct ideas. Either one can be used, but not both, because together they blur the focus of the speech. Julia will have to make a decision:

(a) Does she want to focus her talk on aspects of the problem? Then the following goal is the better statement:

I would like the audience to understand three major aspects of illiteracy in the workplace.

(b) Does she want to focus on how harmful it is? Then the following goal is preferable.

I would like to prove that illiteracy is detrimental to the individual and to industry.

4. Revise the infinitive or infinitive phrase until it indicates the specific audience reaction desired. If you regard your ideas as useful but noncontroversial, then your intent is primarily informative, and the infinitive that expresses your desired audience reaction should take the form "to understand" or "to appreciate." If, however, the main idea of your speech is controversial, a statement of belief, or a call to action, then your intent is persuasive and will be reflected in such infinitives as "to believe" or "to change."

5. Write at least three different versions of the goal. The clearer your specific goal, the more purposeful and effective your speech is likely to be. Even if Julia likes her first sentence, she should write at least two additional versions. The second or third version may prove to be an even clearer statement. For instance, on a second try, she might write,

I would like the audience to understand three major effects of the problem of illiteracy in the workplace.

Changing "three aspects" to "three major effects" gives the goal a different emphasis. She may decide she likes that emphasis better.

Analyze the following five specific speech goals. Place a check mark by those that are well worded; revise the wording of those that don't meet one or more of the five tests.

_____ I intend to persuade my audience that parents should educate their children about sex.

_____ I want to inform the audience about how they can improve the environment.

_____ I want to entertain as well as inform my audience about different types of children's literature.

_____ I want to persuade my audience that they should be responsible citizens and how to start a community action group.

_____ I want the audience to know about increasing memory.

Writing Speech Goals

Following the five-step procedure outlined in the text, write a speech goal for the topic you selected for your first speech.

Anticipating a Thesis Statement

Before you begin your research, you may want to try to refine your goal by writing a thesis statement. Whereas the specific goal is a statement of how you want your audience to respond, the **thesis statement** is a sentence that outlines the specific elements of the speech supporting the goal statement. For example, for a speech on evaluating diamonds, Sandy wrote:

> **Specific goal:** "I would like the audience to understand the major criteria for evaluating a diamond."
>
> **Thesis statement:** "Diamonds are evaluated on the basis of carat (weight), color, clarity, and cutting."

Notice that the specific goal clearly states what Sandy wanted the audience to do (understand the major criteria), but it does not *identify* the criteria for actually evaluating. Since Sandy had worked in a jewelry store, she already had the information about criteria available to her, so she was able to write a thesis statement that listed the criteria of carat, color, clarity, and cutting.

Let's consider another example. Amad had strong feelings about the benefits of donating money to the United Way. So, for his specific goal he wrote:

> I would like my audience to donate money to the United Way.

Because he had done volunteer work for the local United Way drive, he also had the necessary information to formulate the following thesis statement:

> You should donate to the United Way because it covers a wide variety of charities with one contribution, it spends a very low percentage on overhead, and it allows you to designate your dollars to specific agencies if you so desire.

thesis statement *a sentence that outlines the specific elements of the speech supporting the goal statement*

FIGURE 4.2 Relationship among subject, topic, general goal, and specific goal

Subject Area:	Career counseling
Topic:	Networking
General Speech Goal:	Informative
Specific Goal:	I want the audience to understand the procedure for networking in career development.
Tentative Thesis Statement:	You can use networking most effectively if you make networking a high priority, position yourself in places of opportunity, advertise yourself, and follow up on your contacts.
Subject Area:	Finance
Topic:	Debt
General Speech Goal:	Informative
Specific Goal:	I would like the audience to understand two major factors that are increasing the problem of personal debt in the United States.
Tentative Thesis Statement:	Personal debt is facilitated by easy access to credit and need for instant gratification.
Subject Area:	National Collegiate Athletic Association (NCAA)
Topic:	Sanctions
General Speech Goal:	Persuasive
Specific Goal:	I would like the audience to believe that sanctions are an ineffective means of punishing colleges that violate NCAA rules.
Tentative Thesis Statement:	NCAA sanctions do not deter colleges from violating rules, they do not make it difficult for schools to field winning teams, and they do not prevent sanctioned colleges from receiving financial support.

If you do have enough material to write a tentative thesis at this time, then go ahead. You may find, however, that at this stage you don't have the specific information necessary to write such a statement. If so, let your specific speech goal guide your research, and finish refining the thesis statement when you have enough information to work with. Regardless of how far you have come in writing your thesis statement, you'll still want to be sure that the wording meets the tests. In Chapter 6, Organizing and Outlining the Body of the Speech, we'll discuss the process for constructing and testing the thesis statement in more detail.

What, then, is the overall relationship among subjects, topics, goals, and thesis statements? As we have seen, a single subject area contains many potential speech topics. A topic, in turn, can be the basis for three general goals (to entertain, inform, or persuade) and many different specific goals. Finally, a specific goal can be explained in a thesis statement. The examples in Figure 4.2 illustrate this relationship among subject, topic, general goal, specific goal, and thesis statement.

Summary

The first step of effective speech preparation is to determine your speech goal. You begin by selecting a subject that you know something about and are interested in, such as a job, a hobby, or a contemporary issue of concern to you. To arrive at a specific topic, brainstorm a list of related words under each subject heading. When you have brainstormed at least 20 topics, you can check the specific topic under each heading that is most meaningful to you.

Although Glen and Adam were taking the same speech course, they were in different sections. One evening when Adam was talking with Glen about his trouble finding a topic, Glen mentioned that he was planning to speak about affirmative action. Since the number of different speech goals from this topic seemed unlimited, he didn't see any harm in showing Adam his bibliography, so he brought it up on his computer screen.

As Adam was looking at it, Glen went down the hall to get a book he had lent to a friend earlier that morning. While Glen was away, Adam thought he'd take a look at what else Glen had in the file. He was soon excited to see that Glen had a complete outline on the goal "I want the class to understand the steps in designing a home page." Figuring he could save himself some time, Adam printed the outline—he justified his action on the basis that it represented a good start that would give him ideas. As time ran short, Adam decided to just use Glen's outline for his own speech.

Later in the week, Glen's instructor happened to be talking to Adam's about speeches she had heard that week. When she mentioned that Glen had given a really interesting speech on home pages, Adam's teacher said, "That's interesting. I heard a good one just this morning. Now what did you say the goal of the speech you heard was?" When the goals turned out to be the same, Glen's instructor went back to her office to get the outline that she would be returning the next day. As the two instructors went over the outlines, they saw that the two speeches were exactly the same. The next day, they left messages for both Adam and Glen to meet with them and the department head that day.

1. What is the ethical issue at stake?

2. Was there anything about Glen's behavior that was unethical? Anything about Adam's?

3. What should be the penalty, if any, for Glen? For Adam?

The next step is to analyze the audience to decide how to shape and direct your speech. Audience analysis is the study of your audience's knowledge, interests, and attitudes. Gather specific data about your audience to determine how its members are alike and how they differ. Use this information to predict audience interest in your topic, level of understanding of your topic, and attitude toward you and your topic. At times, you may want to validate your predictions by surveying your classroom audience using two-sided, multiple-choice, scaled, or open-ended questions.

The third step is to consider the setting of the speech, which will affect your overall speech plan.

The final step is to write and test your speech goal. The general goal of a speech is to entertain, to inform, or to persuade. The specific goal is a complete sentence that specifies the exact response the speaker wants from the audience. Writing a specific speech goal involves the following five-step procedure: (1) Write a first draft of your speech goal that includes the infinitive phrase that articulates the response you want from your audience. (2) Revise your first draft until you have written a complete sentence that specifies the nature of the audience response. (3) Make sure that the goal contains only one idea. (4) Revise the infinitive or infinitive phrase until it indicates the specific audience reaction desired. (5) Write out at least three different versions of the goal before deciding on one.

At this time, you may want to write a tentative draft of your thesis statement—a sentence that outlines the specific elements of the speech supporting the goal statement. If you do not have enough information to write the thesis statement, wait until you've completed your research.

An empty bag cannot

stand upright.

Benjamin Franklin, *Poor Richards Almanac,* 1740

Researching Your Speech in the Information Age

Jeremy was concerned. He was scheduled for his first speech in a week, but he

hadn't begun to find information. He remembered discussing the subject of

media violence in a class in high school, and he was really taken with the sub-

ject. Just a couple of months ago, he had read an article in a magazine at the

doctor's office, but he couldn't remember the issue of the magazine the article

was in. He decided he'd better get to the library, but he wasn't sure how he

should proceed to find information.

eremy's experience is not unlike that of many of us. We believe that our topic is an important one that we're really interested in, but we just don't know how to go about finding the information we need. Libraries—especially at large universities—can seem threatening. So can the Internet. But even if you feel comfortable with library or Internet sources, you are likely to find information in this chapter that will make your job a little bit easier.

In this chapter, which pursues the action step of finding information, we consider where to look for information and what kinds of information to look for.

Where to Look: Traditional and Electronic Sources of Information

Where should you look for the best material available on your topic? A great deal depends on your topic and the kinds of information you need. For instance, we began this chapter with a vignette about Jeremy's concerns as he prepares for a speech on the effects of media violence. Where he looks for information may well differ from where Erin would look if she were planning to talk about how to spike a volleyball, or where Rhonda would look if she were planning to talk about the dangers of the drug Rohypnol. Because of these kinds of differences, in this section we'll use three speech topics to contrast approaches to research.

Effective speakers develop a research strategy that starts by considering their own knowledge and experiences; moves on to potential information from books, relevant periodicals, and other specialized sources that can be accessed manually or through electronic databases such as InfoTrac College Edition; and considers the possibility of seeking information by means of interviews.

ACTION STEP two

Gather Information
Discover, gather, and evaluate information you can use in your speech.

A. Survey sources manually and electronically that are most likely to yield quality information.

B. Record information that is relevant to your specific speech goal on note cards.

Personal Knowledge, Experience, and Observation

If you have chosen to speak on a topic you know something about, you may already have some material that you can use in your speech. For instance, athletes have special knowledge about their sports, entrepreneurs about starting up their own businesses, cancer survivors about health systems, marine biologists about marine reserves, musicians about music and instruments, and camp counselors about camping. For many of your speeches, then, you are likely to have information that may be usable in your speech—especially examples drawn from your personal experiences. Your firsthand knowledge will contribute to the development of imaginative and original speeches.

If Erin, a member of the varsity volleyball team, plans to give her first speech on "How to Spike a Volleyball," we would expect her to draw a great deal of her material from her own experience and the experiences of her teammates. Discussing such personal volleyball experiences is likely to be especially important in helping her gain interest and/or adapt her information to audience needs. This does not mean that Erin should not consult other sources (we'll consider additional choices for her in other sections). For any speech, we expect a person to consult several sources of information.

For many topics, your personal knowledge from experience can be supplemented with careful observation. If, for instance, you are planning to talk about how a small claims court works or how churches are helping the homeless find shelter, food, job training, and hope, you can learn more about these subjects by attending small claims sessions or visiting a church's outreach center. Observation adds a personal dimension to your speeches that can make them more

Robert W. Ginn/Picture Cube

Careful observation is an often-overlooked research strategy. In addition to facts, observation can provide the kinds of specific details that make your topic come alive for an audience.

informative as well as more interesting. Focusing attention on specific behaviors and taking notes of your observations will provide a record of specifics that you can use in your speech.

Research

Since the best material for many speeches will come from research, you'll want to be able to draw information from books, periodicals, and other specialized sources that can be accessed either manually or via electronic databases. Today, the question is not only which research sources to draw from, but also how to access that material.

In the past, you did research by going to your library and accessing catalogs and indexes that led you to various parts of the library where the relevant materials were housed. Although you can still use this method (in fact, many people still enjoy "getting their hands dirty" thumbing through books, magazines, almanacs, and newspapers), in the 21st century you must also be electronically literate. You should know how to use electronic sources to find information, to manipulate or present it on screen, and to download it for your personal files.

In this section, for each of the topics, we will first talk about sources that you can access manually, such as books, encyclopedias, and periodicals. Then we will discuss electronic means of accessing those same materials, as well as material that would not be available in a physical form in any library.

College and university libraries often use their own particular systems. My examples are based on the system used at the University of Cincinnati. If your library is of a comparable degree of sophistication, you may find that you are able to do everything at your library that I and my students can do at the University of Cincinnati. But whether your library is similar or more or less sophisticated, it is still likely to be different in some ways. Moreover, library methods change frequently, because of increased usage of electronic means of research. In August, for example, I tried to access an electronic database that I had used the previous week, only to discover that I had to learn a whole new way to access it. As a result, please heed the following advice: Whenever you're confused, don't hesitate to ask your library staff for assistance.

Helping library patrons is a major professional responsibility, and librarians will gladly offer their assistance. Within a short period of time, you can learn about *all* of your library's resources with the help of its staff. If for some reason they cannot meet all of your needs quickly, they will refer you to one of the many workshops and learning programs that are sponsored by college and university libraries to "bring you up to speed" with their unique systems.

Books In the past, libraries featured a card catalog for accessing books the library held. Although some libraries may still have a physical card catalog, most of them have transferred records of their holdings to a computer on-line catalog system. Whether you are looking in a card catalog or on a computer, books are listed by title, author, and subject. Thus, if like Jeremy, you are looking for a book about the topic "the effects of media violence on viewers," and you know the *author* of such a book is Sissela Bok, you can look under Bok, Sissela. If you know that the *title* of the book you want is *Mayhem*, you can look under that title. Or if you are just looking to see whether there are any relevant books in your library, you can look under the appropriate *subject*, "violence, mass media." In all cases, you would find the card shown in Figure 5.1.

Author:	Bok, Sissela
Title:	Mayhem: Violence as public entertainment
Pub Info:	Reading, Mass: Addison-Wesley, c 1998
Description:	x, 194p.; 24 cm
Note	"A Merloyd Lawrence" book
	Includes bibliographical references (p. 159-181) and Index
Subject:	Violence in Mass Media
OCLC#:	38218736
ISBN:	0201489791
LCCN:	97048620

Location	Call No.	Status
1) Langsam stacks	P96 V5 B65 1998	Available

Although some of the information is irrelevant, you certainly want the location (for instance, the University of Cincinnati has several college libraries and one all-university library on campus), the call number, and the book's availability. The other bit of useful information is under "Note." In this case, that heading tells you that the book includes bibliographical references and an index.

In addition to being able to search by author, title, and subject, most on-line catalogs now also include search capabilities that allow you to enter "keywords" that you are likely to find most useful for your topic searches.

At the University of Cincinnati, for example, many of the computer terminals in the library are already set up for book searches. To conduct a search, you select "keyword," type in the word or words related to your topic, and the computer will access a list of available books. Even with this user-friendly system, you may find that you need to exercise some creativity in discovering the best keyword(s) to use in the search.

For instance, if Jeremy looks for books on his topic using one or two keywords and is shown zero sources, with a few minutes of creative thinking he should be able to come up with additional keywords that will bring a variety of "hits" (books available). Notice the differences in hits Jeremy found using each of the following headings:

effects of mass media violence 1

media violence 39

violence in mass media 28

violence media 39

violence television 45

crime mass media 21

aggression mass media 2

Finding books on your topic yields many benefits. First, as suggested in Figure 5.1, the books themselves are likely to yield a bibliography of many sources. For instance, Sissela Bok's book *Mayhem* has 22 pages of sources. Jeremy might find several excellent additional sources from the *Mayhem* bibliography alone.

Second, the books are likely to have valuable insights on the subject. Books can provide you with many useful quotes, and may lead you to some new ideas on the topic.

Although many believe that using electronic access is the quickest way to find the most appropriate book or books, sometimes it is not. For instance, if you have the call number for a book, you can then go to the section of the library in which books using that general call number are housed and find other books on the same subject. You can then thumb through them quickly to check their relevance. I often find books this way much faster than going book by book through the on-screen data.

You are likely to want to use both methods to help you find the best and most relevant books available.

Periodicals Periodicals are magazines and journals that appear at fixed periods—weekly, biweekly, monthly, quarterly, or yearly. Because material from weekly, biweekly, and monthly magazines is more current than that found in books, a periodical is likely to be your best source when your topic is one that's "in the news." A periodical is also your best source when the topic is so limited in scope that it is unlikely to provide enough material for a book, or when you are looking for a very specific aspect of a particular topic. Periodical indexes are a repository of articles from magazines and journals. They catalog the material, enhancing your access to and retrieval of relevant articles for your speech topic. These indexes are published each year and in monthly and current supplements for the current year.

The following are basic indexes that you can access manually or electronically, covering a wide variety of magazines and journals available in most major libraries. These indexes can lead you to an abundance of relevant information not only for preparing speeches but also for writing papers in various classes.

The Readers' Guide to Periodical Literature is an index of articles in some 150 popular magazines and journals, such as *Business Week*, *Ebony*, *Newsweek*, *Reader's Digest*, and *Vital Speeches*. The on-line version is called the *Reader's Guide Abstract*.

The Humanities Index and *The Social Sciences Index*, available both manually and on-line, will lead you to articles in more than 300 scholarly journals, such as *The American Journal of Sociology*, *The Economist*, *Modern Language Quarterly*, and *Philosophical Review*. *The Education Index*, also available on-line, will lead you to articles in 350 English-language periodicals, yearbooks, and monographs.

The print versions of these indexes are housed in the reference area of your library. Your library is likely to have many other specialized periodical indexes that might be more relevant for your specific topic. For instance, many libraries will also have such indexes as the *Business Periodicals Index*, the *Psychology Index*, the *Music Index*, the *Art Index*, the *Applied Science and Technology Index*, and many more. Check with your librarian regarding their on-line accessibility.

If you are doing a manual search, in order to find appropriate articles about your topic, you need to determine when the events occurred or when the topic was actively discussed. If you were preparing a speech on the effects of negative political commercials, you would start at the present and work back through the years. But if you were preparing a speech on "blacklisting" of authors and television writers during the McCarthy era, and you wanted material published during that time period, you'd begin your research in the index for 1953, the height of the McCarthy era.

If you are accessing the indexes electronically, you begin by typing in the subject heading that you are researching. The computer will access the index's database and bring up citations that are related to your subject. You can then choose to access the individual articles and read or print them off the computer or use the list of citations to locate the original articles in your library's periodical section. We will be talking more about electronic databases such as these later in this chapter.

Encyclopedias Most libraries have a recent edition of *Encyclopaedia Britannica*, *Encyclopedia Americana*, or *World Book Encyclopedia*. An encyclopedia can be a good starting point for research. Encyclopedias give an excellent overview of many subjects, but you certainly should never limit your research to encyclopedias. Your library is likely to have a wide variety of specialized encyclopedias to choose from in such areas as religion, philosophy, and science. For instance your library is likely to have the *African American Encyclopedia*, *Latino Encyclopedia*, *Asian American Encyclopedia*, *Encyclopedia of Computer Science*, *Encyclopedia of Women*, and *Encyclopedia of Women in American Politics*, as well as many more.

Many libraries now have *Encyclopaedia Britannica* on-line. If so, you will be able to access it just as you did the periodical sources.

Statistical Sources Statistical sources present numerical information on a wide variety of subjects. When you need facts about demography, continents, heads of state, weather, or similar subjects, refer to one of the many single-

Steve Dunwell/The Image Bank

Library research is essential for many speech topics, but the fact that something is in print doesn't make it good supporting material. The evidence you uncover needs to be evaluated for its trustworthiness and relevance to your topic and specific purpose.

volume sources that report such data. Two of the most popular sources in this category are *The Statistical Abstract of the United States* (now available on-line), which provides reference material and numerical information on various aspects of American life, and *The World Almanac and Book of Facts*. You'll find many other almanacs in the same section of the reference material that you find these two sources.

Biographical Sources   When you need accounts of a person's life, from thumbnail sketches to reasonably complete essays, you can turn to one of the many biographical sources available. In addition to full-length books and encyclopedia entries, consult such books as *Who's Who in America* and *International Who's Who*. Your library is also likely to carry *Contemporary Black Biography, Dictionary of Hispanic Biography, Native American Women, Who's Who of American Women, Who's Who Among Asian Americans*, and many more.

Books of Quotations   Since a good quotation can be especially provocative as well as informative, you might also want access to books of quotations. You're most likely to be familiar with *Bartlett's Familiar Quotations*, which has quotations from historical as well as contemporary figures. But your library is also likely to have *The International Thesaurus of Quotations, Harper Book of American Quotations, My Soul Looks Back, 'Less I Forget: A Collection of Quotations by People of Color, The New Quotable Woman*, and *The Oxford Dictionary of Quotations*.

Newspapers   Newspaper articles are excellent sources of facts about and interpretations of both contemporary and historical issues. At a minimum, your library probably holds both an index of your nearest major daily and the *New York Times Index*.

Three electronic newspaper indexes that are most useful if they are available to you are (1) *National Newspaper Index*, which indexes five major newspapers—*New York Times, Wall Street Journal, Christian Science Monitor, Washington Post*, and *Los Angeles Times*; (2) *Newsbank*, which not only indexes but also gives you the text of articles from more than 450 U.S. and Canadian newspapers; and (3) InfoTrac College Edition's *National Newspaper Index*.

United States Government Publications   Two government publications that are especially useful for locating primary sources are the *Federal Register* and the *Monthly Catalog of United States Government Publications*. The *Register* publishes daily regulations and legal notices issued by the executive branch and all federal agencies. It is divided into sections, such as rules and regulations and Sunshine Act meetings. Of special interest are announcements of hearings and investigations, committee meetings, and agency decisions and rulings.

The *Monthly Catalog* covers publications of all branches of the federal government. It has semiannual and annual cumulative indexes by title, author/agency, and subject.

Electronic Databases   In addition to some of the electronic indexes just discussed, several other electronic databases will be particularly useful to you. Most university libraries have licenses to these databases, and provide students with access to them (sometimes at a fee, which is often included in their tuition cost).

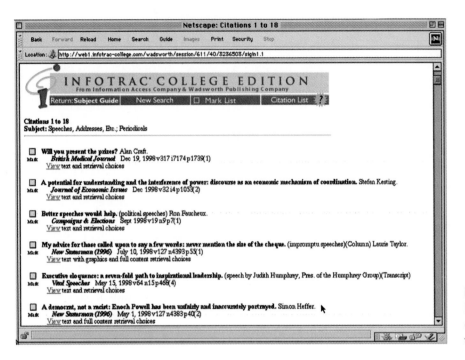

An **electronic database** is information stored so that it can be retrieved from a computer terminal. According to Rubin, Rubin, and Piele, compilers of research sources, "A researcher who is reluctant to use computers to find information or who does not know how to do so effectively will be severely handicapped."[1] The advantages of college library electronic databases are that they can be searched much more quickly than their print counterparts and results can be printed or downloaded onto a floppy disk.

At your school, you are likely to have two choices for conducting electronic searches of library sources. One is to go to the library, where you have access to computer terminals that are already wired into major databases. The other choice is to access library electronic databases via your own personal computer or computer stations housed in special computer rooms around campus.

Of special importance to students who use this book is InfoTrac College Edition, an electronic database of more than 700 periodicals that can be searched and downloaded in ways similar to those already described. InfoTrac College Edition consists of well-known magazines as well as scholarly publications, such as *Vital Speeches*, professional association pamphlets, and encyclopedias. It features full-length articles and images from such popular publications as *Audobon, Discover, Ebony, Omni Online, Popular Science, Science, Sky Telescope, Smithsonian, U.S. News & World Report,* and *Working Woman.* Other electronic databases include ProQuest, Eric, Medline, and PSYCHLIT, to name a few.

Using these databases, you can compile bibliographies and view abstracts, or even full articles, on the computer screen. If you go to the library, reference librarians should know to which databases your library subscribes and can help you learn to access them.

Now let's see how Rhonda might take advantage of the library's on-line database to research her speech topic. On her brainstorming list, Rhonda identified Rohypnol, a strong sedative also known as the "date rape" drug, as a topic under the heading "Social Concern." She had heard stories of women who had

electronic database *information stored so that it can be retrieved from a computer terminal*

been abused after being secretly given this drug by their dates. She was very concerned about possible misuse of this drug and wanted to alert her classmates to the danger.

Tentatively, Rhonda had written, "I want my audience to understand the dangers of the drug Rohypnol." Recall that at this stage of preparation you may have a well-written speech goal and even a tentative thesis statement; or, like Rhonda, you may have only a tentative goal—enough to give your research direction, but leaving the door open for revision depending on the information you find.

At this stage, Rhonda needs a strategy. As she studied research methods, she thought she would start with a book search, then go to a periodical search, and finally, access the University of Cincinnati's on-line database. She began, as Jeremy did, by using a computer terminal that was linked directly to "Telnet," which gave her access to the University Electronic Card Catalog. Under "Keyword" she typed "Rohypnol." She quickly saw that the university had no books on this subject.

Next, Rhonda moved to the bank of computers that were linked to the University of Cincinnati's electronic database, "Ohio Link Research Databases." She clicked on "General Sources." Then, when her choices appeared on the screen, she clicked on "Periodical Abstracts." On the screen that appeared next, she typed "Rohypnol" in the box titled "Keyword." She found she had access to 15 titles, listed in order from most recent to least recent. Most systems keep at least ten years of data in their systems; with the adding of each new year's sources, sources that are more than ten years old are dropped. If Rhonda thought that there might be important periodical sources before the mid-1980s, after she finished her electronic search she would go to the library to search hard copies of *Readers' Guide to Periodical Literature*. But since this topic is "new," she didn't see any need to do that.

In her search, Rhonda decided she needed access to three of the articles:

Labianca, Dominick A. "Rohypnol: Profile of the 'date-rape drug.'" *Journal of Chemical Education*, June 1998, pp. 719–722.

Monroe, Judy. "'Roofies': Horror drug of the '90's." *Current Health*, 2, September 1997, 24–26.

Daum, Meghan. "Coming down hard." *GQ: Gentlemen's Quarterly*, 67, September 1997, 261–271.

For the first two, Rhonda elected to print the entire articles. For the third, she printed only the abstract. Since this was a ten-page article, she thought she would go back to it if she thought she was short on information.

As you use your system, you may find some articles that you can't print out. In that case, you will need to go to your library's journal and magazine index to see whether the library has hard copies of the articles you want.

Skimming   Since you are likely to uncover far more articles and books than you can use, you will want to skim sources to determine whether or not to read them in full. **Skimming** is a method of rapidly going through a work to determine what is covered and how.

skimming   *a method of rapidly going through a work to determine what is covered and how*

If you are evaluating a book, read the table of contents carefully, look at the index, and skim pertinent chapters to determine whether it really presents information on the exact area of the topic you are exploring and whether it contains any documented statistics, examples, or quotable opinions. If you are evaluating a magazine article, spend a minute or two asking the same questions as you would for a book.

If you are compiling a periodical bibliography on computer, you will discover that the services your library subscribes to are likely to include a short abstract for each article that comes up on the computer screen. A look at these abstracts will help you determine which sources you want to read in their entirety. Once you have the sources in hand, however, you'll still need to follow a skimming procedure.

Skimming helps you decide which sources should be read in full, which should be read in part, and which should be abandoned. Minutes spent in such evaluation will save hours of reading.

The Internet

Whatever your topic, you'll want to begin with library sources. More than likely, you'll find plenty of material that you can access manually at the library or electronically through the indexes and other on-line databases just described.

In addition, you may want to access the **Internet**—an international electronic collection of thousands of smaller networks. The World Wide Web (WWW) is such a network and is used widely in getting information on a broad range of topics. Created in 1991 by a group of scientists, it has experienced explosive growth over the years.

Internet *an international electronic network of networks*

Today, most students with access to a university library or to computer labs or terminals at various locations on campus have access to this vast supply of information. Public libraries also often provide Internet access. This access connects you to databases and bulletin boards, scholarly and professional electronic discussion groups, library holdings at colleges and universities (like the Ohio Link Research Databases) across the United States and abroad, and even allows you to take on-line courses.

If your school or public library does not have access to the Internet and you have your own personal computer (Mac or PC) and a modem, you can purchase access by subscribing to a commercial **server** or **service provider** such as America Online (AOL), Compuserve, or Prodigy. They will give you the modem software you need to connect to the Internet and will charge you a monthly access fee, which can range from about $10 to $20. With this subscription, you get features such as an e-mail address, customer support services, up-to-date news and stock prices, access to countless computer games, and even the ability to shop for almost anything you can think of on-line. Note that some databases have an additional connection charge or are available only to those who subscribe to their particular service.

server or **service provider** *an agency that provides the necessary software for you to interface with electronic systems*

University of Cincinnati students are fortunate because they have access to the Internet from the university library or from their home computer through the University of Cincinnati server called Bearcat Online. Your college or university may make such servers available to you as part of your tuition or for a small fee. It's well worth the cost!

In order to better understand how to make the best use of the Internet, let's consider a couple of relevant terms:

Browser A **browser** is a device that gives you access to the information across millions of Web sites on the World Wide Web. At the University of

browser *a device that serves as a kind of directory for accessing documents on the World Wide Web*

Cincinnati, Bearcat Online automatically connects the user to Netscape, a browser that is very common at most colleges and universities. Another browser growing in usage among the general public is Microsoft's Internet Explorer.

To understand how a browser works, let's see how Erin uses Netscape to access documents in the university's electronic database. Erin types in the path name of the document, which is also called the Uniform Resource Locator, or **URL.** Every document on the Web has a unique URL, which is more commonly known as the "address." It consists of three parts: (1) the transfer format (protocol://); (2) the host name of the machine that holds the file (server/); and (3) the document path name (directory/filename).[2]

The URL for the University of Cincinnati Library Research Base is http://www.libraries.uc.edu

When Erin types in this URL, she is connected to the university database. Because she may use this site every day, she should take advantage of the Bookmark feature, available on all browsers. If she clicks on the word Bookmark on the menu bar and then selects Add Bookmark from the pull-down menu, the URL for the library's database (which is on the screen) will be stored. Then, when she wants to go back to that Web site again, she can pull up the site by going to Bookmark and clicking on the name of the site (URLs are normally stored using a simple code name—in this case, Cincy). It's that easy! Note: URLs can and often do change. Typically, but not always, the new address will be listed, and you might even be connected to it automatically.

Search Engines   Search engines identify Web sites, with their URLs, that lead to information on a selected topic. Some search engines accessible through the University of Cincinnati system are Yahoo! (http://www.yahoo.com), Alta Vista (http://www.altavista.digital.com), and Lycos (http://www.lycos.com). An advantage of search engines is that they provide some organization to the bountiful information that keyword searches can find on the Web.

Now let's return to Rhonda's search for information on the topic of Rohypnol, using the search engine Yahoo! While in Netscape, Rhonda typed in the address for Yahoo! and then typed "Rohypnol" in the keyword search area. She had seven "hits," or site matches. After looking at the seven, she decided to download two of the items, Rohypnol Fact Sheet (http://www.lec.org/Drug Search/Documents/Rohypnol.htm) and Rohypnol Alert (http://www.usdoj.gov/dea/pubs/rohypnol/rohypnol.htm).

Finally, Rhonda looked up "Flunitrazepam," a word that appeared as a heading on one of her source sheets, in the *Encyclopaedia Britannica*, and found an article of several pages. She recorded this source as "Flunitrazepam," *Encyclopaedia Britannica* (1997), pp. 199–208.

Between her searches of library sources and the Internet, Rhonda now had five complete sources and one abstract to work with for her speech.

Final Tips When Using the Internet

• Have a strategy, and organize your search. Go first to the library print and on-line resources, and then do research on the Web.

• When you type in a keyword for your search, find out which computer symbols help limit and focus your search. For example, if Jeremy is using Alta Vista and puts quotation marks around the words "media violence," he will only get hits in which these two words appear together. If he does not use quo-

TECHNOLOGY tips

On-line indexes and databases available through libraries as well as the Internet can be used to find sources for supporting material for your speeches. Check with your college or public library to see what indexes and databases you can access through them. For instance, using the Internet, you can access *The Statistical Abstract of the United States* at http://www.census.gov. As practice, visit this site and key in "crime statistics." Spend a few minutes acquainting yourself with this site. How might you use this information in a speech on mandatory sentencing?

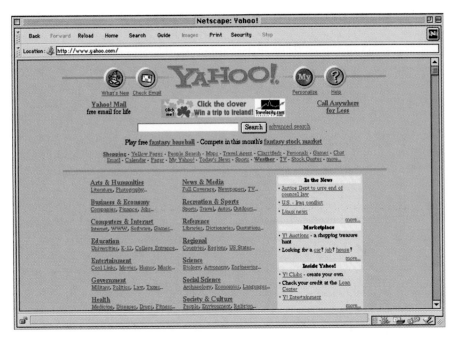

Search engines such as Yahoo! help you find Web sites and corresponding URLs that lead to information on a topic.

tation marks, he will get hits in which *either* word appears, which gives him a lot of information that is not useful to his speech.

• Be aware that if you wait until the last minute to finish researching your speech topic and you plan to use the Internet for source material, you may have to wait to get on-line. Modems connect via telephone lines, and many people may be "dialing in" at the same time you are. Rather than hits, you may get only a busy signal. Start early on your research!

Evaluating On-line Sources   The Internet has no research librarian either organizing information or ensuring that it is up-to-date or even correct. Remember that the Internet contains information that is self-published!

With this in mind, it's important to evaluate the information and authorship of the material. When evaluating on-line sources, you will use many of the same criteria that you use for any source. In their *Guide to the Internet*, John Courtright and Elizabeth Perse focus on three major questions that are especially important for Internet evaluation: Who is the source? Are the data primary or secondary? How old is the information?[3]

1. Source: When a source is given, you need to pay attention to the qualifications. For instance, for the Rohypnol Fact Sheet mentioned previously, the article indicates that the fact sheet was prepared by the Haight Ashbury Free Clinics, Inc., 3330 Geary Boulevard, San Francisco, CA. In addition, it lists the names of two doctors who were involved in preparing the fact sheet.

In contrast, the publication that was listed as Rohypnol Alert is simply titled "Flunitrazepam." No author is given, although the site is listed as U.S. Department of Justice, Drug Enforcement Administration.

From some sites you will find information that is anonymous or credited to someone whose background is not clear. Unless you can get other sources to validate the information, information from such anonymous sources is best not used.

2. Primary versus secondary data. Data are primary when they come from the original source; they are secondary when they come from a source that cites another source. Primary data are preferable; use secondary data when you can trust the source. In well-conducted searches, you can find a great deal of primary data on the Internet. But you still must be concerned with where it came from and how old it is.

3. Age of source. Even some recent publications use old data. With statistics, especially, you want to know when the data were true. If, for instance, you are talking about the number of women in Congress, you don't want to be using data that are more than two years old. Since Congressional elections occur every two years, even data from a recent publication could be wrong.

4. Special interest information. In addition to the three standard issues, you should also be especially wary of Web documents that have been created under the sponsorship of a business, government, or public-interest group. Because sponsored information is likely to reflect the biases of the sponsor, you'll want to make sure that you can verify the credentials of the author of sponsored material. If you can't, then don't use that material in your speech.

Interviews

interviewing *the skillful asking and answering of questions*

Like media reporters, you may get some of your best information for your speech from **interviewing**—the skillful asking and answering of questions. How relevant interviewing is to getting information for your speech will of course depend on your topic. To be effective, you'll want to select the best person to interview and have a list of good questions to ask.

Selecting the Best Person Somewhere on campus or in the larger community are people who have information you can use in your speech. Usually a few telephone calls will lead you to the person who would be best to talk with about your topic. For instance, for a speech on "The Eeffects of Media Violence on Viewers," Jeremy could interview a professor of mass communication or sociology. When you have decided whom you should interview, make an appointment—you cannot walk into an office and expect the prospective interviewee to drop everything just to talk to you. Be forthright in your reasons for scheduling the interview. Whether your interview is for a class speech or for a different audience, say so.

Before going into the interview, make sure that you have done some research on the topic. Interviewees are more likely to talk with you if you appear informed; moreover, familiarity with the subject will enable you to ask better questions.

If you were trying to get an interview with someone on campus, you might proceed as follows:

> Hello, my name is _____. I am taking a course in fundamentals of speech, and I'm preparing a speech on the effects of mass media violence on viewers. If possible, I'd like to make an appointment to talk with you. Would you be available for 15 or 20 minutes during your office hours during the next few days?

At the end, thank the person, repeat the date and time of the interview, and confirm the office number. If you make the appointment more than a few days ahead, it is usually wise to call the day before the interview to confirm the appointment.

Writing Good Questions The heart of an effective interviewing plan is a list of good questions. They are likely to be a mix of open and closed questions, both primary and follow-up, phrased to be neutral rather than leading.

Primary questions are those main-point questions that the interviewer plans ahead of time. **Follow-up questions** are designed to pursue the answers given to primary questions. Although some follow-ups are planned ahead by anticipating possible answers, more often than not they are composed as the interview goes along. Some ("And then?" "Is there more?") encourage further comments; others ("What does 'frequently' mean?" "What were you thinking at the time?") probe; still others ("How did it feel to get the prize?" "Were you worried when you didn't find her?") plumb the feelings of the interviewee. All are designed to motivate a person to enlarge on an answer.

Open questions ask the interviewee to provide whatever information he or she wishes ("What kinds of people are likely to be most affected by television violence?" "What are some kinds of behaviors that viewers exhibit as a result of viewing violence?" "What research studies would you recommend?"). Through the open question, the interviewer finds out about the person's perspectives, values, and goals, but they do take time to answer.[4]

primary questions *questions the interviewer plans ahead of time, serving as the main points for the interview outline*

follow-up questions *questions designed to pursue the answers given to primary questions*

open questions *broad-based questions that ask the interviewee to provide whatever information he or she wishes*

Bob Daemmrich/Stock, Boston

When you need to know how people feel about a particular political, economic, or social issue, you can conduct an interview to get their opinions.

Closed questions range from those that require a simple yes or no ("Are young children affected by TV violence more than older children?") to those that require only a short answer ("What behavior seems to be most affected by television violence?"). By asking closed questions, interviewers can control the interview and obtain large amounts of information in a short time. On the other hand, the closed question seldom enables the interviewer to know *why* a person gave a certain response, nor is the closed question likely to yield much voluntary information.[5]

For the most part, questions should be phrased neutrally. **Leading questions** are phrased in a way that suggests the interviewer has a preferred an-swer—for example, "Television violence has a major effect on children's behav-ior, doesn't it?" **Neutral questions** are phrased without direction from the interviewer, as in "Do you believe television violence has a major effect on chil-dren's behavior?"

The content of your questions will depend on what information you want to get. Try to formulate a list that stays on the subject so that you can get the information you need without taking up too much time.

How many questions you plan to ask depends on how much time you have for the interview. Keep in mind that you never know how a person will re-spond. Some people are so talkative and informative that in response to your first question they answer every question you were planning to ask in great de-tail; other people will answer each question with just a few words.

Early in the interview, plan to ask some questions that can be answered easily and that will show your respect for the person you are interviewing. In an interview with a professor, you might start with background questions such as "How did you get interested in doing research on the effects of media vio-lence?" The goal is to get the interviewee to feel at ease and to talk freely.

The body of the interview includes the major questions you have prepared. You may not ask all the questions you planned to, but you don't want to end the interview until you have the important information you intended to get. The questions are designed to get the information necessary to achieve your goal.

Figure 5.2 shows some of the questions you might ask to get information on the effects of television violence on viewers.

FIGURE 5.2   Sample interview questions

Background Information
How did you get interested in doing research on the effects of media violence?

Findings
Does your research show negative effects of television violence on viewers?
Are heavy viewers more likely to show negative effects than light viewers?
Have you found evidence that shows major effects on aggressiveness? Desensitization?
Have you found evidence that shows effects on civility?

Action
Are the effects great enough to warrant limiting children's viewing of violent programming?
Do you have any recommendations to offer the viewing public?

Listing Sources

The goal of this exercise is to help you compile a list of potential sources for your first speech.

For the topic you selected for your first speech, fill in the following information:

1. Name a person, an event, or a process that you could observe to broaden your personal knowledge base.

2. Working with manual or computerized versions of your library's card catalog or periodical indexes discussed in this chapter, list a total of six specific books and/or magazine articles that appear to provide information on your topic.

3. Name a person you could interview for additional information on this topic.

Conducting the Interview   The following are some communication behaviors that you'll want to follow during the interview.

1. Be courteous during the interview. Start by thanking the person for taking the time to talk to you. Throughout the interview, respect what the person says regardless of what you may think of the answers.

2. Listen carefully. In addition to listening to what is said, also pay attention to how it is said. A person's tone of voice, facial expression, and gestures often communicate as much or more than what the person says. If you don't understand, take time to ask questions. If you're not sure you understand, tell the person what you think he or she meant, such as "If I understand you correctly, you're saying that older and younger children react differently to television violence."

3. Keep the interview moving. Although some people will get so involved that they will not be concerned with the amount of time spent, most people will have other important business to attend to.

4. Make sure that your nonverbal reactions—facial expressions and gestures—are in keeping with the tone you want to communicate. Maintain good eye contact with the person. Nod to show understanding. And smile occasionally to maintain the friendliness of the interview.

Processing the Interview   As soon as possible after the interview, sit down with your answers to the questions and make note cards of the key points you want to use in the speech. Since it's likely that your notes were taken in an outline or shorthand form, make sure that you can make sense out of them. If at any point you are not sure whether you have accurately transcribed what the person said, take a minute to telephone the person to make sure.

What Information to Look For

Whatever the source, your task will be to look for factual statements and expert opinions.

Factual Statements

Factual statements are those that can be verified. "Conference USA now has 12 schools playing basketball," "The Macintosh (Performa) comes with a CD-ROM port," and "Johannes Gutenberg invented printing from movable type in the 1400s" are all statements of fact that can be verified.

When you find what appears to be factual information, you need to be concerned with the degree of confidence of the information. One way to verify whether the information is factual is to check it against material from another source on the same subject.

You'll want to be especially skeptical of "facts" that are asserted on the Internet. Although some Internet sites will refer you to published information, many provide information that has not been evaluated. Since anyone can say virtually anything on-line, you should never use any information that is not carefully documented unless you have corroborating sources.

Expert Opinions

Expert opinions are interpretations and judgments made by authorities in a particular subject area. "Having 12 basketball teams in a conference is far too many to have an equitable schedule," "Having a CD-ROM port on your computer is a necessity," and "The invention of printing from movable type was for all intents and purposes the start of mass communication" are all *opinions* based on the factual statements cited previously. Whether they are *expert opinions* or not depends on who made the statements.

The quality of an opinion depends on whether its source is an expert on the matter at hand. How do you tell an expert from a "quack"? First, the expert is recognized by others in his or her field. Second, the expert must be a student of the matter at hand. For instance, if a pediatrician who has gained a reputation specializing in the care of at-risk newborns has studied the relationship between drug use and birth defects and asserts that such defects occur in higher numbers when the mothers are drug users, then her opinion is expert, because she meets both criteria.

Of course, opinions are most trustworthy when they are accompanied by factual data. If the pediatrician can cite data from reputable scientific studies, her opinion is worth even more.

If you plan to use expert opinions in your speech, identify them as opinions and indicate to your audience the level of confidence that should be attached to them. For instance, an informative speaker may say, "The temperatures throughout the 1990s were much higher than average. Paul Jorgenson, a space biologist, believes that these higher-than-average temperatures represent the first stages of the greenhouse effect, but the significance of these temperatures is not completely accepted as fact."

While opinions cannot entirely take the place of documented facts, expert opinion can be used to interpret and give weight to facts that you have discovered. Moreover, in situations where you cannot get facts, where they are inconclusive, or where they need to be supplemented, you will have to support your claims with expert opinion.

Verbal Forms of Information

Factual information and expert opinions may be presented in the form of examples and illustrations, statistics, anecdotes and narratives, comparisons and contrasts, or quotable explanations and opinions.

Examples and Illustrations **Examples** are specific instances that illustrate or explain a general factual statement. One or two short examples like the following can help make a generalization meaningful.

examples *specific instances that illustrate or explain a general factual statement*

> One way a company increases its power is to buy out another company. Just last week Kroger bought out Fred Meyer Inc., making it the largest grocery firm in the country.
> Professional billiard players practice many long hours every day. Jeanette Lee practices as much as 10 hours a day when she's not in a tournament.

Examples are useful because they provide concrete detail that makes a general statement more meaningful to the audience.

Although most of the examples you find will be real, you may find hypothetical examples you can use. Hypothetical examples are those drawn from reflections about future events—they develop the idea "What if . . . ?" In the following excerpt, John Ahladas presents hypothetical examples of what it will be like in the year A.D. 2039 if global warming continues:

> In New York, workers are building levees to hold back the rising tidal waters of the Hudson River, now lined with palm trees. In Louisiana, 100,000 acres of wetland are steadily being claimed by the sea. In Kansas, farmers learn to live with drought as a way of life and struggle to eke out an existence in the increasingly dry and dusty heartland. . . . And reports arrive from Siberia of bumper crops of corn and wheat from a longer and warmer growing season.[6]

Now let us consider guidelines for selecting and using examples.

First, the examples should be clear and specific enough to create a clear picture for the audience. Suppose we offered the following generalization and support.

Generalization: Electronics is one of the few areas in which products are significantly cheaper today than they were in the 1980s.

Supporting Example: Cellular phones cost less than they did then.

Even though the support statement is a type of example, it is not a very good one. Listeners do not have a clear picture. "Cost less" is not specific; nor does it exemplify the assertion of being "significantly cheaper."

Look at the difference in the following supporting example.

Generalization: Electronics is one of the few areas in which products are significantly cheaper today than they were in the 1980s.

Supporting Example: In the mid-1980s, Motorola sold cellular phones for $5,000 each; now a person can buy a Motorola cellular phone for under $150.

With this single example, the listener has a vivid picture of a tremendous difference in about a 15-year period.

Second, the examples you use should not be misleading. This cellular phone example that is so vivid would be misleading, and thus unethical, if in fact cellular phones were the *only* electronics product whose prices had declined dramatically over the same period. Any misuse of data is unethical, especially if the user knows better.

Third, examples should relate to the generalization they are intended to support.

So, as you gather examples to use in your speeches, make sure that they are clear, that they are vivid (ear catching), that they don't mislead, and that they are truly relevant to the generalization as stated.

Because good examples can give a clear, vivid picture in a relatively few words, it's a good idea to follow this rule of thumb in preparing your speeches: Never let a generalization stand without at least one example.

statistics   *numerical facts*

Statistics   **Statistics** are numerical facts: "Only six out of every ten local citizens voted in the last election." "The cost of living rose 2.5 percent last year." "This year, African Americans, Asian Americans, and Hispanic Americans will represent more than 32 percent of the population of the United States." Such statistical statements enable you to pack a great deal of information into a small package. Statistics can provide impressive support for a point, but when they are poorly used in the speech, they may be boring and, in some instances, downright deceiving. Following are some general guidelines on using statistics effectively.

1. Record only statistics whose reliability you can verify. Taking statistics from only the most reliable sources and double-checking any startling statistics with another source will guard against the use of faulty statistics. For example, it is important to double-check statistics that you find in such sources as paid advertisements or publications distributed by special-interest groups. Be especially wary if your source does not itself provide documentation of the statistics it reports.

2. Record only recent statistics, so that your audience will not be misled. For example, if you come across the statistic that only 2 of 100 members (or 2 percent) of the U.S. Senate are women, you would be misleading your audience if you used that statistic in a speech, because it is way out of date. If you want to make a point about the number of women in the Senate, find the most recent statistics. Check for both the year and/or the range of years to which the statistics apply.

3. Look for statistics that are used comparatively. By themselves, statistics are hard to interpret, but when used comparatively, they have a much greater impact.

Charles Gupton/Stock, Boston

Use statistics from only the most reliable sources, and double-check any startling statistics with another source.

In a speech on chemical waste, Donald Baeder pointed out that whereas in the past chemicals were measured in parts per million, today they are measured in parts per billion or even parts per trillion. Had he stopped at that point the audience would have had little sense of the immensity of the figures. Notice how he goes on to use comparisons to put the meaning of the statistics in perspective:

> One part per billion is the equivalent of one drop—one drop!—of vermouth in two 36,000 gallon tanks of gin and that would be a very dry martini even by San Francisco standards! One part per trillion is the equivalent of one drop in two thousand tank cars.[7]

4. Do not overuse statistics. Although statistics may be an excellent way to present a great deal of material quickly, be careful not to overuse them. A few pertinent numbers are far more effective than a battery of statistics. When you believe you must use many statistics, try preparing a visual aid, such as a chart, to help your audience visualize them.

Although use of statistics can be a great addition to your speech, statistics must always be used with great care. The old statement "Figures don't lie, but liars figure" is one to keep in mind as you evaluate the statistics (figures) that you are considering for your speech.

In short, using statistics tends to be far more complicated than we might believe. You must take into account several variables. When were the statistics true? Exactly what do the statistics cover? Do they purport to cover every instance or just a sample? If they cover a sample, is it a statistically accurate sample? Do the statistics report averages or some other number?

When well used, and well presented, statistics can be most illuminating. Consider this picture of global demographic data presented by William Franklin, President of Franklin International, LTD.

> I recently saw some demographic information which may help to bring perspective to your opportunities and responsibilities, some perspective on your place or role in the world.
>   If we shrink the world's 5.7 billion population to a village of 100 people . . . with all existing human ratios remaining the same, here is the resulting profile.
>
> Of those 100 people, 57 are Asian, 21 European, 14 from North and South America, and 8 from Africa
>
> 51 female, 49 male
>
> 80 live in sub-standard housing
>
> 70 cannot read
>
> Half suffer from malnutrition
>
> 75 have never made a phone call
>
> Less than one is on the Internet
>
> Half the entire village's wealth would be in the hands of 6 people
>
> Only one of the hundred has a college education
>
> You are in a very elite group of only 1% who have a college education.[8]

Anecdotes and Narratives   **Anecdotes** are brief, often amusing stories; **narratives** are tales, accounts, personal experiences, or lengthier stories. Each presents material in story form. Because holding audience interest is so important in a speech and because audience attention is likely to be captured by a story, anecdotes and narratives are worth looking for, creating, and using. In a

anecdotes   *brief, often amusing stories*

narratives   *tales, accounts, personal experiences, or lengthier stories*

5-minute speech, you have little time to tell a detailed story, so one or two anecdotes or a very short narrative would be preferable.

The key to using stories is to make sure that the point of the story states or reinforces the point you are making in your speech. In a speech about telecommunication, Randall Tobias, vice chairman of AT&T, made a point about the promise and the threat of technology.

> A lighthearted story I heard from a scientist-colleague illustrates the point.
> A theologian asked the most powerful supercomputer, "Is there a God?" The computer said it lacked the processing power to know. It asked to be connected to all the other supercomputers in the world. Still, it was not enough power. So the computer was hooked up to all the mainframes in the world, and then all the minicomputers, and then all the personal computers. The theologian asked for the final time, "Is there a God?" And the computer replied: "There is now."[9]

Neither the anecdote nor the narrative needs to be humorous to be effective so long as it is vivid, meaningful, and relevant to the point being made. But, as the previous example shows, humorous anecdotes get attention as they make their point.

Comparisons and Contrasts One of the best ways to give meaning to new ideas is through comparison and contrast. Comparisons illuminate a point by showing similarities. Although you can easily create comparisons using information you have found, you should still keep your eye open for creative comparisons developed by the authors of the books and articles you have found.

Comparisons may be literal or figurative. Literal comparisons show similarities of real things:

> The walk from the lighthouse back up the hill to the parking lot is equal to walking up the stairs of a 30-story building.

Figurative comparisons express one thing in terms normally denoting another:

> I always envisioned myself as a four-door sedan. I didn't know she was looking for a sports car!

Comparisons make ideas not only clearer but also more vivid. Notice how Stephen Joel Trachtenberg, in a speech to the Newington High School Scholars' Breakfast, used a figurative comparison to demonstrate the importance of being willing to take risks even in the face of danger. Although the speech was given years ago, the point is timeless:

> The eagle flying high always risks being shot at by some hare-brained human with a rifle. But eagles and young eagles like you still prefer the view from that risky height to what is available flying with the turkeys far, far below.[10]

Whereas comparisons suggest similarities, contrasts highlight differences. Notice how the following humorous contrast dramatizes the difference between "participation" and "commitment."

> If this morning you had bacon and eggs for breakfast, I think it illustrates the difference. The eggs represented "participation" on the part of the chicken. The bacon represented "total commitment" on the part of the pig![11]

Quotations When you find an explanation, an opinion, or a brief anecdote that seems to be exactly what you are looking for, you may quote it directly in your speech. Because audiences want to listen to your ideas and arguments, they do not want to hear a string of long quotations. Nevertheless, a well-selected quotation might be perfect in one or two key places.

Quotations can both explain and vivify. Look for quotations that make a point in a particularly clear or vivid way. For example, in her speech "The Dynamics of Discovery," Catherine Ahles, former vice president for college relations at Macomb Community College, used the following quotation from Helen Keller to show the detrimental effects of pessimism:

> No pessimist ever discovered the secrets of the stars . . . or sailed to an uncharted land . . . or opened a new heaven to the human spirit.[12]

Frequently, historical or literary quotations can reinforce a point vividly. C. Charles Bahr, chairman of Bahr International, in a speech on telling the truth to sick companies, quoted Mark Twain on the importance of telling the truth:

> Always do right. It will amaze some people and astonish the rest.[13]

To take advantage of such opportunities, you need access to one or more of the many books of quotations mentioned earlier in this chapter. Most books of quotations are organized by topic, which helps in finding a particularly appropriate quote to use in your speech.

Keep in mind that when you use a direct quotation, it is necessary to credit the person who formulated it. Using any quotation or close paraphrase without crediting its source is plagiarism.

Recording Data and Citing Written and Electronic Sources

Whether the research materials you find are factual statements or opinions, you need to record the data accurately and keep a careful account of your sources so that they can be cited appropriately.

Recording Data

It is important to record data so that you can provide the information and its source in a speech or report the documentation to anyone who might question the information's accuracy. When question periods are provided at the end of a speech, members of an audience will often ask for sources of information. Whether or not there is a question period, however, listeners need the assurance that they can find the material used in your speech if they should decide to look for it.

How should you record the materials you uncover in your research, including information not only from printed and on-line sources but also from personal knowledge, observation, and interviews? Because most speakers use only some of their research material and are never sure of the final order in

INFOTRAC COLLEGE EDITION

For further evidence that quotations can be provocative and add interest to your speech, use InfoTrac College Edition to locate the article "How to Stop Boring Your Audience to Death: Databases, Anecdotes and Humor." (Hint: It was published in *Vital Speeches* on February 15, 1996.) Read how three famous statesmen and gifted speakers used quotations with great effectiveness. Learn tips on how to gather quotations that you can have readily available for your next speech.

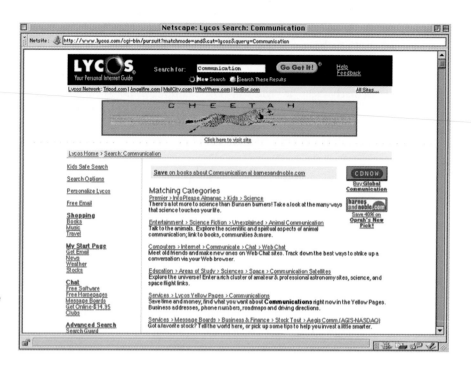

Search engines, such as Lycos shown here, can help you locate and organize information through the use of keyword searches.

which it will be used, it's best to record the material so that it can be easily selected and moved around. The note card method is probably the best.

In the note card method, each factual statement or expert opinion, along with source documentation, is recorded on a separate 4-by-6-inch or larger index card. Although it may seem easier to record all material from one source on a single sheet of paper (or to photocopy source material), sorting and arranging material is much easier when each item is recorded separately. On each card, indicate the topic of the recorded information, the information, and the publication data. Any part of the information that is quoted directly should be enclosed in quotation marks. In general, source documentation includes (1) the name of the author or authors; (2) the title of the article, if the source is a periodical, a newspaper, or an online publication; (3) the title of the book, periodical, or newspaper; (4) the date of publication; (5) the page number; and (6) for Internet sources, the document URL. Specifics and samples for preparing source citations (including interviews) for inclusion in the complete outline are shown in Chapter 6, pp. 113–116. In all cases, list source information in enough detail so that the information can be found later if needed. Figure 5.3 illustrates a useful note card sample.

As your stack of information grows, you then can sort the material. Each item goes under a heading to which it is related. For instance, for a speech on Ebola, the deadly disease that has broken out in Africa, you might have note cards related to causes, symptoms, and means of transmission. The card in Figure 5.3 would be indexed under the heading Deadliness of Disease.

The number of sources that you should use depends in part on the type of speech. For a narrative of a personal experience, you obviously will be the main, if not the only, source. For reports and persuasive speeches, however,

FIGURE 5.3 Example of a note card recording information

Topic: Ebola
Heading: Deadliness of disease

"After a few days the virus's victims begin vomiting blood and bleeding profusely, both internally and from the nose, eyes, and gums. Between 50 and 90 percent of them die within two weeks—some within days—from blood loss and shock."

Josie Glausiusz, "Ebola's Lethal Secrets," *Discover*, July 1998, p. 24. (On-line source, InfoTrac College Edition)

speakers ordinarily use several sources. For a speech on Ebola in which you plan to talk about causes, symptoms, and means of transmission, you should probably have two or more note cards under each heading. Moreover, the note cards should come from at least three different sources. One-source speeches often lead to plagiarism; furthermore, a one- or two-source speech simply does not give sufficient breadth of material. Selecting and using information from several sources will enable you to develop an original approach to your topic.

Citing Sources in Speeches

In your speeches, as in any communication in which you use ideas that are not your own, try to work the source of your material into your presentation. Such efforts to include sources not only help the audience evaluate the content but also add to your credibility. In addition, citing sources will give concrete evidence of the depth of your research. Failure to cite sources, especially when you are presenting information that is meant to substantiate a controversial point, is unethical.

FOCUS ON skills

Preparing Note Cards

The goal of this exercise is to help you prepare note cards that you can use to record information for your first speech.

From the sources that you identified in "Listing Sources," p. 85, complete at least six note cards that provide information related to your specific speech goal. Include at least one specific factual statement, one expert opinion, and four others from among examples and illustrations, statistics, anecdotes and narratives, comparisons and contrasts, and quotations.

On your note cards from magazine articles, cite the name of the author if one is given, the title of the article, the title of the magazine, the publication data, and the page on which the information appears.

On your note cards from books, cite the name of the author if one is given, the title of the book, the publication data (including publisher and year), and the page on which the information appears.

According to an article about Japanese workers in last week's *Time* magazine…

In the latest Gallup poll cited in the February 10 issue of *Newsweek*,…

But to get a complete picture we have to look at the statistics. According to the 1996 *Statistical Abstract*, the level of production for the European Economic Community rose from…

In a speech on business ethics delivered to the Public Relations Society of America last November, Preston Townly, CEO of the Conference Board, said…

According to Gloria Hollister, women's basketball coach, whom I interviewed last week,…

According to statistics that were included on the U.S. Department of Justice Drug Enforcement Administration Web site report on Rohypnol,…

In a written report, ideas taken from other sources are credited in foot-notes; in a speech, these notations must be included in your statement of the material. Although you do not want to clutter your speech with bibliographical citations, be sure to mention the sources of your most important information. These citations need not be complete bibliographical references. Figure 5.4 gives several examples of appropriate source citations.

R E F L E C T   O N   ethics

"Dan, I was wondering whether you'd listen to the speech I'm giving in class tomorrow. It will only take about five minutes."

"Sure."

Tom and Dan found an empty classroom, and Tom went through his speech.

"What did you think?"

"Sounded pretty good to me. I could follow the speech—I knew what you wanted to do. But I was wondering about that section where you had the statistics. You didn't give any source."

"Well, the fact is I can't remember the source."

"You remember the statistics that specifically, but you don't remember the source?"

"Well, I don't remember the statistics all that well, but I think I've got them about right."

"Well, you can check them, can't you?"

"Check them? Where? That would take me hours. And after all, I told you I think I have them about right."

"But Tom, the accuracy of the statistics seem pretty important to what you said."

"Listen, trust me on this—no one is going to say anything about it. You've already said that my goal was clear, my main points were clear, and I sounded as if I know what I'm talking about. I really think that's all Goodwin is interested in."

"Well, whatever you say, Tom. I just thought I'd ask."

"No problem, thanks for listening. I thought I had it in pretty good shape, but I wanted someone to hear my last practice."

"Well, good luck!"

1. What do you think of Tom's assessment of his use of statistics, that "no one is going to say anything about it"?

2. Does Tom have any further ethical obligation? If so, what is it?

Summary

Effective speaking requires high-quality information. You need to know where to look for information, what kind of information to look for, how to record it, and how to cite your sources in your speeches.

To find material, begin by exploring your own knowledge and work outward through observation, written and electronic sources, and interviewing. Look for material in books, periodicals, encyclopedias, statistical sources, biographical sources, newspapers, government publications, electronic databases, and on the Internet. Skim materials to evaluate sources quickly and determine whether or not to read them in full.

Two major types of supporting material for speeches are factual statements and expert opinions. Factual statements report verifiable occurrences. Expert opinions are interpretations of facts made by qualified authorities. Although you will use some of your material as you find it, you may want to present the information in a different form. Depending on your topic and speech goal, you may use facts and opinions orally in the form of examples, illustrations, statistics, anecdotes, narratives, comparisons, contrasts, and quotations.

A good method for recording material that you may want to use in your speech is to write each item of information, along with its bibliographical documentation, on a separate note card. As your stack of information grows, sort the material under common headings. During the speech, cite the sources for your information. You'll want to include a complete list of sources for the speech on your completed outline.

Every discourse like a living creature, should be put together that it has its own body and lacks neither head nor feet, middle nor extremities, all composed in such a way that suit both each other and the whole.

Plato, *Phaedrus*

Peter Chapman

Organizing and Outlining the Speech Body

"Troy, that was a terrific speech that Mareka gave on how we can recycle paper on campus. I didn't realize the efforts that other universities are making to help the environment. I haven't heard so many good stories in a long time."

"You're right, Brett, the stories were interesting, but, you know, I had a hard time following the talk. What did you make of it?"

"Well, she was talking about ways that we can help save the environment—but, you're right, I can't seem to remember anything but that one point about recycling. Let's see, what were the other key points?"

t roy and Brett's experience is not that unusual, for even some well-known speakers give speeches that aren't as clearly organized as they could be. Plato, the classical Greek philosopher whose quotation begins this chapter, was one of the first people to recognize the organic nature of a speech. We can rephrase his advice in a way that follows the old military guideline: First you tell them what you're going to tell them, then you tell them, then you tell them what you told them.

You'll recall that an effective speech plan is a product of seven action steps. So far, we've looked at determining a specific speech goal and finding information. In these next two chapters, we consider the third action step: Organize and develop material in a way that is best suited to your goal and your particular audience. This chapter focuses on outlining the body of the speech; the next chapter focuses on adding the introduction, conclusion, and other necessary elements to complete the speech outline.

Think of an outline not as an entire speech written in outline form, but as a road map for the audience to follow as you consider ways to present the speech. The value of working with an outline is that you can test the logic, development, and overall strength of the structure of your speech before you prepare the wording or begin practicing its delivery. Although the entire outline includes the elements shown in Figure 6.1, in this chapter we focus on outlining your main points and organizing your supporting material around these main points.

Although some professional speakers have learned alternate means of planning speeches and testing structure that work for them, over the years I have seen ample proof that for student speeches there is a direct relationship between the quality of the outline and the effectiveness of the speech. Also, I have found that students with well-organized speeches seem to increase their credibility with an audience, improve their own sense of self-confidence, and enhance what I might call the "listener-friendliness" of their speech.

The process of outlining the body of your speech is likely to include writing a thesis statement, selecting main points, stating the main points, determining the best order, and finally, adding supporting material for the main points.

FIGURE 6.1

Elements of a complete outline

Title (optional)
Specific speech goal
Introduction
Thesis statement
Body (including main points
    and transitions)
Conclusion
Sources

ACTION STEP three

Organize Information

Organize, outline, and develop your material in a way that is best suited to your particular audience.

A. Write a thesis statement that indicates the specifics of the speech goal.

B. Outline main points as complete sentences that are clear, parallel, and meaningful.

C. Order the main points following an organizational pattern that meets audience needs.

D. Create section transitions to serve as guideposts.

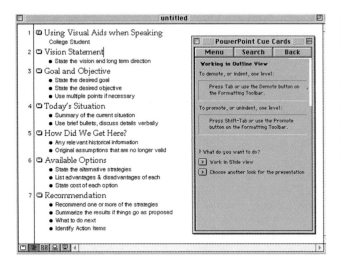

Writing a Thesis Statement

Since at this stage of your preparation you have a tentative speech goal and information drawn from many types of sources, you can focus on framing a thesis statement. Or, if you have already written a tentative statement, you can focus on analyzing the wording of your thesis statement. In either case, the time you spend working on the thesis statement is time well spent, for the clearer your thesis statement, the easier it is to select, state, and begin to build your main points.

In review, you'll recall that whereas the specific goal is a statement of how you want your audience to respond, the **thesis statement** is a sentence that outlines the specific elements of the speech supporting the goal statement. For instance, if Erin's speech goal is "I would like the audience to understand the three steps for executing an effective volleyball spike," she might then write her thesis statement as "The three steps for executing an effective volleyball spike are to have a good approach, a powerful swing, and a good follow-through."

Because Erin is a member of the women's varsity volleyball team, and thus is well aware that an effective spike depends on a good approach, a powerful swing, and a good follow-through, she was probably able to write at least a tentative thesis statement before she began gathering the information that she would use in her speech. So, if you were as well prepared as Erin, you may already have written a tentative thesis statement.

But often, your specific speech goal has many potential aspects, and you have to make decisions about which three (or so) are the most important. So, let's consider a different example to show how you might proceed to select the three you want to talk about, now that you have found most of the information you will use in your speech.

Emming has written the specific goal "I want audience members to be able to find the credit card that is most suitable for them." When he wrote that goal, he had a few ideas about what he might focus on in the speech, but it wasn't until he completed most of his research that he really had enough information to help his audience make good decisions about finding a suitable credit card.

thesis statement *a sentence that outlines the specific elements of the speech supporting the goal statement*

As he looked over his research material, he came up with the following list of criteria for making credit card decisions:

interest rate
convenience
discounts
annual fee
rebates
institutional reputation
frequent flyer points

So, at this stage, Emming has seven potential criteria related to his goal.

Depending on the amount of information you have for your topic, you may be able to list six or eight or even more potential topics for main points. Once you've made a list of all the elements related to your speech goal, you can then begin to evaluate them in order to select the most relevant ones for your thesis statement.

To continue with our example, Emming may notice that several of his sources talk about interest rate and annual fee, and nearly every source also talks about at least one inducement like rebates. So, Emming can cross out those criteria (topics) that don't have as much support and then combine individual inducements under a single heading. Now his list looks like this:

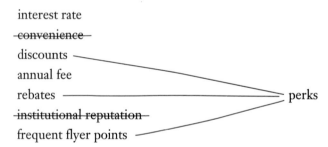

Using these topics, he can now write the following tentative thesis statement: "Three criteria that will enable audience members to find the credit card that is most suitable for them are level of real interest rate, annual fee, and advertised perks."

Outlining Main Points

main points *complete-sentence representations of the ideas used in the thesis statement*

Once you've determined a thesis statement, you can begin outlining the main points that will make up the body of your speech. **Main points** are complete-sentence representations of the ideas that you have used in your thesis statement. Think of your main points as the key building blocks of a speech—the ideas you want your audience to remember if they remember nothing else.

Write Main Points as Complete Sentences

Why should main points be written as complete sentences? Because only sentences can fully express the relationships associated with the key elements of the thesis statement.

Let's consider Roxanne's speech, in which her goal is "I want my audience to understand elements involved in ridding our bodies of harmful toxins." After

Writing Thesis Statements

The goal of this exercise is to help you arrive at a well-worded thesis statement for your speech.

1. Write your specific speech goal. For instance, Emming's was "I want audience members to be able to find the credit card that is most suitable for them."

2. List the elements of your speech goal—elements that might become the main points of your speech. For instance, Emming's were interest rate, convenience, discounts, annual fee, rebates, institutional reputation, and frequent flyer points.

3. After selecting the specific elements that best reflect your speech goal, combine them into a complete sentence that will be your thesis statement.

analyzing the information from her research on "body toxins," she wrote the following thesis statement: "Three proven elements involved in ridding our bodies of harmful toxins are reducing animal foods, hydrating, and eating natural whole foods."

When we look at her thesis statement, we see that the elements she plans to consider are "reducing animal foods, hydrating, and eating natural whole foods." Why shouldn't Roxanne simply state her three main points as follows?

I. Reducing intake of animal foods

II. Hydrating

III. Eating natural whole foods

Think of yourself as an audience member who hears only these words. Would you really understand what they meant? Not likely, because these words alone do not capture the meanings expressed in the thesis statement. These elements only make sense insofar as they are elements involved in ridding our bodies of harmful toxins.

So, as her first attempt at complete-sentence main points, she might write the following:

I. One proven element involved in ridding our bodies of harmful toxins is reducing our intake of animal products.

II. A second proven element involved in ridding our bodies of harmful toxins is keeping well hydrated.

III. A third proven element involved in ridding our bodies of harmful toxins is eating more natural whole foods.

This outline represents the three main points in complete-sentence form.

Now let's recall Emming's thesis statement: "Three criteria that will enable audience members to find the credit card that is most suitable for them are level of real interest rate, annual fee, and advertised perks."

Again, using Roman numerals to represent main point designations, he might write a first draft of the main points of his speech as follows:

I. Examining the interest rate is one criterion that you can use to find a credit card that is suitable for where you are in life.

II. Another criterion that you can use to make sure that you find a credit card that is suitable for where you are in life is to examine the annual fee.

III. Finding a credit card can also depend on weighing the advertised perks, which is the third criterion that you will want to use to be sure that it is suitable for where you are in life.

Notice that, in both of these examples, we have referred to "a first draft of the main points." Sometimes, your first draft will actually become the wording you want to use. Often, however, you will find that your first wording needs revision.

Revise Main Points

As you consider revising your main points, ask yourself the following questions:

- Are they clear?
- Are they parallel in structure?
- Are they meaningful?
- Are they limited to five or less in number?

In order to see how these questions might actually be used, let's consider Emming's main points more carefully. Emming has made a pretty good start. His three main points are complete sentences that capture the essence of the thesis statement. Now let's see how Emming might use the four questions to assure himself that he has achieved the best wording for his points.

clear (main points) *wording that is likely to call up the same images in the minds of all audience members*

1. Are the main points clear? Main points are **clear** when their wording is likely to call up the same images in the minds of all audience members. Emming has drafted his third main point as follows:

III. Finding a suitable credit card can also depend on weighing the advertised perks, which is the third criterion that you will want to use to be sure that it is suitable for where you are in life.

As he reviews the wording of this point, he notices that it is repetitive ("suitable . . . suitable"), too general ("where you are in life"), and wordy ("which is the third criterion that you will want to use to be sure that it is suitable").

Emming could eliminate several of the problems by cutting all the words before "weighing the advertised perks," cutting "which," and changing the rest of the sentence to "is the third criterion for finding a suitable credit card." After these changes, Emming would then have a main point written as follows:

III. Weighing the advertised perks is the third criterion for finding a suitable credit card.

parallel (main points) *wording that follows the same structural pattern, often using the same introductory words*

2. Are the main points parallel in structure? Main points are **parallel** when their wording follows the same structural pattern, often using the same introductory words. Parallel structure helps the audience recognize main points by recalling a pattern in the wording.

Emming notices that each of his main points begins with different wording. He now decides to begin each main point with the words "One criterion for finding a suitable credit card." To keep everything in order, he would first go back and refine the wording of his thesis statement so that it reads: "Three criteria that will enable audience members to find the credit card that is most suitable for them are level of real interest rate, annual fee, and advertised perks." Then, echoing the wording of his thesis statement, his revised draft of the main points would be as follows:

    I. One criterion for finding a suitable credit card is to examine the interest rate.

    II. A second criterion for finding a suitable credit card is to examine the annual fee.

    III. A third criterion for finding a suitable credit card is to weigh the perks.

Parallelism can be achieved in many other ways. A second common way is to start each sentence with an active verb. To take a different example, suppose Kenneth wants his audience to understand the steps involved in antiquing a table. He might write the following first draft of his main points:

    I. Clean the table thoroughly.

    II. The base coat can be painted over the old surface.

    III. A stiff brush, sponge, or piece of textured material can be used to apply the antique finish.

    IV. Then you will want to apply two coats of shellac to harden the finish.

After further consideration, Kenneth might revise his main points to make them parallel in structure. Note the parallel active verbs (italicized) used in his final draft:

    I. *Clean* the table thoroughly.

    II. *Paint* the base coat over the old surface.

    III. *Apply* the antique finish with a stiff brush.

    IV. *Harden* the surface with two coats of shellac.

Notice how the similarity of structure clarifies and strengthens the message. The audience can immediately identify the key steps in the process.

3. Are the main points meaningful? Main points are **meaningful** when they are informative. If the main points are not really meaningful, even if the audience remembers them, what is remembered may not be significant.

meaningful (main points) *wording that is informative*

For instance, let's go back to Emming's first main point. Suppose he had written it as follows:

    I. Thinking about the interest is one thing.

If he really decided to word his first point this way, and if his audience remembered it, what would they know? This phrasing just isn't very meaningful. Obviously, the following is a much better choice:

    I. One criterion for finding a suitable credit card is to examine the interest rate.

Following is a classic example of total failure to achieve the goal of meaningfulness.

Specific Goal: I want the audience to understand different characteristics of bears.

Thesis Statement: Black bears, grizzly bears, and polar bears all have different characteristics.

    I. There are facts about the American black bear.

    II. There are facts about grizzly bears.

    III. There are facts about polar bears.

Obviously, remembering these main points does nothing for the audience. In a case like this, the speaker may have to scrap the tentative main points and start over with the phrasing of the thesis statement.

4. Are the main points limited in number? Main points are limited in number when the total is five or less. As you begin to phrase prospective main points, you may find your list growing to six, seven, or even ten points that seem to be main ideas. A list that long is usually a clue that some points are really subpoints or repeat other points. Because every main point must be developed in some detail, it is usually impractical to have more than five main points; three or four are more manageable. If you have more than five, rework your speech goal to limit the number of main points, group similar points under a single heading, or determine whether some points are subpoints that can be included under main points.

Suppose you were giving a speech on shooting an effective foul shot. You might start with the following points:

I. Face the basket before shooting.
II. Hold your shoulders parallel to the foul line.
III. Spread your feet comfortably, with your knees bent.
IV. Put your foot that is opposite to your shooting arm slightly forward.
V. Hold the ball in your shooting hand, with your elbow bent.
VI. Concentrate on a spot just over the rim.
VII. Straighten your knees as you shoot the ball.
VIII. Follow through after the ball is released.

Now notice how you can make the steps even more meaningful by grouping them under three headings:

I. First, square yourself to the basket.
    A. Face the basket before shooting.
    B. Hold your shoulders parallel to the foul line.
II. Second, have proper balance.
    A. Spread your feet comfortably, with your knees bent.
    B. Put your foot that is opposite to your shooting arm slightly forward.
III. Third, deliver the ball smoothly.
    A. Hold the ball in your shooting hand, with your elbow bent.
    B. Concentrate on a spot just over the rim.
    C. Straighten your knees as you shoot the ball.
    D. Follow through after the ball is released.

Notice that this organization actually results in more items (11 versus 8). Yet it is easier to remember two to four items under each of three subheadings than it is to remember eight separate items.

Determining the Best Order

Well-constructed speeches will follow some identifiable organizational pattern. Although your thesis statement will suggest the type of organization you will be using, there are times when you may decide to revise the thesis statement (or even the goal) to achieve a different organization. Your objective is to find or *create* the structure that will help the audience make the most sense of the material and so achieve your speech goal. Although "real speeches" come with many types of organization, four basic orders that are useful for the beginning speaker to master are topic, time, space, and logical reasons.

Topic Order

Topic order organizes the main points of the speech by categories or divisions of a subject. This is an extremely common way of ordering main points because nearly any subject can be subdivided or categorized in many different ways. The order of the topics may go from general to specific, least important to most important, or in some other logical sequence. The order in which you choose to discuss the topics can often have a great effect on the success of the speech.

topic order   organizing the main points of a speech by categories or divisions of a subject

If topics vary in weight and importance—to the audience or to the goal of the speech—how you order them may influence your audience's understanding or acceptance of them. For example, audiences will often perceive the last point as the most important. In the example that follows, the topics vary in weight. They are presented in the order that the speaker believes is most suitable for the audience and speech goal, with the most important point at the end.

> **Specific Goal:** I want the audience to understand three proven elements for ridding our bodies of harmful toxins.
>
> **Thesis Statement:** Three proven elements involved in ridding our bodies of harmful toxins are reducing animal foods, hydrating, and eating natural whole foods.
>
>   **I.** One proven element involved in ridding our bodies of harmful toxins is reducing our intake of animal products.
>
> **II.** A second proven element involved in ridding our bodies of harmful toxins is eating more natural whole foods.
>
> **III.** A third proven element involved in ridding our bodies of harmful toxins is keeping well hydrated.

Emming's speech on the three criteria that will enable the audience to find the credit card that is most suitable is another example of a speech using topic order.

Time Order

Time order, or **chronological order,** follows a sequence of ideas or events; it focuses on what comes first, second, third, and so on. When you select a chronological arrangement of main points, the audience understands that there is a particular importance to both the sequence and the content of those main points. Time order is most appropriate when you are explaining how to do something, how to make something, how something works, or how something happened. Kenneth's speech on steps in antiquing a table is one example of time order.

time order (chronological order) organizing the main points of a speech as a sequence of ideas or events, focusing on what comes first, second, third, and so on

In the following example, notice how the order of main points is as important to the logic of the speech as the wording.

Specific Goal: I want the audience to understand the four steps involved in developing a personal network.

Thesis Statement: The steps involved in developing a personal network include analyzing your current networking potential, positioning yourself in places for opportunity, advertising yourself, and following up on contacts.

   I. First, analyze your current networking potential.
  II. Second, position yourself in places for opportunity.
 III. Third, advertise yourself.
  IV. Fourth, follow up on contacts.

Although the designations first, second, and so on, are not necessary to the pattern, their inclusion helps the audience to understand that the sequence is important.

Space Order

space order *organizing the main points of a speech by following a spatial or geographic progression*

Space order follows a spatial or geographic progression of main points. It is most helpful when you want the audience to understand that there is a special significance to the positioning of the information. Although space order is far less popular than either topic or time, it is likely to be used in descriptive, informative speeches. In explanations of a scene, a place, a person, or an object, a space order helps to create an orderly visual picture for your audience. To form a coherent, logical description, you can proceed from top to bottom, left to right, inside to outside, or in any constant direction that the audience can picture. In the following example, notice how the spatial order helps us visualize the three layers of the atmosphere.

Specific Goal: I want the audience to picture the three layers that make up the earth's atmosphere.

Thesis Statement: The earth's atmosphere comprises the troposphere, the stratosphere, and the ionosphere.

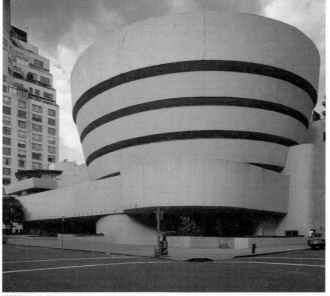

Organizing a speech by space (top to bottom, inside to outside, left to right, north to south) is often effective. How might you discuss a complex building like the Guggenheim Museum in New York pictured here?

CORBIS/Angelo Hornak

I. The troposphere is the inner layer of the atmosphere.

II. The stratosphere is the middle layer of the atmosphere.

III. The ionosphere is the succession of layers that constitute the outer regions of the atmosphere.

In Chapter 12, Principles of Informative Speaking, we consider some other informative speaking orders.

Logical Reasons Order

Logical reasons order emphasizes why the audience should believe something or behave in a particular way. Unlike the other three arrangements of main points, the logical reasons order is most appropriate for a persuasive speech, as in the following example.

> **Specific Goal:** I want the audience to donate money to the United Way.
>
> **Thesis Statement:** Donating to the United Way is appropriate because your one donation covers many charities, you can stipulate which specific charities you wish to support, and a high percentage of your donation goes to charities.
>
> **I.** When you donate to the United Way, your one donation covers many charities.
>
> **II.** When you donate to the United Way, you can stipulate which charities you wish to support.
>
> **III.** When you donate to the United Way, you know that a high percentage of your donation will go directly to the charities you've selected.

In Chapter 13, Principles of Persuasive Speaking, we consider additional ways of phrasing and ordering reasons for persuasive speeches.

logical reasons order *organizing the main points of a speech with statements that indicate why the audience should believe something or behave in a particular way*

Other Choices

As we mentioned earlier, the organizational patterns that we have discussed are the most common but not the only ones. As you develop your public speaking skill, you may find that you will need to revise an existing pattern or create a totally different one to meet the needs of your particular subject matter or audience.

For instance, the latter part of Martin Luther King's most famous speech was organized around the speech title, "I Have a Dream." By constantly repeating "I have a dream," he was able to focus on and develop many elements of his vision of a better society.

Many speakers have organized their entire speeches around the repetition of a key phrase. On the other hand, speakers may create variations of patterns such as the topical speech pattern. Thus, for different audiences, the speaker might present different topics or present the topics in different orders.

In summary, then, to organize the body of your speech, follow these three steps:

1. Turn your speech goal into a thesis statement that forecasts main points.

2. State main points in complete sentences that are clear, parallel, meaningful, and limited to a maximum of five in number.

FIGURE 6.2 Goal, thesis statement, and main points

Specific Goal:	I would like the audience to understand the major criteria for finding a suitable credit card.
Thesis Statement:	Three criteria that will enable audience members to find the credit card that is most suitable for them are level of real interest rate, annual fee, and advertised perks.

    I. One criterion for finding a suitable credit card is to examine the interest rate.

    II. A second criterion for finding a suitable credit card is to examine the annual fee.

    III. A third criterion for finding a suitable credit card is to weigh the perks.

3. Organize the main points in the pattern best suited to your material and the needs of your specific audience.

At this point, you have the structure for your complete outline: a speech goal, a thesis statement, and an outline of the main points of the speech.

Figure 6.2 shows what Emming's outline would look like at this stage of preparation. Notice that his specific speech goal is written at the top of the page. His thesis statement comes right after the goal because later it is likely to become part of his introduction.

The time and thought that you put into finding the most relevant and informative supporting material for your speech will pay off in audience interest and understanding.

Steve Dunwell/The Image Bank

Selecting and Outlining Supporting Material

The main points outline the structure of your speech. Whether your audience understands, believes, or appreciates what you have to say usually depends on how well those main points are explained and supported.

As we saw in Chapter 5, factual statements and expert opinions are the principal types of research information used in speeches. Once the main points are in place, you can select the most relevant of those materials and decide how to build each main point.

List Supporting Material

First, write down a main point. Then, under that main point, list all the information you have found that you believe is related to that main point. Don't worry if ideas are out of order or don't seem to relate to each other. Your goal at this point is to see what you have to work with. For example, Emming might write support for the first main point of his speech as follows:

> **I.** One criterion for finding a suitable credit card is to examine the interest rate.
>
> Most credit cards carry an average of 18%.
>
> Some cards carry an average of as much as 21%.
>
> Some cards offer a grace period.
>
> Department store rates are often higher than bank rates.
>
> Average rates are much higher than ordinary interest rates.
>
> Variable rate means that the rate will change from month to month.
>
> Fixed rate means that the rate will stay the same.
>
> Many companies quote very low rates (6% to 8%) for specific periods.

Organize Supporting Material

Once you have listed the items of information that make the point, look for relationships between and among ideas. As you analyze, you may draw lines connecting information that fits together logically, you may cross out information that seems irrelevant or doesn't really fit, and you may combine similar ideas using different language. For instance, Figure 6.3 depicts Emming's analysis of the information listed under his first main point.

In most cases, similar items that you have linked can be grouped under broader headings. For instance, Emming has four statements related to specific percentages and two statements related to types of interest rate. For the four statements related to specific percentages, he might create the following heading:

> Interest rates are the percentages that a company charges you to carry a balance on your card past the due date.

FIGURE 6.3   Editing of material supporting main point

I. One criterion for finding a suitable credit card is to examine the interest rate.

Most credit cards carry an average of 18%.

Some cards carry an average of as much as 21%.

~~Some cards offer a grace period.~~

~~Department store rates are often higher than bank rates.~~

Average rates are much higher than ordinary interest rates.

Variable rate means that the rate will change from month to month.

Fixed rate means that the rate will stay the same.

Many companies quote very low rates (6% to 8%) for specific periods.

Then under that heading, he can list the relevant items:

> Most credit cards carry an average of 18%.
> Some cards carry an average of as much as 21%.
> Many companies quote very low rates (6% to 8%) for specific periods.

For the two statements related to types of interest rates, he might create the following heading:

> Interest rates can be variable or fixed.

Then, under that heading, he can list the two types:

> Variable rate means that the rate will change from month to month.
> Fixed rate means that the rate will stay the same.

You are also likely to have listed information that you decide not to include in the outline:

> Department store rates are often higher than bank rates.
> Some cards offer a grace period.

Emming decided to cut the department store point because his emphasis was not on who was offering the rates, but on what percentages were being charged. Likewise, he thought that the grace period point wasn't directly related to either of the main ideas he wanted to emphasize.

Sometimes you'll find you have stated the same point two different ways:

> Most credit cards carry an average of 18%.
> Average rates are much higher than ordinary interest rates.

Emming might combine the two to read:

> Most credit cards carry an average of 18%, which is much higher than ordinary interest rates.

In outline form, then, a main point will have two or more subdivisions, and each subdivision may have two or more sub-subdivisions.

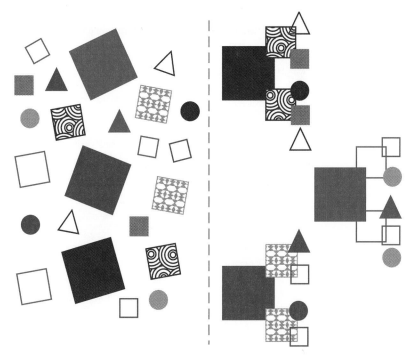

Subordination creates order.

When you outline, you need to follow a consistent form. The form we suggest is to designate main points with Roman numerals, major subpoints with capital letters, and supporting points with regular (Arabic) numbers.

The items of information listed for Emming's first main point might be grouped and subordinated as follows:

I. One criterion for finding a suitable credit card is to examine the interest rate.

    A. Interest rates are the percentages that a company charges you to carry a balance on your card past the due date.

        1. Most credit cards carry an average of 18%, which is much higher than ordinary interest rates.

        2. Some cards carry an average of as much as 21%.

        3. Many companies quote very low rates (6% to 8%) for specific periods.

    B. Interest rates can be variable or fixed.

        1. A variable rate means that the rate will change from month to month.

        2. A fixed rate means that the rate will stay the same.

As we said, the outline lists supporting material; it doesn't include all of the development. For instance, in this speech, Emming might build points by using personal experiences, examples, illustrations, anecdotes, statistics, quotations, and other forms of supporting material. The outline only needs to include enough supporting information to ensure that you can explain and clarify the point you are making. Later, if you believe that some of the other supporting material needs to be included in the outline, you can add it.

Figure 6.4 shows the progress of Emming's outline. It now contains the specific goal, the thesis statement, the three main points, and the tentative development of the first main point. Notice that main points are designated by Roman numerals, subpoints by capital letters, and supporting points by regular (Arabic) numbers.

FIGURE 6.4 Goal, thesis statement, main points, and partial outline

Specific Goal:	I would like the audience to understand the major criteria for finding a suitable credit card.
Thesis Statement:	Three criteria that will enable audience members to find the credit card that is most suitable for them are level of real interest rate, annual fee, and advertised perks.

I. One criterion for finding a suitable credit card is to examine the interest rate.
  A. Interest rates are the percentages that a company charges you to carry a balance on your card past the due date.
    1. Most credit cards carry an average of 18%, which is much higher than ordinary interest rates.
    2. Some cards carry an average of as much as 21%.
    3. Many companies quote very low rates (6% to 8%) for specific periods.
  B. Interest rates can be variable or fixed.
    1. A variable rate means that the rate will change from month to month.
    2. A fixed rate means that the rate will stay the same.
II. A second criterion for finding a suitable credit card is to examine the annual fee.
III. A third criterion for finding a suitable credit card is to weigh the perks.

Outlining Section Transitions

transitions *words, phrases, or sentences that show a relationship between other words, phrases, or sentences*

section transitions *complete sentences that link major sections of a speech*

Transitions are words, phrases, or sentences that show a relationship between other words, phrases, or sentences. In this chapter, we focus on what we call section transitions; we'll consider other types of transitions in Chapter 10, Practicing Speech Wording.

Section transitions are complete sentences that link major sections of a speech. They summarize what has gone before and/or show movement to the next main idea. These transitions act like a tour guide leading the audience through the speech and are helpful when you do not want to take a chance that the audience might miss something.

Section transitions work best at breaks from one part of the speech to another or from one main point to another. For example, in his speech on antiquing tables, suppose Kenneth has just finished the substance of his introduction and is now ready to launch into his main points. Before stating his first main point, he might say:

Antiquing a table is a process that has four steps—now let's consider the first of those four steps.

When his listeners hear this transition, they are mentally prepared to listen to the wording of the first main point. Then, perhaps, when he finishes talking about the first main point, he might use another section transition:

Now that we see what is involved in cleaning the table, let's move on to the second step.

You might be thinking, "This sounds repetitive to me. If I used all these transitions my audience will think I'm treating them like four-year-olds!" Nothing could be further from the truth.

Section transitions are important for several reasons. First, they help the audience follow the flow of the speech. If every member of the audience were able to pay 100% attention to every word, then perhaps section transitions wouldn't be needed. But as people's attention rises and falls during a speech, they often find themselves wondering where they are. Section transitions give them a mental jolt that says "Pay attention."

Second, section transitions are important in helping people retain information. They may well remember something that was said once in a speech. But their retention is likely to increase markedly if they hear something more than once. Even in writing, good transitions are important, but they're even more important in speaking. If listeners get lost or think they've missed something, they can't go back as they can with writing. So, by using good transitions, speakers actually help listeners stay with them and thus remember more of the information.

So, in a speech, if we forecast main points, then state each main point, and use transitions from one point to the next, not only are audiences more likely to follow, they are also more likely to remember the organization.

In your speech outlines, section transitions are written in parentheses at the junctures of the speech.

Listing Sources

Regardless of the type of speech or how long or how short it will be, you'll want to list your sources in the outline. The two standard ways of listing sources are alphabetically by author's last name or by category, with items listed alphabetically within each category. I recommend the first, but your professor may prefer the second, or may leave the choice up to you.

Written Sources

Although the specifics of listing sources differ depending on whether the source is a book, a periodical or newspaper, or an Internet source or Web site, certain common elements are essential to all: author, name of article, title of publication, date of publication, and page numbers. Now let's consider the specifics of listing sources of each type.

Books   For a book, write the name of the author (last name first), the title of the book, the chapter or article if the book is a collection of chapters or articles written by different people, place of publication, publisher's name, and date of publication. For example:

> Fuhrman, Joel, *Fasting and Eating for Health* (New York: Simon & Schuster, 1995).
> Janzen, Rod, "Five Paradigms of Ethnic Relations," in Larry Samovar and Richard Porter, eds., *Intercultural Communication*, 8th ed. (Belmont, CA: Wadsworth, 1997), pp. 63-72.

Magazines and Periodicals   For a periodical or newspaper, write the name of the author (last name first) if one is given, the title of the article, the name of

INFOTRAC COLLEGE EDITION

The body of the speech contains the main points of the speech. Although clearly stated main points are important, you help your audience understand the relationship between your main points by using section transitions between your main points.

To practice phrasing section transitions, access InfoTrac College Edition and click on PowerTrac. From the search index, choose Journal Name (jn). Type in "Vital Speeches" and click Submit. Under search results, view Vital Speeches and find Clark, Katherine K., "The Great Equalizers: Six Secrets to Success for All Entrepreneurs."

Identify the speech goal and the main points. Then, before the statement of each main point, create section transitions. How would these transitions make this speech even better?

the periodical or newspaper, the date, and the page number from which the information was taken. Examples:

Magazine

> Quinn, Jane Bryant, "Should You Be Worried?" *Newsweek*, August 17, 1998, 40–42.

Academic Journal

> Labianca, Dominick, "Rohypnol: Profile of the 'Date-Rape Drug.'" *Journal of Chemical Education* 75 (June 1998), 719–722.
>
> Smith, Craig R., and Lybarger, Scott, "Bitzer's Model Reconstructed," *Communication Quarterly* 44 (Spring 1996), 197–213.

Newspaper

> DiFilippo, Dana, "Year-round Schools Gaining Popularity," *The Cincinnati Enquirer*, August 1, 1998, B5, B7.

Electronic Databases

When you're taking material from the Web or some other electronic source, try to include as much documentation as possible so that another person can find what you've cited.

> http://ballyfitness.com/ Dr. Paul Kennedy, "Muscle Soreness," May 12, 1998.

FIGURE 6.5 Sample speech outline (incomplete)

Specific Goal: I would like the audience to understand the major criteria for finding a suitable credit card.

Thesis Statement: Three criteria that will enable audience members to find the credit card that is most suitable for them are level of real interest rate, annual fee, and advertised perks.

Introduction

Body

   I. One criterion for finding a suitable credit card is to examine the interest rate.

      A. Interest rates are the percentages that a company charges you to carry a balance on your card past the due date.

         1. Most credit cards carry an average of 18%, which is much higher than ordinary interest rates.

         2. Some cards carry an average of as much as 21%.

         3. Many companies quote very low rates (6% to 8%) for specific periods.

      B. Interest rates can be variable or fixed.

         1. A variable rate means that the rate will change from month to month.

         2. A fixed rate means that the rate will stay the same.

          (Now that we have considered rates, let's look at the next criterion.)

  II. A second criterion for finding a suitable credit card is to examine the annual fee.

  III. A third criterion for finding a suitable credit card is to weigh the perks.

Conclusion

Sources

---

http://www.lec.org/DrugSearch/Documents/Rohypnol.htm David Smith, Donald R. Wesson, and Sarah R. Calhoun, "Rohypnol (Flunitrazepam) Fact Sheet," October 1998.

Experience and Observation

If you're drawing from your own experience or observation, you will want to list the nature of that experience or observation. For instance, if Margot, who is preparing a speech on diamonds, worked at a jewelry store part-time for one or two years, she can list that experience as a source.

Work experience: Fegel's Jewelry, senior year of high school, 1998–1999.

Likewise, if Marquez, who is preparing a speech on brewing, visited a bottling plant in order to observe various stages of the process, he would list that observation as a source.

Observation: Visited Schoenling Brewery, April 22, 1999. Spent an hour on the floor observing the use of various machines in the total process and employees' responsibilities at each stage.

Interviews

If you have conducted an interview, you will want to list the name of the person, the person's position, and the date of that interview. If, for instance,

Carson had done a variety of computer searches for his speech on cloning and had come up with more than seven major articles, but time was getting short. He had had three tests the week before his assigned speech, and even though he had taken the time to get an excellent list of sources, the speech itself was due the next morning.

As Carson thought about his problem, it occurred to him that one magazine article he had read really said it all. In fact, as far as he could see, most of the key ideas he had noticed in his scanning of the other articles were pretty well sketched out in this one source. Suddenly a "plan" for his speech hit him. He would use *only* this one magazine article as the source of his speech material. He would cite the other articles in his list of sources, and would only have to change one of the three main ideas in his thesis statement. Moreover, the article had three references to other sources, so his list really did reflect what was in the speech.

Quickly then, Carson took three key paragraphs from the article and put them in outline form for his speech. He thought of a way he could start the speech, and he wrote a short summary for the conclusion. "Great," he thought, "in just about 15 minutes, I've got my speech for tomorrow." He even had time to read through the three paragraphs about four times before he went to bed—he knew he was in great shape for the speech.

1. Was Carson behaving ethically? If not, what ethical guideline did he violate?

2. What could Carson do that would make his use of this key article ethically beyond reproach?

Margot interviewed one of the diamond cutters at Fegel's Jewelry where she had worked part-time, she would list the interview as follows:

Interview with Bruno Mueller, diamond cutter at Fegel's Jewelry, March 19, 1999.

Summary

Take the time to organize your speech. Develop an outline for the body first, as discussed in this chapter, and then go on to complete a plan and an outline for the introduction and conclusion. Your audience will appreciate the effort, and you will feel more confident when you talk.

First, write a thesis statement based on your speech goal. When you have the potential main points, select the ones you will use. Then, write the main points in complete sentences that are clear, parallel in structure, meaningful, and limited to a maximum of five.

A speech can be organized in many different ways, depending on the type of speech and the nature of the material. Some of the most common organizational patterns are topic, time, space, and logical reasons. Look at your speech and determine whether you have organized it in a meaningful way consistent with one of the common patterns.

The next step is to develop your main points with supporting material. A useful approach is to list the potential material, then subordinate the material in a way that clarifies the relationships between and among subpoints and main points.

Prepare sectional transitions to be used between points. Sectional transitions are complete sentences that link major sections of a speech. Finally, list the sources you have used for your speech.

You now have an outline of the body of the speech, and are ready to begin planning your introduction and conclusion.

To lose our fluency of speech has nowhere a worse effect than at the commencement . . . that pilot is surely one of the worst who runs his vessel aground as it is leaving the harbor.

Quintilian, *Institutes of Oratory,*
Book IV, 1, 61

Organizing and Outlining Introductions and Conclusions

Margot had asked Donna to listen to her rehearse her speech. As she stood in front of the classroom where she was practicing, she began, "Today I want to tell you some things about diamonds. There are several criteria you can use in evaluating a diamond."

"Whoa, Margot," Donna said. "That's your introduction?"

"Yes," Margot replied. "People know what diamonds are. Why shouldn't I just get on with the speech?"

argot's question sounds reasonable—most people know what diamonds are. But this doesn't mean that everyone in the audience is ready to listen to a speech about evaluating diamonds. People might think the topic is boring, irrelevant to them, or for some other reason, not worth their time. For most speeches, how well you start the speech may determine whether most members of the audience even listen, and how well you start and how well you finish your speech can play a major role in the speech's overall success.

In the previous chapter, we discussed organizing and outlining the body of the speech. In this chapter, we complete the outline by organizing and developing an introduction that both gets attention and leads into the body of the speech, developing a conclusion that both summarizes the material and leaves the speech on a high note, writing a title, and listing sources.

Outlining the Introduction

At this stage of preparation, the body of the speech is sufficiently well developed that you can concentrate on how to begin your speech. Although your introduction may be only a few sentences, it is still especially important, for, as Quintilian, the great Roman rhetorician, reminds us with his comparison of speechmaking to captaining a ship, "that pilot is surely one of the worst who runs his vessel aground as it is leaving the harbor." Here we consider what a speech introduction should accomplish and how to craft effective introductions.

Goals of the Introduction

Unlike Margot's "Today I want to tell you," a good introduction serves to (1) get attention, (2) set the tone for a speech, (3) create a bond of goodwill between speaker and audience, (4) establish your credibility, and (5) lead into the content of a speech.

ACTION STEP

Organize Information

Organize, outline, and develop your material in a way that is best suited to your particular audience.

A. Create an introduction that gets attention, sets the tone, creates goodwill, builds your credibility, and leads into the body of the speech.

B. Create a conclusion that both summarizes the material and leaves the speech on a high note.

C. Review and complete the speech outline.

D. Prepare speaker notes from the outline.

Getting Attention An audience's physical presence does not guarantee that people will actually listen to your speech. Your first goal, then, is to create an opening that will win your listeners' attention by arousing their interest and providing them a need to know the information you will present. Even if you are giving a speech to an audience that already knows what you're going to be talking about and has a real need to absorb what you will be saying, it is still useful to start with an attention-getter. Later in this chapter, we discuss several types of attention-getting devices you can use.

Setting a Tone A humorous opening will signal a lighthearted tone; a serious opening signals a more thoughtful or somber tone. A speaker who starts with a rib-tickling ribald story is putting the audience in a lighthearted, devil-may-care mood; if that speaker then says, "Now let's turn to the subject of abortion (or nuclear war, or drug abuse)," the audience will be confused, and the speech may be doomed.

Creating a Bond of Goodwill In your first few words, you often establish how an audience will feel about you as a person. If you're enthusiastic, warm, and friendly and give a sense that what you're going to talk about is in the audience's best interest, it will make them feel more comfortable with spending time listening to you.

Establishing Your Credibility Regardless of your topic or goal, your audience is going to wonder why they should pay attention to what you have to say. Although credibility is built and maintained throughout the speech, it is a good idea to say something at the beginning about your right to talk on this topic. For instance, when Erin starts her speech on the volleyball spike, her audience is likely to feel more comfortable with her as an authority if she mentions that she's a member of the women's varsity volleyball team. In Jeremy's introduction to his speech about violence in the media, he might say that he has had a long-time interest in the effects of television and has looked for the best research available on the subject. If your credibility is built primarily on the quality of the material you will present, then build your credibility as the speech goes along.

Leading into Content Since audiences want to know what the speech is going to be about, it's useful to forecast your organization in the introduction. If you have a well-written speech goal and thesis statement, then you have the

Charles Gupton/The Stock Market

An effective speech introduction will not only get attention and lead into the body of the speech but will also build goodwill and set the tone for the speech.

material necessary to meet this goal. For instance, in a speech on campaigning, just before you actually state your first main point, you might draw from your specific goal and say, "In this speech, I'll explain the four stages of a political campaign." A clear forecast of the main points is appropriate unless you have some special reason for not revealing the organization; such a forecast is almost always called for in an informative speech.

Although meeting five goals sounds like a great deal, in many cases you will find that you can accomplish all of them in a few sentences. If you can't meet all five goals in your brief opening, then be sure that you create an appropriate tone, develop goodwill, and establish your credibility as the speech moves along.

Types of Introductions

Ways to begin a speech are limited only by your imagination. To find the most effective opening, try two or three different introductions in practice and pick the one that seems best suited to your purpose and meets the needs you have identified in your analysis of audience and setting.

Because you will be giving very short speeches this term, we give special attention to adapting types of openings to short speeches. In real-life speeches, you will have more leeway in developing introductions using startling statements, rhetorical questions, stories, personal references, quotations, and suspense.

Startling Statement   One excellent way to grab your listeners' attention and focus on the topic quickly is to open with a startling statement that will override the various competing thoughts in your listeners' minds. The following example illustrates the attention-getting effect of a startling statement:

> If I pointed a pistol at you, you would be justifiably scared. But at least you would know the danger to your life. Yet every day we let people fire away at us with messages that are dangerous to our pocketbooks and our minds, and we seldom say a word. I'm talking about television advertisers.
> Today I want to look at our choices in how we can go about letting our feelings about advertising be heard.

In just 76 words—about 30 seconds—this introduction grabs attention and leads into the speech.

Rhetorical Question   Asking a rhetorical question—a question seeking a mental rather than a vocal response—is another appropriate opening for a short speech. Notice how a student began her speech on counterfeiting with three short questions:

> What would you do with this ten-dollar bill if I gave it to you? Take your friend to a movie? Treat yourself to a pizza and drinks? Well, if you did either of these things, you could get in big trouble—this bill is counterfeit!
> Today I want to share with you the extent of counterfeiting of American money worldwide and what our government is doing to curb it.

Again, a short opening (just 70 words—less than 30 seconds) gets attention and leads into the speech.

Now let's consider a longer opening that shows the potential for using rhetorical questions in a major speech. Notice how Wendy Liebermann, President of WSL Strategic Retail, gets the attention of her audience—members of the Non-Prescription Drug Manufacturers Association—and leads into her speech with a series of short questions:

> Have you wondered of late what's going on with consumers? Why they are so full of contradictions when it comes to spending money? Why they will buy a $500 leather jacket at full price but wait for a $50 sweater to go on sale? Will buy a top-of-the-line sports utility vehicle then go to Costco to buy new tires? Will eagerly pay $3.50 for a cup of coffee but think $1.29 is too expensive for a hamburger? Will spend $2.00 for a strawberry-smelling bath soap but wait for a coupon to buy a $0.99 twin pack of toilet soap?
>
> The economy is booming. Unemployment is at a 25-year low. Real income has increased. Why isn't everyone out spending like they did in the 1980s— shopping everywhere, buying everything? Why are so many companies struggling? What is this paradox? Is there a paradox?
>
> Well, that's what we are going to talk about today. This apparent consumer paradox: what it is; what it means and how to make sense out of it. Because if we don't understand it and respond to it, there's a very good chance we won't attract the consumers we want, and a very, very good chance we won't build long-term profitable sales, and a very, very, very good chance we won't all be sitting here this time next year.[1]

This 221-word opening (well under 2 minutes) would work for a 10- to 15-minute speech or longer. Notice that the series of questions in the first paragraph touches the behavior of many of us and even introduces some light humor. Right away, the speaker is not only getting attention but gaining goodwill. In addition, the lighthearted approach sets the tone for her speech. The second series of questions starts to really get the audience to think with her. Both series set up the subject matter of the speech. The third paragraph then tells the audience exactly what she will be looking at in reference to these questions.

So, we can see that rhetorical question openings can be adapted to speeches of any length.

Story If you have a good story that gets an audience's attention and is really related to the goal of the speech, you probably have an unbeatable opening. Because many good stories take time to tell, they are generally more appropriate for longer speeches. However, you will occasionally find or think of a story that is just right for your speech, as was this one on balancing stakeholder interests:

> A tightrope walker announced that he was going to walk across Niagara Falls. To everyone's amazement, he made it safely across, and everybody cheered. "Who believes I can ride a bicycle across?" And they all said, "Don't do it, you'll fall!" But he got on his bicycle and made it safely across. "Who believes I can push a full wheelbarrow across?" Well, by this time the crowd had seen enough to make real believers of them, and they all shouted, "We do! We do!" At that he said, "OK . . . Who wants to be the first to get in?"
>
> Well, that's how many investors feel about companies who have adopted the philosophy that balancing the interests of all stakeholders is the true route to maximum value. They go from skeptics to believers, but are very reluctant to get in that wheelbarrow.
>
> What I would like to do this afternoon is share with you Eastman's philosophy of stakeholder balance, give you some specific examples of how we're putting this philosophy into practice, and then I'll give you some results.[2]

Most people understand the need to get attention. What better way than to tell a good story? But the goal of telling a story to open the speech is not just to get attention; it is to get attention on the subject matter of the speech. Notice that Deavenport's opening story focuses on the issue of balance—then notice that his speech is about "stakeholder balance" as his organization's philosophy.

So, if a person has heard a really funny story that relates to the subject of dogs, and if the speech is about dogs, then telling that funny story may really help the speaker focus audience attention *on the speech*. But if the speech is about the economy, the audience is going to laugh at the dog story and then mentally drift when they discover that the speech is about something else. So, if you have a relevant story, use it in your speech—but if it does not relate to your topic, don't use it.

Personal Reference   Although any good opening should engage the audience, the personal reference to audience experience is directed solely to that end. In addition to getting attention, a personal reference can be especially effective at engaging listeners as active participants in a speech. A personal reference opening like this one on exercise may be suitable for a speech of any length:

> Say, were you panting when you got to the top of those four flights of stairs this morning? I'll bet there were a few of you who vowed you're never going to take a class on the top floor of this building again. But did you ever stop to think that maybe the problem isn't that this class is on the top floor? It just might be that you are not getting enough exercise.
>
> Today I want to talk with you about how you can build an exercise program that will get you and keep you in shape, yet will only cost you three hours a week, and not one red cent!

Although this 112-word opening can be presented in less than a minute, you can build the personal reference into an opening for a major speech. Let's see how Dana Mead, Chairman and Chief Executive Officer of Tenneco, used personal reference in the opening to his speech to the Executives' Club of Chicago:

> Thank you and good afternoon. It's great to be back in Chicago, the city of new beginnings. In 1893, Chicago hosted the world's fair—the Columbian Exposition—commemorating one of the world's greatest beginnings, the 400th anniversary of Columbus' voyage to America. (Actually, it took 401 years before Chicago completed the exhibition—but it was so grand no one was nitpicking!)
>
> The fair had a real second purpose—to demonstrate to the world what progress Chicago had made since the fire of 1871—and of course it succeeded in truly impressing the world.
>
> Chicago continues to impress the world. As one of the global economy's industrial titans, your hosting of the Transatlantic Business Dialogue, in my recent experience, was the catalyst for the impressive progress which that meeting produced. So, when I talk about the new American economy, my remarks should be familiar—you are already part of it.[3]

Although this personal reference was only the first part of Mead's speech introduction, it gives you a good idea of the kinds of information you can use to relate to your audience.

Quotation   A particularly vivid or thought-provoking quotation makes an excellent introduction to a speech of any length. You will need to use your imagination to relate the quotation to your topic so that it yields maximum benefits. For instance, in the following beginning of his introduction, notice how David Boaz, a libertarian, uses a quotation to get the attention of his audience attending the Libertarian National Convention focused on political behavior:

> In the 18th century British parliament, the Earl of Sandwich said to the great libertarian John Wilkes, "I do not know whether you will die on the gallows or

of some dread disease." Wilkes responded, "That depends, sir, on whether I embrace your principles or your mistress."

In Washington more politicians have been embracing mistresses than principles recently.[4]

As the introduction progresses, he introduces the topic of his speech, liberty versus power.

In the following excerpt from her speech to the annual meeting of the American Medical Association, AMA President Nancy Dickey exemplifies the way a clever speaker can use a quotation in the opening to serve as the theme for the entire speech:

> A wise person once said, "Always have your bags packed, you never know where life's journey is going to take you." I couldn't agree more. In fact, as you can see, I have my bag with me tonight [she holds up her standard medical bag for the audience to see]. I've chosen to bring that traditional black bag that physicians have carried with them for generations. And I'm here to tell you— my bag is packed and ready to go as I prepare for this year-long journey of my AMA presidency.
>
> Of course, having your bag packed isn't really about having a change of clothes ready. It's about being prepared to take advantage of the opportunities that come your way in life. And I am prepared.
>
> . . .
>
> I've also packed some more tangible items in my bag tonight. Symbolic items, really, which represent my presidential priorities for the year ahead. And tonight I want to share these items and priorities with you—and ask for your help in making them a reality during the next 12 months.[5]

I think you would agree that if you were a physician in her audience, you would be intrigued by what she had to say about her priorities for the year.

Suspense   If you can start your speech in a way that gets the audience to ask, "What is she leading up to?" you may well get them hooked for the entire speech. The suspense opening is especially valuable when the topic is one that the audience might not ordinarily be willing to listen to if the speech were opened less dramatically. Consider the attention-getting value of the following:

> It costs the United States more than $116 billion per year. It has cost the loss of more jobs than a recession. It accounts for nearly 100,000 deaths a year. I'm not talking about cocaine abuse—the problem is alcoholism. Today I want to show you how we can avoid this inhumane killer by abstaining from it.

Notice that by putting the problem "alcoholism" at the end, the speaker encourages the audience to try to anticipate the answer. And since the audience may well be thinking "narcotics," the revelation that the answer is alcoholism is likely to be that much more effective.

Selecting an Introduction

Because the introduction is critical in establishing your relationship with your audience, it's worth investing the time to compare different openings. Try working on two or three different introductions; then pick the one you believe will work best for your specific audience and speech goal.

For instance, Emming created the following three introductions for his speech on evaluating credit cards:

> Have you seen the number of agencies that have showered the campus with credit card applications. Sounds good, doesn't it? Take just a few minutes to fill out a statement, and you'll be in control of your economic destiny. But wait a

Writing Speech Introductions

The goal of this practice is to help you create choices for how you will begin your first speech.

1. For the speech body you outlined in the previous chapter, prepare three separate introductions that you believe would be appropriate, and present them aloud.

2. Which one do you believe is the best? Why?

minute. The road down consumer credit lane is not as smooth as the companies would have you believe. Today I'm going to share with you the criteria gained from my reading and personal experience that you'll want to consider for selecting a credit card. (86 words)

Each of these pieces of plastic I hold in my hand is a credit card. They look about the same, don't they? They're not. Before you travel into credit card land, you had better consider what you're getting into. Today I'm going to share with you the criteria gained from my reading and personal experience that you'll want to consider for selecting a credit card. (64 words)

Banks and credit unions are willing to shower us with incentives in order to get us to sign up for our own credit card. But we'd be wise to look before we leap. P.T. Barnum said, "There's a sucker born every minute." Today I'm going to share with you the criteria that you'll want to consider for selecting a credit card so that you won't end up being one of those "suckers." (72 words)

Which one do you prefer?

Each of these possibilities is an appropriate length. Most introductions range from 5 to 10 percent of the speech. Thus, for a 5-minute speech (approximately 750–800 words), an introduction of 40 to 75 words is appropriate; for a 30-minute speech, an introduction of 2 to 4 minutes is appropriate.

Whether or not your speech introduction meets all five of the goals directly, it should be long enough to put listeners in a frame of mind that will encourage them to hear you out, without being so long that it leaves too little time to develop the substance of your speech. Of course, the shorter the speech, the shorter the introduction.

The introduction will not make your speech an instant success, but it can get an audience to look at and listen to you and to focus on your topic. That is about as much as a speaker can ask of an audience during the first minute or two of a speech.

Outlining the Conclusion

Shakespeare said, "All's well that ends well," and nothing could be truer of a good speech. The conclusion offers you one last chance to hit home with your point. Too many speakers either end their speeches so abruptly that the audience is startled or ramble on aimlessly until they exhaust both the topic and the audience. A weak conclusion—or no conclusion at all—can destroy much of the impact of an otherwise effective speech. Even the best conclusion cannot save a poor speech, but it can heighten the impact of a good speech.

Goals of the Conclusion

A conclusion has two major goals: (1) to wrap up the speech so that it reminds the audience of what you have said and (2) to hit home so that the audience will remember your words or consider your appeal. Even though the conclusion will be a relatively small part of the speech—seldom more than 5 percent (35 to 40 words for a 5-minute speech)—it is worth the time and effort to make it effective.

Types of Conclusions

The following are four basic types of conclusions that you will want to master.

Summary By far the easiest way to end a speech is to summarize the main points. Thus, the shortest appropriate ending for a speech on the warning signs of cancer would be, "So remember, if you experience a sudden weight loss, lack of energy, or blood in your urine or bowels, then you should see a doctor immediately." Such an ending restates the key ideas the speaker wants the audience to remember. Summaries are appropriate for either informative or persuasive speeches.

Although effective speakers often summarize to achieve the first goal of wrapping up the speech so that it reminds the audience of what they have said, they are likely to supplement their summaries with material designed to achieve the second goal: hitting home so that the audience will remember their words or consider their appeal. The following represent several ways to supplement or replace the summary.

Story Storylike, or anecdotal, material that reinforces the message of the speech works just as well for the conclusion as for the introduction. In his speech on banking, Edward Crutchfield ends with a personal experience showing that bankers must be ready to meet competition coming from any direction:

> I played a little football once for Davidson—a small college about 20 miles north of Charlotte. One particularly memorable game for me was one in

INFOTRAC COLLEGE EDITION

In an article in InfoTrac College Edition, "Happy Endings," a prizewinning journal writer is quoted as saying that a "story with a strong lead and a strong conclusion is 'like some kind of basket where you've got to have a handle at both ends.'" Indeed, many speakers forget that people tend to remember what they heard first and what they heard last.

Using InfoTrac College Edition, conduct a search using the keywords "introductions, conclusions." What points does the above citation make that are applicable to speech preparation? Use the Link button to discover references to Closure. What will you do to ensure that your speeches begin and end with a bang?

Jeffry Myers/Stock, Boston

The conclusion offers you one last chance to hit home with your point. Supplementing a summary with a quote or a short anecdote is often a good way of emphasizing what you want the audience to get from the speech.

which I was blindsided on an off-tackle trap. Even though that was 17 years ago, I can still recall the sound of cracking bones ringing in my ears. Well, 17 years and three operations later my back is fine. But I learned something important about competition that day. Don't always assume that your competition is straight in front of you. It's easy enough to be blindsided by a competitor who comes at you from a very different direction.[6]

Storylike conclusions will work for either informative or persuasive speeches.

Appeal to Action   The appeal to action is a common way to end a persuasive speech. The **appeal** describes the behavior that you want your listeners to follow after they have heard your arguments. Notice, for example, how William Franklin, President of Franklin International, ends his speech on "Careers in International Business" with an appeal. After summarizing the five main ideas of his speech—learn from other cultures; be true to your personal values; take any opportunity to experience leadership; persevere; network—he concludes with the following statement:

> Baron Charles Montesquieu said a couple of hundred years ago, "Commerce is the best cure for prejudice, peace is the natural effect of trade." If that was true in the 18th century it will be even more true in the 21st century. Trade and investment bring more than just money and goods, they bring ideas. As 21st century leaders you have great opportunity to help us all to overcome prejudice and bring about understanding and peace for all people. I have great confidence that is what you will do.[7]

By their nature, appeals are most relevant for persuasive speeches, especially when the goal is to motivate an audience to act.

Emotional Impact   No conclusion is more impressive than one that drives home the most important points with real emotional impact. Consider the following example, in which Richard Lamm, of the Center for Public Policy and Contemporary Issues, ends his speech on unexamined assumptions with a powerful emotional appeal for unity.

> Diverse people must unify or they have conflicts. Melting pots that don't melt become pressure cookers. A country is not a rooming house where we just live while we make our living. What is the social glue that holds diverse people together? Beware of "pyrrhic victories." Listen to John Gardner: "If a community is lucky, and fewer and fewer are, it will have a shared history and tradition. It will have its 'story,' its legends and heroes and will retell those stories often. It will have symbols of group identity—a name, a flag, a location, songs and stories in common—which it will use to heighten its merciless sense of belonging. To maintain the sense of belonging and the dedication and commitment so essential to community life, members need inspiring reminders of shared goals and values."[8]

Like the appeal, the emotional conclusion is likely to be used for a persuasive speech where the goal is to reinforce belief, change belief, or motivate an audience to act.

Selecting a Conclusion

Speakers select the type of conclusion to use on the basis of the speech goal and the likely appeal to the audience. To determine how you will conclude your speech, try out two or three conclusions, then choose the one that you believe will best reinforce your speech goal with your audience.

For his speech on evaluating credit cards, Emming created the following three for consideration. Which do you like best?

appeal   type of conclusion that describes the behavior you want your listeners to follow

> So, if you decide to apply for a credit card, you'll now be able to make some evaluation based upon interest rates, annual fee, and perks.
>
> I think you can see that by examining interest rates, annual fee, and perks, you can be sure of getting a credit card that is right for you.
>
> Before making your final credit card selection, make sure that you have examined interest rates, annual fee, and perks.

Because this first speech is relatively short, Emming decided to end his speech with just one sentence. For speeches that are no longer than 5 minutes, a single-sentence conclusion is often appropriate. You're likely to need as much of your time as possible to do a good job of presenting the main points. But as speeches get even a little longer, you'll want to consider supplementing the summary to give the conclusion more impact.

Writing a Title

In many classroom situations, speeches are not required to have titles. But in most speech situations outside the classroom, it helps to have a title that lets the audience know what to expect. A title is probably necessary when you will be formally introduced, when the speech is publicized, or when the speech will be published. A good title may be especially important in attracting an audience. A good title will be brief, descriptive of the content, and if possible, creative. Most speakers don't settle on a title until the rest of the speech preparation is complete.

Three kinds of titles are (1) a simple statement of subject—a shortened version of the speech goal, (2) a question, and (3) a creative title.

1. Simple statement of subject. This straightforward title captures the subject of the speech in a few words.

> Courage to Grow
> Selling Safety
> The Dignity of Work
> America's Destiny

2. Question. To spark greater interest, you can phrase your speech goal as a question. A prospective listener may then be motivated to attend the speech to find out the answer.

> Do We Need a Department of Play?
> Are Farmers on the Way Out?

> What Is the Impact of Computers on Our Behavior?
> Are We Living in a Moral Stone Age?

3. Creative title. A more creative approach is to combine a familiar saying or metaphor with the simple statement of subject.

> Teaching Old Dogs New Tricks: The Need for Adult Computer Literacy
> Promises to Keep: Broadcasting and the Public Interest
> The Tangled Web: How Environmental Climate Has Changed
> Freeze or Freedom: On the Limits of Morals and Worth of Politics

The simple statement of subject gives a clear idea of the topic, but is not especially eye- or ear-catching. Questions and creative titles capture interest but may not give a clear idea of content unless they include subtitles.

Once you are comfortable with your goal, you can begin thinking about a title. When you are trying to be creative, you may find a title right away or not until the last minute.

Completing the Outline

Now that you have all the parts, it's time to put everything together in complete outline form. The following checklist helps you make sure that you have an outline that will be most useful to you as you move into the rehearsal phase.

1. Have I used a standard set of symbols to indicate structure? Main points are usually indicated by Roman numerals, major subdivisions by capital letters, minor subheadings by Arabic numerals, and further subdivisions by lowercase letters.

2. Have I written main points and major subdivisions as complete sentences? Complete sentences help you to see (1) whether each main point actually develops your speech goal and (2) whether the wording makes your intended point. Unless the key ideas are written out in full, it will be difficult to follow the next guidelines.

3. Do main points and major subdivisions each contain a single idea? This guideline ensures that the development of each part of the speech will be relevant to the point. Thus, rather than

I. The park is beautiful and easy to get to.

divide the sentence so that both parts are separate:

I. The park is beautiful.
II. The park is easy to get to.

This two-point example sorts out distinct ideas so that the speaker can line up supporting material with confidence that the audience will see and understand its relationship to the main points.

4. Does each major subdivision relate to or support its major point? This principle is called *subordination*. Consider the following example:

I. Proper equipment is necessary for successful play.
    A. Good gym shoes are needed for maneuverability.

B. Padded gloves will help protect your hands.

C. A lively ball provides sufficient bounce.

D. And a good attitude doesn't hurt.

Notice that the main point deals with equipment. A, B, and C (shoes, gloves, and ball) all relate to the main point. But D, attitude, is not equipment and should appear somewhere else, if at all.

5. Are the total words in the outline limited to no more than one-third the total number of words anticipated in the speech? An outline is only a skeleton of the speech—not a manuscript with letters and numbers. The outline should be short enough to allow you to experiment with methods of development during practice periods and to adapt to audience needs during the speech itself. An easy way to judge whether your outline is about the right length is to check that it contains no more than one-third the number of words in the actual speech. Because approximate figures are all you need, to compute the approximate maximum words for your outline, start by assuming a speaking rate of 160 words per minute. (Last term, the speaking rate for the majority of speakers in my class was 140 to 180 words per minute.) Thus, using the average of 160 words per minute, a 3- to 5-minute speech would contain roughly 480 to 800 words, and the outline should be 160 to 300 words. An 8- to 10-minute speech, roughly 1,280 to 1,600 words, should have an outline of approximately 426 to 533 words.

Now that we have considered the various parts of an outline, let us put them together for a final look. The sample outline in Figure 7.1 illustrates the principles in practice. The commentary in the margin relates each part of the outline to the guidelines we have discussed.

Readying Notes for Practice

At this time, you may want to begin readying notes for your speech rehearsals and speech delivery.

The way to start is to reduce your speech to an **abbreviated outline** of key sentences, phrases, and words. Later, if you have anything in the speech for which you must have a perfectly accurate representation—such as a specific example, a quotation, or a set of statistics—it can be written out and placed in the appropriate spot within your final speaking notes.

abbreviated outline *speaker's outline of key sentences, phrases, and words*

Making this abbreviated outline helps in at least two ways. First, the act of compiling the abbreviated outline helps to cement the flow of the speech in your mind. Second, it gets you to think about key ideas and phrasings. Notice that this outline does not yet include such developmental material as personal experiences, examples, illustrations, quotations, statistics, and other types of material that you will use to bring life to the speech and adapt to your audience.

As Emming works with his credit card outline, he arrives at the first draft of a speaker's outline, shown in Figure 7.2.

Once Emming has reached this stage, he's ready to consider what he will use to fill out the speech.

In Chapter 11, Practicing Delivery, we will talk about rehearsing the speech. At that time, Emming will move the speaker outline to note cards and prepare separate cards with quotations and/or statistics that must be presented word for word.

Analysis

Write your specific goal at the top of the page. Refer to the goal to test whether everything in the outline is relevant.

The heading *Introduction* sets the section apart as a separate unit. The introduction attempts to (1) get attention, (2) set a tone, (3) gain goodwill, (4) establish credibility, and (5) lead into the body.

The thesis statement states the elements that are suggested in the specific goal. In the speech, the thesis serves as a forecast of the main points.

The heading *Body* sets this section apart as a separate unit. In this example, main point I begins a topical pattern of main points. It is stated as a complete, meaningful sentence.

The two major subdivisions designated by A and B indicate the equal weight of these points.

The second-level subdivisions—designated by 1, 2, and 3 for the major subpoint A, and 1 and 2 for the major subpoint B—give the necessary information for understanding the subpoints. The number of major and second-level subpoints is at the discretion of the speaker. After the first two levels of subordination, words and phrases may be used in place of complete sentences in further subdivisions.

This transition reminds listeners of the first main point and forecasts the second.

Outline

Specific Goal: I would like the audience to understand the major criteria for finding a suitable credit card.

Introduction

I. How many of you have been hounded by credit card vendors outside the Student Union?

II. They make a credit card sound like the answer to all of your dreams, don't they?

III. Today I want to share with you three criteria you need to consider carefully before deciding on a particular credit card.

Thesis Statement: Three criteria that will enable audience members to find the credit card that is most suitable for them are level of real interest rate, annual fee, and advertised perks.

Body

I. One criterion for finding a suitable credit card is to examine the interest rate.

 A. Interest rates are the percentages that a company charges you to carry a balance on your card past the due date.

 1. Most credit cards carry an average of 18%, which is much higher than ordinary interest rates.

 2. Some cards carry an average of as much as 21%.

 3. Many companies quote very low rates (6% to 8%) for specific periods.

 B. Interest rates can be variable or fixed.

 1. A variable rate means that the rate will change from month to month.

 2. A fixed rate means that the rate will stay the same.

(Now that we have considered rates, let's look at the next criterion.)

II. A second criterion for finding a suitable credit card is to examine the annual fee.

    A. The annual fee is the cost the company charges you for extending you credit.

    B. The charges vary widely.

        1. Some cards advertise no annual fee.

        2. Most companies charge fees that average around 25 dollars.

(After you have considered interest and fees, you can weigh the benefits that the company promises you.)

III. A third criterion for finding a suitable credit card is to weigh the perks.

    A. Perks are extras that you get for using a particular card.

        1. Some companies promise rebates.

        2. Some companies promise frequent flyer miles.

        3. Some companies promise discounts on "a wide variety of items."

    B. Perks don't outweigh other criteria.

Conclusion

I. So, getting the credit card that's right for you may be the answer to your dreams.

II. But only if you exercise care in examining interest rates, annual fee, and perks.

Sources

Bankrate Monitor, http://www.Bankrate.com

Lloyd, Nancy, "Charge Card Smarts," *Family Circle*, February 1998, pp. 32–33.

Orman, Suze, "Minding Your Money," *Self*, February 1998, p. 98.

Rose, Sarah, "Prepping for College Credit," *Money*, September 1998, pp. 156–157.

Speer, Tibbett L., "College Come-ons," *American Demographics*, March 1998, pp. 40–45.

Main point II, continuing the topical pattern, is a complete, meaningful statement paralleling the wording of main point I. Furthermore, notice that each main point considers only one major idea.

This transition summarizes the first two criteria and forecasts the third.

Main point III, continuing the topical pattern, is a complete, meaningful statement paralleling the wording of main points I and II.

Throughout the outline, notice that main points and subpoints are factual statements. The speaker adds examples, experiences, and other developmental material during practice sessions.

The heading *Conclusion* sets this section apart as a separate unit.

The content of the conclusion is intended to summarize the main ideas and leave the speech on a high note.

A list of sources should always be a part of the speech outline. The sources should show where the factual material of the speech came from. The list of sources is not a total of all sources available—only those that were used, directly or indirectly.

Each of the sources is shown in proper form.

Completing the Speech Outline

The goal of this practice is to help you complete the outline for your first speech.

1. Using information from the Focus on Skills exercises on pages 65, 101, and 114, complete the sentence outline for your first speech. Include your list of sources at the end of the outline.

2. Compare what you have written to the sample outline in Figure 7.1 to make sure that it conforms to the guidelines discussed in this chapter. Check to see whether you have included your speech goal, the thesis statement (to be placed at the end of the introduction), clearly written main points, and transitions between main points.

F I G U R E 7.2 First draft of speaker's outline

Intro

How many hounded by vendors?
Make CC sound like answer your dreams?
If yes, need criteria to evaluate.
Three criteria: (1) interest rate, (2) annual fee, and (3) perks.

Body

The 1st C: Examine the interest rate.

    IR's are % that a company charges to carry balance.

- Average of 18%
- As much as 21%
- Start at very low rates (6–8%) for periods—but restrictions

    IR's variable or fixed

- Variable: change month to month
- Fixed: stay the same

    T (Now considered rates, look at next C.)

The 2d C: Examine the annual fee.

    AF is cost company charges to extend you credit.
    AF varies widely.

- Some cards no annual fee
- Most companies average around $25

    T (After considered interest and fees, weigh benefits promised.)

The 3d C: Weigh the perks.

    Perks are extras for using a card.

- Rebates
- Frequent flyer miles
- Discounts on items

    Perks don't outweigh other factors.

Con

So, interest rates, annual fee, perks.

As Marna and Gloria were eating lunch together, Marna happened to ask Gloria, "How are you doing in Woodward's speech class?"

"Not bad," Gloria replied. "I'm working on this speech about product development. I think it will be really informative, but I'm having a little trouble with the opening. I just can't seem to get a good idea for getting started."

"Why not start with a story—that always worked for me in class."

"Thanks, Marna, I'll think on it."

The next day, when Marna ran into Gloria again, she asked, "How's that introduction going?"

"Great. I've prepared a great story about Mary Kay—you know, the cosmetics woman? I'm going to tell about how she was terrible in school and no one thought she'd amount to anything. But she loved dabbling with cosmetics so much that she decided to start her own business—and the rest is history."

"That's a great story. I really like that part about being terrible in school. Was she really that bad?"

"I don't know—the material I read didn't really focus on that part of her life. But I thought that angle would get people listening right away. I did it that way because you suggested starting with a story."

"Yes, but . . ."

"Listen, she did start the business. So what if the story isn't quite right? It makes the point I want to make: If people are creative and have a strong work ethic, they can make it big."

1. What are the ethical issues here?

2. Is anyone really hurt by Marna's opening the speech with the story?

3. What are the speaker's ethical responsibilities?

Summary

The introduction serves to gain attention, set the tone for the speech, create goodwill, establish credibility, and lead into the body of the speech. Types of speech introductions include startling statements, rhetorical questions, stories, personal references, quotations, and suspense.

A well-designed speech conclusion ties the speech together and ends it on a high note. Types of conclusions include summaries, stories, appeals to action, and emotional impact.

Although most classroom speeches may not require a title, in most speech situations outside the classroom it helps to have an informative and appealing title. Three kinds of titles are the simple statement of subject, the question, and the creative title.

To complete and refine your speech outline, use a standard set of symbols, use complete sentences for main points and major subdivisions, limit each point to a single idea, relate minor points to major points, and make sure the outline length is no more than one-third the number of words of the final speech.

Finally, prepare an abbreviated speaker's outline, using key sentences, phrases, and words. You will use this abbreviated outline later as you practice and deliver your speech.

You persuade a man only insofar as you can talk his language by speech, gesture, tonality, order, image, attitude, idea, *identifying* your ways with his.

Kenneth Burke, *A Rhetoric of Motives*, 1950

Adapting to Audiences

Jeremy had asked his friend Gloria to listen to one of his speech rehearsals. He finished the speech, "So, violence does affect people in several ways. It not only desensitizes them to violence, it also contributes to making them behave more aggressively." Then he turned to Gloria and asked, "What do you think?"

"You're giving the speech to your classmates, right?"

"Yeah."

"Well, you had a lot of good material, but I didn't hear anything that showed that you had members of the class in mind. You could have been giving the speech to any audience!"

loria saw that Jeremy had forgotten something that has been recognized as long as speeches have been given: that a speech is intended for a specific audience. In previous chapters, you've learned how to build the basic structure of the speech. In this chapter, we focus on the fourth of seven action steps of speech preparation: developing a strategy for adapting material to your specific speech audience. Recall that in Chapter 4, you completed a Focus on Skills exercise, Analyzing Your Audience, in which you predicted audience reactions. Now we will consider how you can use that analysis to develop common ground, build and maintain audience interest, relate to audience level of understanding, and reinforce or change audience attitude toward you and your specific goal. Then, in the following chapters, we will continue to emphasize means of adapting through the selection and use of visual aids, speech wording, and delivery.

Developing Common Ground

The effective speaker recognizes that listeners want to be talked *with*, not *at*. The first and perhaps the easiest way that speakers recognize their audiences' presence is to develop **common ground**—an awareness that the speaker and audience share the same or similar information, feelings, and experiences.

common ground *awareness that the speaker and audience share the same or similar information, feelings, and experiences*

Let's look at four ways of developing common ground that you can use in all of your speeches.

Use Personal Pronouns

personal pronouns *pronouns referring directly to the person speaking, spoken to, or spoken about*

One way of developing common ground is to use **personal pronouns**—pronouns referring directly to the person speaking, spoken to, or spoken about. By talking in terms of *you*, *us*, *we*, and *our*, you give listeners verbal signs that you

ACTION STEP four

Determine a Strategy
Develop a strategy for adapting material to your specific speech audience

A. Establish common ground.

B. Adapt to audience level of interest.

C. Adapt to audience level of understanding.

D. Adapt to audience attitude toward you.

E. Adapt to audience attitude toward your topic.

are talking with them. In Jeremy's speech on the effects of television violence, for example, instead of saying,

> When *people* think about violence on TV, *they* often wonder how it affects viewers.

Jeremy could say,

> When *you* think about violence on TV, *you* may wonder how it affects viewers.

The use of just these two personal pronouns in the sentence may not seem like much, but it can mean the difference between audience attention and audience indifference to you and your speech.

Ask Rhetorical Questions

A second way of developing common ground is to ask **rhetorical questions**—questions phrased to stimulate a mental response rather than an actual spoken response on the part of the audience. Although public speaking is not direct conversation with your audience, by asking rhetorical questions you can create the impression of conversation. For instance, in the preceding example, one more change in the sample sentence would increase the sense of audience participation in the speech. Instead of saying,

rhetorical questions *questions phrased to stimulate a mental response rather than an actual spoken response on the part of the audience*

> When you think about violence on TV, you may wonder how it affects viewers.

Jeremy might ask,

> When you watch a particularly violent TV program, have you ever asked yourself, "I wonder whether watching such violent programs has any negative effects on viewers"?

Rhetorical questions generate audience participation; once the audience participates, it becomes more involved in the content. Since rhetorical questions must be sincere to be effective, practice them until you can ask questions naturally and sincerely.

Share Common Experiences

A third way of developing common ground is to share common experiences by selecting and presenting personal experiences, examples, and illustrations that *show* what you and the audience have in common. For instance, suppose you are talking about leadership and in your speech you say,

> Leaders are sometimes oblivious to signs of trouble or think that any troubles that do exist just can't make a real difference.

To make this statement more meaningful, you could add the following example:

> Remember in the movie *Titanic* when the captain, who knows that his ship is going to encounter icebergs, turns the controls over to a subordinate and goes off to bed? Recall that he did this because he believed the *Titanic* was so big and so powerful that a few icebergs weren't going to bother it, right? Wrong!

Personalize Information

A fourth way of creating common ground is to **personalize** information by relating it to specific audience references. Rather than using information in the same form as they found it, effective speakers look for ways to express informa-

personalize *relate information to specific audience references*

Romilly Lockyer/The Image Bank

Such reactions as applause, laughter, head nodding, and smiles are all signs that the audience is relating well to what you are saying.

tion using audience information. Suppose you are giving a speech on the Japanese economy and its effects on U.S. markets to your student chapter of the American Marketing Association at a university in California. You want to begin by helping listeners understand geographic data about Japan. You could just cite the following statistics from the 1999 *World Almanac:*

> Japan is small and densely populated. The nation's 126 million people live in a land area of 146,000 square miles, giving them a population density of 863 persons per square mile.

Although this passage provides the necessary information, it does not show that you had this specific audience in mind. Let's see how you could state the same information in a way that would be both more interesting and more meaningful to your California audience.

> Japan is a small, densely populated nation. Its population is 126 million—less than half that of the United States. Yet the Japanese are crowded into a land area of only 146,000 square miles—roughly the same size as California. Just think of the implications of having half the population of the United States living here in California, instead of the 30-odd million who live here now. In fact, Japan packs 863 persons into every square mile of land, whereas in the United States we average about 74 persons per square mile. Overall, then, Japan is about 12 times as crowded as the United States.

This revision includes an invented comparison of the unknown, Japan, with the familiar, the United States and the audience's home state of California. Even though most Americans do not have the total land area of the United States on the tip of their tongue, they do know that the United States covers a great deal of territory. Likewise, a California audience would have a mental picture of the size of their home state compared to the rest of the nation. If you were speaking to an audience from another part of the country, you could make your comparison to a different state, such as Texas, New York, or Florida. Such detailed comparisons allow the audience to visualize just how small and crowded Japan is.

Reworking information so that it creates common ground will take time, but the effort will pay big dividends, for your listeners are always going to be asking, "What does this have to do with me?" And unless the way you present your information answers that question, your speeches are not going to be as effective as they should be.

Now that we have considered ways of creating common ground, let's consider specifics of creating interest, increasing understanding, and developing credibility.

Creating and Maintaining Audience Interest

Since listeners' interest depends on whether they believe that information has personal impact (that it speaks to the question, "What does this have to do with me?"), let's consider strategies you can use to build and maintain audience interest.

Timeliness

Listeners are more likely to be interested in information they perceive as **timely**—they want to know how they can use the information *now*. Even for topics that seem timely, you will still want to call audience attention to the fact. For instance, in Rhonda's speech about Rohypnol, she might say,

> Perhaps you've never heard of the drug Rohypnol. But far too many people our age, and especially women, have become aware of it too late and with tragic consequences. For Rohypnol, or "roofies" as it's called on the street, has become known as the "date rape drug."

No matter what your topic, you can create a way of showing its timeliness.

timely   *relating to now*

Proximity

Listeners are more likely to be interested in information that has **proximity**— a relationship to their personal space. Psychologically, we pay more attention to information that affects our "territory" than information we perceive as remote. You've heard speakers say something like, "Let me bring this closer to home by showing you. . . ." Statements like these work because information becomes important to people when they perceive it as affecting "their own backyard." If, for instance, you were giving a speech on the EPA's difficulties with its environmental cleanup campaigns, you would want to focus on examples in the audience's own community. If you don't have that kind of information, take time to find it. For instance, for the EPA topic, a well-placed telephone call to the local or regional EPA office, or even to your local newspaper, will get the information you need to make the connection.

proximity   *a relationship to one's personal space*

Seriousness

Listeners are more likely to be interested in information that is **serious**—that has a physical, economic, or psychological impact on them. To build or maintain interest during a speech on toxic waste, you could show serious *physical*

serious   *having physical, economic, or psychological impact*

impact by saying "Toxic waste affects the health of all of us"; you could show serious *economic* impact by saying "Toxic waste cleanup and disposal are expensive—they raise our taxes"; or you could show serious *psychological* impact by saying "Toxic waste erodes the quality of our life and the lives of our children."

Think of how dramatically your classroom attention picks up when the professor reveals that a particular piece of information is going to "be on the test." The potential serious economic impact (not paying attention can cost us a lowered grade) is often enough to jolt us into attention. Most of us just don't put our attention into high gear unless we see the seriousness of information.

Adapting to Audience Level of Understanding

If you predict that your listeners do not have the necessary background to understand the information you will present in your speech, you will need to orient them. If you predict that your audience does have sufficient background, you will need to present the information in a way that will ensure continued understanding.

Orienting Listeners

Since your listeners are likely to stop paying attention if they are lost at the start of your speech, a good rule of thumb is to err on the side of expecting too little knowledge rather than expecting too much. So, if there is any reason to believe that some people may not have the necessary background knowledge, take time to review basic facts. For instance, for a speech about changes in political and economic conditions in Eastern Europe, although you can be reasonably sure that everyone in your audience is aware of the breakup of the Soviet Union and Yugoslavia, they may not remember all the specific countries that have been created. Before launching into changing conditions, remind your listeners of the names of the nations you are going to be talking about.

Since some of your listeners may be well oriented, a good way to present that information without insulting their intelligence is to give the impression that you are reviewing information that the audience already knows. By saying, "As you will remember," "As you know," or "As we all learned in our high school courses," you phrase your orientation in a way that will be accepted as a review and not a putdown. For instance, for the speech on changes in political and economic conditions in Eastern Europe, you might say, "As you will recall, the old Soviet Union now consists of the following separate states." If listeners already know the information, they will see your statements as reminders; if they do not know it, they are getting the information in a way that doesn't call attention to their information gaps—they can act as if they do in fact remember.

How much orientation you can give depends on how much time is available. When you don't have the time to give a complete background, determine where a lack of information will impinge on your ability to get through to your audience and fill in the crucial information that closes those gaps.

Bob Daemmrich/Stock, Boston

Audiences will learn more from your information if you adapt material to their prior experience and level of understanding.

Presenting New Information

Even when we predict that our audience has the necessary background information, we still need to work on ways of presenting new information that ensures continued understanding. Speakers can use such devices as defining, describing, exemplifying, and comparing to help clarify information that may be confusing or difficult for some audience members. A speaker must keep in mind that an audience is made up of individuals, and an effective speaker anticipates the different comprehension styles of those individuals. As you plan your speech, ask yourself the following questions.

1. Have I defined all key terms carefully? For instance, if your speech goal is "I want my audience to understand four major problems faced by those who are functionally illiterate," in the opening of your speech you might present the following definition:

> By "functionally illiterate," I mean a person who has trouble accomplishing transactions involving reading and writing in which that person wishes to engage.

TECHNOLOGY tips

Watch two workout videos—one made specifically for novices and the other specifically for fitness buffs. Focus on the talk, not on the workout. Note the differences in the way the trainers speak to their intended audiences. What guidelines for adaptation can you draw from this experience?

Define
"A sphere is a solid that is
bounded by. . . ."

Exemplify
"This soccer ball is an example of a
sphere."

Compare
"A sphere is like our planet
. . . or . . . like a baseball."

**Three ways of developing the
concept *sphere***

2. Have I supported every generalization with at least one specific example? For instance, suppose you made the statement,

> Large numbers of Americans who are functionally illiterate cannot read well enough to understand simple directions.

You could then use the example,

> For instance, a person who is functionally illiterate might not be able to read or understand a label that says "Take three times a day after eating."

3. Have I compared and/or contrasted new information to information my audience already understands? For instance, if you want to give the audience a sense of what it feels like to be functionally illiterate, you might compare the problems of functional illiterates to problems they've experienced, such as dealing with a foreign language. Perhaps you have had a personal experience that you could use to make such a comparison.

> Many of us have taken a foreign language in school. As a result, we figure that we can visit a place where that language is spoken and "get along," right? But as we enter a "foreign" territory, we often discover that even road signs can be difficult to comprehend when we're under even a little pressure. For instance, when I was fortunate enough to visit Montreal last summer, I saw a sign that said the place I was looking for was "à droite." Now I took French in school and I thought I could handle simple directions, yet for just a minute I found myzelf puzzling whether "à droite" was "to the right" or "to the left." Just imagine what it must be like if, for many such "simple" ideas or directions, you had to puzzle for a while and then run the risk that you were making a major mistake.

In short, at any point in a speech where there appears to be any difficulty in understanding an idea or a concept, be prepared to define, exemplify, and compare or contrast.

4. Have I used more than one means of development for significant points I want the audience to remember? This final bit of advice is based on a sound psychological principle: The more different kinds of explanations a speaker gives, the more listeners will understand.

Let's go back to a significant statement we made earlier:

> Large numbers of Americans who are functionally illiterate cannot read well enough to understand simple directions.

To this statement we added an example:

> For instance, a person who is functionally illiterate might not be able to read or understand a label that says "Take three times a day after eating."

The example makes the statement more meaningful. Now let's see how we can build that statement even further:

> A significant number of Americans are functionally illiterate. That is, large numbers of Americans—about 20 percent of the adult population, or around 35 million people—have serious difficulties with common reading tasks. They cannot read well enough to understand simple cooking instructions, directions on how to work an appliance, or rules on how to play a game. For instance, a person who is functionally illiterate might not be able to read or understand a label that says "Take three times a day after eating."

The first statement, "A significant number of Americans are functionally illiterate," consists of eight words that are likely to be uttered in slightly less than five seconds! A listener who coughs, drops her pencil, or happens to remember an appointment she has during those five seconds will miss the entire sentence. The first example adds 25 words. Now it is likely that more people will get the point. But the expanded example contains 85 words. Now, even in the face of some distractions, it is likely that most listeners will have heard and registered the information.

In short speeches, you can't fully develop every bit of information. What you can do is to identify two or three of your highest-priority bits of information and build them fully, using two or three different kinds of development.

Building a Positive Audience Attitude toward You as the Speaker

If you predict that the audience will have a positive attitude toward you as a speaker, then you need only try to maintain that attitude; if, however, you predict that the audience has no opinion or for some reason has a negative attitude toward you, then you will want to change that attitude.

Audience attitude toward you relates to your **credibility** with the audience—the level of trust that an audience has or will have in you. As you recall from the discussion in Chapter 1, your credibility is based primarily on the listener's perception of your knowledge/expertise on the particular subject and your trustworthiness and personality.

credibility *the level of trust that an audience has or will have in the speaker*

Knowledge and Expertise

One way of building credibility is to build audience perception of your **knowledge and expertise,** which you'll recall includes your qualifications or capability, or what is referred to as your "track record."

The first step in building a perception of knowledge and expertise is to go into the speaking situation fully prepared. Audiences have an almost instinctive knowledge of when a speaker is "winging it," and most audiences lose respect for a speaker who hasn't thought enough of them or the situation to have a well-prepared message.

The next step is show your audience that you have a wealth of high-quality examples, illustrations, and personal experiences. Recall how much more favorably you perceive professors who have an inexhaustible supply of supporting information as opposed to those professors who present, and seem to have, only the barest minimum of facts.

The third step is to show any direct involvement you have had with the topic area. In addition to increasing the audience's perception of your depth of knowledge, your personal involvement increases the audience's perception of your practical understanding of the issues and your personal concern for the subject. For example, if you are speaking on toxic waste, your credibility will increase manifold by sharing with the audience your personal experiences in petitioning for local environmental controls.

knowledge and expertise *qualifications or capability—a track record*

Trustworthiness

A second way of building credibility is to build audience perception of your **trustworthiness,** which, you'll recall, refers to both your character and your apparent motives for speaking. The more your listeners see you as one of them,

trustworthiness *both character and apparent motives for speaking* the easier it will be for you to establish your trustworthiness; the more your listeners see you as different, the more difficult it will be. Whether people *should* be or not, they are more distrustful of those they see as different. Thus, women are generally more trusting of other women than of men; African Americans are more trusting of other African Americans than of European Americans or Asian Americans; Christians are more trusting of other Christians than of Jews or Muslims. Part of building your credibility, then, depends on your ability to bridge gaps between you and members of your audience.

First, listeners will make value judgments of your character based on their assessment of your moral and ethical traits. What are your character strengths? Are you an honest, industrious, dependable, morally strong person? As you plan your speech, you need to ask yourself what you can do in the speech to demonstrate these moral and ethical traits. For instance, how can you convince your audience that you have presented your information honestly?

In addition listeners will consider your apparent motives. Early in your speech, it's important to show why listeners need to know your information. Then, throughout the speech, you can emphasize your sincere interest in their well-being. For a speech on toxic waste, for example, you could explain *how* a local dumpsite affects the community. As you present documented facts and

The audience's perception of your trustworthiness results from their assessment of your character and your apparent motives for presenting the information.

Jose Carrollo/PhotoEdit

figures showing the extent of danger to individuals, your audience is likely to form the belief that you have a sincere interest in the well-being of the community.

Personality

A third way of building credibility is to build audience perception of your **personality,** which you'll recall is the impression you make on your audience based on such traits as enthusiasm, friendliness, warmth, and a ready smile.

Because audience perceptions of your personality are likely to be based on their first impressions of you, try to dress appropriately, groom yourself carefully, and carry yourself in an attractive manner. The old compliment "He/she cleans up real good" is one to remember. It is surprising how much an appropriately professional dress and demeanor will increase audience perception of personality.

In addition, audiences react favorably to a speaker who acts friendly. A smile and a pleasant tone of voice go a long way in showing a warmth that will increase your listeners' comfort with you and your ideas.

We will discuss three additional features of personality—enthusiasm, eye contact, and vocal expressiveness—in the chapter on Practicing Your Delivery.

Although you are primarily responsible for building your credibility in your classroom speeches, in real-life speeches there is likely to be someone assigned to introduce you and your speech. For those speeches, you will want to enlist the help of that person. Well before the day of the speech, provide the person with information about you. If the introducer asks you to write an introduction for him or her to present, by all means take advantage of that opportunity. Include information that shows your experience in the subject area. If, for example, you are speaking about literacy to a Parents and Teachers Association meeting, include accounts of your experience in tutoring children and adults.

> **personality**   *the impression you make on your audience based on such traits as enthusiasm, friendliness, warmth, and a ready smile*

Adapting to Audience Attitude toward Your Speech Goal

Although adapting to listeners' attitudes toward your speech goal is especially important for persuasive speeches, it can be important for informative speeches as well. An audience **attitude** is a predisposition for or against people, places, or things, usually expressed as an opinion. For a speech on refinishing wood furniture, for example, your listeners may hold the opinion "Refinishing furniture is too hard."

At the outset, try to predict whether listeners will view your topic positively, negatively, or have no opinion. If, for instance, you think your listeners would view refinishing furniture positively or neutrally, then you can move forward with your speech; if, however, you think your listeners really view refinishing furniture as too hard or unimportant, then you'll need to take time early in the speech to change their opinion. In Chapter 13, Principles of Persuasive Speaking, we will consider strategies for dealing with listeners' attitudes in more detail.

> **attitude**   *a predisposition for or against people, places, or things, usually expressed as an opinion*

Forming a Plan of Audience Adaptation

speech plan   *a written strategy for determining how you will use common ground, develop and maintain interest, ensure understanding, and cope with potential negative reactions to you as a speaker and/or your topic or goal*

Now that you have a complete outline of your speech, it's time to determine a specific speech plan for adaptation. A **speech plan** is a written strategy for determining how you will use common ground, develop and maintain interest, ensure understanding, and cope with potential negative reactions to you as a speaker and/or your topic or goal. Adaptation is relatively easy when the majority of the audience members are like you—that is, similar to you in age, race, religion, academic background, and so forth. As you face more diverse audiences, however, problems of adaptation become more complex. As a result, you must think through your strategy carefully.

Specifics of the Speech Plan

To begin a plan of adaptation, you need to assemble a specific audience analysis for each speech situation (see Audience Analysis Checklist, p. 58). Analyze your information on audience age, education, occupation, income, race, religion, nationality, group affiliation, and geographic uniqueness to determine the significant characteristics of your audience. Recall that you are predicting whether or not your audience is interested in the topic, likely to understand your material, and likely to have a positive attitude toward you and your topic or speech goal. Direct audience adaptation may be relevant for all three of these assessments. When you have reviewed your predictions, you can consider strategies for adaptation.

INFOTRAC COLLEGE EDITION

This chapter has stressed the importance of tailoring your speech to your audience. Using InfoTrac College Edition, locate Frank Grazian's article on this subject, "Gaining Knowledge about the Audience Is Vital." (Hint: Click on PowerTrac. Under Search Index, choose author. Type his name in the entry box and click Submit.) After reading the article, see if you can explain Grazian's stated formula "[The audience's] expectation of reward relates to the [listening] effort required." In addition, write down what you consider to be one or two key points of the article. Then, when you are listening to speeches in class or in public, evaluate if the speakers have tailored their speeches to the audience as effectively as they could have.

1. What will you do to establish common ground? Consider where and how you will use personal pronouns and rhetorical questions, common experiences, hypothetical situations, and personalizing information.

2. What will you do to build and maintain interest? Consider where you will use personal experiences, stories, examples, illustrations, comparisons, and contrasts.

3. What will you do, if anything, to ensure that the audience has enough background information? Show what you will do to orient your listeners if they have insufficient background to understand your speech.

4. What will you do to build and maintain your credibility? Write how you will attempt to show your knowledge/expertise, trustworthiness, and appealing personality.

5. What will you do to build and maintain a positive attitude toward your topic? Write about how you will show the importance of your information to the audience.

Examples of Speech Plans

Let us first look at a sample audience analysis and, based on it, a sample plan for adaptation. Then we'll consider two contrasting cases—one in which audience factors are known and in your favor, and one in which audience factors have to be inferred from the data available and are less favorable to your success.

FIGURE 8.1 Emming's audience analysis

Data

My audience will consist of about 20 college students, 12 women and 8 men. Three of the 20 are African American, and one is Asian American. They are of different religions. Eighteen of them range in age from 18 to 20, and the other two are about 23 to 25.

Predictions

Audience Interest   Audience interest is likely to be high because my classmates are at an age where credit cards are starting to become important to them.

Audience Understanding   Because of their general familiarity with credit cards as a means of shopping, audience preparation for understanding the information is likely to be high.

Attitude toward Speaker   While my audience's attitude toward me may be generally positive, members may not be sure of my expertise on credit cards.

Attitude toward Topic   Although audience attitude about getting credit cards now may vary, they still are likely to be open to hearing about criteria because they are likely to be interested in investigating getting a card in the near future. Even those who already have credit cards may find my speech useful as a means of determining whether they should switch to a different card.

Sample Audience Analysis and Speech Plan   Recall that Emming is planning a speech to inform his class about the criteria for evaluating credit cards. Using information from the Audience Analysis Checklist in Chapter 4, he has prepared the detailed audience analysis shown in Figure 8.1. Based on that analysis, he might then write the strategy shown in Figure 8.2.

Now let's consider the two examples that are not classroom related—one with favorable conditions, and the other less so.

Case 1. Audience Factors Known and in Your Favor   Lana Jackson, the immediate supervisor for all clerical staff at her company, is speaking to inform

FIGURE 8.2 Emming's speech plan

Common Ground   Throughout the speech I will use personal pronouns and ask appropriate rhetorical questions. Whenever possible, I will try to personalize information.

Interest   Although interest is likely to be present, I will still try to stimulate interest in the introduction, but I will place my emphasis on maintaining that interest throughout the speech. I will present a couple of examples of people who have had difficulties in paying balances at the end of each month, which I believe will heighten interest. I will also use visual material to show my listeners what I am talking about.

Understanding   Since students are familiar with the idea of credit cards, I won't have to spend time explaining them. But because most will not be familiar with how people can get caught up in credit card debt, I will use specific examples to show what can happen if users are not careful. I will use overhead projections to help explain the criteria.

Attitude toward Speaker   Audience attitude toward me may be skeptical. As an Asian American, I may be seen as different from the majority of the class. But since I am used to associating with people of all races and ethnic backgrounds without difficulty, I'm not concerned with any problems of adapting to the class. Still, since they are likely to question my expertise on the use of credit cards, I will have to be especially careful to present information accurately.

Attitude toward Topic or Speech Goal   Although their attitude toward the speech goal is likely to be favorable, I will still attempt to feature good information to keep their attitude toward the subject positive.

them about the installation of a new word processing program on all computers.

Because Lana is the supervisor, she knows that the audience will be comprised of about 25 Cincinnati women and men of mixed race, religion, and nationality, ages 19 to 40, with educational levels ranging from high school graduate to graduates of two-year college programs.

Based on that information, her analysis could include the following predictions:

1. Audience interest is likely to be high because they will have to become proficient with the new program in a short period of time.

2. Because of their familiarity with the company, the types of computers, and the previous package, audience preparation for understanding the information is likely to be high.

3. While their attitude toward her may be generally positive, her audience may not be sure of her expertise with the new package.

4. Although audience attitude about changing programs may vary, they still are likely to be open to the information if they can be convinced that the new package will enable them to accomplish their goals more easily.

Based on these predictions, Lana might write the strategy shown in Figure 8.3.

Case 2. Audience Factors Inferred and Less Favorable   Lana Jackson has been asked to talk about computer software packages to the monthly meeting of a local community organization comprised of adults. Because members of the speaker committee of this organization want to be "up to date," they thought it would be worthwhile to have a speech on this topic so that their members could learn to "surf the net" and understand how to find material on any topic they want.

If the only information Lana has about the audience is that they are adult members of a community organization who have agreed to schedule a speech

FIGURE 8.3   Speech plan: Audience factors known and favorable

Common Ground   Throughout the speech, I will use personal pronouns and ask appropriate rhetorical questions. Whenever possible, I will try to personalize information.

Interest   Because interest is likely to be high, I will place my emphasis on maintaining that interest. Since staff members are familiar with word processing packages, I can focus on several of the features that will enable them to produce better copy more easily. I will also use visual material to show my listeners what I am talking about.

Understanding   Since they understand computer packages, I will use comparisons of the key features of the new package to operations they are familiar with. And where possible, I will share common experiences and personalize information. I will use overhead projections to help clarify difficult ideas.

Attitude toward Speaker   Audience attitude toward me may be skeptical. Because I am "management," they may be a little cynical about my intentions. I will have to stress that what is good for the company is also good for them. They may also wonder about my expertise with the new package. I will have to be especially careful to present information smoothly and accurately.

Attitude toward Topic or Speech Goal   Although their attitude toward the speech goal is likely to be favorable, I will still attempt to feature improvements so that they will understand why they need to spend their time and energy learning the new system. I will show them that the improvements are significant.

on computer software, she can still infer data about them that will help her determine a speech strategy.

Because it is an adult organization, Lana can infer that the audience will be comprised of both males and females of mixed race, religion, and nationality, with a mixed educational background, whose ages range from about 25 upward. Moreover, she can infer that many have homes and families and, because they are members of a local community organization, that they have a geographic bond.

Even though her data are inferred, Lana can still make predictions about interests, understanding, and attitude. Based on that information, her analysis might include the following predictions:

1. The audience's interests are likely to vary, because they are likely to have no natural need for information about computer packages other than some natural curiosity. Still, they wouldn't come if they didn't have some interest.

2. Because their background knowledge probably ranges widely, it is likely that their level of understanding of the specifics of software packages is relatively low.

3. Their attitude toward the speaker is likely to be neutral because they won't know that much about her.

4. Their attitude about software packages is likely to range from favorable to neutral or even slightly negative. Some will be very positive about what the software can do for them; others will be fearful and will see the computer as an intrusion into their privacy.

Based on these predictions, Lana might develop the strategy shown in Figure 8.4.

FIGURE 8.4 Speech plan: Audience factors inferred and less favorable

Common Ground Throughout the speech, I will use personal pronouns and ask appropriate rhetorical questions. Whenever possible, I will try to personalize information.

Interest Because interest levels will vary, I will have to begin the speech with an anecdote or a personal experience about "surfing" that will capture initial interest. Very early in the speech, I will also try to focus on the ease with which these packages enable people to find out information they want on any topic relatively quickly. I will stress aspects of software packages that would be useful immediately to a general adult audience and would have a real impact on them. And of course, I will develop visual aids to reinforce key points.

Understanding Because the audience members are unlikely to share the same background information on computers, early in the speech I will ask how many have had any experience in "surfing." Then, based on the percentage of positive responses, I will determine how much background information I have to give before I can get into the meat of the speech. I must keep language on an elementary level, and I must define all terms carefully. I must also take into account the perceptions of people of different races and cultural backgrounds. I will need a variety of examples, illustrations, and anecdotes that relate to a racially and culturally diverse audience. And of course, wherever possible, I will try to personalize information. I will also give them a simple example that demonstrates the ease of use.

Attitude toward Speaker Because they know little about me, I will have to demonstrate my expertise and assure them that my intentions are to help them learn more about technology that could be useful to them. Moreover, since they may perceive themselves as being different from me, I'm going to have to demonstrate my trustworthiness. I will be especially careful with the way I present information so that they will see me as reliable. I will also try to keep the speech light and somewhat humorous.

Attitude toward Topic or Speech Goal Because these attitudes are also likely to vary, I will use examples and illustrations of "average Americans" who have found interest in computer packages.

Adapting to the Audience

The goal of this exercise is to help you begin developing strategies for your speech plan.

Working with your speech goal and audience checklist from Chapter 4, write an audience adaptation strategy. Be sure to include specifics about how you will adapt to your audience in the following areas: (1) common ground, (2) audience interest, (3) audience level of understanding, (4) audience attitude toward you as speaker, and (5) audience attitude toward your speech goal. Pattern your written strategy after those in Figures 8.2, 8.3, and 8.4.

Special Problems of Speakers from Different Cultures

This chapter has been written with the assumption that you have been raised in the United States. But you may be from another country or culture, and English may be your second language. Two problems with audience adaptation you may face, then, are difficulty with the English language and lack of a common set of experiences to draw from. Difficulty with the language includes both difficulty with pronunciation and difficulty with vocabulary and idiomatic speech. Both of these could make you feel self-conscious. But the lack of a common set

"Kendra, I heard you tell Jim about the speech you're giving tomorrow. You think it's a winner, huh?"

"You got that right, Omar. I'm going to have Bardston eating out of the palm of my hand."

"You sound confident."

"This time I have reason to be. See, Prof. Bardston's been talking about the importance of audience adaptation. These last two weeks that's all we've heard—adaptation, adaptation."

"What does she mean?"

"Talking about something in a way that really relates to people personally."

"OK—so how are you going to do that?"

"Well, I checked with several people in class and found that they're really in favor of the city's controversial plan to expand the Convention Center facility. Moreover, recently Bardston herself let it slip that she thinks it's a good idea. So I'm going to discuss the major reasons that people give for supporting the plan—in a way that will make her think that I'm a supporter."

"But the other day you told me that you thought it was a stupid idea to soak the taxpayers for another expansion."

"You're absolutely right. But by keeping the information positive, she'll think I'm a supporter. It isn't as if I'm going to be telling any lies or anything."

1. In a speech, is it ethical to adapt in a way that resonates with your "audience," but isn't in keeping with what you really believe?

2. Could Kendra have achieved her goal by using different methods? How?

of experiences to draw from may be even more significant. So much of our information is gained through comparison and examples that the lack of common experiences may make drawing comparisons and using appropriate examples much more difficult.

What can you do to help you through the public speaking experience? Difficulty with language may require you to speak more slowly and articulate as clearly as possible. Also, make sure that you are comfortable with your topic. You may want to consider talking about aspects of your homeland. Since you would be providing new information, your classmates would likely look forward to hearing you speak. It would be useful for you to practice at least once with a person raised in the United States. You can ask the person to help make sure that you are using language, examples, and comparisons that the audience will be able to relate to.

On the other hand, you'll find that most American students are much more tolerant of mistakes made by people who are speaking in what is for them their second or even third language than they are of mistakes made by American-born students. Also, keep in mind that the more practice you can get speaking to people from this culture, the more comfortable you will become with the language and with your ability to adapt to them.

Summary

Speakers adapt to their audiences by creating common ground and by planning strategies that create or build audience interest, adapt to audience levels of understanding, and adapt to audience attitudes toward the speaker and the speech goal.

Creating common ground includes using personal pronouns, rhetorical questions, common experiences, hypothetical situations, and information that is personalized to relate to common audience characteristics.

Most people's interest is determined by whether they believe that information relates specifically to them. Strategies include stressing the timeliness of the information, stressing the impact on the audience's personal space, and stressing the seriousness of the personal impact.

Strategies for adapting to audience understanding of information depend on the audience's existing knowledge level. If the audience lacks specific topic knowledge, then fill in necessary background information. During the remainder of the speech use definitions, examples, and comparisons.

If the audience has a positive attitude toward you, try to maintain that attitude; if, however, it is neutral or for some reason negative, then work to change that attitude. Attitude toward the speaker is based on audience perception of speaker credibility, or the level of trust the audience has. Although a positive introduction by another person can help, speakers build their credibility by going into the speech fully prepared, by emphasizing sincere interest in the audience's well-being, by dressing, grooming, and presenting themselves attractively, and by smiling and talking in a pleasant tone of voice.

Audience attitudes toward the speech goal can be classified as no opinion, in favor, or opposed. If the audience has no opinion, is in favor, or is only slightly opposed to your topic, efforts to create and build attention and relate to level of understanding will also work to improve attitude. If the audience is opposed to your topic or goal, you'll need to work to change their opinion.

For your first few speeches, it may help to write out a speech plan that specifies how you will adapt your speech to the specific audience.

A picture is worth a thousand words.

Anne Dowie

Visual Aids: From Models to Computer Graphics

"How's it going with the speech, Jeremy?"

"Well, I'm getting frustrated."

"Why's that?"

"Well, we're supposed to think about using visual aids with this speech. But I can't think of anything that I could use."

"Well, what's your topic?"

"I'm giving a speech on the effects of media violence, but I don't see any sense in showing any act of violence."

"No, but there are lots of other things you could show."

"Like what?"

"Well, I'll bet that you have statistics about the amount of violence."

"Sure."

"Well, wouldn't the class understand them better if you *showed* them the statistics?"

"But wouldn't showing statistics be just as boring as giving them?"

n the chapter opening dialog, Jeremy makes a good point. It is probable that just showing some statistics would be boring. But the question he needs to answer is what he could do to show the statistics in an interesting, meaningful way. In this chapter the focus is on developing a strategy for adapting to your audience visually. And although there are times when visual aids may not be necessary, having them will help capture your audience's attention and make your speech more interesting.

visual aid *a form of speech development that allows the audience to see as well as hear information*

A **visual aid** is a form of speech development that allows the audience to see as well as hear information. You'll want to consider using visual aids because of their potential for adapting to audiences by clarifying and dramatizing verbal information. And using good visual aids can pay off for you. Research has shown that people are likely to remember features of visual aids even over long periods,[1] and people are likely to learn considerably more when ideas appeal to both eye and ear than when they appeal to the ear alone.[2] In my own classes, a great many students report that during the round of speeches in which I require the use of visual aids, they enjoy the speeches more and remember more information than in any other round. In addition, when speakers use visual aids, it tends to reduce their anxiety and thus give them more confidence.[3]

In this chapter, we will consider the types of visual aids, the criteria for making choices about which and how many visual aids to use, ways of designing visual aids to best adapt to your audience's needs, and methods for using them in your speech.

Types of Visual Aids

The first step in developing a strategy for adapting to your audience visually is to consider what visual aids you could use. When making your selection, it's essential to consider the situation in which you are presenting. A speech in class, a presentation given to clients in a business setting, or an after-dinner talk all invite different types of visual aids. Let's consider those that involve self,

A C T I O N S T E P five

Create Visual Aids
Create visual aids to clarify, emphasize, and dramatize verbal information.

objects, models, charts, flipcharts, graphs, pictorial representations, projections, chalkboards or markerboards, handouts, and computer graphics.

Yourself

On occasion, *you* can become your own best visual aid. What you do and how you look may well reinforce or supplement what you say. Through descriptive gestures, you can show the size of a soccer ball or the height of a tennis net; through your posture and movement, you can show the motions involved in swimming the butterfly stroke or administering artificial respiration; through your own attire, you can illustrate the native dress of a foreign country, the necessary equipment for a cave explorer, or the uniform of a firefighter. In every one of these examples, what you do and what you look like help you get your point across.

Objects

Not only what you do or look like, but what you bring with you can serve as a visual aid. The objects you are talking about make good visual aids if (1) they are large enough to be seen (consider how far away people will be sitting) and (2) small enough to carry around with you. A cell phone, a basketball, or a braided rug is the kind of object that can be seen by the audience and manipulated by the speaker. In her speech on spiking a volleyball, Erin used a volleyball throughout much of her speech. Avoid passing the object around, though, because the audience can become distracted.

Models

When an object is too large to bring to the speech site or too small to be seen, a three-dimensional model may prove a worthwhile substitute. If you were to talk about a turbine engine, a suspension bridge, an Egyptian pyramid, or the structure of an atom, a model might well be the best visual aid. Working models are especially interesting—for example, a pickup truck or a jet plane.

Charts

A **chart** is a graphic representation that distills a lot of information and presents it to an audience in an easily interpreted format. The most common are word charts and organizational charts.

Word charts are often used to preview material that will be covered in a speech, to summarize material, and to remind an audience of speech content.

chart *graphic representation that presents information in an easily interpreted format*

word chart *a summary, list, or outline*

FIGURE 9.1 **A sample word chart**

Criteria for Evaluating Credit Cards
1. Interest Rate
2. Annual Fee
3. Perks

Charles Gupton/Stock, Boston

For his speech on credit cards, for example, Emming might make a word chart that lists his main points, as shown in Figure 9.1. An outline can also be considered a word chart.

organizational chart   *symbols and connecting lines used to diagram a complicated system or procedure*

Organizational charts use symbols and connecting lines to diagram step-by-step progressions through a complicated procedure or system. The chart in Figure 9.2 illustrates the organization of a student union board.

F I G U R E 9.2   **A sample organizational chart**

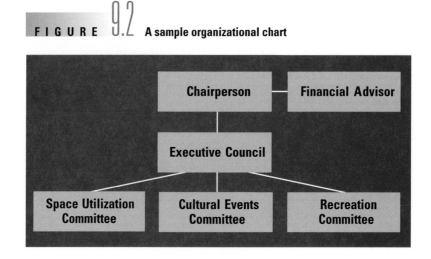

Flipcharts

A **flipchart** is a large pad of paper mounted on an easel and is a popular method of displaying key words and outlines. Flipcharts (and easels) are available in many sizes. For a presentation to four or five people, a small tabletop version works well; for a larger audience, it is wise to use a larger size, such as 30 by 40 inches.

In preparing flipcharts, leave several pages between each chart in the pad. If you discover a mistake or decide to revise a chart, you can tear out that sheet without disturbing the order. After you have finished all the charts, tear out all but one sheet between each chart. The one sheet serves as both a transition page and a cover sheet. Because you want your audience to focus on your words and not on visual material that is no longer being discussed, you can flip to the empty page while you are talking about material not covered by charts. Also, the empty page between charts ensures that heavy lines or colors from the next chart will not show through.

flipchart *large pad of paper mounted on an easel, used for visual displays*

Graphs

Graphs are diagrams that compare information.

Bar graphs use vertical or horizontal bars to show relationships between two or more variables at the same time or at various times on one or more dimensions. For instance, if you were giving a speech on gold, you could use the bar graph in Figure 9.3 to show the relative holdings in gold of the major International Monetary Fund (IMF) member nations.

graph *a diagram that compares information*

bar graph *a diagram that uses vertical or horizontal bars to show relationships between two or more variables at the same time or at various times on one or more dimensions*

FIGURE 9.3 **Bar graph**

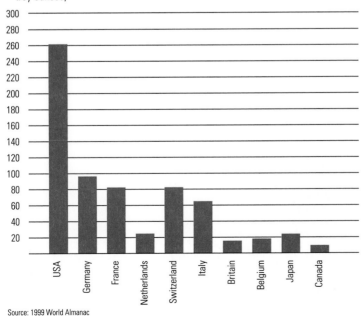

Comparative holdings of gold in 1997 by IMF member nations (in millions of fine troy ounces)

Source: 1999 World Almanac

FIGURE 9.4 Line graph

U.S. population increase from 1810 to 1990 (in millions)

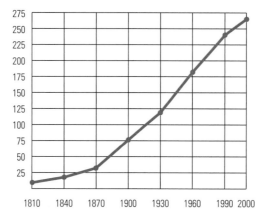

line graph *a diagram that uses connected points to indicate changes in one or more variables over time*

pie graph *a circular diagram that shows the relationship among parts of a single unit*

Line graphs indicate changes in one or more variables over time. In a speech on the population of the United States, for example, the line graph in Figure 9.4 helps by showing the population increase, in millions, from 1800 to 1997.

Pie graphs help audiences to visualize the relationships among parts of a single unit. In a speech on the nature of external funding for the University of Cincinnati in 1998, the speaker might use a pie graph such as the one in Figure 9.5.

Pictorial Representations

In addition to charts and graphs, other types of graphic visuals include pictorial representations such as diagrams, drawings, maps, and photographs.

Diagrams and drawings are popular visual aids because they are easy to prepare. If you can use a compass, a straightedge, and a measure, you can draw well enough for most speech purposes. For instance, if you are making the

FIGURE 9.5 Pie graph

Percentage distribution of external funding among major university programs

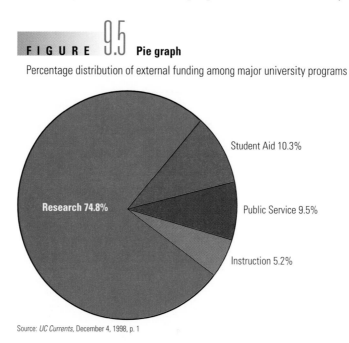

Source: *UC Currents*, December 4, 1998, p. 1

point that water skiers must hold their arms straight, with the back straight and knees bent slightly, a stick figure (see Figure 9.6) will illustrate the point. Stick figures may not be as aesthetically pleasing as professional drawings, but they work just as well. In fact, elaborate, detailed drawings are not worth the time and effort and actually may obscure the point you wish to make. If your

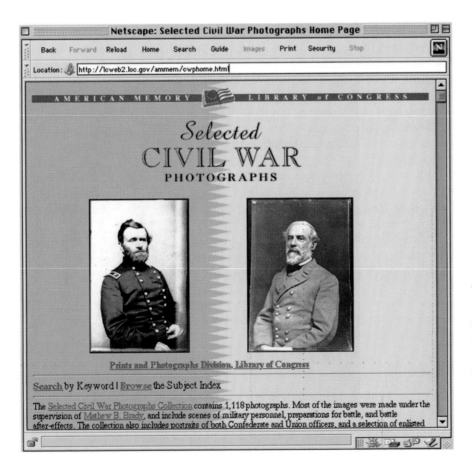

The Internet is a rich source of images to download for your visual aids. Make sure you take care not to violate any copyright restrictions posted at the Web sites. In general, students can use images for a class speech without copyright problems. For example, the Library of Congress is one excellent source of historical images.

FIGURE 9.7 A sample map

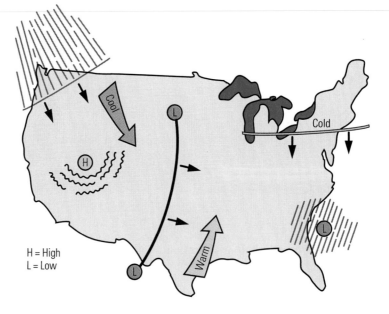

H = High
L = Low

prospective drawing is too complicated for you to handle personally, then you may need professional help. A major advantage of drawings is that you can often sketch cartoon figures to help you make a point humorously. You can also use computer software clip art and the Internet to find a visual representation of almost anything. Computer graphics will be discussed later in this chapter.

map *pictorial representation of a territory*

Maps are pictorial representations of a territory. Well-prepared maps allow you to focus on landforms (mountains, deserts, rivers, lakes), states, cities, land routes, or weather systems. The map in Figure 9.7 focuses on weather systems.

Photographs and downloaded visual images are useful visual aids when you need an exact reproduction. To be effective, photographs and computer images need to be large enough to be seen from the back of the room and simple enough to make your point at a glance.

Given the nature of free speech issues, it is now possible to find and download pictures and images that are disquieting to say the least. It is possible to obtain images of virtually anything these days, especially from the Internet. Always keep in mind your audience and the goal of your speech. Although there may be times when a disturbing image is relevant, do not be tempted to present anything for shock value. The Reflect on Ethics feature at the end of this chapter provides an interesting case in point.

Projections

LCD *liquid crystal display panel that sits on top of an overhead projector for displaying electronic visuals*

Almost any kind of graphic or pictorial visual aid can be prepared for projection onto a screen. Projection media include overhead transparencies, slides, films, and **LCDs**—liquid crystal display panels that sit on top of an overhead projector for displaying electronic visuals.

Courtesy of InFocus Systems, Inc.

If you have access to an LCD (liquid crystal display panel) that allows you to project your visual aid directly from your computer, make sure that the lighting in the room isn't so bright that it competes with your presentation.

Overhead transparencies are projected onto a screen via an overhead projector. A major advantage of overheads is that you can make them rather easily and inexpensively if you have access to a computer, a copy machine, and overhead (acetate) sheets. If you own a computer, you are likely to have the software (Microsoft Word, PowerPoint, or PageMaker) that you need; if you don't own your own computer, your college computer lab is likely to have the necessary equipment and software to help you. Once you've made the visual aid, and if you have access to an ink-jet or laser printer, you can print it on acetate sheets and display it via the overhead projector. If you have access to a dot matrix printer, you will have to print it on regular paper and take it to a copy service to be converted to a transparency.

Overheads can also be made by hand (traced or hand-lettered) or by machine (copy machine, thermographic, color lift).

Overheads work well in nearly any setting, and unlike other kinds of projections, they don't require dimming the lights in the room. Overheads can be especially useful for showing how formulas work, for illustrating various computations, or for analyzing data because it is possible to write, trace, or draw on the transparency while you are talking. This is best left to experienced presenters, however. I advise that your overheads be complete, so you can concentrate on your speech and not on adding data during your speech.

Slides are mounted transparencies that can be projected individually. The advantage of slides over film is that you can control when each image will be shown. Most carousel projectors have a remote control device that allows you to pace your showing of slides and to talk about each one as long as necessary,

overhead transparency acetate sheet projected onto a screen via an overhead projector

slide mounted transparency that can be projected individually

Slides and overhead transparencies not only get and hold attention but can be seen by the entire audience.

as well as reverse if needed. But, as with films, because slides require darkening the room while they are projected, novice speakers may lose the attention of their audience or their place in their notes.

Perhaps the single biggest potential problem is that slides can become out of order. When you have finished rehearsing your speech (be sure to rehearse using the slides as you plan to use them in your speech), double-check that the slides are in the right order. Also, make sure you have an extra light bulb for the projector.

Although films may be beautifully done, they are seldom appropriate for speeches, mostly because films so dominate that the speaker loses control. Occasionally, during a longer speech, you may want to use short clips of a minute or two each. Still, because projecting film requires a darkening of the room for that portion of time, I do not advise using films as visual aids.

Chalkboard or Markerboard

Chalkboards or markerboards are readily available in almost every classroom. Nevertheless, I would avoid using these media unless you are drawing a very simple figure or writing a single keyword to emphasize a point.

Common errors in using either type of board include writing too much material while you are talking, obscuring the material with your body as you are writing, or spending too much time talking to the board rather than your audience. I'm sure you have experienced these behaviors in your high school and college classes.

If you plan to draw or write while talking, practice doing it. If you are right-handed, stand to the right of what you are drawing. Try to face at least part of the audience while you work. Although it may seem awkward at first, your effort will allow you to maintain contact with your audience and will allow the audience to see what you are doing while you are doing it.

Handouts

Among the first visual aids that come to mind for many speakers are handouts. On the plus side, you can prepare handouts quickly, and all the people in the audience can have their own professional-quality material to refer to and take with them from the speech. On the minus side is the distraction of distributing handouts and the potential for losing the audience's attention when you want it to be looking at you. Before you decide on handouts, consider each of the other types of visual aids discussed previously. If you do decide on handouts, it is a good idea to distribute them at the end of the speech.

Computer Graphics

The availability of software designed especially for producing "presentation graphics" is rapidly changing how many speakers prepare charts, diagrams, and other visual aids. With the right equipment, graphics can be displayed directly on a screen or TV monitor as a computer "slide show," printed out and enlarged, photographed to make slides, or used to create overhead transparencies or handouts. Except for complex multimedia presentations, then, computer graphics are not so much a new type of visual aid as a new way of producing the kinds of visuals already discussed. They do have the ability to add a very polished look to your speech, and because using computer graphics in presentations is getting to be commonplace in many business environments, it is important to be familiar with this method.

The ever-growing capabilities of personal computers and popular software packages are rapidly making computer graphics a regular part of many speakers' repertoires. Today's computers are so easily accessible and so advanced in capabilities that any professional speaker should experiment with one of the many computer graphics systems—such as Microsoft PowerPoint, Adobe Persuasion, or Lotus Freelance—to prepare visual material for speeches.

Today, many colleges and universities have dedicated classrooms that house or are user-ready for advanced electronic equipment. If your school is one of these, then it probably offers workshops you can sign up for. If you have not tried a presentation graphics package, or if you are unsure of which one to try and what its capabilities might be, look through computer magazines for reviews of graphics software. When you learn to use one of the many computer graphics packages, you will find that with a few computer keystrokes or the click of a "mouse," you can change lines of facts and figures into a variety of graphic displays.

Additionally, access to the Internet enables you to download and store your own "library" of images. Depending on the presentation graphics software you have, you can insert virtually any image from your "library" into your presentation. If you have access to a scanner, you can also transfer a photograph from a book or magazine directly to your computer library.

Preparing good presentations using computer graphics does take time and practice, however. It is best to start simple and become more elaborate by importing images as you get more comfortable with the software capabilities.

If you do experiment with computer graphics, keep in mind that all the guidelines for using visual aids still apply. In particular, be wary of the temptation to produce overly fancy graphics that actually obscure the information you want the audience to assimilate. With the ability the computer gives you to

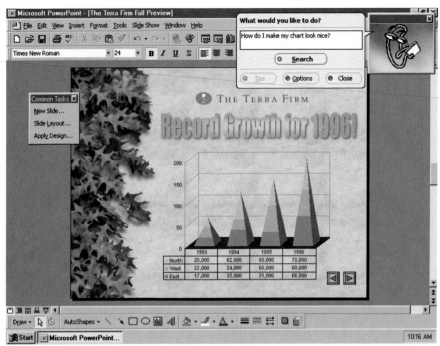

Reprinted by permission of Microsoft Corporation

Several computer graphics systems are available for use in creating effective visual aids. This is a sample screen from Microsoft PowerPoint.

manipulate graphics—for example, to easily create complex three-dimensional bar charts or combine several images and typefaces in a single display—it is easy to let the medium overpower the message.

Also keep in mind that just because you can use computer graphics doesn't mean that you have to. Your speech may be such that a different form of visual aid would be more effective for the audience. Erin's speech on volleyball, for instance, may be extremely interesting and engaging without the use of computer graphics.

Making Choices

Now that we've considered the various types of visual aids, you have to make choices before you start collecting or creating the visual aids you plan to use. In this section, we focus on some of the key questions you need to answer to help you make visual aid choices.

1. What are the most important ideas in helping me achieve my speech goal? These ideas are the ones you will want to enhance with visual aids. Visual aids are likely to be remembered. So, you want to make sure that what you present visually is what you want your audience to remember.

2. How large is the audience? The kinds of visual aids that will work for a small group of 20 or less differ from the kinds that will work for an audience of 100 or more. For an audience of 20 or less, as in most of your classroom speeches, you can show relatively small objects and use relatively small models and everyone will be able to see. For very large audiences, you'll want projections that can be seen from 100 or 200 feet away with ease.

3. Is necessary equipment readily available? At times, you may be speaking in an environment that is not equipped for electronic displays. At the University of Cincinnati, for example, most rooms are equipped with only a chalkboard, an overhead projector, and electrical outlets. Anything else you want to use you will have to bring yourself or schedule through the appropriate university office. Be prepared! In any situation in which you have scheduled equipment from an outside source, you need to prepare yourself for the possibility that the equipment may not arrive on time or may not work the way you thought it did. Call ahead, get to your speaking location early, and have an alternative visual aid to use, just in case.

4. Is the time involved in making or getting the visual aid and/or equipment cost effective? Visual aids are supplements. Their goal is to accent what you are doing verbally. If you believe that a particular visual aid will help you better achieve your goal, then the time spent is well worth it.

You'll notice that most of the visual aids we've discussed can be obtained or prepared relatively easily. But because some procedures are "so easy," we find ourselves getting lost in making some of them. Visual aids definitely make a speech more interesting and engaging. However, I've found that the best advice is to "keep it simple."

5. How many visual aids should I consider? Unless you are doing a slide show in which the total focus of the speech is on visual images, the number of visual aids you use is likely to be relatively few. For the most part, you want the focus of the audience to be on you, the speaker. You want to use visual aids when their use will hold attention, exemplify an idea, or help the audience remember. For each of these goals, the more visual aids used, the less value they will contribute. For a 5-minute speech, using three visual aids at crucial times will get attention, exemplify, and stimulate recall far better than using six or eight.

There is another reason for keeping the visual aids to a small number. A couple of really well crafted visual aids may well maximize the power of your statements, whereas several poorly executed or poorly used visual aids may actually detract from the power of your words.

In summary, use the following guidelines when choosing visual aids:

- Take a few minutes to consider your visual aid strategy. Where would some kind of visual aid make the most sense? What kind of visual aid is most appropriate?

- Adapt your visuals to your situation, speech topic, and audience needs.

- Choose visuals with which you are both comfortable and competent.

- Check out the audiovisual resources of the speaking site before you start preparing your visual aids.

- Be discriminate in the number of visual aids you use and the key points that they support.

Designing Visual Aids

The visual aids that you are most likely to design for a classroom presentation are charts, graphs, diagrams, and drawings written on poster board or flipcharts or projected on screens using overheads or slides. However simple you may think your visual aids will be, you still have to determine their design features.

Selecting Visual Aids

The goal of this exercise is to help you determine what, if any, visual aids you will use in your speech.

1. Carefully study the verbal information you are planning to use in the speech. Where do you believe visual aids would be effective in creating audience interest, facilitating understanding, or increasing retention?

2. What kinds of visual aids would be most effective in each of the places you have identified? Yourself? Objects? Models? Charts? Pictorial representations? Projections? Chalkboard? Handouts? Computer graphics?

First, we'll suggest nine design principles. Then, we'll look at several renderings of material to illustrate these principles.

1. Use printing or type size that can be seen easily by your entire audience. If you're designing a hand-drawn poster board, check your lettering for size by moving as far away from the visual aid you've created as the farthest person in your audience will be sitting. If you can read the lettering and see the details from that distance, then both are large enough; if not, draw another sample and check it for size.

When you project a typeface from an overhead onto a screen, the lettering on the screen will be much larger than the lettering on the overhead itself. So, what's a good rule of thumb for overhead lettering? Try 36-point type for major headings; 24-point for subheadings; and 18-point for text. Figure 9.8 shows how these sizes look on paper. The 36-point type will project to about $2\frac{1}{2}$ to 3 inches on the screen; 24-point will project to about 1 to 2 inches; 18-point will project to $\frac{1}{2}$ to 1 inch.

2. Use a typeface that is pleasing to the eye. Modern software packages, such as Microsoft Word, come with a variety of typefaces. Yet only a few of

FIGURE 9.8 **Visual aid print sizes**

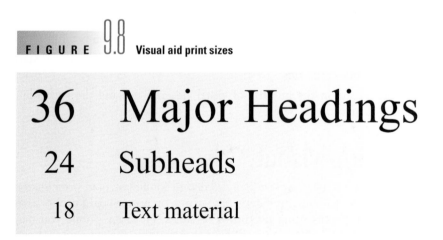

36 Major Headings

24 Subheads

18 Text material

FIGURE 9.9 Typefaces in 18-point regular and boldface

Courier	Selecting Typefaces **Selecting Typefaces**
Times	Selecting Typefaces **Selecting Typefaces**
Souvenir	Selecting Typefaces **Selecting Typefaces**
Helvetica	Selecting Typefaces **Selecting Typefaces**

them will work well in projections. Figure 9.9 shows a sample of four standard typefaces in regular and boldface 18-point size. Most other typefaces are designed for special situations.

Which of these typefaces seem most pleasing to you? Perhaps you'll decide that you'd like to use one typeface for the heading and another for the text. In general, you will not want to use more than two typefaces—headings in one, text in another. You want the typefaces to call attention to the material, not to themselves.

3. Use upper- and lowercase type. The combination of upper- and lowercase is easier to read. Some people think that printing in all capital letters creates emphasis. Although that may be true in some instances, ideas printed in all capital letters are more difficult to read—even when the ideas are written in short phrases (see Figure 9.10).

4. Try to limit the lines of type to six or less. Because you don't want the audience to spend a long time reading your visual aid—you want them listening to you—it's a good idea to limit the total number of lines to six or less, if possible. The visual aid is a reinforcement and summary of what you say, not the exact words you say. You don't want the audience to have to spend more than 6 or 8 seconds "getting" your visual aid.

FIGURE 9.10 All capitals versus upper- and lowercase

CARAT—THE WEIGHT OF A DIAMOND

Carat—The Weight of a Diamond

FIGURE 9.11 Sample visual aid: Draft #1

> I WANT YOU TO REMEMBER THE THREE R'S OF RECYCLING
>
> Reduce the amount of waste people produce by overpacking or using material that won't recycle.
>
> Reuse by relying on cloth towels rather than paper towels, earthenware dishes rather than paper or plastic plates, and glass bottles rather than aluminum cans.
>
> Recycle by collecting recyclable products, sorting them appropriately, and getting them to the appropriate recycling agency.

Suppose Kendra, who is preparing a speech on "The Three R's of Recycling," is beginning the process of drafting samples of a visual aid she wants to use. Her first two drafts are represented by Figures 9.11 and 9.12. Notice that Figure 9.12 is an improvement over Figure 9.11 solely in terms of limiting the number of lines, making it much easier to read quickly.

5. Present information in short phrases rather than complete sentences. Again, you want audience attention focused on you and your words—the visual aid is meant to be a reinforcement. As Kendra continues trying to improve her visual, she further edits it by presenting her information in short phrases rather than complete sentences.

Although the number of words is reduced by only a few, this third draft, shown in Figure 9.13, is much easier to read.

6. Focus on items of information that you will emphasize in your speech. Since we often get ideas for visual aids from other sources, the tendency is to include all the material that was originally included. But for speech purposes, you'll want to keep the aid as simple as possible, clearly focused on the key information.

As you develop your visual aids, try to eliminate anything that distracts or takes emphasis away from the point you want to make. Notice how Kendra has tried to improve the focus of her visual aid, as shown in Figure 9.14. Although

FIGURE 9.12 Sample visual aid: Draft #2

> I WANT YOU TO REMEMBER THE THREE R'S OF RECYCLING
>
> Reduce the amount of waste people produce.
>
> Reuse by relying on cloth towels, earthenware dishes, and glass bottles rather than disposables.
>
> Recycle by collecting, sorting, and delivering recyclable material.

FIGURE 9.13 Sample visual aid: Draft #3

Remember the three R's of recycling

Reduce the amount of waste

Reuse by avoiding disposables

Recycle by collecting, sorting,
and delivering recyclables

she actually has several more lines of type, the improved focus on key words makes it a potentially stronger visual aid. Notice that she has also improved the focus by indenting and using different type sizes to show the relative importance of items.

Because the tendency to clutter is likely to present a special problem on graphs, let's use another example to illustrate this principle. Suppose you wanted to show college enrollment by age of students, based on figures reported in *The Chronicle of Higher Education*. The graph in Figure 9.15a shows all eleven age categories for which data were reported; Figure 9.15b simplifies by combining age ranges with small percentages. The graph in Figure 9.15b is not only easier to read, but it also emphasizes the highest percentage classifications.

7. Make sure information is laid out on the aid in a way that is aesthetically pleasing. Layout involves leaving white space around the whole message, indenting subordinate ideas, and using different type sizes as well as different treatments, such as bolding and underlining. Kendra's fourth draft (Figure 9.14) shows improvement over her earlier versions in better spacing, indentation, and use of different type sizes.

FIGURE 9.14 Sample visual aid: Draft #4

Remember the three R's of recycling

Reduce waste

Reuse

cloth towels
dishes
glass bottles

Recycle

collect
sort
deliver

FIGURE 9.15 Pie charts

College enrollment by age of students

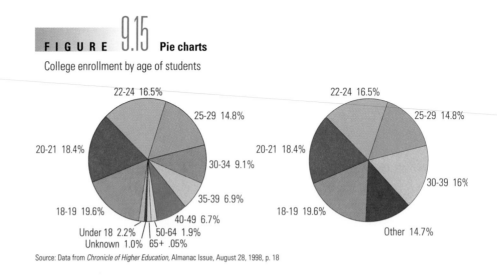

Source: Data from *Chronicle of Higher Education*, Almanac Issue, August 28, 1998, p. 18

8. Add clip art where appropriate. If you are working with computer graphics, consider adding clip art. Most computer graphics packages have a wide variety of clip art that you can import to your document. You can also buy relatively inexpensive software packages that contain thousands of clip art images. A relevant piece of clip art can make the image look both more professional and more dramatic. Notice that Kendra's next effort, shown in Figure 9.16, includes clip art. It also uses fewer words and uses underlining for emphasis. Be careful, though; clip art can be overdone. Don't let your message be overpowered by unnecessary pictures.

Figures 9.11, 9.12, 9.13, 9.14, and 9.16 show one potential word chart in five different forms. Of the five, Kendra would probably use either 9.14 or 9.16. If she chooses 9.14, she might reconfigure it slightly to add underlining and perhaps the clip art used in 9.16.

9. Consider using color. Although black and white will work well for most of your visual aids, you may want to experiment with using color. As with clip art or graphics, however, don't go overboard. Poorly used color can be a distraction, not an enhancement.

FIGURE 9.16 Sample visual aid: Draft #5

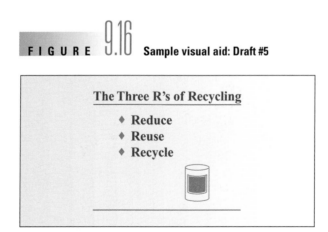

With that said, here are some tips for using color in your visual aids:

- Use the same color background for each visual. Avoid dark backgrounds.
- Use bright colors, such as red, to highlight the most important information.
- Use black or blue for lettering, especially on flipcharts.
- Do not use yellow or orange for lettering—they can't be seen well from a distance.
- Leave lots of white space around your lettering and clip art.
- If you want to get into more complex color usage, use a color wheel to select harmonizing colors.
- Use no more than four colors; two or three are even better.
- Always make a quick template before you prepare all your visual aids. Pretend you are your audience. Sit as far away as they will be sitting, and evaluate the colors you have chosen for their appeal and readability.

Using Visual Aids in Your Speech

Many speakers think that once they have prepared good visual aids, they will have no trouble using them in the speech. However, many speeches with good visual aids have become shambles because the speaker neglected to practice with them. As a general rule of thumb, you will want to make sure that you practice using visual aids in your rehearsals. During practice sessions, indicate on your notes exactly when you will use each visual aid (and when you will remove it). Work on statements for introducing the visual aids, and practice different ways of showing the visual aids until you are satisfied that everyone in the audience will be able to see them. Following are several guidelines for using visual aids effectively in your speech.

1. Plan carefully when to use visual aids. As you practice your speech, indicate on your outline when and how you will use each visual aid.

2. Carefully consider audience needs. If your audience would find a graphic helpful in understanding and remembering a portion of your speech, then a visual aid at that point is appropriate. On the other hand, regardless of how exciting a visual may be, if it does not contribute directly to the audience's attention to, understanding of, or retention of information on your topic, then reconsider its use.

3. Show visual aids only when talking about them. Visual aids will draw audience attention. The basic rule of thumb is: When the visual aid is no longer the focus of attention, remove it, turn it off, or get rid of it.

If you use an overhead projector, it may come with a lid or cover on the light. If yours doesn't, then either turn the machine off or cover your transparency with a blank sheet of paper. If you are using an LCD and a computer, show your visual and then advance to a blank screen. You can insert blank pages in areas where you know you will need them.

Often a single visual aid contains several bits of information. In order to keep audience attention where you want it, you can prepare the visual aid with

Don't display visual aids when you're not referring to them.

cover-ups. Then, as you move from one portion of the visual aid to another, you can remove covers to expose the portion of the visual aid that you are then discussing.

4. Talk about the visual aid while showing it. Since you know what you want your audience to see in the visual aid, tell your audience what to look for, explain the various parts, and interpret figures, symbols, and percentages.

When you show your visual—for example, a transparency projected onto a screen in front of the class—use the following "turn-touch-talk" technique.

When you display the visual, walk to the screen—that's where everyone will look anyway. Slightly *turn* to the visual and *touch* it—that is, point to it with your arm or a pointer (use carefully). Then, with your back to the screen and your body still at a slight 45-degree angle to the group, *talk* to your audience about the visual.

When you finish making your comments, return to the podium or your speaking position, and turn off the projector or otherwise put the visual away.

5. Display visual aids so that everyone in the audience can see them. If you hold the visual aid, position it away from your body and point it toward the various parts of the audience. If you place your visual aid on a chalkboard or easel or mount it in some way, stand to one side and point with the arm nearest the visual aid. If it is necessary to roll or fold the visual aid, bring some transparent tape to mount it to the chalkboard or wall so that it does not roll or wrinkle.

6. Talk to your audience, not to the visual aid. You may need to look at the visual aid occasionally, but it is important to maintain eye contact with your audience as much as possible—in part so that you can gauge how they are reacting to your visual material. When speakers become too engrossed in their visual aids, looking at them instead of the audience, they tend to lose contact with the audience entirely.

REFLECT ON ethics

Karen is planning to give her speech on late-term "partial birth" abortions. As she thinks about what she should do, she decides to go onto the Web to see whether she can come up with any visual ideas. Along the way, she finds a picture of an aborted fetus. She downloads it into her computer and into her PowerPoint file. Later that day, she tells Paula what she has done and asks her what she thinks of her plan.

"Hey," Paula replies, "that'll knock their socks off. Go for it."

As Karen rehearses her speech, she is still wondering whether using that visual aid is a good idea. But, with Paula's apparent encouragement, she uses it in her speech.

During oral critiquing of the speeches, one classmate raises the question of the ethics of showing a graphic picture like the aborted fetus.

1. What ethical arguments support the use of disquieting graphic images?

2. What arguments would hold the use of these images to be unethical?

3. What do you believe is the ethical principle you will follow in making decisions like this?

7. Avoid passing objects around the audience. People look at, read, handle, and think about whatever they hold in their hands. While they are so occupied, they are not likely to be listening to you.

Summary

Visual aids are useful for any kind of speech. The most common types of visual aids are yourself, objects, models, charts, flipcharts, graphs, pictorial representations, projections, chalkboard or markerboard, handouts, and computer graphics. Advancements in computer graphics give the speaker a wide range of flexibility in creating professional-quality visual materials.

Before you start collecting or creating the visual aids you plan to use, you need to consider a number of questions. What are the most important ideas in helping me achieve my speech goal? How large is the audience? Is necessary equipment readily available? Is the time involved in making or getting the visual aid and/or equipment cost effective? How many visual aids should I consider?

Take time to design your visual aids with the following principles in mind: Use printing or type size that can be seen easily by your entire audience. Use a typeface that is pleasing to the eye. Use upper- and lowercase type. Try to limit the lines of type to six or less. Present information in short phrases rather than complete sentences. Make sure information is laid out in a way that is aesthetically pleasing. Focus on items of information that you will emphasize in the speech. Add clip art where appropriate. Consider using color.

When you plan to use visual aids in a speech, make sure that you practice using them in rehearsal. Keep the following suggestions in mind: Plan carefully when you will use each visual aid. Carefully consider audience needs. Show visual aids only when talking about them. Talk about the visual aid while showing it. Display visual aids so that everyone in the audience can see them. Talk to your audience, not to the visual aid. Avoid passing objects around the audience.

**A speech reminds us
that words, like chil-
dren, have the power to
make dance the dullest
beanbag of a heart.**

Peggy Noonan, *What I Saw at the
Revolution,* 1990

Practicing Speech Wording

As Rhonda was listening to the recording she had made of her first speech practice session, she listened carefully to the section on the effects of Rohypnol. She stopped the tape as she heard herself saying:

> "Rohypnol leaves many bad effects on people. And a lot of these are really, really treacherous. I mean, you can be totally out of it for a long time."

> "That's just not very meaningful," Rhonda said to herself. "First, it's really not that specific. I say, 'leaves bad effects,' but I don't mention any. And 'really, really treacherous' isn't very exciting."

When you are ready to begin thinking about presenting your speech, the emphasis switches from what you plan to say to how you plan to say it. In the chapter opening, Rhonda is beginning to consider the first important issue of presenting your speech, practicing the wording; in the next chapter we consider the counterpart of wording, practicing the delivery.

You'll recall that an effective speech plan is a product of seven action steps. In this chapter we consider the sixth one: Practice the presentation of the speech until the wording is clear, vivid, emphatic, and appropriate. In this chapter we begin with the overall goal of developing an oral style, then we move to the specifics of practicing your speech to increase clarity, vividness, emphasis, and appropriateness. As you consider this material, you should be able to make the kinds of changes during practice sessions that will make the language of your speeches much better.

Developing an Oral Style to Communicate Meaning

oral style *language that is instantly intelligible to the ear*

Oral style is language that is instantly intelligible to the ear. Unlike written communication, where wording evolves through editing and finally appears on the printed page, wording in speech communication develops through oral practice. Think of the process of wording this way. By carefully outlining your speech, you have produced a skeleton that includes anywhere from 20 to 40 percent of the words that could be used in the speech. During the first practice, you fill out the outline to speech length. Then, through several practice periods, you sample various wordings. Your mind retains wordings that seem especially effective and seeks to modify awkward, hesitant, or otherwise ineffective phrasings. You continue until you are confident that the speech itself will do what you intend.

The steps of speech practice—including a discussion of how this practice is handled *without resulting in memorization*—are the subject of Chapter 11,

A C T I O N S T E P **six**

Practice Wording
Practice the speech until the wording is clear, vivid, emphatic, and appropriate.

Practicing Delivery. The question in this chapter is, What criteria can you use to measure whether or not the words you are using in practice will result in an effective oral style that is appropriate for your audience?

As we have said, oral style is language that is instantly intelligible to the *ear*, so that the audience receives the same meanings as the speaker intends. If a written sentence is too long or unclear, the reader can go back to reread it and puzzle out its meaning. If a speech sentence is too long or unclear, the listener cannot go back. The speaker must focus on how to help the audience understand the meaning as the speech is given. Moreover, your speech must affect the ear of a *specific* audience. Language that is intelligible to one culture may not be intelligible to another; language that is intelligible to adults may not be to children.

Richard Weaver, a major figure in contemporary rhetorical theory, tells us that language is "sermonic."[1] That is, whether or not we are aware of it, we can strike special and sometimes unique chords in each member of an audience by how we word our ideas. Wording is not to be taken lightly. Each of us has an ethical responsibility to use language with care, for mindless, sloppy, or unknowingly provocative language can create images over which we have no control.

Before we examine the specific criteria of clarity, vividness, emphasis, and appropriateness in the use of oral language, we will look briefly at language and meaning.

Language and Meaning

On the surface, the relationship between language and meaning seems perfectly clear: We select the correct word, and people will interpret our meaning correctly. In fact, the relationship between language and meaning is not nearly so simple, for two reasons: Language must be learned, and the use of language is a creative act.

First, we are not born knowing a language. Rather, each generation within a language community learns the language anew from older members. But each generation may learn only a portion of the words used by the previous generation or may only learn some of the word meanings used by previous generations, because some words and meanings are no longer useful for conveying meaning.

In addition, younger generations will invent new words or assign different meanings to the words they learn. For instance, such words as *mediagenic* (attractive and appealing to viewers and readers of the news media) and *hip-hop* (street subculture language including rap) have come into common usage to express ideas that were unthinkable to your grandparents.

Changes also occur because of the need to create words to communicate perceptions. If we encounter a situation that no word in our vocabulary can describe, we are likely either to form a new word or to use an old word in a new way to describe it. Likewise, if we see an object that is different from any object we have a word for, we choose a new word to label it. Speakers of English in the 1940s would have been puzzled by the expression *couch potato*, for example, because only recently have we used this term to describe people who are chronic television viewers.

The Denotative and Connotative Meaning of Words

When Melissa tells Trish that her dog died, what Melissa means depends on both word denotation and connotation.

denotation *direct, explicit meaning of a word; dictionary definition*

Denotation **Denotation** is the direct, explicit meaning people have agreed to give to a word; in short, denotation is the dictionary meaning. So denotatively, when Melissa says that her dog died, she means that her domesticated canine passed from physical life. But in some situations, even the denotative meaning of a word may not be clear. First, the dictionary definitions reflect current and past practice in the language community; second, they use words to define words; and third, each dictionary author is engaging in the creative act of communicating. The end result is that words are defined differently in various dictionaries and may include multiple meanings that change over time.

Moreover, meaning may vary depending on the context in which the word is used. For example, the dictionary definition of *gay* includes both having or showing a merry, lively mood and homosexual. Thus, **context**—the position of a word in a sentence and the other words around it—is important in interpreting which denotation of a word is meant. Not only will the other words and the syntax and grammar of a verbal message help us to understand the denotative meaning of certain words, but so will the situation in which they are spoken. Whether the comment "He's really gay," is understood to be a comment on someone's sexual orientation or on his merry mood may depend on the circumstances in which it is said.

context *the surrounding verbal elements that help determine the specific meaning of a word*

connotation *the feelings or evaluations associated with a word*

Connotation Whereas denotation refers to the standard dictionary meaning given to a word, **connotation** is the feelings or evaluations associated with the word, and may be even more important to our understanding of meaning.

C. K. Ogden and I. A. Richards were among the first scholars to consider the misunderstandings resulting from the failure of communicators to realize that their subjective reactions to words will be a product of their life experiences.[2] For instance, when Melissa tells Trisha that her dog died, Trisha's understanding of the message depends on the extent to which her feelings about pets and death—her connotations of the words—correspond to the feelings that Melissa has about pets and death. So whereas Melissa, who sees dogs as truly indispensable friends, may be trying to communicate a deep sense of grief, Trisha, who doesn't particularly care for pets in general or dogs in particular, may miss the sense of Melissa's statement.

Why should you understand the relationship of denotation and connotation to message meaning? Because the only message that counts is the message that is understood, regardless of whether it is the one you intended.

Variations in Meaning across Subgroups

As we mentioned earlier, a language community may include within it subgroups with unique cultures. Hecht, Collier, and Ribeau point out, "Cultural groups define themselves in part through language, and members establish identity through language use."[3] Subgroups thus develop variations on the core language that allow them to share meanings that are unique to their cultural experiences. Because people from different cultures approach the world from different perspectives, they are likely to experience difficulty sharing meaning when they talk with each other. One of the most confounding aspects of language and its interpretation for people from different cultures is the use of idioms. For instance, people from different cultures have an impossible time understanding such common idioms as "He bought the farm" and "She really sent me on a wild goose chase."

In addition to subgroups based on race, religion, and national origin, we are also experiencing an unprecedented growth in subgroup cultures and language differences associated with generation, social class, and political interests. The need for awareness and sensitivity in applying our communication skills doesn't depend on someone's being an immigrant or from a different ethnic background. Rather, the need for being aware of potential language differences is important in every type of communication. Developing your language skills so that the messages you send are clear and sensitive will increase your communication effectiveness in every situation.

General and abstract words invite different interpretations.

Speaking Clearly

Message clarity is improved by reducing ambiguity and confusion. Compare the clarity of the following two descriptions of the same incident:

> Some nut almost got me a while ago.

> An older man in a banged-up Honda Civic ran the light at Calhoun and Clifton and almost hit me while I was waiting to turn left at the cross street.

You can clarify your language by using specific, concrete, precise, and simple words.

Use Specific, Concrete, Precise, Simple Words

Specific words clarify meaning by narrowing what is understood from a general category to a particular group within that category. The first words that come to mind as we try to express our thoughts are often general and abstract, allowing the listener to choose from many possible images rather than picturing the single, focused image that the speaker has. The more listeners are called on to provide their own images, the more likely they are to see meanings different from what the speaker intends.

For instance, if Nevah says that Ruben is a "blue-collar worker," you may picture an unlimited number of occupations that fall within this broad category. If, instead, she says he's a "construction worker," the number of possible images you can picture is reduced. But if she says Ruben is "a bulldozer operator," this image snaps into focus and is likely to align with the one she intended you to have.

So, think of general to specific as a continuum going from most general to most specific. Using the previous example, the continuum goes from blue-collar worker to construction worker to construction vehicle operator to bulldozer operator. Figure 10.1 further illustrates the continuum of general to specific.

Concrete words are not only more specific, but they are also likely to appeal to our senses—to conjure up a picture. Often we can see them, hear them, smell them. The word *speak*, for example, is a general/abstract term. To make it more concrete, we can use words like *mumble, whisper, bluster, drone, jeer,* or *rant.* Say these words aloud. Notice the different sound of your voice when you say *whisper* as opposed to *bluster, jeer,* or *rant.*

specific words *words that clarify meaning by narrowing what is understood from a general category to a particular group within that category*

concrete words *words that appeal to the senses or conjure up a picture*

FIGURE 10.1 **From general to specific**

Art
Painting
Oil painting
Impressionist oil painting
Renoir's *La Promenade*

precise words *words that most accurately or correctly capture the sense of what we are saying*

Finally, we seek words that are **precise**—that most accurately or correctly capture the sense of what we are saying. Suppose I seek the most precise word to describe Phillip's speech. I might say, "Phillip blustered. Well, to be more precise, he ranted." Notice that we're not talking general to specific—both words are on roughly the same level of abstraction; nor are we talking about one word being more concrete—as we have seen, both are concrete. Now we are concerned with precision of meaning. *Blustering* means talking in a way that is loudly boastful; *ranting* means talking in a way that is noisy or bombastic. So, what we're considering here is shades of meaning: Depending on how the person was talking, *blustering* or *ranting* would be the more precise word. Let's try another one. "Susan laughed at my story—well, to be more precise, she chuckled." A *laugh* is a loud show of mirth; a *chuckle* is a more gentle sound expressing suppressed mirth. Similar? Yes. But, different—indicating shades of meaning.

In the examples that follow, notice how the use of specific, concrete, and precise language in the right-hand column improves the clarity of the messages in the left-hand column.

The senator brought *several things* with her to the meeting.	The senator brought *recent letters from her constituency* with her to the meeting.
He lives in a *really big house.*	He lives in a *fourteen-room Tudor mansion.*
The backyard has *several different kinds* of trees.	The backyard has *two large maples, an oak, and four small evergreens.*
Morgan is a *fair grader.*	Morgan *uses the same standards for grading all students.*
Many students *aren't honest* in class.	Many students *cheat on tests* in class.
Judy *hits* the podium when she wants to emphasize her point.	Judy *pounds on* the podium when she wants to emphasize her point.

While specific, concrete, and precise words help reduce ambiguity and sharpen meaning, there are times when clarity is best achieved by adding a detail or an example. For instance, suppose Linda says, "Rashad is very loyal." Since the meaning of *loyal* (faithful to an idea, person, company, and so on) is

Pablo Corral V/Corbis

To differentiate among individuals in this picture, you would have to be precise, specific, and concrete in your description.

abstract, to avoid ambiguity and confusion Linda might add, "He never criticizes a friend behind her back." By following up her use of an abstract concept with a concrete example, Linda makes it easier for her listeners to "ground" their idea of loyalty in a concrete or "real" experience.

In your effort to find specific, concrete, precise words, make sure that you use common or simple words—words that your listeners will understand. Some speakers think that to be effective they must impress their audience with their extensive vocabularies. As a result, instead of looking for common or simple words, they use words that appear pompous, affected, or stilted to the listener. Speaking precisely and specifically does not mean speaking obscurely. So when you have a choice, select the simplest, most familiar words that convey your specific meaning. The following story illustrates the problem with pretentious, unfamiliar words:

A plumber wrote to a government agency, saying that he found that hydrochloric acid quickly opened drain pipes but that he wasn't sure whether it was a good thing to use. A scientist at the agency replied, "The efficacy of hydrochloric acid is indisputable, but the corrosive residue is incompatible with metallic permanence."

The plumber wrote back thanking him for the assurance that hydrochloric acid was all right. Disturbed by this turn of affairs, the scientist showed the letter to his boss, another scientist, who then wrote to the plumber: "We cannot assume responsibility for the production of toxic and noxious residue with hydrochloric acid and suggest you use an alternative procedure."

The plumber wrote back that he agreed, hydrochloric acid worked fine. Greatly disturbed by this misunderstanding, the scientists took their problem to the top boss. She wrote to the plumber: "Don't use hydrochloric acid. It eats the hell out of pipes."

FIGURE  **10.2** **Choosing simple words**

To simplify your language, use:

building	instead of	edifice
clothing	instead of	apparel
bury	instead of	inter
engagement	instead of	betrothal
begin	instead of	commence
avoid	instead of	eschew
wedding	instead of	nuptials
predict	instead of	presage
beauty	instead of	pulchritude
home	instead of	residence
view	instead of	vista
use	instead of	utilize

The decision rule is to use a more difficult word *only* when you believe that it is the very best word for a specific context. Suppose you wanted to use a more precise or specific word for *building*. Using the guideline of simplicity, you might select *house, apartment, high-rise,* or *skyscraper,* but you would avoid *edifice.* Each of the other choices is more precise or more specific, but *edifice* is neither more precise nor more specific, and in addition to being less well understood, it will be perceived as affected or stilted. Figure 10.2 gives some examples of needlessly fancy words and simpler equivalents.

Eliminate Clutter

verbal clutter *use of extraneous words, unnecessary repetition of words, repetitious modifiers, and empty adjectives*

One of the greatest enemies of clarity in speech is **verbal clutter,** which includes extraneous words, unnecessary repetition of words, repetitious modifiers, and empty adjectives. Clutter not only obscures meaning but also drives listeners crazy. Although we tolerate such clutter in conversation, we are far less likely to accept it in public speeches.

Clutter is particularly noticeable in the early stages of rehearsal, when speakers are still unsure of what they will say. The following examples illustrate four ways to eliminate clutter.

1. Eliminate repetitions that do not add emphasis.

Wordy: He found that the bill that he supported is not a bill that he should have supported.

Better: He found he should not have supported that particular bill.

2. Eliminate empty words and phrases—especially pointless modifiers—that add nothing to the meaning of the sentence.

Wordy: Kim Li became the leader she is through very, very hard work and just a whole lot of attention to, you know, detail.

Better: Kim Li became an accomplished leader through hard work and attention to detail.

3. Edit long sentences into shorter, harder-hitting ones.

Wordy: A few of the people who had become very angry with what Councilman Ortega said rose to take the opportunity of refuting the arguments set forth by Councilman Ortega.

Better: A few angry people rose to refute Councilman Ortega's arguments.

4. Combine sentences or simplify phrases and clauses that include the same ideas.

Wordy: The speeches that were prepared by Martin Luther King, Jr., are different from those speeches that were prepared by other Civil Rights speakers of the period.

Better: Martin Luther King, Jr.'s speeches are different from those of other Civil Rights speakers.

During your first practice sessions, your speaking may not appear to be natural. You may concentrate so heavily on speaking without clutter that meaning may suffer. But the more you practice, the more easily you will find yourself reducing clutter. Just as an athlete works on skills in practice but concentrates on the game in competition, so you can stress techniques in practice but concentrate on ideas and the audience when you give a speech. Eventually, if practice is successful, you will be able to monitor even public speaking without conscious effort.

Develop Your Ability to Speak More Clearly

Being able to speak more clearly requires building your working vocabulary and brainstorming to generate word choices from your active vocabulary.

Vocabulary Building As a speaker, the larger your vocabulary, the more choices you have from which to select the word you want; as a listener, the larger your vocabulary, the more likely you are to understand the words used by others.

One way to increase your vocabulary is to study one of the many vocabulary-building books on the shelves of most any bookstore. You might also study magazine features, such as "Word Power" in the *Reader's Digest*. By completing this monthly quiz and learning the words with which you are not familiar, you might increase your vocabulary by as many as 20 words per month.

A second way to increase your vocabulary is to make note of words that people use in their conversations with you that you are not able to define precisely. For instance, suppose you hear, "I was inundated with phone calls today!" If you can't define *inundated*, write it down. Later, look it up in the dictionary and then say the sentence with a synonym—in this case, *overwhelmed* or *flooded*. If you then say to yourself, "She was inundated—overwhelmed or flooded—with phone calls today," you are likely to remember that meaning and apply it the next time you hear the word. You can follow the same procedure when you read.

Elle Schuster/The Image Bank

The larger your vocabulary, the more chance you have of communicating effectively. One way to enrich your vocabulary is through study of basic vocabulary books and books of synonyms.

brainstorming *uncritical, nonevaluative process of generating alternatives*

Mental Brainstorming   Having a larger vocabulary won't help your speaking if you don't have a procedure for using it. One way to practice accessing choices from your memory is to brainstorm during practice sessions and later in conversation. **Brainstorming,** you'll recall, is an uncritical, nonevaluative process of generating alternatives. Suppose you were practicing a speech on registration and said, "Preregistration is awful." If you don't think that *awful* is the right word, you might be able to quickly brainstorm the words *frustrating, demeaning, cumbersome,* and *annoying.* Then, in your next practice, you might say, "Preregistration is overly cumbersome."

Speaking clearly impromptu is hard work, but as you build your vocabulary and learn to mentally brainstorm, you will find that you are able to make your public speaking clearer. You will really know that you have made strides in improving specificity, precision, and concreteness when you find that you can form clear messages even under pressure of presenting your speeches.

Be Sensitive to Cultural Differences

Verbal communication rules and expectations about clarity of language vary from culture to culture. One major dimension used by theorists to explain similarities and differences in language and behavior is individualism versus

Specific, Concrete, and Precise

1. For each word listed, find three words or phrases that are more specific, or more concrete.

implements	building	nice	education
clothes	colors	chair	bad
happy	stuff	things	car

2. Make the following statements clearer by editing words that are not precise or not specific and concrete:

"You know I love basketball. Well, I'm practicing a lot because I want to get better."

"Paula, I'm really bummed out. Everything is going down the tubes. You know what I mean?"

"Well, she just does these things to tick me off. Like, just a whole lot of stuff—and she knows it!"

"I just bought a beautiful outfit—I mean, it is really in style. You'll love it."

"I've really got to remember to bring my things the next time I visit."

collectivism.[4] In general, in *individualistic cultures*, individuals' goals are emphasized more than group goals, because these cultures value uniqueness. Many of the individualistic cultures are nations of western Europe and the United States. In contrast, in *collectivistic cultures*, group goals are emphasized more than individual goals, because these cultures value harmony and solidarity. Many of the collectivistic cultures are nations of Asia, Africa, and South America.[5]

Individualistic cultures tend to use *low-context communication*, in which information is (1) embedded mainly in the messages transmitted and (2) presented directly. Collectivistic cultures tend to use *high-context communication*, in which people (1) expect others to know how they're thinking and feeling and (2) present messages indirectly. Thus, low-context cultures operate on the principle of saying what you mean and getting to the point, whereas high-context cultures communicate in ways that are often ambiguous and indirect. Typically, Asians are comfortable talking for hours without clearly expressing an opinion; they may be suspicious of direct verbal expressions of love and respect. In contrast, people from low-context cultures prize clear and direct communication. Their approach may be characterized by such expressions as "Say what you mean" and "Don't beat around the bush."[6]

What does this mean to public speaking students? When you are a member of a culture that differs from that of the majority of your audience, you need to ask yourself whether language that seems clear to you will seem equally clear to your audience. If there is any question, then during your practice periods ask a person from the same culture as the majority of your audience to listen to the parts of your speech in which your wording is raising questions. Also keep in mind that people from different cultures may have different meanings for the words you are using. For example, saying that the government wants what is "best for the people" can and does mean many different things depending on one's politics, priorities, and culture.

Jonathan Nourok/PhotoEdit/PNI

People from different cultures are often able to communicate clearly with each other in informal settings. However, they may encounter misunderstandings in their communication in public speaking resulting from their differing perspectives.

If problems are apparent, then you can reword those sections of the speech. For low-context audiences, this is likely to mean using more concrete examples so that your listeners will be more likely to get the same meanings that you intend. For high-context audiences, this may mean refraining from too many examples. In this opposite case, I would be cautious about trying to be purposely ambiguous—you may only confuse yourself and your audience.

Speaking Vividly

vivid *full of life, vigorous, bright, intense*

While clear language helps the audience grasp the meaning, vivid language paints meaning in living color. **Vivid** means full of life, vigorous, bright, and intense. Vivid speech begins with vivid thought. You must have a striking mental picture before you can communicate one to your audience. If you can feel the bite of the wind and the sting of the nearly freezing rain, if you can hear the thick, juicy sirloin steaks sizzling on the grill, if you can feel the exhilaration as the jet climbs from takeoff, then you will be able to describe these sensations vividly. The more imaginatively you can think about your ideas, the more vividly you can state them.

The contrast between the following two passages illustrates the value of vivid language.

A great deal of potential was seen in Helen Keller by Anne Sullivan. She worked hard on Helen until the potential that enabled Helen to help people such as herself all over the world was realized.

Anne Sullivan saw great potential in Helen Keller. "She loved her, disciplined her, played, prayed, pushed, and worked with her until the flickering candle

Lawrence Migdale/Photo Researchers

Vivid speech begins with vivid thought. The more imaginatively you can think about your ideas, the more likely you can state them vividly.

that was her life became a beacon that helped light the pathway and lighten the burdens of people all over the world."[7]

The first passage describes what Sullivan did with and for Helen Keller. The second passage, from Beverly Chiodo's speech "Choose Wisely," vivifies the passage through active rather than passive voice, specific, active verbs that create mental pictures, and figurative language. Let's consider each of these methods for increasing vividness.

1. Use active rather than passive voice. Voice is the form of a transitive verb that tells whether the grammatical subject performs the action stated in the verb or is acted on. Casting all your sentences in active voice will lay a foundation for vivid speech. "Too many have been caught unaware" is passive voice because "many," the grammatical subject, is acted upon. "Yet many have slept through it" is active voice because "many," the grammatical subject, performs the action stated in the verb.

2. Use specific, active verbs that form sharp mental pictures. In the Helen Keller example, the general phrase "worked hard" in the first passage does not create a sharp mental picture of what Anne did. In contrast, Chiodo's "disciplined her, played, prayed, pushed" uses specific verbs that each evoke a different image.

3. Use figurative language. Figurative language involves using a word or words in an imaginative rather than a literal sense. The first passage—Anne's work "enabled Helen to help people such as herself"—states Helen's contribution literally. Chiodo's version—"the flickering candle that was her life became a beacon that helped light the pathway and lighten the burdens of people all over the world"—contains figurative language that uses words imaginatively. The "flickering candle" is a figurative expression for a life that contained potential; "her life became a beacon" is a figurative expression for a life that served as a role model.

Although there are many types of figurative language,[8] two common devices that work well in speeches are similes and metaphors.

Using Similes

Perhaps the easiest comparative figure to create is the **simile,** which is a direct comparison of dissimilar things. Similes usually contain the word *like* or *as.* Many common clichés are similes. To make a point about lack of speed, we may say, "He runs like a turtle" or "She's slow as molasses." Likewise, to dramatize a negative description, we may say, "He swims like a rock" or "She's built like a pencil." The problem with using clichés in your speeches is that their familiarity destroys the vividness they once possessed. Similes are vivid when the basis for the direct comparison is imaginative or different. Thus, "Trucks are like monstrous boxcars that eat highways for breakfast"[9] is a vivid simile. Likewise, an elementary school teacher said that being back at school after a long absence "was like trying to hold 35 corks under water at the same time"[10]—a fresh, imaginative simile for the nature of a public school teacher's task after a long holiday.

Using Metaphors

A second common comparative figure of speech is the metaphor. A **metaphor** is much like a simile, but instead of a direct comparison using *like* or *as,* a metaphor builds a direct identification between the objects being compared. Metaphors are such a common part of our language that we seldom think of them as special. We call problem cars "lemons"; we describe a baseball team's infield as a "sieve."

As you create metaphors for your speeches, avoid the trite or hackneyed. Note the creativity shown in the following examples:

Human progress is a chain, and every generation forges a little piece of it.[11]

(Replying to the statement that TV is just a toaster with pictures.) This particular toaster is not just browning bread. It is cooking our country's goose.[12]

It is imperative that we weave our fabric of the future with durable thread.[13]

And my personal favorite, describing New Orleans:

I can attest to the fact that this fair city must surely be the one place on earth where sound travels faster than light. Here is a circus of curved mirrors and distorted images of lights and shadows, of leads and red herrings—where it daily becomes more difficult to separate fact from fiction.[14]

Speaking Emphatically

In your speech, you know which words and phrases are especially important. It's up to you to help your listeners recognize their importance by emphasizing them. In this section, we consider three verbal means of emphasis: placement and sequencing, repetition, and transition.

FOCUS ON skills

Vividness

1. Revise each of the following five sentences by substituting more vivid words or phrases and by using active verbs. The first one has been done for you.

   We've got to *generate income* to enable us to *improve education.*

   (Revision: We need to *raise taxes* to *pay for smaller class size.*)

   The day *broke dark and dismal.*

   Don surprised everyone by *making a great catch.*

   A *lot of damage* to Homestead, Florida, *was caused by* Hurricane Andrew.

   Writers have found that working at a word processor *really helps them a lot.*

2. For each of the following clichés, create a fresher image.

   as cold as ice

   as happy as a lark

   selling like hot cakes

   he's playing with fire

   we have to nip that in the bud

Emphasize through Placement and Sequencing

Placement and sequencing mean constructing a list of items in such a way that the most important item comes last. If a speaker says that the president is the chief of foreign relations, commander in chief of the armed forces, head of a political party, and head of the executive branch, there is a natural tendency for the audience to perceive the last role as the most important.

placement and sequencing
constructing a list of items in such a way that the most important item comes last

Unfortunately, many speakers list items with no consideration of order. If the last item turns out to be the most trivial, the audience will perceive that item as anticlimactic. To take advantage of the natural tendency to look for the most important idea to come last, emphasize by building a sequence that moves from least important to most important.

Emphasize through Repetition or Restatement

Repetition means saying the same words again. If you say, "An analysis of more than 5,000 hours of programming on cable and broadcast television found that violence went unpunished 73% of the time—that's 73% of violent TV behavior that goes unpunished," a listener will perceive the repetition as an indication that the point must be important and should be remembered. Repetition is widely used because it is easy to practice and quite effective.

repetition *saying the same words again*

If you want the audience to remember your exact word, then repeat it once or twice: "The number is 572638—that's 5, 7, 2, 6, 3, 8," or "A ring-shaped coral island almost or completely surrounding a lagoon is called an atoll—the word is *atoll.*"

If you want the audience to remember an idea but not necessarily the specific language, you can restate, rather than repeat, it. Whereas repetition is the exact use of the same words, **restatement** means echoing the same idea but in different words—for instance, "The population is 975,439—that's roughly 1 million people," or "The test will be composed of four essay questions; that is, all the questions on the test will require you to discuss material in some detail."

restatement *echoing the same idea in different words*

Emphasize through Transition

Transitions are the words, phrases, and sentences that show relationships between and among ideas. Transitions summarize, clarify, forecast, and in almost every instance, emphasize. Of the three methods of emphasis discussed here, transition is perhaps the most effective and yet the least used.

transitions *words, phrases, and sentences that show relationships between and among ideas*

Internal Transition Internal transitions are words and phrases that link parts of a sentence in ways that help people see the relationships of the parts. In the following sentences, notice how internal transition words clarify and emphasize the relationships between ideas.

internal transitions *words and phrases that link parts of a sentence in ways that help people see the relationships of the parts*

1. Miami gets a lot of rain. Phoenix does not.
   Miami gets a lot of rain, *but* Phoenix does not.
   or
   Although Miami gets a lot of rain, Phoenix does not.
2. You should consider donating money to United Way. It will make you feel better.
   You should consider donating money to United Way *because* it will make you feel better.
3. Buckeye Savings is in good financial shape. Buckeye pays high interest.
   Buckeye Savings is in good financial shape; *moreover,* it pays high interest.

The English language contains many words that show idea relationships. Figure 10.3 lists many of the common transition words and phrases that are appropriate in a speech.[15]

Sectional Transition Recall from the discussion in Chapter 7 that sectional transitions are complete sentences placed between major sections of a speech to indicate shifts in meaning, degree of emphasis, and movement from one idea to another. Sectional transitions tell the audience exactly how it should respond.

In addition to acting as a tour guide leading the audience through the speech ("Now that we've seen how people learn to cope with hostile environments, let's consider how these coping strategies affect our perception"), sectional transitions can announce the importance of a particular word or idea. As the speaker, you know which ideas are most important, most difficult to understand, or most significant. If you state that information, the audience will know how to react. For example, you might say any of the following:

Now I come to the most important idea in the speech.

If you don't remember anything else from this presentation, make sure you remember this.

FIGURE 10.3 Common transition words and phrases and their uses

Transitions	Uses
■ also ■ and ■ likewise ■ again ■ in addition ■ moreover	■ Use these words to add material.
■ therefore ■ and so ■ so ■ finally ■ all in all ■ on the whole ■ in short	■ Use these expressions to add up consequences, to summarize, or to show results.
■ but ■ however ■ yet ■ on the other hand ■ still ■ although ■ while ■ no doubt	■ Use these expressions to indicate changes in direction, concessions, or a return to a previous position.
■ because ■ for	■ Use these words to indicate a reason for a statement.
■ then ■ since ■ as	■ Use these words to show causal or time relationships.
■ in other words ■ in fact ■ for example ■ that is ■ more specifically	■ Use these expressions to explain, exemplify, or limit.

But maybe I should say this again, because it is so important.

Pay particular attention to this idea.

These examples represent only a few of the possible expressions that interrupt the flow of ideas and interject keys, clues, and directions to stimulate audience memory or understanding.

Speaking Appropriately

During the past few years, we have seen great controversy over "political correctness," especially on college campuses. Although several issues germane to the debate on political correctness go beyond the scope of this chapter, at the heart of this controversy is the question of what language behaviors are appropriate—and what language behaviors are inappropriate.

Speaking appropriately means using language that adapts to the needs, interests, knowledge, and attitudes of the listener, and avoiding language that alienates. Appropriate language has the positive value of cementing the bond of trust between the parties in a communication transaction. When people like and trust you, they are likely to believe you. The more hostile people are to you and your ideas, the more care you need to take to use language that is sensitive to their needs. Yet, under strain, or in your eagerness to make a point, you can sometimes say things you do not really mean or express feelings that are unlikely to be accepted by strangers. If you do that, you may lose all that you have gained. In this section, we look specifically at appropriate and inappropriate language.

Formal versus Informal Language

Language is appropriate when it is neither too formal nor too informal for the situation. Your goal is to adapt your language to the specific audience to which you are speaking. Thus, we are likely to use more informal language when speaking to an audience of colleagues and more formal language when speaking to the Board of Directors.

Some people may think that adapting to an audience means speaking the way the speaker believes the members of the audience speak. Rather than being helpful, this approach is likely to be counterproductive. For instance, when an adult is giving a speech to teenagers, there is no need for that adult to try to use teen slang or street talk. Teens will recognize such attempts as phony. Likewise, an African American talking to a Hispanic audience, a European American talking to an African American audience, or a Northerner talking to a Southern audience will not improve adaptation by trying to adopt what he or she believes is the vocabulary, sentence structure, or dialect of the audience. Again, members of the audience will perceive this as condescending and question the speaker's motives.

Freedom from Jargon and Unnecessary Technical Expressions

Language is appropriate when it is free of jargon and unnecessary technical expressions. Many of us become so immersed in our work or hobbies that we forget that people who are not in our same line of work or who do not have the same hobbies are not going to understand language that seems to be such a part of our daily communication. For instance, when a computer whiz gets into a conversation with a computer-illiterate friend about computers, the whiz is going to want to carry on about RAM, bits, bytes, and other technical jargon. But

unless the whiz can learn to express ideas in language that his friend understands, little communication will take place. In short, anytime you are talking with people outside your specific work or hobby area, you need to carefully explain, if not abandon, the technical jargon and speak in language that is recognized by the person to whom you are talking.

Sensitivity in Language Use

Language is appropriate when it is sensitive to usages that others perceive as offensive. Some of the mistakes in language that we make result from using expressions that are perceived as sexist, racist, or otherwise biased—that is, any language that is perceived as belittling any person or group of people by virtue of their sex, race, age, disability, or other identifying characteristic. Three of the most prevalent linguistic uses that communicate insensitivity are generic language, nonparallel language, and stereotyping.

Generic Language   Generic language is a problem because it excludes a group of people, grammatically or connotatively, on the basis of sex. English-language examples include the generic use of *he* and *man*.

1. Generic *he*. Traditionally, English grammar called for the use of the masculine pronoun *he* to stand for the entire class of humans regardless of sex. So, in the past, standard English called for such usage as "When a person shops, he should have a clear idea of what he wants to buy." Even though such statements are grammatically correct, they are now considered sexist because they inherently exclude females.

Guideline: Do not construct sentences that use only male pronouns when no gender-specific reference is intended. You can generally avoid this usage in one of two ways. One is by using plurals. For instance, instead of saying, "Since a doctor has high status, his views may be believed regardless of topic," you could say, "Since doctors have high status, their views may be believed regardless of topic." The second method is to use both the male and female pronoun: "Since a doctor has high status, his or her views may be believed regardless of topic." These changes may seem small, but they can mean the difference between alienating or not alienating the people with whom you are speaking.

2. Generic *man*. A second problem results from the traditional use of the generic *man*. Many words that have become a common part of our language are inherently sexist because they seem to apply to only one gender. Consider the term *man-made*. What this really means is that a product was produced by human beings, but its underlying connotation is that a male human being made the item. Using such terms when speaking about all human beings is troubling, but using them to describe the behavior or accomplishments of women (as in "Sally creates and arranges man-made flowers") is ludicrous.

Guideline: Avoid using words that have built-in sexism, such as *policeman, postman, chairman, man-made,* and *mankind.* For most expressions of this kind, you can use or create suitable alternatives, such as *police officer, mail carrier,* and *chairperson.* For man-made, you might substitute *synthetic.* For *mankind,* you may need to change the construction—for example, from "All of mankind benefits," to "All the people in the world benefit."

Nonparallel Language   Nonparallel language treats groups of people differently, and as a result is belittling. Two common forms of nonparallelism are marking and unnecessary association.

marking   *adding gender, race, age, or other designations unnecessarily to a general word*

1. Marking. Marking means adding gender, race, age, or other designations unnecessarily to a general word. For instance, *doctor* is a word that represents all people with medical degrees. To describe Jones as a doctor is to treat Jones linguistically as a member of the class of doctors. For example, you might say, "Jones, a doctor, contributed a great deal to the campaign." If, however, you said, "Jones, a female doctor" (or "a black doctor," or "an old doctor," or "a handicapped doctor"), you would be marking. By marking, you are trivializing a person's role by emphasizing an irrelevant characteristic of the person. For instance, if you say "Jones is a really good female doctor" (or "black doctor," or "old doctor," or "handicapped doctor"), you may be intending to praise Jones. In reality, your audience can interpret the sentence as saying that Jones is a good doctor for a female, but not necessarily good compared to a male.

Guideline: Avoid markers by treating all groups equally. If it is relevant to identify the person by gender, race, age, and so on, do so, but leave out such markers when they are irrelevant. One test of whether a characteristic is relevant and appropriate is whether you would mention the person's sex, race, age (and so on) regardless of what sex, race, or age the person happens to be. It is relevant to specify "female doctor," for example, only if in that context it would be equally relevant to specify "male doctor." In general, leave sex, race, age, and other markers out of your labeling.

2. Unnecessary association. Another form of nonparallelism is emphasis on a person's association with another when you are not talking about the other person. Often you will hear a speaker say, "Gladys Thompson, whose husband is CEO of Procter and Gamble, is the chairperson of this year's United Way campaign." In response to this sentence, you might say that the association of Gladys Thompson with her husband gives further credentials to Gladys Thompson. But using the association seems to imply that Gladys Thompson is important not in herself but because of her relationship with her husband. The following illustrates a more flagrant example of unnecessary association: "Anita Marquez, the award-winning principal at Central High School, and wife of Juan Marquez, a local contractor, is chairperson for this year's United Way campaign." Here Juan Marquez's occupation and relationship to Anita Marquez is clearly irrelevant. In either case, the pairing takes away from the person who is supposed to be the focus.

Guideline: Avoid associating a person irrelevantly with his or her partner. If the person has done or said something noteworthy, you should recognize it without making unnecessary associations.

stereotyping   *assigning characteristics to people solely on the basis of their class or category*

Stereotyping   **Stereotyping** consists of assigning characteristics to people solely on the basis of their class or category. Stereotyping represents a shortcut in thinking. By developing an attitude or a belief about an entire group and then applying that attitude to every member of the group, a person no longer has to consider the potential for individual differences—the stereotype applies to all persons in the group. It provides some people with a certain comfort to talk about social issues in a way that states or implies that African Americans

Heather had agreed to listen to a portion of Terry's speech on nutrition. Terry said to her, "I think you'll love this opening—it's a little risky, but I think it will really get people's attention."

"It's obvious that several of you are getting pretty fat—and I know that you'd like to be looking more like normal people. Well, today I'm going to talk about nutrition and how even those of you who aren't as overweight as some others in class can still profit from following the advice that I've got to offer."

"Whoa, Terry—are you listening to what you're saying?"

"Come on, I'm just trying to get people to take a good look at themselves. My startling statement is designed to give people a jolt. And anyway, they know me and know that I don't mean anything by it."

"Terry, saying, 'It's obvious that several of you are pretty fat—and I know that you'd like to be looking more like *normal* people' isn't funny. It's flat out offensive, and you know it!"

"I still don't think most people would take it wrong. But, OK, I'll be more politically correct. How about this: 'It's obvious that a lot of you are overweight—in fact I'm sure that you'd like to get rid of some of that fat. Well, today I'm going to talk about nutrition and how even those of you who aren't so overweight can still profit from following the advice that I've got to offer.' There, that's better, isn't it?"

1. Is it better? Has Terry made sufficient changes in the opening?

2. If not, how can Terry revise further to get people to think about themselves but not be offended by his wording?

are lazy, Italians are naturally hotheaded, old people are cantankerous, or European Americans are racist.

Guideline: Avoid making statements that treat groups of people as if they can be identified by the same characteristics. Thus, in a speech, if you must make value judgments about people, make them about specific individuals, and make such statements without reference to any group with which the specific person may be associated.

You have heard children shout, "Sticks and stones may break my bones, but words will never hurt me." I think this rhyme is so popular among children because they know it is a lie, but they do not know what else to say. Whether we are willing to admit it or not, words do hurt—sometimes permanently. Consider the great personal damage done to individuals throughout history as a result of being called "hillbilly," "nigger," "fag," "yid." Consider the fights started by one person calling another a "whore." Of course, we all know that it is not the words alone that are so powerful; it is the context of the words—the situation, the feelings about the participants, the time, the place, or the tone of voice. You may recall circumstances in which a friend called you a name or used a four-letter word to describe you and you did not even flinch; you may recall other circumstances in which someone else made you furious by calling you something far less offensive.

We should always be aware that our language has repercussions. When we do not understand or are not sensitive to our listeners' frame of reference, we may state our ideas in language that distorts the intended communication. Many times a single inappropriate sentence may be enough to ruin an entire interaction. For instance, if you say "And we all know the problem originates downtown," you may be alluding to the city government. However, if your listeners associate downtown not with the seat of government but with the residential area of an ethnic or social group, the sentence will have an entirely different meaning to them. Being specific will help you avoid such problems; recognizing that some words communicate far more than their dictionary meanings will help even more.

Very few people can escape all unfair language. By monitoring your usage, however, you can guard against frustrating your attempts to communicate by assuming that others will react to your language the same way you do, and you can guard against saying or doing things that offend others and perpetuate outdated sex roles, racial stereotypes, and other biased language.

Summary

Your overall language goal is to develop a "personal" oral style that captures your uniqueness. Language usage should be guided by the knowledge that words are only representations of ideas, objects, and feelings. Meaning is often a product of word denotation (dictionary meaning), word connotation (the thoughts and feelings that words evoke), and complications arising from cultural differences.

Specific goals of language use are to state ideas clearly, vividly, emphatically, and appropriately.

Ideas are clarified through precise, specific, concrete, simple language that is devoid of clutter. Precise words are those that accurately depict your meaning. Specific and concrete words are those that call up a single image. Simple words are the least pretentious but most precise words you can find. Avoid clutter by eliminating repetitions that do not add emphasis; eliminating empty phrases; editing long sentences into shorter, emphatic sentences; and combining sentences and phrases with like ideas. A speaker must also take into account how audience members might mistake meaning if they represent a different culture from the speaker.

Vividness means full of life, vigorous, bright, and intense. Increase the vividness of your language by using active rather than passive voice, by using specific, active verbs that form sharp mental pictures, and by using figurative language, especially similes and metaphors.

Emphasis means giving certain words and ideas more importance than others. One way to emphasize is through placement and sequencing, arranging points from least to most important. A second way is through repetition or restatement. A third way is through transitions, using words and phrases that show relationships between ideas.

Appropriateness means using language that adapts to the audience's needs, interests, knowledge, and attitudes and that avoids alienating listeners. Appropriateness dictates formal versus informal language, freedom from jargon and unnecessary technical expressions, and sensitivity. Inappropriate and exclusionary language can be minimized by avoiding generic language, nonparallel language, and stereotyping.

**Delivery I say has the
sole and supreme power
of oratory.**

Cicero, *DeOratore,* III, 56

Practicing Delivery

As Nadia sat down, everyone in the audience burst into spontaneous applause.

"I don't understand it, Marv. I thought my speech was every bit as good as Nadia's, but when I got done, all I got was the ordinary polite applause that everyone gets regardless of what they've done. Of course, I'm not as pretty as Nadia."

"Come on, Syl, she's good looking, but that's not why she got such a reception. Your speech was good. You had a good topic, lots of good information, and solid organization. But, I'll tell you, buddy, you didn't deliver your speech anywhere near as well as she did."

arv recognized what has been well documented through the ages: Good delivery is a necessity of effective speaking. Why? Primarily because delivery is the source of the audience's contact with the speaker's mind. Although delivery cannot improve the ideas of a speech, it can help to make the most of those ideas. And even if you are not by nature a gifted speaker, you can improve your delivery immensely if you are willing to practice.

Although speeches may be presented impromptu (on the spur of the moment without prior preparation), by manuscript (completely written out and then read aloud), or by memory (completely written out and then memorized), the material you have been reading is designed to help you present your speeches extemporaneously. An **extemporaneous** speech is carefully prepared and practiced, but the exact wording is determined at the time of utterance.

You'll recall that speech preparation is a product of seven action steps. In this chapter, we consider the final step: practicing your speech delivery. We'll discuss characteristics of voice, articulation, and bodily action; strategies for using your voice and bodily action to achieve a conversational quality—one that shows enthusiasm, vocal expressiveness, fluency, spontaneity, and eye contact; and guidelines for effective practice. Then we will look at a sample speech.

extemporaneous *a speech that is carefully prepared and practiced, but with the exact wording determined at the time of utterance*

Physical Elements of Delivery

The physical elements of delivery include voice, articulation, and bodily action.

Voice

Your voice is the vehicle that communicates the words of your speech to the audience. How you sound may emphasize the meaning, supplement the meaning, and at times even contradict the meaning of the words you speak. As a result, how you use your voice can make the difference between the success or failure of a speech. To use it well, it is important to understand how your voice works.

Voice is produced in the larynx. As you exhale, you bring your vocal folds (muscles that protect the trachea opening) together closely enough to vibrate

ACTION STEP **seven**

Practice Delivery

Practice the speech until the delivery is enthusiastic, vocally expressive, fluent, spontaneous, and direct.

A. Use voice and bodily action to develop a conversational quality.

B. Rehearse the speech until you can deliver it extemporaneously within the time limit.

Myrleen Ferguson/PhotoEdit

Rehearsing is an essential part of preparing an effective speech. To make your practice sessions most useful, try to make them as similar as possible to the actual speech situation.

the air as it passes through them (see Figure 11.1). This vibration (called phonation) produces a weak sound that is then built up or resonated as it travels through the pharynx (throat), mouth, and in some cases, nasal cavity. The resonated sound is then shaped by the articulators (tongue, lips, palate, and teeth) to form the separate sounds of our language system. These individual sounds are then put together into words, or distinguishable oral symbols.

The four major characteristics of voice are pitch, volume, rate, and quality. Once you learn to control these characteristics, you can create vocal variety and emphasis that will help communicate your meaning effectively.

Pitch refers to the highness or lowness of your voice. As noted previously, your voice is produced in the larynx by the vibration of your vocal folds. To feel this vibration, put your hand on your throat at the top of the Adam's apple and say "ah." Now, just as the pitch of a violin string is changed by making it tighter or looser, so the pitch of your voice is changed by tightening and loosening the vocal folds. Most people have a working pitch range of more than an octave—eight full notes on a musical scale.

pitch *the highness or lowness of your voice*

Most people speak at a pitch level that is about right for them. A few, however, have pitch difficulties—that is, they talk using tones that are too high or too low for their best voice. If you have questions about your pitch level, ask your instructor about it. If you are one of the few people with a pitch difficulty, your instructor can refer you to a speech therapist for corrective work. For

FIGURE 11.1

Section of the head area and breathing apparatus, showing the relationship of the nose, mouth, pharynx (throat), larynx (which houses the vocal folds), and lungs

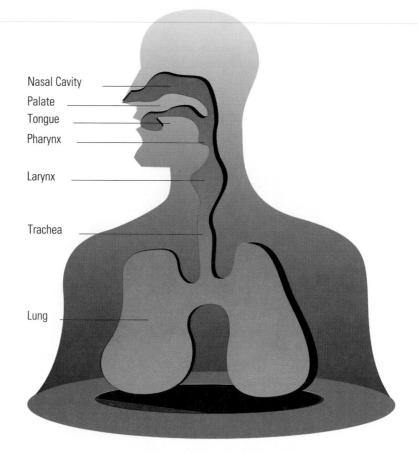

Nasal Cavity
Palate
Tongue
Pharynx
Larynx
Trachea
Lung

most people, the question is not whether they have a satisfactory pitch range but whether they are making the best use of their pitch range.

volume *the loudness of the tone you make*

Volume is the loudness of the tone you make. When you exhale normally, the diaphragm relaxes, and air is expelled through the trachea. When you speak, you supplement the force of the expelled air on the vibrating vocal folds by contracting your abdominal muscles. This greater force behind the air you expel increases the volume of your tone.

To feel how these muscles work, place your hands on your sides with your fingers extended over the stomach. Say "ah" in a normal voice. Now say "ah" as loudly as you can. If you are making proper use of your muscles, you should feel an increase in stomach contractions as you increase volume. If you feel little or no stomach muscle contraction, you are probably trying to gain volume from the wrong source; such a practice can result in tiredness, harshness, and lack of sufficient volume to be heard in a large room.

Each person, regardless of size, can make his or her voice louder. If you have trouble talking loudly enough to be heard in a large classroom, work on increasing pressure from the abdominal area while exhaling.

rate *the speed at which you talk*

Rate is the speed at which you talk. Although most people utter between 130 and 180 words per minute in normal conversation, the rate that is best for anyone is a highly individual matter. An acceptable rate of speech is determined by whether listeners can understand what you are saying. Usually, even very fast talking is acceptable when words are well articulated and when there is sufficient vocal variety and emphasis.

If your instructor believes you talk too rapidly or too slowly, he or she will tell you and may suggest ways you can improve. If you want to change your speaking rate, start by working with written passages—it makes it easier to compute your speaking rate. First, read aloud for exactly 3 minutes. When you have finished, count the number of words you have read and divide by 3 to compute the number of words you read per minute. If you perceive your reading as too fast or too slow, reread the same passage for another 3-minute period, consciously decreasing or increasing the number of words you read. Again, count the words and divide by 3.

At first, it may be difficult to change speed significantly, but with practice, you will see that you can read much faster or much slower when you want to. You may find that a different rate, whether faster or slower, will sound strange to you. To show improvement in your normal speaking, you have to learn to adjust your ear to a more appropriate rate of speed. But if you practice daily, within a few weeks you should be able to accustom your ear to changes so that you can vary your rate with the type of material you read. As you gain confidence in your ability to alter your rate, you can practice with portions of speeches. You will talk faster when material is easy or when you are trying to create a mood of excitement; you will talk more slowly when the material is difficult or when you are trying to create a somber mood.

Quality is the tone, timbre, or sound of your voice. The best vocal quality is a clear and pleasant tone. Difficulties with quality include nasality (too much resonance in the nose on vowel sounds), breathiness (too much escaping air during phonation), harshness (too much tension in the throat and chest), and hoarseness (a raspy sound). If your voice tends to have one of these undesirable qualities, consult your instructor. Although you can make some improvement on your own, significant improvement requires a great deal of work and extensive knowledge of vocal anatomy and physiology. Severe problems of vocal quality should be referred to a speech therapist.

quality *the tone, timbre, or sound of your voice*

Articulation

Articulation is the shaping of speech sounds into recognizable oral symbols that combine to produce a word. Articulation is often confused with **pronunciation**—the form and accent of various syllables of a word. In the word *statistics*, for instance, articulation refers to the shaping of the ten sounds (s-t-a-t-i-s-t-i-k-s); pronunciation refers to the grouping and accenting of the sounds (sta-tis'-tiks). If you are unsure of how to pronounce a word in a speech, consult a dictionary for the proper pronunciation.

Many speakers suffer from minor articulation problems of adding a sound where none appears (*athalete* for *athlete*), leaving out a sound where one occurs (*libary* for *library*), transposing sounds (*revalent* for *relevant*), and distorting sounds (*truf* for *truth*). Although some people have consistent articulation problems that require speech therapy (such as substituting *th* for *s* consistently in speech), most of us are guilty of carelessness that is easily corrected.

Two of the most common articulation faults for most students are slurring sounds (running sounds and words together) and leaving off word endings. Spoken English always contains some running together of sounds. For instance, most people are likely to say "tha-table" for "that table." It is simply too

articulation *the shaping of speech sounds into recognizable oral symbols that combine to produce a word*

pronunciation *the form and accent of various syllables of a word*

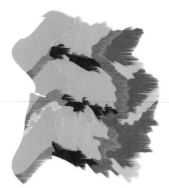

Slurring

Articulation

accent *the inflection, tone, and speech habits typical of the natives of a particular country, region, state, or city*

difficult to make two *t* sounds in a row. But many of us slur sounds and drop word endings to excess. "Who ya gonna see?" for "Who are you going to see?" illustrates both of these errors. If you have a mild case of "sluritis" caused by not taking the time to form sounds clearly, you can make considerable improvement by taking 10 to 15 minutes three days a week to read passages aloud, trying to overaccentuate each sound. Some teachers advocate "chewing" your words—that is, making sure that lips, jaw, and tongue move carefully for each sound you make. As with most other problems of delivery, speakers must work conscientiously several days a week for months to improve significantly.

Because constant mispronunciation and misarticulation may suggest ignorance or carelessness (or both), it is important to correct mistakes. Table 11.1 lists many common problem words that people are likely to mispronounce or misarticulate.

A major concern of speakers from different cultures and different parts of the country is their **accent**—the inflection, tone, and speech habits typical of the natives of a country, a region, or even a state or city. Thus, one doesn't have to be from a foreign culture to have an accent. In reality, nearly everyone speaks with some kind of an accent, since "accent" means any tone or inflection that differs from the way we and our neighbors speak. For instance, natives of a particular city or region will speak with inflections and tones that they believe are "normal" North American speech (for instance, people from the Northeast who drop the *r* sound (saying *Havad* for *Harvard*) or people from the South who "drawl." But when they visit a different city or region, they will be accused of having an "accent," because the people living in the city or region they visit hear inflections and tones that they perceive as *different* from their own speech.

When should people work to lessen or eliminate an accent? Only when the accent is so "heavy" or different from people's expectations that they have difficulty in communicating effectively, or if they expect to go into teaching, broadcasting, or other professions where an accent may have an adverse effect on their performance.

TABLE 11.1 Problem Words

WORD	INCORRECT	CORRECT
arctic	ar'-tic	arc'-tic
athlete	ath'-a-lete	ath'-lete
family	fam'-ly	fam'-a-ly
February	Feb'-yu-ary	Feb'-ru-ary
get	git	get
larynx	lar'-nix	ler'-inks
library	ly'-ber-y	ly'-brer-y
nuclear	nu'-kyu-ler	nu'-klee-er
particular	par-tik'-ler	par-tik'-yu-ler
picture	pitch'-er	pic'-ture
recognize	rek'-a-nize	rek'-ig-nize
relevant	rev'-e-lant	rel'-e-vant
theater	thee-a'-ter	thee'-a-ter
truth	truf	truth
with	wit *or* wid	with

Bodily Action

How effective you are in communicating your meaning may well depend on how your nonverbal bodily actions supplement your voice. The principal nonverbal variables that affect meaning are facial expression, gestures, movement, poise, and posture.

Facial expression refers to eye and mouth movement. The eyes and mouth communicate far more than we might realize. We need only recall the icy stare, the warm smile, or the hostile scowl we have received to understand that the eyes (and the mouth as well) mirror the mind. Your facial expression should be appropriate to what you are saying. If, for example, you get a stern look on your face when you say "City Council is not listening to the people," your facial expression adds power to your words. If, on the other hand, you smile or show no expression, your audience will be confused. Audiences look for facial expressions that seem to be reflecting your thoughts and feelings. Think actively about what you are saying, and your face will probably respond appropriately.

Gestures are movements of hands, arms, and fingers. We use gestures consciously to describe or to emphasize. When a person says "about this high" or "nearly this round," we expect to see a gesture accompanying the verbal description. Likewise, when a person says, "Put that down" or "Listen to me," we look for a pointing finger, a pounding fist, or some other gesture that reinforces the point. If you gesture in conversation, you will usually gesture in speech. If you do not gesture in conversation, it is probably best not to force yourself to gesture in a speech. Leave your hands free at all times to help you "do what comes naturally." If you clasp them behind you, grip the sides of the speaker's stand, or put your hands in your pockets, then you are not free to gesture naturally even if you want to.

facial expression *eye and mouth movement*

gestures *movements of hands, arms, and fingers*

© Joel Gordon 1995

When a person speaks emphatically, we expect to see gestures and facial expression that reinforce the words.

If you wonder what to do with your hands at the start of the speech so that they do not seem conspicuous, either rest them on the speaker's stand partially clenched or hold them relaxed at your sides—perhaps with one arm slightly bent at the elbow. Once you begin speaking, forget about your hands—they will be free for appropriate gestures. If, however, you discover that you have folded your arms in front of you or clasped them behind you, put them back in one of the two original positions. After you have spoken a few times, your instructor will suggest whether you need to be more responsive or somewhat restrained with your hands and arms.

movement   *motion of the entire body*

Movement refers to motion of the entire body. Some speakers stand perfectly still throughout an entire speech. Others are constantly on the move. In general, it is probably best to remain in one place unless you have some reason for moving. A little movement, however, adds action to a speech, so it may help hold attention. Ideally, movement should help to focus on a transition, emphasize an idea, or call attention to a particular aspect of a speech. Avoid such unmotivated movement as bobbing and weaving, shifting from foot to foot, or pacing from one side of the room to the other. At the beginning of your speech, stand up straight on both feet. If you find yourself in some peculiar posture during the course of the speech, return to the upright position with your weight equally distributed on both feet.

poise   *assurance of manner*

Poise refers to assurance of manner. A poised speaker is able to avoid mannerisms that distract the audience, such as taking off or putting on glasses, smacking the tongue, licking the lips, or scratching the nose, hand, or arm. As a general rule, anything that calls attention to itself is negative, and anything that helps reinforce an important idea is positive. Likewise, a poised speaker is able to control speech nervousness. As we discussed in Chapter 2, all speakers show varying amounts of nervousness. Poised speakers have learned to push the thought of their nervousness aside and concentrate on communicating with the audience.

posture   *the position or bearing of the body, which gives further evidence of poise*

Posture refers to the position or bearing of the body. Good posture—upright stance and squared shoulders—communicates a sense of poise to an audience. Speakers who slouch may give an unfavorable impression of themselves, including the impressions of limited self-confidence and unconcern.

Bodily action is a natural part of effective speaking. If you are thinking actively about what you are saying, your bodily action probably will be appropriate. If you use either too much or too little bodily action, your instructor can give you pointers for limiting or accenting your normal behavior. Although you may find minor errors, do not be concerned unless your bodily action calls attention to itself; then find ways of controlling or changing the behavior.

During speech practice sessions, try various methods to monitor or alter your bodily action. Videotape provides an excellent means of monitoring your bodily action. You may want to practice before a mirror to see how you look to others when you speak. (Although some speakers swear by this method, others find it a traumatic experience.) Perhaps the best method is to get a willing listener to critique your bodily action and help you improve. Once you have identified the behavior you want to change, tell your helper what to look for. For instance, you might say, "Raise your hand every time I begin to rock back and forth." By getting specific feedback when the behavior occurs, you can make immediate adjustments.

Achieving a Conversational Quality

INFOTRAC COLLEGE EDITION

Good delivery depends on excellent verbal skills, as well as excellent nonverbal communication. Using InfoTrac College Edition, conduct a search using the words "nonverbal communication" for the Subject Guide. Locate three articles that would be helpful in preparing you to develop your nonverbal behavior in your next speech.

In your speech practice, as well as in the speech itself, the final measure of your presentation is how well you use your vocal and nonverbal components to develop a **conversational quality**—a style of presentation that sounds like conversation to your listeners. Five components of conversational quality are enthusiasm, vocal expressiveness, spontaneity, fluency, and eye contact.

conversational quality   *a style of presentation that sounds like conversation to your listeners*

Enthusiasm

Enthusiasm is excitement or passion about your speech. If sounding enthusiastic does not come naturally to you, make sure you have a topic that really excites you. Even normally enthusiastic people can have trouble sounding enthusiastic when they choose an uninspiring topic. Then, focus on how your listeners will benefit from what you have to say. If you are convinced that you have something worthwhile to communicate, you are likely to feel and show more enthusiasm.

enthusiasm   *excitement or passion about a topic*

To validate the importance of enthusiasm, think of how your attitude toward a class differs depending on whether the professor's presentation says "I'm really excited to be talking with you about geology (history, English lit)" or "I'd rather be anywhere than talking to you about this subject." A speaker who looks and sounds enthusiastic will be listened to, and that speaker's ideas will be remembered.

Vocal Expressiveness

The greatest sign of enthusiasm is **vocal expressiveness**—the vocal contrasts in pitch, volume, rate, and quality that affect the meaning audiences get from the sentences you present. Read the following sentence:

> We need to prosecute abusers.

vocal expressiveness   *vocal contrasts in pitch, volume, rate, and quality that affect the meaning audiences get from the sentences you present*

What did the writer intend that sentence to mean? Without a context, who knows? Now, to illustrate how vocal expressiveness affects meaning, read the sentence aloud four times. The first time emphasize *We*, the second time emphasize *need*, the third time emphasize *prosecute*, and the fourth time emphasize *abusers* (see Figure 11.2).

When you emphasize *We*, it answers the question "Who will do it?" When you emphasize *need*, it answers the question "How important is it?" When you emphasize *prosecute*, it answers "What are we going to do?" When you emphasize *abusers*, it answers "Who will be prosecuted?" Thus, to ensure

> **We** *need to prosecute abusers.*
>
> *We* **need** *to prosecute abusers.*
>
> *We need to* **prosecute** *abusers.*
>
> *We need to prosecute* **abusers.**

audience understanding, your voice must be expressive enough to delineate shades of meaning.

monotone *a voice in which the pitch, volume, and rate remain constant, with no word, idea, or sentence differing significantly from any other*

A total lack of vocal expressiveness produces a **monotone**—a voice in which the pitch, volume, and rate remain constant, with no word, idea, or sentence differing significantly from any other. Although few people speak in a true monotone, many severely limit themselves by using only two or three pitch levels and relatively unchanging volume and rate. An actual or near monotone not only lulls an audience to sleep, but more important, diminishes the chances of audience understanding. For instance, if the sentence "Congress should pass laws limiting the sale of pornography" is presented in a monotone, listeners will be uncertain whether the speaker is concerned with who should be responsible for the laws, what Congress should do with the laws, or what the subject of the laws should be.

The following Focus on Skills exercise can help you develop your vocal expressiveness.

Spontaneity

spontaneity *being so responsive to your ideas that the speech seems as fresh as a lively conversation, even though it has been well practiced*

Spontaneity means being responsive to your ideas and their meaning while you are speaking. A spontaneous speech is fresh; it sounds as if the speaker is really thinking about both the speech and the audience as he or she speaks. In contrast, a monotonous speech that sounds like a rote recitation decreases the audience's attention to both speaker and speech.

FOCUS ON skills

Vocal Expressiveness

1. Prepare a short explanation (how to play a game or run a computer program, for example). As you prepare, concentrate on the meaning, and determine which words you will try to emphasize.

2. Have a classmate listen to your explanation and make note of which words were higher in pitch, or louder, or slower and which words were given special emphasis.

3. Compare the listener's reaction with your plan. If you spoke in such a way that the person selected the words you were trying to emphasize, you are using vocal expressiveness to clarify meaning.

Lack of spontaneity often results when speakers try to memorize their speeches. Because people who try to memorize often have to struggle so hard to remember the words, their delivery tends to become monotonous. Although talented actors can make lines that they have spoken literally hundreds of times sound spontaneous and vocally expressive, most public speakers cannot.

How can you make your outlined and practiced speech sound spontaneous? Learn the *ideas* of the speech—*don't memorize words*. Suppose someone asks you about the route you take on your drive to work. Because you are familiar with the route, you can present it spontaneously. You have never written out the route, nor have you memorized it—you "know it." You develop spontaneity in public speaking by getting to know the ideas in your speech as well as you know the route you take to work. Study your outline and absorb the material you are going to present, but do not try to memorize how you are going to present it. We will consider spontaneity further when we get to methods of speech rehearsal.

Fluency

Effective delivery is not only expressive and spontaneous; it is also **fluent**—devoid of hesitations and vocal interferences. Although most of us are occasionally guilty of using some vocal interferences (extraneous sounds or words that interrupt fluent speech), these interferences become a problem when they are perceived by others as excessive and when they begin to call attention to themselves and so prevent listeners from concentrating on meaning. The most common interferences that creep into our speech are *uh, er, well,* and *OK,* along with those nearly universal interrupters of Americans' conversation, *you know* and *like.*

Vocal interferences are difficult to eliminate from speech, but they can be reduced through awareness and practice. Vocal interferences are often caused by a fear of momentary silence that may lead to being interrupted. To avoid silent gaps in speaking, many people fill the "dead air time" with such filler sounds as *uh, er, well,* and *um.* Although the chance of being interrupted may be real (some people will seek to interrupt at any pause), the intrusion of an excessive number of fillers is a high price to pay to prevent an occasional interruption.

Equally prevalent, and perhaps even more disruptive than filler sounds, is the incessant use of *you know* and *like.* The *you know* habit may begin as a way to find out whether what we are saying is already known by others. For some, *you know* may be a source of identification—a way of showing that we and those to whom we are talking share common knowledge. For most people, however, the flooding of sentences with *you know* is simply a bad habit, resulting in such incoherent statements as "You know, Maxwell is, you know, a good, you know, lecturer."

Similarly, the use of *like* may start from making comparisons such as "He's hot, he looks like Tom Cruise." Soon the comparisons become shortcut, as in "He's like really hot!" Finally, the use of *like* becomes pure filler: "Like, he's really cool, like I can't really explain it, but I'll tell you he's like hot!"

Curiously, listeners are unlikely to acknowledge their irritation with a speaker's use of *you know* or *like,* even when the use affects their attention to your ideas. So, if you want to know whether your use of these interferences is excessive, you need to ask your listeners directly. The following steps can help you decrease your use of interferences.

fluent *devoid of hesitations and vocal interferences*

interestingly
...grammed immediately. Anything t...
utilizes a formula, no matter how to
For example, we can make any sort
from one mathematical system of the
another, we can interpret data, we can
stigate mathematical models of physic
curances. Pascal allows us to progr
s a super calculator. As long as
...n algorithm, or design, or formula
at calculates

HOW CAN WE JUSTIFY

If you're *not* using safety belts *now,* it's time to start. **Safety belts save lives!**

Variety: Which of these speakers would you rather listen to?

Fluency

Work in groups, taking turns. Each person selects his or her own topic — such as a current event in the news, a critique of a recent movie, or a description of a job/course problem — and tries to talk continuously for 2 minutes. Whenever the speaker uses a vocal interference, the other members of the group raise their hands. One group member should be assigned the task of counting and recording the number of times that hands were raised (if two hands were raised at the same time, count it as only one vocal interference). Give everyone two chances. Work to eliminate vocal interferences.

1. Train yourself to hear your interferences. Even people with a major problem seem unaware of the interferences they use. You can train your ear in at least two ways:

a. Tape-record yourself talking for several minutes about any subject — the game you saw yesterday, the course you plan to take next term, or anything else that comes to mind. Before you play it back, estimate the number of times you think you peppered your speech with *uh*, *you know*, and *like*. Then compare the actual number with your estimate. As your ear becomes trained, your estimates will be closer to the actual number.

b. Have a close friend listen to you and raise a hand every time you use a filler such as *uh* or *you know*. The experience may be traumatic or nerve-wracking, but your own ear will soon start to pick up the vocal interferences as fast as the listener's.

2. Practice seeing how long you can talk without using a vocal interference. Begin by talking for 15 seconds. Gradually increase the time until you can talk for 2 minutes without a single interference. Meaning may suffer, and you may spend a disproportionate amount of time avoiding interferences. Still, it is good practice.

3. Mentally note your interferences in conversation and in speech making. You will make real headway when you can recognize your own interferences in real communication settings. When you reach this stage, you will find yourself avoiding and limiting interferences.

Eye Contact

eye contact *looking at various groups of people in all parts of an audience throughout a speech*

Eye contact, or directness, involves looking at various groups of people in all parts of an audience throughout a speech. As long as you are looking at people (those in front of you, in the left rear of the room, in the right center of the room, and so on) and not at your notes or the ceiling, floor, or window, everyone in the audience will perceive you as having good eye contact.

One way of ensuring eye contact is to think of your audience as a collection of groups sitting in various places in the audience. Then, at random, talk for 4 to 6 seconds with each group. Perhaps start with a Z pattern. Talk with the group in the back left for a few seconds, then glance at people in the far right for a few seconds, and then move to a group in the middle, a group in the front left, and then a group in the front right. Then perhaps reverse the order, starting in the back right. Eventually you'll find yourself going in a random pattern in which you look at all groups over a period of a few minutes. Such a pattern ensures that you do not spend a disproportionate amount of your time talking with those in front of you or in the center of the room.

Maintaining eye contact is important for several reasons.

1. Maintaining eye contact helps audiences concentrate on the speech. If speakers do not look at us while they talk, we are unlikely to maintain eye contact with them. This break in mutual eye contact often decreases concentration on the speaker's message.

2. Maintaining eye contact increases the audience's confidence in you, the speaker. Just as you are likely to be skeptical of people who do not look you in the eye as they converse, so too audiences will be skeptical of speakers who do not look at them. Eye contact is perceived as a sign of sincerity. Speakers who fail to maintain eye contact with audiences are perceived almost always as ill at ease and often as insincere or dishonest.[1]

3. Maintaining eye contact helps you gain insight into the audience's reaction to the speech. Because communication is two-way, your audience is speaking to you at the same time you are speaking to it. In conversation, the audience's response is likely to be both verbal and nonverbal; in public speaking, the audience's response is more likely to be shown by nonverbal cues alone. Audiences that pay attention are likely to look at you with varying amounts of intensity. Listeners who do not pay attention are likely to yawn, look out the window, and slouch in their chairs. By monitoring your audience's behavior, you can determine what adjustments, additions, and deletions you should make in your plans. As speakers gain greater skill, they can make more and better use of the information they get about listeners through eye contact with them.

Rehearsal

Now that you have your outline and an overall plan of what you need to do to ensure interest and understanding, you are ready to begin **rehearsing**—practicing the presentation of your speech aloud. In this section, we consider a timetable for preparation and practice, the use of speech notes, and some specifics of individual rehearsal sessions.

rehearsing *practicing the presentation of a speech aloud*

Timetable for Preparation and Practice

Too often, speakers believe that they are ready to present the speech once they have finished their outline. But if you are scheduled to speak at 9 A.M. Monday and you don't finish the outline until 8:45, the speech is likely to be far less effective than it would have been had you allowed yourself sufficient practice time. It is only through practicing the speech aloud that you can assure effective presentation.

You might think it's asking a lot to actually practice your speech a few times. Let's put this in perspective. Michael Jordan has been acknowledged to be the best basketball player of his day, and perhaps of all time. Why, he's so good that he doesn't have to practice, right? Wrong! His coach and fellow players attest to the fact that Jordan practices as long or longer than any of the players on the team. Or let's consider an even more astounding example. In the book *Iron and Silk*, an American goes to live in China and teach English. While there, he studies Kung Fu with a Chinese master, who teaches him for 5 min-

7 days before	Select topic; begin research
6 days before	Continue research
5 days before	Outline body of speech
4 days before	Work on introduction and conclusion
3 days before	Finish outline; find additional material if needed; have all visual aids completed
2 days before	First rehearsal session
1 day before	Second rehearsal session
Due date	Give speech

TECHNOLOGY tips

Arrange to videotape yourself rehearsing your speech. As you review the videotape, focus on your enthusiasm, vocal expressiveness, fluency, spontaneity, and eye contact. Identify the sections where your delivery was particularly effective and the sections where you need to improve. Then, practice the sections that you believe need the most work. After a few run throughs, re-record those sections of the speech. You will be pleased with the improvement.

speech notes   *a word or phrase outline, plus hard-to-remember information such as quotations and statistics*

utes a day and then tells to practice. "How long?" Mark asks him. "For six hours a day!" That's right, 5 minutes of class and six hours of practice!

In general, try to complete your outline at least two days before a speech is due so that you have sufficient practice time to revise, evaluate, and mull over all aspects of the speech. Figure 11.3 suggests an appropriate timetable for preparing a classroom speech.

Is there really a relationship between practice time and speech effectiveness? A study by Menzel and Carrell offers tentative confirmation for the general hypothesis that more preparation time leads to better speech performance. They concluded, "The significance of rehearsing out loud probably reflects the fact that verbalization clarifies thought. As a result, oral rehearsal helps lead to success in the actual delivery of a speech."[2]

Using Notes during Your Speech

Speech notes consist of a word or phrase outline of the speech, plus hard-to-remember information such as quotations and statistics. Appropriate notes are composed of key words or phrases that help trigger your memory. Notes will

When a speaker's notes are really a complete outline or a manuscript, chances for effective delivery are lessened considerably. Prepare a few note cards that can be used to refresh memory, not as a crutch.

Peter Chapman

be most useful to you when they consist of the fewest words possible, in lettering large enough to be seen instantly at a distance. Many speakers condense their written preparatory outline into a brief word or phrase outline.

For a speech in the 3- to 5-minute range, one or two 3-by-5-inch note cards are all you will need. For a speech in the 5- to 10-minute range, three to four note cards should be enough: one card for goal and introduction, one or two cards for the body, and one card for the conclusion. When your speech contains a particularly good quotation or a complicated set of statistics, you may want to write them in detail on separate 3-by-5 cards.

Let's return to the example of Emming's speech on credit cards. First, review the first draft of his abbreviated outline, shown in Figure 7.2 (page 134). Now let's see how Emming might put this reduced outline on two 3-by-5 note cards. Figure 11.4 represents a phrase outline, Figure 11.5 a key word outline. You may be more comfortable with one or the other, or perhaps a mix of the two. Then, if Emming has a quotation or some statistics that he wants to be sure to state accurately, he can put those on another card or two.

During practice sessions, use your notes as you would in the speech. Either set the notes on the speaker's stand or hold them in one hand and refer to them only when needed. Speakers often find that the act of making a note card is so

FIGURE 11.4 Phrase Note Cards

How many hounded by vendors?
Three criteria: IR, Fee, Perk
1st C: examine IR's
IR's are % charged
• Average of 18%
• As much as 21%
• start 6–8%, but restrictions
IR's variable or fixed
• Variable changes
• Fixed stays same
T considered IR's: next C
2d C: examine annual fee
AF cost company charges
Vary
• Some no annual
• Most av $25
T IR's, fees, weigh bens
3d C: weigh perks—extras
• rebates
• freq flyer miles
• discounts
P's not outweigh factors
So, 3 C's IR, Fee, Perk

FIGURE 11.5 Word Note Cards

Hounded?
3 C's
IR's
percents
18 av
21 high
6–8
variable/fixed
change
stay same
T
Ann Fee
charges
vary
from no
av $25
T
Perks—extras
rebates
freq flyer
discounts
not outweigh
So, 3 C's

effective in helping cement ideas in the mind that during practice, or later during the speech itself, they do not need to use the notes at all.

Remember that you will also want to make sure that you practice using visual aids in your rehearsals. As we said in Chapter 9, you should indicate on your notes exactly when you will use each visual aid (and when you will remove it). Work on statements for introducing the visual aids, and practice different ways of showing the visual aids until you are satisfied that everyone in the audience will be able to see them.

Rehearsal Sessions

A good rehearsal session involves practicing the speech, analyzing it, and practicing it again.

First Practice   Your initial rehearsal should include the following steps.

1. Tape-record your practice session. If you do not own a recorder, try to borrow one. You may also want to have a friend sit in on your practice.

2. Read through the outline once or twice to refresh ideas in your mind. Then put the outline out of sight.

3. Make the practice as similar to the speech situation as possible, including using any visual aids you've prepared. Stand up and face your imaginary audience. Pretend that the chairs, lamps, books, and other objects in your practice room are people.

4. Write down the time that you begin.

5. Begin speaking. Keep going until you have presented your entire speech.

6. Write down the time you finish. Compute the length of the speech for this first practice.

Analysis   Replay the tape. Look at your outline again. Did you leave out any key ideas? Did you talk too long on any one point and not long enough on another? Did you clarify each of your points? Did you try to adapt to your anticipated audience? (If you had a friend or relative listen to your practices, then have that listener help with your analysis.)

Second Practice Go through the six steps outlined for the first practice. By practicing a second time right after your analysis, you are more likely to make the kind of adjustments that begin to improve the speech.

Additional Rehearsals After you have completed one full rehearsal, consisting of two sessions of practices and analysis, put the speech away until that night or the next day. Although you may need to go through the speech one or several more times, there is no value in cramming all the practices into one long rehearsal time. You may find that an individual practice right before you go to bed will be very helpful; while you are sleeping, your subconscious will continue to work on the speech. As a result, you are likely to find significant improvement in your mastery of the speech when you practice again the next day.

How many times you practice depends on many variables, including your experience, your familiarity with the subject, and the length of your speech.

Ensuring Spontaneity When practicing, try to learn the speech, not memorize it. Recall that memorizing the speech involves saying the speech the same way each time until you can give it word for word without notes. **Learning the speech** involves understanding the ideas of the speech, but having the freedom to word the ideas differently during each practice.

learning the speech under-standing the ideas of the speech, but having the freedom to word the ideas differently each time

Let us illustrate the method of learning a speech by using a short portion of the speech outline on pages 132–133 of Chapter 7 as the basis for rehearsal. That portion of the outline reads as follows:

A. Interest rates are the percentages that a company charges you to carry a balance on your card past the due date.

   1. Most credit cards carry an average of 18%.

Now let's consider three practices that focus on this small portion of the outline.

First practice: "Interest rates are the percentages that a company charges you to carry a balance on your card past the due date. Most credit cards carry an average of 18%. Did you hear that? 18%!"

Second practice: "Interest rates are the percentages that a company charges you when you don't pay the balance in full and thus still owe the company money. Most credit cards carry an average of 18%. Did you hear that? 18%! So, if you leave a balance, every month before you know it, you're going to be paying a lot more money than you thought you would."

Third practice: "Interest rates are the percentages that a company charges you when you don't pay the balance in full and thus still owe the company money. Most credit cards carry an average of 18%. Did you hear that? A whopping 18%, at a time when you can get about any kind of a loan for less than 10%. Of course, if you pay off your balance, there's no cost—but high percentages of credit card holders don't, and thus rack up a lot of extra costs."

Notice that points A and 1 of the outline are in all three versions; the essence of the outline will be part of all your practices. But because you have made slight variations each time, when you finally give the speech there will be that sense of spontaneity. In your speech, you will probably use a wording that is most meaningful to you. At the same time, you will be assured that you are likely to get the key point across.

Criteria for Evaluating Speeches

As we said in Chapter 3, in addition to learning to prepare and present speeches, you are learning to analyze critically the speeches you hear. From a pedagogical standpoint, critical analysis of speeches not only provides the speaker with both an analysis of where the speech went right and where it went wrong but also gives you, the critic, insight into the methods that you want to incorporate, or perhaps avoid, in presenting your own speeches.

In the past several chapters, you have been learning not only the steps involved in speech preparation but also the criteria by which speeches are measured. The critical assumption is that if a speech has good content, is well organized, and is well presented, it is more likely to achieve its goal. Thus, the critical apparatus for evaluating any speech comprises questions that relate to the basics of content, organization, and presentation.

For this first major speech, we recommend using the Speech Evaluation Checklist on page 219, which includes a series of questions covering all aspects of speech preparation and delivery. But for this first speech, the principal emphasis will be on clarity of goal, clarity and appropriateness of main points, and delivery.

Summary

Delivery refers to the use of voice and body to communicate the message of the speech; it is what the audience sees and hears.

Although speeches may be delivered impromptu, by manuscript, or memorized, in this course we focus on speeches that are presented extemporaneously—prepared and practiced, but with the exact wording determined at the time of speaking.

The physical elements of delivery include voice, articulation, and bodily action. The four major characteristics of voice are pitch, volume, rate, and quality. Pitch refers to the highness or lowness of a voice. Volume is the loudness of tone. Rate is the speed at which a speaker talks. Quality is tone, timbre, or sound of a voice.

Effective speakers also are careful with their articulation, the shaping of speech sounds, and their pronunciation, the form and accent of various syllables.

Check items that were accomplished effectively.

Content

_____ **1.** **Was the goal of the speech clear?**

_____ **2.** Did the speaker have high-quality information?

_____ **3.** Did the speaker use a variety of kinds of developmental material?

_____ **4.** Were visual aids appropriate and used well?

_____ **5.** Did the speaker establish common ground and adapt the content to the audience's interests, knowledge, and attitudes?

Organization

_____ **6** Did the introduction gain attention, gain goodwill for the speaker, and lead into the speech?

_____ **7.** **Were the main points clear, parallel, and meaningful complete sentences?**

_____ **8.** Did transitions lead smoothly from one point to another?

_____ **9.** Did the conclusion tie the speech together?

Presentation

_____ **10.** Was the language clear?

_____ **11.** Was the language vivid?

_____ **12.** Was the language emphatic?

_____ **13.** **Did the speaker sound enthusiastic?**

_____ **14.** **Did the speaker show sufficient vocal expressiveness?**

_____ **15.** **Was the presentation spontaneous?**

_____ **16.** **Was the presentation fluent?**

_____ **17.** **Did the speaker look at the audience?**

_____ **18.** Were the pronunciation and articulation acceptable?

_____ **19.** Did the speaker have good posture?

_____ **20.** Was speaker movement appropriate?

_____ **21.** Did the speaker have sufficient poise?

Based on these criteria, evaluate the speech as (check one):
_____ excellent, _____ good, _____ satisfactory, _____ fair, _____ poor.

Nonverbal bodily actions affect a speaker's meaning. Facial expression, gestures, movement, poise, and posture all work together in effective speaking.

Effective speeches achieve a conversational quality, including enthusiasm, vocal expressiveness (variety, emphasis, and freedom from monotonous tone), spontaneity (sounding fresh, not memorized), fluency (freedom from such vocal interferences as *uh, um, well, you know,* and *like*), and eye contact.

Between the time the outline is completed and the speech is given, it is important to practice the speech several times, weighing what you did and how you did it after each practice. During these practice periods, you will work on presenting ideas spontaneously and using notes effectively.

Ridding the Body of Toxins[3]

The following outline, approximately 325 words, is an appropriate length when considering that the specific goal, thesis statement, and transitions that are written out in full are included in the count. As you then read the speech that follows, you'll notice how Roxanne uses other material to build the speech and adapt to her audience.

Outline

Specific Goal: I want my audience to understand the elements involved in ridding the body of toxins.

Introduction

I. Hippocrates said that every one of us has a doctor within ourselves—we just have to help him with his work.

II. We can help that doctor within us by working to reduce toxins that make us sick.

Thesis Statement: Three important elements in eliminating toxins from the body are eliminating or reducing animal foods from the diet, keeping our bodies well hydrated, and eating natural whole foods.

Body

I. The first element is eliminating or reducing animal foods from the diet.

    A. Animal foods are filled with toxins.

        1. Toxins develop from microorganisms.

        2. Toxins are added in processing.

        3. Toxins exist in packaging.

    B. Animal foods are also difficult for our bodies to digest.

        1. Meat may sit in our intestines for days.

        2. Toxins that develop eventually escape into our systems, making us ill.

    C. Eliminating animal foods keeps our bodies from absorbing toxins.

(And now that we know the value of eliminating animal foods, let's go on to the second element that's involved in ridding ourselves of toxins.)

II. The second element is keeping ourselves well hydrated.

    A. Drinking four to six glasses of water per day keeps our feces moistened so they move through the system more quickly.

    B. Drinking water prevents waste material from hanging around too long.

(Now we can move on to the third element of ridding ourselves of toxins.)

III. The third element is using natural whole foods.

    A. Natural whole foods work to eliminate toxins.

B. To get maximum value, leave the skin on foods.

    1. The skin of vegetables adds roughage and bulk.

    2. Roughage and bulk also help waste move through the system quickly.

Conclusion

I. The three elements of eliminating body toxins are eliminating or reducing animal foods, keeping ourselves well hydrated, and adopting a natural whole food diet.

II. Because "Wellness starts within ourselves," we have to be our own physician.

Sources

Afrika, Llailo O. *Afrikan Holistic Health*, 4th ed. Brooklyn, NY: A & B Books, 1993.

Fuhrman, Joel. *Fasting and Eating for Health*. New York: Simon and Schuster, 1995.

Monte, Tom. *How to Stay Young*. New York: Rodale Press, 1994.

Tierra, Michael. *The Way of Herbs*. New York: Simon and Schuster, 1989.

Tortora, Gerard. *Principles of Anatomy and Physiology*, 8th ed. New York: HarperCollins, 1996.

Plan for Adapting to Audience

1. Getting and maintaining interest. I plan to begin the speech with a quotation to capture audience attention. During the speech, I will use personal stories and visual aids to help maintain interest and personal pronouns to adapt to my audience.

2. Facilitating understanding. I do not believe the information I will present is difficult to understand. I will work to keep technical jargon to a minimum. I believe that my examples, which are relevant to class experience, as well as my visual aids, will help make the information easy to understand.

3. Organization. I have organized my speech following a topical pattern. All three of my main points are complete sentences, and I will have transitions between points.

4. Building credibility. I plan to build credibility by pointing out that I worked in a doctor's office.

Thinking Critically: Speech Analysis

Read the following speech aloud. Then, analyze it on the basis of key criteria drawn from the Speech Evaluation Checklist on page 219: clear goal; introduction that gets attention and leads into the speech; clear, parallel, meaningful, complete-sentence main points; meaningful development; conclusion that ties the speech together and leaves it on a high note. Compare your thoughts with the speech analysis provided in the margin.

Speech

Thousands of years ago, Hippocrates said that every one of us has a doctor within ourselves—we just have to help him with his work. A natural healing force is the strongest force in getting well. Our food should be our medicine, and our medicine should be our food. But to eat when we are sick is to feed the

Analysis

Roxanne uses a quotation to get audience attention.

In this part of the introduction, she provides us a basis for listening to her speech.

symptoms. Many of us today—here today—suffer from time to time with illness, and we ask ourselves, "Why are we getting sick?" Well, to answer that question in just one word: toxins. Toxins that exist naturally in the environment and toxins that we ingest over time will throw our systems off balance and eventually make us ill.

I'd like to share with you three elements in eliminating toxins from your body.

As you can see, the first element is eliminating or reducing animal foods from your diet.

You see, animal foods are filled with toxins. Toxins that exist—that exist naturally because they develop from microorganisms that are present in decaying flesh. Toxins such as sodium nitrates and sodium nicanotates that are added in processing, and toxins that are in the packaging that cover the meat that we buy.

In addition, animal foods are difficult for our bodies to digest. We are not particularly equipped to move meat from our system because our digestive tract is 30 feet long.

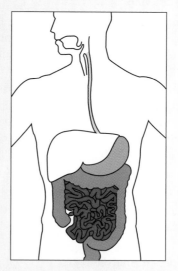

So, when we eat meat, it's often going to sit there for up to three days. It's sitting there for microorganisms to grow and for the toxins to develop from these microorganisms.

And now that we know why meat is one of the primary sources for toxins that we want to eliminate, let's go on to the second element that's involved in ridding ourselves of toxins.

The second element is keeping ourselves well hydrated. Water is vital in eliminating toxins from our body. Why? Because water moistens the feces that are made up of indigestible materials, waste products, such as sloughed off mycoflora cells from the inside of your intestines, as well as the bacteria. And according to Dr. Marvin Shuster, who is a professor and the head of the Division of Digestive Diseases at Johns Hopkins Teaching Hospital, our main source of water is from what we ingest. So he recommends that we drink at least four to

---

Here she previews main points.

Roxanne's first main point on eliminating animal foods is emphasized with her overhead visual aid. Although the visual aid contains the heading and abbreviated statements of her three main points, only the heading and first point could be seen—the other two were covered. Then as she stated each of the other points, she uncovered them. This is a good technique for maintaining focus.

Good specific information, reinforced with a visual aid.

Also notice use of personal pronouns.

Good transition to her second main point.

Roxanne's second main point, also a complete sentence, focuses on keeping hydrated.

Notice how she cites her source.

six glasses of water per day. Enough to keep our feces moistened so that we can have an adequate bowel movement. For if waste material hangs around too long in the intestines, microorganisms grow, adding to toxins that keep us sick.

OK, so we want to rid ourselves of toxins by drinking enough water that we'll moisten the feces. And now that we know to keep ourselves hydrated, let's move on to the third element of ridding ourselves of toxins.

Another good transition.

That third element is using natural whole foods. Now, natural whole foods can rid our body of toxins because they are whole foods. You've seen white rice—it's polished, it's not a whole grain. Brown rice is a whole grain. When we fix vegetables, instead of scraping the skin off, we want to use the complete vegetable. Like we have a carrot, we'll use the whole thing. We clean it, but we don't peel the skin off because that adds roughage and bulk that we need to help move those feces through the intestinal tract, again, so they don't hang around too long and make us ill.

Her third complete-sentence main point focuses on whole foods.

Good explanation. We see why it is important to eat the peel.

Now, another thing about whole foods is that it's based on the concept of wholeness or balance. Yin yang? You've heard of that? OK, that's where we treat the entire body. We just don't go after the symptoms, we treat the whole thing. And that's one thing we need to do when we are sick. Instead of just going toward what we think is making us ill, it's our whole body that's off kilter, so we have to treat the whole body instead of just parts of it.

Notice how she continues to emphasize balance.

Ridding ourselves of toxins can pay big dividends. For instance, I've got a nephew who cleared up his complexion just from eliminating meat from his diet. He had suffered from acne since he was a young teenager. And now he's about 22 years old. Two years ago he tried to eliminate meat from his diet and increase his reliance on natural foods, and his complexion cleared up.

Good use of a personal example to hold attention and give support.

So now we know that the three elements of eliminating body toxins are eliminating or reducing animal foods, keeping ourselves well hydrated, and also adopting a natural whole food diet. Because, as Hippocrates said, "Wellness starts within ourselves." So, we have to be our own physician. Thank you, and be well. ■

She begins her conclusion by reviewing the three elements. Her final sentence repeats her opening to give it additional emphasis. Throughout the speech, Roxanne has clear main points, good explanation, and good transitions. This is a good example of a first speech that follows a topical pattern.

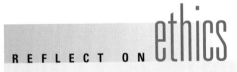

REFLECT ON ethics

**Any piece of knowledge
I acquire today has a
value at this moment ex-
actly proportioned to my
skill to deal with it.**

Ralph Waldo Emerson,
"Natural History of Intellect," 1871

Principles and Practices of Informative Speaking

For several months, a major architectural firm had been working on designs for the arts center to be built in the middle of downtown. Members of the city council and guests from various constituencies in the city, as well as a number of concerned citizens, were taking their seats as the long anticipated presentation was about to begin. As Linda Garner, mayor and presiding officer of the city council, finished her introduction, Donald Harper, the principal architect of the project, walked to the microphone to begin his speech.

S cenarios like this are played out every day as speakers struggle to help us increase our understanding of complex issues. More than a century ago, Ralph Waldo Emerson succinctly captured the challenge of adapting information to a specific audience in the chapter opening quote: "Any piece of knowledge I acquire today has a value at this moment exactly proportioned to my skill to deal with it."

As an informative speaker, your rhetorical goal is to present information in a way that holds interest, facilitates understanding, and increases the likelihood of remembering. We begin by focusing on principles of informing that you can use to consider (1) *how* to create interest so the audience will listen, (2) *how* to explain in a way that will help the audience understand, and (3) *how* to discuss the information in a way that will help the audience remember. The second part of the chapter focuses on the informative speaking skills of exposition, demonstration or explanation of processes, and definition.

INFOTRAC COLLEGE EDITION

Using InfoTrac College Edition, click on "learning, psychology of" in the Subject Guide. Look for articles that discuss "how people learn" and "how people think" in order to gain additional information that is relevant to informative speaking. Read one or more articles to help you better understand how to prepare your informative speech.

Principles of Informing

You will be a more effective informative speaker if you apply principles of credibility, intellectual stimulation, creativity, relevance, and emphasis.

Credibility

Principle 1 Audiences are more likely to listen to you if they like, trust, and have confidence in you.

Although we've already discussed the bases of credibility (knowledge/expertise, trustworthiness, and personality), we emphasize it here because building or maintaining your credibility is essential to your success. If your listeners have faith in you, they'll be more willing to learn. The following three points are mentioned as reminders of what you must do in your speeches.

1. **Demonstrate your expertise.** As an informative speaker, you must talk knowledgeably and fluently with command of your information and without stumbling and making a variety of misstatements.

2. **Emphasize your interest in audience well-being.** Likewise, you must show your listeners that you care about them and what happens to them.

3. **Look and sound enthusiastic.** Finally, you must show enthusiasm for your information.

You will probably see the cumulative effect of credibility during this term. As your class proceeds from speech to speech, some speakers will grow in stature in your mind and others will diminish.

Intellectual Stimulation

Principle 2 Audiences are more likely to listen to information they perceive to be intellectually stimulating.

Information will be perceived as **intellectually stimulating** when it is new to audience members and when it meets deep-seated needs to know.

When we say *new*, we mean information that most of the audience is not familiar with or that presents new insights or twists on familiar topics. If you

intellectually stimulating *information that is new to audience members and/or meets deep-seated needs to know*

Robert Clay/Jeroboam

As an informative speaker, your goal is to present information so that it holds interest and increases understanding and remembering.

really have researched your topic, you are likely to have information that will be new to a majority of your audience.

For example, a topic that is likely to be perceived as new and is very important for college students—especially women—to learn about is the drug Rohypnol. On the one hand, it gives a cheap but dangerous high; on the other hand, some people use it to lower the defenses and resistance of others. Even if the audience has heard about the "date-rape drug," they are unlikely to know much of its history, properties, and other dangers.

But even when you are considering talking about a topic that most of the people in your audience are familiar with, you can brainstorm new angles, new applications, or new perspectives. For instance, during the basketball season, a player (or a real aficionado) who first considers talking about how to shoot a jump shot would be wiser to brainstorm other topics that would give viewers a better understanding of the game as they watch it. For instance, the player might brainstorm "pick and roll," "matchup zone defenses," "using the press," or "breaking a press"—topics that casual fans may have heard of but may not really understand very well.

But just being new is not enough. The information must also meet the audience's deep-seated hunger for knowledge and insight. Part of the informative speaker's job is to feed that hunger. Every day we are touched by ideas and issues that we don't fully grasp. But we often ignore those ideas and issues, partly because we don't have sufficient motivation to find additional information. For instance, several years ago scientists discovered an "ice man"—the well-preserved body of a man who lived between four and five thousand years ago, buried in a glacier of the southern Alps. Newspaper headlines announced the discovery, and while readers were excited by the information, they probably did not pursue the topic. The informative speaker seizes the topic and links the significance of the ice man to an understanding of our own history and development that may well stimulate our natural intellectual curiosity.

Let's consider a more typical example. Suppose you are planning a speech on new cars. From just the data you could draw from the April issue of *Consumer Reports* (the month in which comparative statistics and ratings are given for all new cars), you could find information that would be intellectually stimulating. For instance, we are aware that over time Japanese-made cars have captured an increasingly large share of the American market, at least partly because of perceived quality issues. How are American companies responding to those issues? Are American-made cars achieving higher quality ratings? Are American-made cars "competitive"? Are sales increasing? Equally stimulating speeches could explore information on safety features, mileage data, and styling.

To find a topic, you can still work off your brainstorming list. But for an important informative speech, don't be satisfied with a superficial topic. Brainstorm until you have a new angle that you can pursue.

The following are some topics that meet this important criterion. Keep in mind that the following are just "headings." If one of the following strikes a chord with you, work with it until you can arrive at an aspect of the topic that will be intellectually stimulating.

acupuncture	stock market	global warming	AIDS
hurricanes	sexual harassment	Social Security	cloning
vegetarianism	Special Olympics	homophobia	poverty
child abuse	media violence	environment	welfare
immigration	sports values	censorship	discrimination

Creativity

Principle 3   Audiences are more likely to listen to, understand, and remember information that is presented creatively.

Creativity can be defined as a person's capacity to produce new or original ideas and insights.[1] Although you may be thinking, "I'm just not a creative person," all of us can be creative if we are willing to work at it. Let's consider some guidelines and procedures that can help you become a more creative speaker.

creativity *a person's capacity to produce new or original ideas and insights*

1. Gather enough high-quality information to give you a broad base from which to work. Contrary to what many people think, creativity is more likely a product of perspiration than inspiration. If you have more high-quality information than you really need for the speech, you have more flexibility and choices.

2. Give yourself enough time for the creative process to work. Many students finish their outline just in time to "go over the speech" once before they present it—then they wonder why they're not able to "be creative." Your mind needs time to reflect on your outline and information. This is why we recommend completing your outline for a classroom speech *at least* two days before the actual presentation. With that extra time available, you're likely to find that the morning after an uninspiring practice you suddenly have two or three fresh ideas to work with. While you were sleeping, your mind was still going over the material. When you awoke, the product of unconscious or subconscious thought reached your consciousness. So, you can facilitate creatively simply by giving your mind time to work with your information.

3. Be prepared to pursue a creative idea when it comes. Have you ever noticed how ideas seem to come at odd times, like while you're cleaning your room, mulching the garden, or waiting at a stoplight? Have you also noticed that when you try to recall those "great" ideas, they are likely to have slipped away? Many speakers, writers, and composers carry pencil and paper with them at all times, and when an idea comes, they make a note of it. Not all of these flights of fancy are flashes of creative genius, but some of them are good or at least worth exploring. If you do not make note of your ideas, you will never know whether they are good.

4. Force yourself to practice sections of the speech in different ways. Too many times, when we have finished our outline, we act as if it's cast in stone. Then we keep going over it the same way "to learn it." But if you don't take the time to practice in different ways, you allow yourself to be content with the first way of presenting material that comes to mind, rather than considering alternatives that might be better. If, however, you purposely phrase key ideas in different ways in each of the first few practices, you give yourself choices. Although some of the ways you express a point may be similar, trying new ways will stretch your mind, and chances are good that one or two of the ways will be far superior and much more imaginative than any of the others.

Let's look at an example that gives you a chance to think about alternative choices. Suppose you are planning to give a speech on climatic variation in the United States and that your research has uncovered the data shown in Table 12.1. We will use these data to show that (1) one set of data can suggest several lines of development on one topic and (2) the same point can be made in many different ways.

(1) Study your information, and ask what's unusual or noteworthy and why. For instance, as you look at Table 12.1, you might notice several unusual or noteworthy points. First, you might notice that the *high* temperatures in U.S. cities vary far less than the *low* temperatures. For instance, for the year shown in the table, the summer high temperature was 96 degrees in Miami and 95 degrees in Minneapolis. However, the winter low was 50 degrees in Miami and −27 in Minneapolis—a 77-degree difference! Conventional wisdom would suggest that high temperatures should vary nearly as much as low temperatures. Why is this not so?

You might also notice that it hardly ever rains on the West Coast in the summer. Two of the three West Coast cities, Los Angeles and San Francisco,

TABLE 12.1 Sample Data (Climate)

City	Temperature (in degrees Fahrenheit)		Precipitation (in inches)	
	High	Low	July	Annual
Chicago	95	−21	3.7	35
Cincinnati	98	−7	3.3	39
Denver	104	−3	1.9	15
Los Angeles	104	40	trace	15
Miami	96	50	5.7	56
Minneapolis	95	−27	3.5	28
New Orleans	95	26	6.1	62
New York	98	−2	4.4	42
Phoenix	117	35	0.8	7
Portland, ME	94	−18	3.1	44
St. Louis	97	−9	3.9	37
San Francisco	94	35	trace	19
Seattle	94	23	0.9	38

show only a trace of rain in July, and a third, Seattle, often considered a rainy city, shows only 0.9 inch in July—less than one-third of any eastern city, and less than one-sixth of Miami. Why is there so little rain on the West Coast in July? Why is there so much more in the East?

Finally, you might notice that in almost all the cities in the East and Midwest, July, a month thought to be hot and dry, actually accounts for more than the average one-twelfth of annual precipitation. Conventional wisdom suggests that July is the driest month of the year. Why do we perceive July to be a dry month? Why isn't it?

Thus, as we study the data in this one chart, we can raise questions that suggest at least three different lines of development for a speech on climate: Why are highs so similar but lows so different? Why is there so much more rain in the summer in the Midwest and East than in the West? Why is July wetter in most cities than we'd expect?

(2) Create different ways of making the same point. Using only the information from Table 12.1, let's consider two ways of supporting the point that "Yearly high temperatures in U.S. cities vary far less than yearly low temperatures."

(a) Of the 13 cities selected, ten (77%) had yearly highs between 90 and 100 degrees. However, of the same 13 cities, four (31%) had yearly lows above freezing; two (15%) had lows between 0 and 32 degrees; and seven (56%) had low temperatures below 0.

(b) Chicago, Miami, Minneapolis, New Orleans, Portland (ME), San Francisco, and Seattle—seven cities at widely varying latitudes—all had yearly high temperatures of 94 to 96 degrees. In contrast, the same seven cities had lows ranging from 50 degrees in Miami down to −27 degrees in Minneapolis.

Can you find another way of making the same point?

As we discussed previously, to be creative you must give yourself time to think.

Relevance

Principle 4 Audiences are more likely to listen to and remember information they perceive as relevant.

Rather than acting like sponges that absorb every bit of information, most of us act more like filters: We listen only to that information we perceive to be relevant. **Relevance** is the personal value that people find in information when it relates to their needs and interests. Relevance might be measured by an audience's "need to know."

Finding **vital information**—information the audience perceives as a matter of life or death—may be the ultimate in relevance. Police cadets, for instance, will see information explaining what they should do when attacked as vital. Similarly, students may perceive information that is necessary to their passing a test as vital. When a speaker shows listeners that information is critical to their well-being, they have a compelling reason to listen.

Of course, information does not have to be vital to be perceived as relevant. But always ask yourself in what way the material you plan to present is truly important to the audience, and emphasize that connection in your speech. For example, in a speech on Japan, a topic that may seem distant from the audience's felt needs and concerns, you can increase the perception of relevance by focusing on the importance of Japanese manufacturing to the U.S. economy and local jobs. In a speech on the Egyptian pyramids, you can increase percep-

relevance *the personal value that people find in information when it relates to their needs and interests*

vital information *information the audience perceives as a matter of life or death*

tion of relevance by relating their construction to contemporary building construction. In any speech you give, it is up to you to show how the information relates to the audience's needs and interests.

Although establishing relevance is important throughout the speech, it is especially important during your introduction, when audience members are sure to ask themselves, "Why should I listen to a speech on . . . ?" Notice how the following opening for a speech on high-speed rail transportation establishes relevance:

> Have you been stuck in a traffic jam lately? Have you started what you hoped would be a pleasant vacation only to be trampled at the airport or, worse, to discover when you got to your destination that your luggage hadn't? We're all aware that every year our highways and our airways are getting more congested. At the same time, we are facing a rapidly decreasing supply of petroleum. Today, I'm going to tell you about one of the most practical means for solving these problems—high-speed rail transportation.

Emphasis

Principle 5   Audiences are more likely to understand and to remember information that is emphasized.

Audiences will remember only some of the content presented in a speech—the rest is likely to be lost over time. Part of your challenge is to determine *what* you want the audience to retain and then to give that information proper emphasis. To meet this challenge, you must prioritize your information.

Ordinarily, the highest-priority information in your speech includes the specific goal, the main points, and key facts that give meaning to the main points. So, if you were giving a speech on evaluating credit cards, you would want to make sure the audience remembered

- **the goal:** to understand the three criteria for evaluating a credit card offer
- **the main points:** Three criteria for evaluating credit cards are know the real interest rates, know the annual fees, and know the unique benefits.
- **important facts:** Interest rates tend to be quite high—up to 18% or more. Fees range from 20 to 30 dollars on most cards. Many offer unique benefits such as frequent flyer miles, cash-back rebates, or coupons.

Once you have prioritized your information, plan a strategy for increasing your audience's retention of these items. In previous chapters, we have discussed various methods of emphasizing information. Let's remind ourselves of the importance of visual aids, repetition, transitions, and humorous stories, and then add one more method, mnemonics.

1. Use visual aids. Recall that visual aids emphasize because we remember more when we can associate pictures with words. Especially for informative speeches, you will want to think very carefully about the kinds of visual aids that will work best for you.

2. Repeat important words and ideas. Recall that just because a word is spoken does not necessarily mean that it is perceived. One of the best ways of breaking through is sheer repetition. Also recall that you can repeat a word or you can restate an idea in a slightly different way. But remember that when repetition is overdone, it loses its effectiveness. So, repeating a few important words and ideas will pay dividends—but repeating too many words or ideas will backfire.

3. Use transitions to guide audience thinking. Since listeners cannot go back if they get lost, it is especially important for speakers to do what they can to help audiences see where they have been and where they are going. Thus, in the introduction of the speech on credit cards, you tell the audience what you will cover: "In this speech, we will look at the three criteria for evaluating a credit card." Then, as you proceed through a long main point, you might remind your listeners where you are going by saying, "So we've seen the importance of looking at interest rates; now let's consider annual fee." And before the end of the speech, you might review: "So, in this speech, we've looked at the three criteria for evaluating a credit card—interest rate, annual fee, and benefits."

The value of such clarifying structure is tremendous. Because listeners' minds may wander, you must exercise control in how you want the audience to perceive what you say. I have heard listeners swear that a speaker never stated the second main point of the speech, when in reality the point was stated—but in a way that had no effect on the audience. Clarifying structure through transitions helps your audience recognize where you are in the speech and why your point is significant.

4. Use humor to stress key points. Our own experience shows that of all the forms of presenting information, we are most likely to remember information in humorous story form. For instance, suppose you were giving a speech on the importance of having perspective. Your main point might be that because a problem that seems enormous at the moment may turn out to be minor in a few days, being able to put events into perspective saves a great deal of psychological wear and tear. To cement the concept of *perspective*, you might tell the following story:

> A first-time visitor to the races bet two dollars on the first race on a horse that had the same name as his elementary school. The horse won, and the man was ten dollars ahead. In each of the next several races he bet on horses such as Apple Pie, his favorite, and Kathie's Prize, after his wife's name, and he kept winning. By the end of the sixth race, he was 700 dollars ahead. He was about to go home when he noticed that in the seventh race, Seventh Veil was scheduled in the number seven position, and was currently going off at odds of seven to one. The man couldn't resist—he bet his entire 700 dollars. And sure enough, the horse came in seventh. When he got home, his wife asked, "How did you do?" Very calmly he looked at his wife and said, "Not bad—I lost two dollars." That's perspective.

5. Create memory aids for your audience. You can help your listeners retain more of your speech by suggesting memory aids, formally called **mnemonics.** For instance, if you were giving a speech on evaluating diamonds, your audience might remember that the four criteria are weight, clarity, tint, and shape. But they would be more likely to remember "carat, clarity, color, and cutting." Why? Because you've created a memory aid—the four criteria all begin with *C*.

mnemonics   *memory aids*

acronym   *a word formed from initial letters of each of the successive parts of a compound term, a common word made up of the first letters of objects or concepts, or a sentence made up of words whose initial letters signal something else*

Mnemonics may be **acronyms**—words formed from initial letters of each of the successive parts of a compound term (NATO, OPEC); common words made up of the first letters of objects or concepts (HOMES for the five great lakes); or sentences made up of words whose initial letters signal something else (Every Good Boy Does Fine for the five notes of the scale). For instance, in her speech on the healing power of listening, Carol Koehler, Professor of Communication and Medicine, offered the word *CARE* to reflect the qualities of the therapeutic communicator: *C* for concentrate, *A* for acknowledge, *R* for response, and *E* for emotional control.[2]

Most memory aids are a form of association. An **association** is the tendency of one thought to stimulate recall of another, similar thought. Suppose that in your speech on evaluating diamonds, you are trying to help the audience remember the value of color. If blue is the most highly prized tint and yellow or brown tints lower a diamond's value, you might associate blue tint with "the blue-ribbon prize" and yellow (or brown) tint with "a lemon." Thus, the best diamond gets the "blue ribbon," and the worst diamond is a "lemon."

Figurative associations like these fall into the two categories of similes and metaphors. Recall that a simile is a comparison using *like* or *as*: "A computer screen is like a television monitor." A metaphor states an identity: "Laser printers are the Cadillacs of computer printers." I still remember vividly a metaphor I heard in a speech more than 20 years ago. A student explained the functioning of a television tube by saying, "A television picture tube is a gun shooting beams of light." If you make your associations striking enough, your audience will remember your point as well as I remember that point about how a television tube works.

association the tendency of one thought to stimulate recall of another, similar thought

Methods of Informing

"Marta, what are you going to be talking about for your informative speech?"

"Well, you know I'm a science buff, and lately I've been getting really interested in meteorology, so I think I'm going to talk about something related to that."

"Didn't you tell me that you were down in Florida when Hurricane Georges hit?"

"That was something. I was in Naples, and it looked like it was going to smack us directly. Fortunately for us, after it hit the Keys it veered into the Gulf and then zoomed into Alabama."

"Then why don't you talk about hurricanes?"

"Well, there's so much. I don't know where to focus."

You may find yourself in a situation much like Marta's. She really wants to talk about something related to meteorology, but she's concerned about how to limit her topic and approach.

In the first part of this chapter, we presented some fundamental principles of informative speaking. In this part, we consider the informative speaking skills of exposition, explanation or demonstration of processes, and definition. Each of these represents both a skill and a type of speech. At times, you may use some or all of these skills in a single speech. Other times, you may prepare an informative speech based primarily on one of the skills.

For instance, in her speech, Marta may decide to talk about hurricanes. If she decides to take a composite approach, she may well use all three types of skills. That is, she might first *define* hurricanes and contrast them with tornadoes and typhoons; next, she might *explain* or *demonstrate* how a hurricane develops; and finally, she might give an *exposition*—a general informative speech—on the devastation of a hurricane and its effects on people as well as on business and industry of the area struck. Alternatively, she might devote her entire speech to *defining* hurricanes or *demonstrating* how hurricanes develop. Her choice will depend on many factors, perhaps the most important of which, for a classroom speech, is the time available.

TECHNOLOGY tips

Informative speeches become more interesting when the information seems relevant and the speaker credible. One way to enhance your credibility and to acquire information that is specific to your speech is to correspond through e-mail with a respected expert on the subject. In your e-mail message you should ask a specific question that is relevant to your topic and not answered in the existing printed material that you have found. Then you can report the answers you receive in your speech as follows: "In an e-mail I recently received from . . . , she told me that . . ."

expository speech *a general informative speech that seeks to convey understanding of an idea and that requires outside source material to give the speech depth*

Because each of these three broad-based skills is a product of somewhat different subskills, we will discuss each one in turn and illustrate each with a sample speech. Your informative speaking strength will grow as you gain a mastery of these three major methods of informing: exposition, process explanation or demonstration, and definition.

Exposition

Throughout history people have had an insatiable need to know. Unanswered questions stimulate research; research yields facts; and facts, when properly ordered and developed, yield understanding. Oral communication of this understanding is achieved through expository speaking.

Although any informative speech is in a sense an expository speech, in this section an **expository speech** is defined as a general informative speech that seeks to convey understanding of an idea and that requires outside source material to give the speech depth. For example, "The Causes of Teen Violence," "The Practice of Islamic Religion," and "The Origin and Classifications of Nursery Rhymes" would all be possible topics for expository speaking.

An expository speech embodies all of the principles that we discussed in the first part of the chapter. Thus, it is an excellent assignment for a major informative speech.

FOCUS ON skills

Expository Speaking

Prepare a 5- to 8-minute general informative speech. An outline and a list of sources are required. Criteria for evaluation include means of ensuring audience interest, audience understanding of information, and retention of information, which focus on speaker credibility, intellectual stimulation, creativity, relevance, and emphasis.

As an addendum to the outline, you may wish to write a plan for adapting the speech to your audience based on predictions you made using the Audience Analysis Checklist on p. 58 of Chapter 4. In your plan, include three short sections discussing strategies for (1) getting and maintaining interest, (2) facilitating audience understanding, and (3) increasing retention. Where appropriate, comment on use of visual aids and the role of language and delivery techniques for implementing your plan. See the sample outline, speech plan, and informative speech that follow.

FOCUS ON skills

Critiquing

Write a critique for at least one of the informative speeches you hear in class. Outline the speech. As you outline, answer the questions on the Expository Speech Evaluation Checklist (page 235).

SPEECH EVALUATION checklist

Expository Speech

Check all items that were accomplished effectively.

Primary Criteria

_____ **1.** Was the specific goal designed to increase audience information?

_____ **2.** Was the speaker effective in establishing his or her credibility on this topic?

_____ **3.** Was the information intellectually stimulating?

_____ **4.** Did the speaker show creativity in idea development?

_____ **5.** Did the speaker show the relevance of the information?

_____ **6.** Did the speaker emphasize the information?

_____ **7.** Was the organizational pattern appropriate for the intent and content of the speech?

General Criteria

_____ **1.** Was the specific goal clear?

_____ **2.** Was the introduction effective?

_____ **3.** Were main points clear?

_____ **4.** Was the conclusion effective?

_____ **5.** Was the language clear, vivid, emphatic, and appropriate?

_____ **6.** Was the speech delivered enthusiastically, with vocal expressiveness, fluently, spontaneously, and directly?

Evaluate the speech as (check one)

_____ excellent, _____ good, _____ average, _____ fair, _____ poor.

Use the information from this checklist to support your evaluation.

SAMPLE speech

Improving Grades[3]

Outline

Specific Goal: I want my audience to understand three techniques for improving grades in college.

Introduction

   I. We all know that good grades are a necessity whether we wish to go on to graduate school or get the best job possible.

  II. Because I'm a returning student, I've felt even more pressure to do as well as I can in all my courses.

 III. I want to share with you three methods for improving grades that I've tried to apply in my own work.

Thesis Statement: Three proven techniques for improving test scores in college are to attend classes regularly, develop a positive attitude, and study efficiently.

Body

I. The first proven technique for improving grades in college is to attend classes regularly.

    A. The primary difference between A students and C students is regular attendance.

        1. A students average one absence a term.

        2. C students average four absences a term.

    B. If your motivation lags, remember that each day of classes is worth $1,000.

(Now that we've seen the importance of attendance, let's consider the second technique.)

II. The second proven technique is to develop a positive attitude.

    A. The mind has power over behavior.

        1. Go into class relaxed.

        2. Be confident.

    B. Visualize success on the exam.

        1. Once the subconscious mind accepts an idea, it executes it.

        2. Use affirmations.

(Now let's consider the third technique.)

III. The third proven technique is to study systematically.

    A. Read assignments thoroughly before each class.

    B. Process information presented in class.

    C. Review assignments after class.

Conclusion

I. If you attend class regularly, study efficiently, and prepare yourself psychologically for every class, you'll reap the rewards of an improved GPA.

Sources

Jewler, A. Jerome, and Gardner, John N. *Step by Step to College Success.* Belmont, CA.: Wadsworth, 1987.

Kalish, Richard A. *Guide to Effective Study.* Monterey, CA: Brooks/Cole, 1979.

Murphy, Joseph. *The Power of Your Subconscious Mind.* New York: Bantam, 1985.

Olney, Claude W. *Where There's a Will There's an A.* Paoli, PA: Chesterbook Educational Publishers, 1989.

Wipperman, R. P. Personal interview, 2 November 1992.

Plan for Adapting to Audience

1. Getting and maintaining interest. I plan to begin the speech by showing the monetary rewards of study. During the speech, I believe that my quotations and examples as well as my clear and vivid language will help maintain interest. Likewise, I hope to show the relevance of the topic for all of us—I will focus on all of our interests in improving grades. I will also use personal pronouns and rhetorical questions. I further believe that my enthusiastic delivery will help to maintain interest.

2. Facilitating understanding. Even though the class should perceive the techniques as relatively simple, I believe listeners will find the information intellectually stimulating. I believe my listeners appreciate the clarity of the information that I present. I also will use repetition and comparison to help listeners see the information more clearly. Foremost, I will clarify structure with good transitions. I will also use repetition and comparison.

3. Increasing retention. My primary means of increasing retention will be emphasis through repetition and transitions. I will preview the three techniques in the introduction, state each clearly as main points, and then repeat them again in the conclusion. I also believe that by relating the techniques to their needs as students, they are likely to want to remember them.

Thinking Critically: Speech and Analysis

Read the following speech aloud at least once. Examine it to see whether information has been presented in a way that is credible, intellectually stimulating, creative, relevant, and emphatic. Most important, assess the speech for its informative value.

Speech

We all know the importance of good grades for either getting into graduate school or getting the best possible job. R. P. Wipperman, a section head for Procter & Gamble, told me that good grades "are the calling card that get you in the door."

Because I've been away from college for more than 17 years, I've been particularly concerned about getting back into the studying groove, so I've been reading study guides looking for specific techniques that are most likely to help with my grades. Today I'd like to share with you three relatively easy, proven techniques for improving your GPA that I've learned from my study: attend classes regularly, maintain a positive attitude, and study systematically.

The first proven technique is to attend classes regularly. It sounds so simple, doesn't it, but it turns out to be really important. According to Dr. Claude Olney, who is highly regarded for his publications on grades, one of the most significant differences between an A and a C in a course is attendance. Olney did a study of 800 students and found that, on average, people who got A's missed less than one class per term, and people who got C's missed more than four classes per term. During class, professors clarify difficult concepts, emphasize key information, and give insights that can't be gotten any other way. Regular attendance is important to learning in general *and* to doing well on tests in particular.

If you need further motivation to attend class, think of it this way: Every day you attend class is worth $1,000 to you—that's a thousand dollars! According to a Census Bureau study reported in a recent *Cincinnati Enquirer*, a college diploma hanging on the wall is worth $1,039 a month in extra pay (an average of $2,116 a month for college graduates compared with $1,077 per month for high school graduates). This $12,000+ a year comes to some $600,000 over a lifetime. Since here at UC we spend about 600 days in class over four years, that comes out to about $1,000 for every day we come to school.

Analysis

Notice how Jennifer begins with a statement that we will all agree with. Then she moves to a quotation that reinforces that statement.

In this sentence, we see her laying the groundwork for building her credibility.

She uses her thesis statement as a transition leading into the body of the speech.

Throughout the speech, the speaker leads us through the organization. She begins the body of the speech by identifying the first technique. Although the speaker has given the credentials for her authority, she has not cited the source from which the information came.

Here and throughout the speech, we see excellent information that is clearly presented.

Good adaptation to audience needs and interests. Clear explanation of the basis for the assertion.

Here the speaker points out the source of the study and the source of the information.

Notice the clear transition summarizing the first point and leading us to the second. Good transitions and clearly stated main points not only facilitate understanding, but also help us remember the points.

Notice that the speaker not only presents a relevant quotation but also points out the significance of the quotation.

This second documented source in the section helps to reinforce the importance of positive thinking.

A clear transition to the third technique.

Notice that all three main points are stated with parallel wording: "The first (second, third) technique is. . . ." Also notice the way she previews the three subdivisions of the point.

This section shows good adaptation as the speaker refers to a common behavior—waiting to read the assignment until after class.

Here, adaption both helps to build interest and helps the audience perceive the information as relevant.

Notice that here she tells her listeners that this third subpoint is the most important.

It would have been a good idea to mention the specific source of these statistics.

Jennifer finishes her speech with a brief summary. Although a summary is appropriate, she might have used some additional concluding point to help leave the speech on a high note.

This is an example of a well-organized, highly informative speech. Listeners should not only see the importance of the information to them, but should be encouraged to remember the techniques for improving grades.

Now that we've seen the importance of attendance, let's consider the second technique.

The second technique is to develop a positive attitude toward school in general and each class in particular. Bill Moyers just finished a public television series reemphasizing the power of the mind on all aspects of our behavior. To emphasize this relationship, I love the following quote from Dr. Olney: "If you think you can do it, you're right, and if you don't think you can do it, you're still right." Notice, whether you can do it or not depends a great deal on whether you think you can. So, go into class each day relaxed, confident that you're ready for class, and you're ready to make the most of what the professor chooses to talk about or discuss during that class. This will help the mind work for you. Joseph Murray, who wrote *The Power of Your Subconscious Mind*, said, "Once the subconscious mind accepts an idea, it begins to execute it." Remind yourself of how much you are learning and how that learning is making you a better educated, more interesting person. On test days, say, "I'm ready for this test" or "I know this information." If you have a positive attitude, you'll get better grades.

Now let's consider the third technique.

The third proven technique is to learn to study systematically. Every one of the study sources I consulted suggested the importance of reading, processing, and reviewing.

First, read assignments thoroughly before going to class. Many of us figure that the professor will cover what we need to know in class so we don't really have to read the assignment before class. But learning works a lot better if we have a good idea of the material when we get to class.

Second, process the information in class. When the professor lectures, take careful notes and see how information relates to material you have studied for class; during class discussions, ask questions in order to check definitions and review examples.

Third, and most important, review the assignment material *after class*. This is the key to systematic study. Keep in mind that without reinforcement, we forget half of what we've read within 48 hours and 90 percent of what we've read within two weeks. If the information is reinforced, however, we can remember 80–90 percent of the information we have read. Reviewing assignment material after class provides this important reinforcement. So, tonight, before you begin reading information for tomorrow's classes, review information from today's classes!

So, by attending every class, thinking positively, and studying systematically (read, process, and review), you will improve your GPA. ■

Process Explanation or Demonstration

Many informative speeches involve either demonstrating or explaining a *process*—telling how to do something, how to make something, or how something works. For instance the boss might explain the process of going through various stages in order to be promoted, an engineer can explain how a turbojet works, or an author might explain how to get a book published. In the sample speech at the end of this section, the speaker explains the process of producing a nightly edition of ESPN's SportsCenter.

Whereas a **process explanation** tells how to do something, how to make something, or how something works, often with the help of visual aids, a **demonstration** involves a live, hands-on visual portrayal of the process. For instance, a computer trainer might demonstrate how to use new software, a chef might demonstrate how to bone a chicken, or a golf pro might demonstrate how to hit out of sand traps. Some of these demonstrations are completely hands-on, performing the entire step-by-step procedure; others are partial demonstrations, using various visual aids. To demonstrate effectively, speakers need to delineate clear steps and master the elements of demonstration.

process explanation *telling how to do something, how to make something, or how something works*

demonstration *going through a hands-on process in front of the audience*

Organizing Main Points As we pointed out in Chapter 6, Organizing and Outlining the Body of the Speech, in either a process explanation or demonstration, the speech is likely to follow a chronological (time) order, with each main point representing one step of the process. Although some processes may have only three or four clearly identifiable steps, others may have far more.

Michael Newman/PhotoEdit

Since demonstrations call for having all the necessary materials on hand and making sure everyone can easily see what you are doing, complete demonstrations work best with small audiences.

The question then becomes, What do speakers do when they can identify 9, 11, or even 15 steps to the process? Because no step can be left out, knowledgeable speechmakers subordinate the steps under five or fewer main steps—a number listeners can easily hold in their active consciousness at one time.

One way of reducing the total number of steps is to group like ideas under common headings. Suppose that a process appears to have ten individual steps. Since listeners are more likely to remember three steps with three or four subdivisions than ten individual steps, the effective speaker reorganizes the multistep speech into one with three to five steps. This reorganizing process of grouping like ideas is called **chunking.**

To test this method, look at Figure 12.1. Read the ten steps in column A to a friend and ask him or her to repeat them. Then read the three steps, with subdivisions, in column B and ask the friend to repeat them. Even though column B has a total of 13 items (three steps and ten subdivisions), most people are able to recall them more readily than the ten independent steps. Although both sets of directions are essentially the same, the chunking of steps in column B enables an audience to visualize the process more easily.

If the process you plan to explain seems to have more than five steps, you can probably work out similar groupings. The plan–make–finish organization shown in column B is a common type of grouping for explaining how to make something. A little thought on the best way to group similar steps pays dividends in audience understanding and recall. And using strong transitions between steps helps reinforce the points to aid retention.

Choosing the Type of Demonstration   When the task is relatively simple, such as how to get more power on a forehand table-tennis shot, you may want to try a complete demonstration. If so, practice until you can do it smoothly and easily under the pressure of facing an actual audience. Since the actual demonstration is likely to take longer than in practice (you may have to make some modifications during the speech to enable everyone in the room

FIGURE 12.1   Reducing the total number of steps by grouping like ideas under common headings

A

1. Gather the materials.
2. Draw the pattern.
3. Trace the pattern on wood.
4. Cut out the pattern so that the tracing line can still be seen.
5. File to the pattern line.
6. Sandpaper edge and surface.
7. Paint the object.
8. Sand lightly.
9. Apply a second coat of paint.
10. Varnish.

B

1. **Plan the job.**
   A. Gather the materials.
   B. Draw the pattern.
   C. Trace the pattern on wood.

2. **Cut out the pattern.**
   A. Saw so that the tracing line can still be seen.
   B. File to the pattern line.
   C. Sandpaper edge and surface.

3. **Finish the object.**
   A. Paint.
   B. Sand lightly.
   C. Apply a second coat of paint.
   D. Varnish.

Explaining or Demonstrating a Process

1. Prepare a 4- to 7-minute speech in which you show how something is made, how something is done, or how something works. An outline is required. Evaluation will focus on quality of the topic; selection, construction, and use of visual aids; and skill in organization and presentation. Following are examples of the kinds of topics that would be appropriate for this assignment.

How to Do It	How to Make It	How It Works
racing start	spinach soufflé	zone defense
networking	fishing flies	helicopter
hanging wallboard	paper figures	compact disc
grading meat	wood carvings	photocopier

2. Since explaining or demonstrating a process is a common major speech, as an addendum to the outline, you may wish to write a specific plan for adapting the speech to your audience. In the plan, include four short sections discussing strategies for (1) building credibility, (2) getting and maintaining interest, (3) facilitating understanding, and (4) increasing retention. You may wish to discuss how you will use your creativity to ensure that the speech will be perceived as intellectually stimulating, relevant, clear, and memorable. Where appropriate, comment on the use of demonstration and visual aids and the role of language and delivery techniques for implementing your plan.

3. Write a critique of at least one demonstration you hear in class. As you listen to the speech, take notes outlining its organization, and use the Demonstration Speech Evaluation Checklist on page 242.

to see the demonstration), you may want to make sure that the final practice is somewhat shorter than the maximum time limit you will have for the speech.

For a relatively complicated process, you may want to consider a modified demonstration in which you complete various stages of the demonstration at home and do only part of the actual work in front of the audience. Suppose you were going to demonstrate construction of a floral display. Actually performing the construction from scratch is too complex and time-consuming for a speech-length presentation. Instead, you could prepare a complete set of materials to begin the demonstration, a mock-up of the basic floral triangle, and a completed floral display. During the speech, you would describe the materials needed and then begin demonstrating how to make the basic floral triangle. Rather than trying to get everything together perfectly in a few seconds, you could remove, from a bag or some other concealed place, a partially completed arrangement illustrating the floral triangle. You would then use this in your demonstration, adding flowers as if you were planning to complete it. Then, from another bag, you could remove the completed arrangement to illustrate one of the effects you were discussing. Conducting a modified demonstration of this type is often easier than trying to complete an entire demonstration in a limited time.

Explaining or Demonstrating a Process

Check all items that were accomplished effectively.

Primary Criteria

_____ **1.** Was the specific goal appropriate for a process explanation or demonstration?

_____ **2.** Did the speaker show expertise with the process?

_____ **3.** Did the speaker organize the steps of the process?

_____ **4.** Did the speaker have the necessary materials to explain or demonstrate the process?

_____ **5.** Did the speaker explain or demonstrate the process skillfully?

_____ **6.** Did the speaker select or construct useful visual aids?

_____ **7.** Did the speaker use the visual aids effectively?

_____ **8.** Did the speaker use any special strategies to help the audience remember main points and other key information necessary to understand the process?

General Criteria

_____ **1.** Was the specific goal clear?

_____ **2.** Was the introduction effective?

_____ **3.** Were the main points clear?

_____ **4.** Was the conclusion effective?

_____ **5.** Was the language clear, vivid, emphatic, and appropriate?

_____ **6.** Was the speech delivered enthusiastically, with vocal expressiveness, fluently, spontaneously, and directly?

Evaluate the speech as (check one)

_____ excellent, _____ good, _____ average, _____ fair, _____ poor.

Use the information from this checklist to support your evaluation.

SAMPLE **speech**

Process of Producing a Nightly Edition of ESPN's SportsCenter[4]

Outline

Specific Goal: I want my audience to understand the three steps that go into the process of producing a late night edition of ESPN's SportsCenter.

Introduction

I. This promo I'm holding is a waited-for sight for the more than 5 million viewers of ESPN's SportsCenter, the most popular sports show in America.

II. I'm especially excited about the show because I hope that someday I can be a part of it or one like it.

Thesis Statement: The three steps that it takes to put together an edition of SportsCenter are the preparation of ideas for that night's show, the gathering and organizing of information as it comes in, and finally preparing for the start of the show.

Body

I. The first step that each SportsCenter edition goes through is the idea stage.

    A. The staff talks about what has happened and what is likely to happen in sports that day.

    B. Then the staff discusses the breakdown—the main theme for that night.

(But these are just the ideas.)

II. The second step in producing a SportsCenter edition is to gather and organize information.

    A. During this time period, the hosts are confronted with a massive amount of information from the computer from which stories will be written.

    B. Next, the hosts begin to write the script for that night's show.

        1. The rundown gives the framework for the show.

        2. The hosts have to write the copy and be prepared to ad lib.

    C. As they select stories, they seek verification for them.

        1. Any major story has to be run through the senior management.

        2. Then the hosts seek a second and third source to confirm the original source.

(At this point the structure is set, but there's still a lot to do.)

III. The third step in producing a SportsCenter edition is the final preparation for that show.

    A. By about 7:30, the hosts start watching events, looking for specific material to use that night.

    B. By 9:00 or so, the hosts work on the tease—the assorted clips that are seen before the hosts actually come on.

    C. During the last hour, the hosts work on final details.

        1. They check late scores.

        2. Then they get ready to go on.

Conclusion

I. The three major steps in the production of ESPN's SportsCenter are preparing ideas, gathering and organizing information, and setting up for the start of the show.

Sources

"Every Day Is Game Day." *Sports Illustrated*, December 21, 1992, p. 52.
Kindred, Dave. "Center of Attention." *Sporting News*, May 8, 1995, p. 6.

Olbermann, Keith, and Patrick, Dan. *The Big Show: A Tribute to ESPN's Sports-Center.* New York: Pocket Books, 1997.

Observation: I've watched and analyzed SportsCenter countless times.

Plan for Adapting to Audience

1. Getting and maintaining interest. I plan to begin the speech with startling information that gets the audience excited about listening to the process of getting shows on the air. During the speech, I will also give specific examples that audience members can relate to.

2. Facilitating understanding. I do not believe the information I will present is difficult to understand. I will work to keep technical jargon to a minimum, and I will define technical terms that the audience may not understand. Finally, I will use visual aids both to get attention and to help explain a key part of the speech.

3. Organization. I have organized my speech following the time order. I will have transitions between points.

4. Building credibility. I believe that my examples, which are relevant to class experience, will help make the information easy to understand. Moreover, I will emphasize my understanding of the program.

Thinking Critically: Speech and Analysis

Read the following speech aloud. Then, analyze it in terms of the primary criteria listed on page 242: goal, expertise, organization, materials, skill, and use of visual aids.

Analysis   **Speech**

SportsCenter Is Next on

ESPN

Doug begins the speech by showing a visual aid and documenting the popularity of the show.

This promo I'm holding is an anticipated sight for the more than 5 million viewers of ESPN's late night edition of SportsCenter, which according to an article in *Sports Illustrated* is the most popular sports show in America. This is an amazing fact considering that they only cover one particular thing—sports.

Here he explains why it is so popular.

SportsCenter is popular mostly because it gives more highlights and in-depth information than any other sports show on television.

Doug not only gives insight into his goals, but also starts to build his credibility.

I'm especially excited about the show because I've been a fan for years. In fact, I hope that someday I can be a part of SportsCenter or some show like it.

The three steps involved in putting together an edition of SportsCenter are the preparation of ideas for that night's show, the gathering and organizing of information as it comes in, and the final preparation for the start of the show.

The first step that each SportsCenter edition goes through is the idea stage. This step, which begins early in the afternoon, is where the staff talks about what has happened and what is likely to happen in sports that day. During that time, the hosts learn what pretaped features will be airing that night. Any features that are relevant to that night are researched to the fullest or they don't go on at all. All features are based on what is going on in sports on that particular day.

Then the breakdown of shows for the night is discussed. The breakdown is the main theme for the night. It is an in-depth look at whatever the main event of that particular time of year is. For instance, when Mark McGwire was in the middle of his quest to become the home run champ, SportsCenter broke down everything from the day Roger Maris broke Babe Ruth's record to the day Mark McGwire was expected to break Roger Maris's record. Similarly, when the NBA lockout began, SportsCenter broke down both sides' positions: what the players wanted and what the owners wanted and what it took—would take—for them to get together to start the season. Now the hosts have the key ideas for the show.

The second step in producing a SportsCenter edition is to gather and organize information for that night's show. This is the time when the producer puts the show "rundown" into the computer. The rundown is the exact order of stories and listing of what each story will consist of. The producer must decide on camera—the on-camera segments by either cohost, videotaped highlights with or without a voice-over, and which athletes' comments will be heard on tape. After all, not all will be on the air.

Let's look at a small segment that Keith Olbermann and Dan Patrick showed in their book *The Big Show*, in which they discussed their participation in "SportsCenter."

Order	Camera	Host	Topic	Tape	Content	Time range
1	30S	Keith	Indians/Orioles	41	OTS-VO	2:02–2:26
2			Tribe/O's Post	42	SOT	0:35–0:35
3	10S	Dan	Padres/Cardinals	43	OTS-VO	2:05–2:30

This sketchy "rundown" gives order (1, 2, etc.), camera angle, host who will narrate, subject of cutting, tape machine showing the segment, what actually happens on the tape, and range of time.

Then the hosts begin to write the script for that night's show based on the rundown. They must turn the sketchy rundown into meaningful dialogue—as well as prepare themselves to ad lib to fill time. It might be surprising to you that the person we actually see "on-air" writes the whole show from this rundown—but that's how it goes.

They feel that if they didn't do that, then they would not know all the information and in an emergency, they would not be prepared. Other than the occasional feature piece written by an associate producer, the hosts write the entire show.

As they begin to put the stories together, they need some credibility to back them up. This is when they call to verify the tips they have received. Any story that is a source story has to be run through the senior management and

At the ending of the introduction, Doug previews the three steps of the process.

The first step (the idea stage), stated as a complete sentence, gives an idea of the length of preparation for the show as well as pointing out what is discussed.

Here Doug explains the usage of "breakdown."

Good use of example to show how they proceed.

Then he follows with a more recent example.

Second step, also stated as a complete sentence, focuses on gathering and organizing information. Again, good definition of a term that the audience might not understand.

Doug documents the specific information that is included in the rundown.
Here Doug shows a visual aid that indicates the sketchiness of the information the hosts work with.

He continues with a clear explanation of the process.
Good adaptation to a thought that is likely to be in the minds of audience members.
He continues with a clear explanation of the process.

Good job of demonstrating need and procedure for ensuring credibility.

usually must have a second and third source to confirm the original source. Basically, if one story were to go wrong, they would lose all credibility and probably not be able to air as successfully as they have.

The third step in producing a SportsCenter edition is the final preparation for that show. By about 7:30, they start the final preparation. At this point the games for the night have begun, and the watching starts for highlights. Most of the time, the hosts have to watch many different games and do not have a chance to concentrate on one particular game, even if their favorite team is playing. The record for the number of different game highlights shown in a single one-hour Big Show is 27—you heard that, 27 different games were shown on one hour of SportsCenter.

The next stage of final preparation is the formation of the tease. The tease is a minute or so of assorted clips that are shown before the hosts actually come on and say hello. The production assistant will write a rough script and present a list of video shots that look as if they would be good enough to air as the show is about to start to keep people's interest. The hosts themselves then write the tease. The last step is getting dressed and putting on the makeup for the show. Late scores are written in and readjustments can be made to lead-ins if games have gone in different directs than earlier expected. Take the three-minute walk to the studio, check the microphone and earphone, clear throats repeatedly, take a deep breath, try to get rid of those butterflies, and Sports-Center is about to start.

So, the first step is preparing ideas for that night's show. The second step is gathering and organizing information as it comes in. And of course, the third step is preparing for the start of the show. All of these steps are essential to producing a successful edition of SportsCenter so that 5 million people will be able to watch ESPN from 11 to 12 at night and enjoy the show.

As for people like myself who will someday want to work at SportsCenter or at ESPN on a sports program, all this information is extremely valuable—and I hope you enjoyed it as well. ■

Third step is a complete sentence that focuses on final stages of preparation.

Good attention-getting point— and well emphasized through repetition.

Again, good explanation.

Here Doug reviews the steps.

Good personal reference. This is an example of a well-organized process speech.

Definition

Richard Weaver, a major 20th-century figure in rhetorical theory, labeled definition as the most valuable of all lines of speech development, primarily because of its role in helping audiences understand and relate to key concepts.[5] Since clear vivid definitions are essential in all effective speeches, we begin by looking at the types of short definitions you can use. Then we show how extended definitions can be used as the basis for major informative speeches.

Short Definitions   Short definitions are used to clarify concepts in as few words as possible. Effective speakers learn to define by synonym and antonym, classification and differentiation, use or function, and etymological reference.

1. Synonyms and antonyms. Using a synonym or an antonym is the quickest way to define a word, for you are able to indicate an approximate, if not exact, meaning in a single sentence.

Synonyms are words that have the same or nearly the same meanings; **antonyms** are words that have opposite meanings. Defining by synonym is defining by comparison: For a word that does not bring up an immediate concrete meaning, we provide one that does. Synonyms for *prolix* include *long, wordy,* and *verbose.* Its antonyms are *short* and *concise.* Synonyms are not dupli-

synonyms   *words that have the same or nearly the same meanings*

antonyms   *words that have opposite meanings*

cates for the word being defined, but they do give a good idea of what the word means. Of course, the synonym or antonym must be familiar to the audience or its use defeats its purpose.

2. Classification and differentiation. When you define by classification, you give the boundaries of the particular word and focus on the single feature that differentiates that word from words with similar meanings. Most dictionary definitions are of the classification—differentiation variety. For instance, a dog may be defined as a carnivorous, domesticated mammal of the family Canidae. "Carnivorous," "mammal," and "family Canidae" limit the boundaries to dogs, jackals, foxes, and wolves. "Domesticated" differentiates dogs from the other three.

3. Use or function. A third short way to define is by explaining the use or function of the object represented by a particular word. Thus, when you say "A *plane* is a hand-powered tool that is used to smooth the edges of boards" or "A *scythe* is a piece of steel shaped in a half circle with a handle attached that is used to cut weeds or high grass," you are defining tools by indicating their use. Because the use or function of an object may be more important than its classification, this is often an excellent method of definition.

4. Etymology. Etymology is the derivation or history of a particular word. Because meanings of words change over time, origin may reveal very little about modern meaning. In some instances, however, the history of a word lends additional insight that will help the audience not only better remember the meaning but also bring the meaning to life. For instance, a *censor* was originally one of two Roman magistrates appointed to take the census and, later, to supervise public morals. The best source of word derivation is the Oxford English Dictionary.

etymology *the derivation or history of a particular word*

5. Example and comparison. Regardless of which short definition form you use, most statements need to be supplemented with examples, comparisons, or both to make them understandable. That is especially true when you define abstract words. Consider the word *just* in the following sentence: "You are being *just* in your dealings with another when you deal *honorably* and *fairly*." Although *just* has been defined by synonym, listeners still may be unsure of the meaning. We might add, "If Paul and Mary do the same amount of work and we reward them by giving them an equal amount of money, our dealings will be just; if, on the other hand, we give Paul more money because he's a man, our dealings will be unjust." In this case, the definition is clarified with both an example and a comparison.

For some words, a single example or comparison will be enough. For other words or in communicating with certain audiences, you may need several examples and comparisons.

Extended Definitions   Often a word is so important to a speech that an extended definition is warranted. An extended definition is one that serves as an entire main point in a speech or, at times, an entire speech. Thus, an entire speech can be built around an extended definition of a term such as *freedom, equality, justice, love,* or *impressionistic painting.*

An extended definition begins with a single-sentence dictionary definition or stipulated definition. For example, *Webster's Third New International Dictionary* defines *jazz* as "American music characterized by improvisation, syncopated rhythms, contrapuntal ensemble playing, and special melodic features peculiar to the individual interpretation of the player." This definition suggests four topics ("improvisation," "syncopation," "ensemble," and "special melodies") that could be used as the basis for a topical order for a speech. Assuming you were familiar enough with jazz to talk about it, you might organize your speech as follows.

Specific Goal: I want my audience to understand the four major characteristics of jazz.

I. Jazz is characterized by improvisation.

II. Jazz is characterized by syncopated rhythms.

III. Jazz is characterized by contrapuntal ensemble playing.

IV. Jazz is characterized by special melodic features peculiar to the individual interpretation of the player.

The key to the effectiveness of the speech would be how well you explain each topic. Your selection and use of examples, illustrations, comparisons, personal experiences, and observations will give the speech its original and distinctive flavor.

Wendy Finkleman's sample speech "Impressionistic Painting," which follows, is an example of an extended definition.

SPEECH EVALUATION checklist

Extended Definition

Check all items that were accomplished effectively.

Primary Criteria

_____ **1.** Was the specific goal appropriate for defining?

_____ **2.** Did the speaker use synonym and antonym, classification and differentiation, use or function, or etymology effectively?

_____ **3.** Did the speaker use examples to develop the definition?

_____ **4.** Did the speaker use any special strategies to help the audience remember main points and other key information necessary to understand the concept being defined?

General Criteria

_____ **1.** Was the specific goal clear?

_____ **2.** Was the introduction effective?

_____ **3.** Were the main points clear?

_____ **4.** Was the conclusion effective?

_____ **5.** Was the language clear, vivid, emphatic, and appropriate?

_____ **6.** Was the speech delivered enthusiastically, with vocal expressiveness, fluently, spontaneously, and directly?

Evaluate the speech as (check one)

_____ excellent, _____ good, _____ average, _____ fair, _____ poor.

Use the information from this checklist to support your evaluation.

FOCUS ON SKILLS

Defining

Prepare a 4- to 6-minute extended definition. An outline is required. Evaluation will focus on the definition's clarity and on the organization and quality of the developmental material.

Some of the best topics for extended definition are general or abstract words, words that give you leeway in definition and allow for creative development. The following are examples of the kinds of words for which extended definitions are appropriate:

impressionism	epistemology	fossil	acculturation
existentialism	rhetoric	humanities	extrasensory perception
myth	Epicurean	logic	status

SAMPLE SPEECH

Impressionistic Painting[6]

Outline

Specific Goal: I want the audience to understand the definition of impressionistic painting.

Introduction

I. "I paint as the bird sings"; this quote from Monet describes the light, vibrant nature of impressionistic painting.

II. Through the years, impressionism has become a highly appreciated art form.

III. *Impressionism* is defined as a practice in painting among French painters of the late 1800s in which subject matter was depicted in its natural setting and painted in vibrant hues of unmixed color and with broad, fragmented brush strokes.

Thesis Statement: Impressionistic painting involves unique subject matter, use of color, and technique.

Body

I. Impressionism involves the unique use of natural subject matter.

A. Impressionistic painters painted visual impressions.

1. The painters did not use conventional arrangements.

2. They painted entirely out of doors.

B. The painters used nature as their predominant source of subject matter.

1. They painted the effects of light on water.

2. They enjoyed painting landscapes.

(Now let's consider the second aspect of impressionistic painting.)

II. Impressionistic painting also involves a unique use of color.

    A. The painters tried to record colors as they appeared in natural light.

        1. They used vibrant colors.

        2. The use of colors was nontraditional.

    B. Impressionistic painters were first to use color in shadows.

        1. Colors tended to cast complementary tones on neutral backgrounds.

        2. Effects of shadow can be achieved by contrasts in color.

(Not only does impressionism involve unique subject matter and unique use of color, but most notably it involves unique technique.)

III. Most notably, impressionistic painting involves a unique technique.

    A. The painters developed the technique of using fragmented brush strokes.

        1. They blended colors by placing them side by side on canvas.

        2. The effect is similar to the dots of light in a television picture.

    B. They left their paintings "unfinished" by conventional standards.

        1. There were no clear outlines.

        2. This translated the immediacy and strength of the impression.

Conclusion

I. In its unique use of subject matter, color, and technique, impressionism has made quite an impression on the art world.

Sources

Hayes, Colin. *The Colour Library of Art*. London: Paul Hamlyn Limited, 1961.
Janson, David. *The History of Art*. New York: Harcourt Brace, 1985.
Martini, Alberto. *Monet*. New York: Avenel Books, 1978.
Rouart, Kenis. *Degas*. New York: Rizzoli International, 1988.

Plan for Adapting to Audience

1. Building credibility. I hope to build credibility through my sincere interest in and knowledge of impressionistic painting.

2. Getting and maintaining attention. I will begin the speech with an attention-getting quotation. In several places in the speech I will call for the listeners to refer to their experiences. In addition, I plan to deliver the speech in a sincere, enthusiastic manner.

3. Facilitating understanding. I will state each of the three aspects clearly and discuss them in what I believe will be easy-to-understand language. I am putting special emphasis on clear, vivid language to describe the points I am making.

4. Increasing retention. In addition to clear transitions before main points, I hope to use vivid examples and comparisons that will be memorable to my listeners.

Impressionist Master

Claude Monet
1840-1926

Corbis /Bettmann

Speech

"I paint as the bird sings." This quotation from Claude Monet describes the light, vibrant nature of impressionistic painting. When impressionism first emerged in the late 1800s, it was frowned upon by critics; however, as time has moved on, it has become a highly appreciated art form. *Impressionism* is defined as a practice in painting among French painters of the late 1800s depicting subject matter in its natural setting, painted in vibrant hues of unmixed color, with broad, fragmented brush strokes. Let's consider each of these three aspects of impressionism.

The first aspect that makes impressionism unique is that it involves natural subject matter. Contrary to the practice of the time of arranging a basket of fruit or a basket of flowers or posing a model, impressionists painted natural objects primarily outdoors. In fact, impressionists were the first artists to both start and finish a painting outdoors. Because they didn't bring the painting inside the studio at all, nature was the predominant source of their subjects. Many of their paintings featured landscape views. And since impressionists were particularly fascinated with the effect of light on water, they often painted water scenes. Now let's consider the second aspect of impressionistic painting.

A second aspect of impressionism that defines it is the unique use of color. Again, in contrast to the typical practice of the time, instead of using muted tones impressionists captured the natural colors of nature by using more vibrant hues. More distinctive than just their selection of color was their use of color in shadows. Claude Monet, who was one of the originators of impressionistic painting, found that a color when cast on a neutral background would tend to cast in complementaries. For example, a red when cast on a gray background will tend to cast a bluish-green hue, because red is opposite blue-green on the color wheel. Yellow, on the other hand, would tend to cast a violet hue since yellow is opposite violet on the color wheel. Monet found that this same effect occurred in nature. Thus there was no longer a need to render shadows as dark harsh tones when you could render shadows by using complementary colors. This unique aspect of impressionistic painting was a significant artistic advancement.

Analysis

After using an attention-getting quotation from Monet, the speaker gives a complete definition of impressionism, focusing on the three key aspects that differentiate it from other styles of painting.

Notice the good transition leading into the body of the speech.

Because the definition includes three specific aspects that differentiate impressionism from other painting styles, each main point focuses on one aspect.

This first main point focuses on the use of natural subject matter. In developing the definition, the speaker emphasizes that not only were the subjects natural objects but that the paintings were done in a natural environment.

This second main point develops the second aspect of impressionism, the use of color.

Notice how the speaker uses clear examples to explain how colors are perceived in shadows.

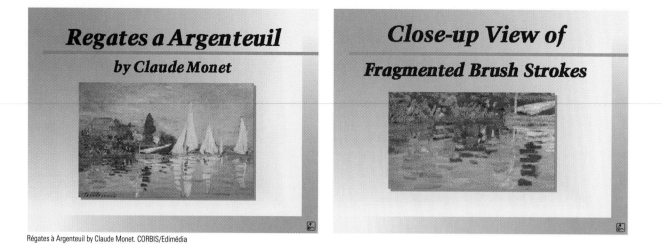

Regates a Argenteuil
by Claude Monet

Close-up View of
Fragmented Brush Strokes

Régates à Argenteuil by Claude Monet. CORBIS/Edimédia

Notice the good transition that reviews the first two aspects and leads into the third, the use of broad, fragmented brush strokes.

   This comparison of the perception of brush strokes and commas is a good one.

   Likewise, the comparison to the way we perceive color on a television screen helps the audience to understand the point.

Not only does impressionism involve unique subject matter and unique use of color, but most notably it involves unique technique. A third aspect of impressionism that defines it is the technique of using broad, fragmented brush strokes. On canvas, these brush strokes looked a little bit similar to a comma or a semicolon. Instead of mixing the colors on a palette or on a plate before putting them on a canvas, impressionists blended them by putting separate flashes of color on the canvas. Their effect was similar in manner to the way a television screen works. When you sit very close to a television screen, you see different tiny dots of color and when you move away those tiny dots of color form a solid visual impression. Because of the nature of these fragmented brush strokes, the paintings looked very unfinished by conventional standards. They didn't have the sharp clear outline that is characteristic of the painting of the time; nor did they leave a smooth appearance. Again this method was often frowned upon by the critics of the time, but it added to the originality of impressionism and it created a sense of immediacy and strength of the impressionists, which was the primary goal of their painting.

So, the next time you hear people refer to *impressionistic* painters, you can picture paintings depicting subject matter in its natural setting, painted in vibrant hues of unmixed color, with broad, fragmented brush strokes. ■

In her conclusion, the speaker reviews the three major parts of her extended definition.

   This speech is a good example of using the aspects of a definition as the framework for an entire speech.

Summary

Informative speeches are those in which the primary goal is to create understanding. As an informative speaker, your rhetorical challenge is to present information in a way that facilitates attending, understanding, and remembering.

   To accomplish these goals, speakers can learn to incorporate several principles: Audiences are more likely to show interest in, understand, and remember information (1) if they like, trust, and have confidence in the speaker, (2) if they perceive the information to be intellectually stimulating, (3) if it is presented creatively, (4) if they perceive it to be relevant, and (5) if it is emphasized.

Speakers are perceived to be credible if they are competent, have good intentions, are of good character, and have a pleasant personality. Information is seen as intellectually stimulating when it is new to audience members and meets a deep-seated need to know. Creativity involves using material in an imaginative way. Information is perceived as relevant if it is vital or important to audience members. Information is likely to be remembered if it is presented with the help of visual aids, if it is repeated, if it is introduced with external transitions, if it is presented humorously, or if it includes mnemonic devices.

Methods of informative speaking include exposition, process explanation or demonstration, and definition.

Exposition is a general informative speech using outside sources of information.

Process explanation or demonstration involves showing how to do something, how to make something, or how something works. Both full and modified demonstrations are often enhanced by visual aids.

Defining is giving the meaning of a word or concept through synonym and antonym, classification and differentiation, use or function, or etymological reference, and is enhanced by the use of examples and comparisons.

Speech is power:

speech is to persuade,

to convert, to compel.

Ralph Waldo Emerson,
"Social Aims," 1875

Principles of Persuasive Speaking

As she finished her speech, the entire audience rose as a body and cheered. Over the din, the chair shouted, "All those in favor, say 'aye'" and as one, everyone roared "aye" as a testament to her lucid and persuasive argument. As she walked to her seat, people reached to pat her on the back, and those who could not touch her chanted her name: "Sheila . . . Sheila . . . !"

"Sheila! Wake up," Denny said as he shook her shoulder. "You're supposed to be working on your speech."

P erhaps you've imagined yourself giving such a stirring speech that your audience cheered wildly at your persuasive powers. Although everything works well in our fantasies, our real-life attempts to persuade are not always so successful. **Persuasive speaking**—a process in which a speaker presents a message intended to affect beliefs or move an audience to act—is perhaps the most demanding speech challenge.

For more than 2,000 years, **rhetoric**—the study of public speaking—has been equated with persuasion. Although some people lament the emphasis of persuasion, on the grounds that all persuasion is by nature manipulative, the fact is that in the 21st century as before, many of the most important speeches given in our society will be persuasive in nature. For instance, preachers will still try to save souls, politicians will still seek reelection, and social reformers will still advocate the need for change. Although we agree that persuasion can be manipulative, one of the reasons to study ethical persuasion is to learn how to be effective within the bounds of ethical behavior.

As we have said, a persuasive speech is one that is designed to change a belief or move people to action. The primary questions are, What happens when one is "persuaded," and how can speakers learn to increase their ability to persuade within ethical boundaries?

The previous chapters have covered the steps involved in preparing and delivering any kind of speech, and the goals, principles, and methods of informative speaking. Let's briefly consider how a persuasive speaker's procedure is related to the informative speaker's:

- Both design their speeches to achieve a specific goal.
- Both attempt to hold audience attention.
- Both attempt to help audiences understand information.
- Both attempt to help audiences remember that information.
- Both seek to be perceived by their listeners as having their best interests in mind.
- Both assume that listeners have the power to act.

Persuasive speeches differ from informative speeches in that

- Persuasive speeches are designed to change audience beliefs or move audiences to action.
- Persuasive speakers use their information to show why the audience should believe or act.

Now let us turn to detailed and specific principles that are especially relevant to persuasive speaking. The following principles, based on the seven action steps, are designed to help increase the likelihood of achieving persuasive speech goals.

persuasive speaking *a process in which a speaker presents a message intended to affect beliefs or move an audience to act*

rhetoric *the study of public speaking, often equated with persuasion*

INFOTRAC COLLEGE EDITION

To learn more about the psychology of persuasion, use InfoTrac College Edition to conduct a subject search on the word "persuasion." Locate the citations under "persuasion, psychology of" in the Subject Guide, and choose two articles to read that you believe will help you understand how to be a better persuasive speaker. Choose two key points from the articles you have chosen and plan to incorporate them in your next persuasive speech.

Writing a Specific Goal That Meets Ethical Standards

Principle 1 You are more likely to persuade audience members when they understand that you believe in your goal and that your goal is in their best interests.

You begin your persuasive speech preparation by writing a persuasive speech goal (often called a **proposition**) that meets the tests discussed in Chapter 4. Let's consider three examples:

proposition *a persuasive speech goal*

I want my audience to believe that the city should build a downtown entertainment center.

I want my audience to believe that late-term abortions should be prohibited.

I want my audience to support the United Way.

Each of these meets the tests because

- Each is a complete sentence.
- Each has an infinitive (*to believe, to support*) that shows the nature of the desired response.
- Each clearly states the nature of the response.

After you have written several tentative persuasive goals, you will notice that they can be classified into two types of general purpose: (1) to affect beliefs and (2) to move an audience to action. Differentiating is important, because the two goals involve different approaches.

Although a speech goal that is phrased *to affect a belief* may result in listeners' acting upon that belief, your primary emphasis is on having them agree with you that the belief you present is reasonable.

The following speech goals seek audience acceptance of a belief:

I want the audience to believe that the city should build a downtown entertainment center.

I want the audience to believe that the federal income tax deduction for house payment interest should be abolished.

I want the audience to believe that the speed limit on all interstate highways should be raised to 70 miles per hour.

Notice that in each case, the speech will be advocating what should or ought to be believed—not what the audience members should or ought to do as a result of that belief.

Speeches that are designed *to move an audience to action* go beyond gaining agreement on a belief—they state exactly what you want your audience to *do*. The following goals all seek action:

I want my audience to donate money to the food bank drive.

I want the members of my audience to write to their congressional representatives to support legislation in favor of gun control.

I want my audience members to attend the school's production of *Grease*.

In her speech on limiting exposure to the sun, which appears at the end of this chapter, Elizabeth Helphinstine had several wording choices for her speech goal. As she thought about her speech, she decided that she didn't just want her classmates to believe that the sun's rays were harmful—she wanted to alter their behavior. As a result, rather than wording her speech goal "I want my audience to recognize the harm caused by the sun's direct rays," she decided on a wording that was designed to move her audience to action: "I want the audience to limit their exposure to the harmful rays of the sun."

Now let's consider the standards that determine how we know our goals are ethical. First, an ethical persuasive speaker gives members of the audience free choices. As Richard Weaver, a leading scholar in ethical rhetorical issues

said many years ago, ethical rhetoric is based upon choice. An audience must be allowed to accept the appeal to persuade *on its merits*. Weaver went on to say, "As rhetoric confronts us with choices involving values, the rhetorician is a preacher to us, *noble* if he tries to direct our passion toward noble ends and *base* [unethical] if he uses our passion to confuse and degrade us."[1] Second, then, it is the goal of the ethical speaker to lead audiences toward choices that are in the best interests of the members of the audience and society, and not just the interests of the speaker. Thus, a speech goal meets the ethical test if

- the speaker truly believes that the goal is important, and
- the goal is in the best interests of the audience.

Adapting to Audience Attitude

Principle 2   You are more likely to be able to persuade when you direct your goal and your information to your audience's attitude.

Persuasion is more likely to take place when your audience has a positive attitude toward your goal, so it is crucial to assess the direction and strength of audience attitudes about your topic in general and your specific goal in particular. You'll recall that an **attitude** is "a general or enduring positive or negative feeling about some person, object, or issue."[2] Your attitude is usually expressed in evaluative terms—you like or dislike something. For instance, in reference to the concept of corporal punishment, if a person is predisposed to favor spanking children who have disobeyed, we could say that this person has a positive attitude toward corporal punishment.

We have said the goal of a persuasive speech is to affect audience beliefs or behavior. But how do beliefs and behaviors relate to attitudes? Most psychologists see a **belief** as the cognitive, or mental, aspect of an attitude; that is, we believe something to be true if someone can prove it to our satisfaction. On the subject of corporal punishment, I might *believe* that spanking children helps to give them respect for school rules. So, if I hold a favorable attitude toward corporal punishment in general, it will be easier for me to hold a belief that spanking children will increase their respect for school rules.

Students of persuasion realize that people's expressions of attitudes or beliefs take the form of opinions. An **opinion** is a verbal expression of an attitude or a belief. "I think corporal punishment is important" is an opinion that reflects a favorable attitude (important rather than unimportant) about corporal

attitude   *a general or enduring positive or negative feeling about some person, object, or issue*

belief   *the cognitive, or mental, aspect of an attitude*

opinion   *verbal expression of a belief or attitude*

punishment. "I think spanking children helps to give them respect for school rules" is an opinion reflecting the belief that spanking is related to developing discipline.

There is a difference between an opinion and a behavior. A **behavior** is an action related to or resulting from an attitude or a belief. As a result of their attitudes or beliefs, people behave in certain ways. For instance, people who believe in the value of corporal punishment may be inclined to spank children who have disobeyed rules. Spanking is the behavior that results from the belief.

Often there is harmony among these elements. For instance, a person may have a favorable attitude toward corporal punishment; the person may then express the opinion that corporal punishment is important; and as a result of the attitude and opinion, the person may spank children when they misbehave. Of course, it is possible for discrepancies to occur: A person may voice the opinion that corporal punishment is important, but then never spank a child who disobeys rules.

Because much of the success of a speech depends on determining how an audience is likely to react to your goal, you must find out where the audience stands. As we said in Chapter 4, you make such judgments based on demographic information and/or opinion polls. The more data you have about your audience and the more experience you have in analyzing audiences, the better are your chances of judging audience attitudes accurately.

Audience attitudes (expressed by opinions) may be distributed along a continuum from highly favorable to hostile (see Figure 13.1). Even though any given audience may have one or a few individuals' opinions at nearly every point along the distribution, audience opinion tends to cluster at a particular point. That cluster point represents the general audience attitude for that topic. Because it would be impossible to direct your speech to all the various shades of attitudes held by the members of your audience, you must classify audience attitude as predominantly "in favor" (already holding a particular belief), "no opinion" (uninformed, neutral, or apathetic), or "opposed" (holding an opposite point of view) so you can develop a strategy that adapts to that attitude.

Now let us consider specific strategies for adapting to audiences. Suppose your goal is "I want audience members to believe that they should alter their intake of saturated fats." In your research, you may have found that consumption of high amounts of saturated fats in the teen years establishes life-long eating habits and begins slow vascular deterioration that people may not begin to notice until later in life. As you will see, your assessment of audience attitude is likely to affect (1) how you phrase your goal and/or (2) how you determine the way you will use your information.

FIGURE 13.1 Opinion Continuum

| Hostile | Opposed | Mildly opposed | Neither in favor nor opposed | Mildly in favor | In favor | Highly in favor |

In Favor

If you believe your listeners already favor your belief, then you may want to change your goal to focus on a specific course of action.

For instance, if members of your audience already favor limiting their intake of saturated fats, it would be a mistake to focus on changing their belief. Since what is likely to keep people who have a favorable attitude from acting is their lack of motivation, your job is to provide a specific course of action around which they can rally. When you believe your listeners are on your side, try to crystallize their attitudes, recommit them to a particular direction, or suggest a specific course of action that will serve as a rallying point. The presentation of a thoughtful and specific solution increases the likelihood of audience action.

Even when audience members are on your side, they may perceive what you want them to do as impractical. If so, they are likely to ignore your appeal regardless of its merits. For instance, if your goal is to have class members increase their exercise, taking the extra time necessary to exercise may seem impractical given their workloads. However, if your on-campus facility has a Nautilus room, you may be able to show them how they can increase their exercise by using otherwise "wasted" time between classes or before or after lunch, in which case they may see the practicality of your goal.

For the speech at the end of this chapter, Elizabeth Helphinstine reasoned that the audience had cognitive knowledge that the sun's rays are harmful, so she elected to write her proposition to move the audience to action.

When you know that your audience is already leaning in your favor, you can focus your speech on a specific course of action.

Jose Carrillo/PhotoEdit

No Opinion

If you believe your listeners have no opinion, then you can focus on goals that establish a belief or goals that move the audience to action.

If you believe your audience has no opinion because it is *uninformed*, the strategy should be to give enough information to help your audience understand the subject before you develop persuasive appeals that are directed toward establishing a belief or moving your listeners to action. For instance, if you believe your audience is uninformed about the need to lower saturated fat intake, then early in the speech you need to define "saturated fat," talk about how cholesterol is formed, and share medical evidence about its effects on the human body. Be careful about how much time you spend on this informative part of the speech. If it takes more than half of your allotted time to explain what you are talking about, you may not have enough time to do much persuading.

If you believe your audience has no opinion because it is *neutral*, then you see your audience as being able to reason objectively and accept sound reasoning. In this case, then, your strategy will involve presenting the best possible arguments and supporting them with the best information you can find. If your assessment is correct, then you stand a good chance of success with that strategy.

If you believe your audience members have no opinion because they are *apathetic*, all of your effort may be directed to moving them out of their apathy. Members of your audience may know what saturated fat is, know how cholesterol is formed, and even understand the medical information on negative effects, but they may not seem to care. Instead of emphasizing the information with this audience, you will emphasize motivation. You will need less material that proves the logic of your arguments and more material that is directed to your listeners' personal needs.

Opposed

If you believe your listeners are opposed, then your strategy will depend upon whether their attitude is slightly negative or totally hostile.

If you believe your listeners are *slightly opposed* to your proposal, you can approach them rather directly with your argument, hoping that its weight will swing them to your side. If your audience is slightly opposed to lowering their saturated fat intake, you can present good reasons and evidence supporting the proposal.

Another part of your strategy should involve presenting arguments in ways that lessen your listeners' negative attitudes without arousing their hostility. With a negative audience, take care to be objective with your material and make your case clearly enough that those members who are only mildly negative will consider the proposal and those who are very negative will at least understand your position.

If you believe your audience is *hostile* toward your goal, you may want to approach the topic indirectly or to consider a less ambitious goal. To expect a complete shift in attitude or behavior as a result of one speech is probably unrealistic. If you present a modest proposal that seeks a slight change in attitude, you may be able to get an audience to at least consider the value of your message. Later, when the idea begins to grow, you can ask for a greater change. For instance, the audience may be comprised of people who are "fed up" with appeals to monitor their diets. If you believe your goal is important to them

Sohm/Stock, Boston

If you believe your listeners are opposed to your proposal, your strategy should include presenting arguments in ways that lessen your listeners' negative attitudes without increasing their hostility.

regardless of their negative attitude, then develop a strategy that will be more subtle. This will involve recognizing their hostility and talking about the topic in a way that will not arouse or increase that hostility.

Figure 13.2 summarizes the strategy choices we have reviewed for audiences with different attitudes toward your topic. Later in this chapter, we will discuss patterns of speech organization that are appropriate for each type of audience.

Giving Good Reasons and Evidence

Principle 3   You are more likely to persuade an audience when the body of your speech contains good reasons and evidence that support your speech goal.

Human beings take pride in being rational; we seldom do anything without some real or imagined reason. Since the 1980s, persuasive speech theory has focused sharply on persuasion as a cognitive activity; that is, people form cognitive structures to create meaning for experiences.[3] To meet this audience need, the main points of a persuasive speech are usually stated as **reasons**—statements that tell why a proposition is justified.

reasons   *statements that tell why a proposition is justified*

FOCUS ON **skills**

Assessing Audience Attitudes

In reference to your specific persuasive speech goal, is your audience's attitude likely to be in favor, neutral, or opposed? What speech strategies will you use to adapt to that attitude?

FIGURE 13.2 Adapting persuasive speech strategies to audience attitudes

AUDIENCE ATTITUDES		STRATEGY CHOICES
If audience members are …	**then they may …**	**so that you can …**
Strongly in favor	■ be ready to act	■ provide practical suggestions
		■ put emphasis on motivation rather than on information and reasoning
In favor	■ already share many of your beliefs	■ crystallize and reinforce existing beliefs and attitudes to lead them to a course of action
Mildly in favor	■ be inclined to accept your view, but with little commitment	■ strengthen positive beliefs by emphasizing supporting reasons
Neither in favor nor opposed	■ be uninformed	■ emphasize information relevant to a belief or move to action
	■ be neutral	■ emphasize reasons relevant to belief or action
	■ be apathetic	■ concentrate on motivating them to see the importance of the proposition or seriousness of the problem
Mildly opposed	■ have doubts about the wisdom of your position	■ give them reasons and evidence that will help them to consider your position
Opposed	■ have beliefs and attitudes contrary to yours	■ emphasize sound arguments
		■ concentrate on shifting beliefs rather than on moving to action
		■ be objective to avoid arousing hostility
Hostile	■ be totally unreceptive to your position	■ plant the "seeds of persuasion"
		■ try to get them to understand your position

Finding Reasons

Reasons are statements that answer *why* you should believe or do something. If you have expertise in the subject matter, you're likely to know some of the reasons. For example, if you want the audience to see a particular movie, you know that two important reasons will be based on (1) plot and (2) acting.

For most of your persuasive speeches, however, you will want to do research to verify and/or discover reasons so that you can choose the best ones for your speech. For example, for a speech goal phrased "I want the audience to believe that the United States should overhaul the welfare system," you might discover these six reasons:

I. The welfare system costs too much to maintain.

II. The welfare system is inequitable.

III. The welfare system does not help those who need help most.

IV. The welfare system has been grossly abused.

V. The welfare system does not encourage recipients to seek work.

VI. The welfare system does not encourage self-support.

Once you have a list of possible reasons, weigh and evaluate them to select three or four good ones, using the following criteria.

1. Good reasons can be supported. Some reasons that sound impressive cannot be supported with facts. For example, the fourth reason, "The welfare system has been grossly abused," sounds like a good one; but if you cannot find facts to support so strong a statement, either modify it or do not use it in your speech. You'll be surprised how many reasons mentioned in various sources have to be dropped from consideration for a speech because they can't be well supported.

2. Good reasons are relevant to the proposition. Sometimes, statements look like reasons but don't supply much proof. For instance, "The welfare system is supported by socialists" may sound like a reason for overhauling it to people who dislike socialism, but it doesn't offer any direct proof that the system needs overhauling.

3. Good reasons will have an impact on the intended audience. Suppose that you have a great deal of factual evidence to back up the statement "The welfare system does not encourage recipients to seek work." Even if it is a well-supported reason, it will not be an ineffective reason to use in a speech if the majority of the audience does not see "seeking work" as a primary criterion for evaluating the welfare system. Although you cannot always be sure about the potential impact of a reason, you can estimate its possible impact based on your audience analysis. For instance, on the topic of welfare reform, some audiences would be more concerned with costs, equity, and abuses of the system.

Finding Evidence to Support Your Reasons

By themselves, reasons are only unsupported statements. Although some reasons are self-explanatory and occasionally have a persuasive effect without further support, most listeners look for factual statements and expert opinions to support the reasons before they will either accept or act on them.

As we learned in Chapter 5, the best support is comprised of verifiable factual statements. Suppose that in a speech designed to motivate people to donate money to Alzheimer's research, you give the reason "Alzheimer's disease is a major killer." The statement "According to statistics presented in last month's *Time* magazine, Alzheimer's disease is the fourth leading cause of death for adults" would be factual support for that reason.

Statements from people who have good reputations for knowledge on the subject represent expert opinions. Thus, expert opinion support for the reason "Alzheimer's disease is a major killer" might be the statement, "According to the Surgeon General, 'By 2050 Alzheimer's disease may afflict 14 million people a year.'"

Let's look at one more example to illustrate the use of fact and opinion evidence to support a proposition:

Proposition: I want the audience to believe that television violence has a harmful effect on viewers.

Reason: Television violence desensitizes people to violence.

Evidence by fact: In a survey of 50 children between the ages of 5 and 10 in Los Angeles, California, the children were asked after watching *Teenage Mu-*

tant Ninja Turtles whether or not violence was acceptable. Thirty-nine of them responded "Yes, because it helps you to win fights."

Evidence by expert opinion: According to Kirsten Houston, writing in the July 1997 *Journal of Psychology*, "Repeated exposure to media violence is a major factor in the gradual desensitization of individuals to such scenes. This desensitization, in turn, weakens some viewers' psychological restraints on violent behavior."

Whether your evidence is a supposed factual statement or an opinion, you'll want to ask at least three questions to assure yourself that what you present is "good" evidence:

1. What is the source of the evidence? This question involves both the people who offered the opinions or compiled the facts *and* the book, journal, or Internet sources where they were reported. Just as some people's opinions are more reliable than others, so are some printed and Internet sources more reliable than others. Be especially careful of undocumented information that comes from the Internet. If evidence comes from a poor source, an unreliable source, or a biased source, you will want to seek verification of it or drop it from the speech.

2. Is the evidence recent? Products, ideas, and statistics are best when they are recent. You must ask when the particular evidence was true. Five-year-old evidence may not be true today. Furthermore, an article in last week's newsmagazine may be using five-year-old evidence in the story.

3. Is the evidence relevant? Make sure that your evidence directly supports the reason. If it does not, then leave it out of the speech.

In the next chapter, we will look at forms of reasoning and fallacies of reasoning, as we offer more specific guidelines for preparing a speech of reasons.

For the speech at the end of this chapter, Elizabeth Helphinstine had several potentially strong reasons to present to her audience. The two that she thought would be most powerful were that exposure to the sun causes premature aging and that it causes skin cancer. She then worked to make sure that she had good support for both reasons.

Organizing Reasons to Meet Audience Attitudes

Principle 4   You are more likely to persuade an audience when you organize your reasons in a way that will be most persuasive to that audience.

Statement of logical reasons, problem/solution, comparative advantages, criteria satisfaction, and motivational are patterns that you are likely to select for your persuasive speech organization. So that you can contrast the patterns and better understand their use, we will use the same proposition (specific goal) and the same (or similar) reasons to illustrate each one. For each pattern, we will describe it, show the audience attitudes for which it is most applicable, and describe the logic of the order.

Statement of Logical Reasons Pattern

statement of logical reasons *a straightforward organization in which you present the best-supported reasons you can find, with your second strongest reason first and strongest reason last*

The **statement of logical reasons** is a straightforward organization in which you present the best-supported reasons you can find, following an order of second strongest first, strongest last, and other reason(s) in between. It will work when your listeners have no opinion on the subject, are apathetic, or are perhaps mildly in favor or opposed.

Proposition: I want my audience to vote in favor of the school tax levy on the November ballot.

I. Income will enable the schools to restore vital programs. (second strongest)

II. Income will enable the schools to give teachers the raises they need to keep up with the cost of living.

III. The actual cost to each member of the community will be very small. (strongest)

In a speech using the statement of logical reasons pattern, the logic of the organization may be stated as follows: When good reasons and evidence are presented supporting a proposal, the proposal should be adopted.

Problem Solution Pattern

problem solution pattern *an organization that first clarifies the nature of the problem, then proposes a solution and shows why it is the best one*

The **problem solution pattern** provides a framework for clarifying the nature of the problem and showing why a given proposal is the best one. The problem solution pattern is often organized around three general reasons: (1) There is a

Effective speakers vary their organizational patterns depending on attitudes of their different audiences.

Harvey Fink/Impact Visuals/PNI

problem that requires action. (2) The proposal will solve the problem. (3) The proposal is the best solution to the problem, because it will lead to positive consequences. This pattern is also a straightforward presentation of reasons, so it is likely to work best for a topic that is relatively unfamiliar to an audience—one in which they are unaware that a problem exists—or for an audience that has no opinion or is only mildly pro or con. A problem solution organization for the school tax proposition might look like this:

Proposition: I want my audience to vote in favor of the school tax levy on the November ballot.

I. The shortage of money is resulting in serious problems for public education. (statement of problem)

II. The proposed increase is large enough to solve those problems. (solution)

III. For now, a tax levy is the best method of solving the schools' problems. (consequences)

In a speech using the problem solution pattern, the logic of the organization showing the relationship between the reasons and the speech goal may be stated as follows: When a problem is presented that is not or cannot be solved with current measures and the proposal can solve the problem practically and beneficially, then the proposal should be adopted.

In the speech at the end of this chapter, Elizabeth Helphinstine had several choices for organizing the speech. She decided on a problem solution pattern. That is, although she thought her audience would already understand that the sun has harmful rays, it would be in her interest to consider two specific dangers of those rays: causing premature aging and causing skin cancer. She also realized that she would have to provide a rationale for the solution (avoid the sun's rays) that would seem practical. So, for her solution she focuses on easy ways to cope with the problem: limiting hours and taking necessary precautions.

Comparative Advantages Pattern

The **comparative advantages pattern** allows you to place all the emphasis on the superiority of the proposed course of action. Rather than presenting the proposition as a solution to a grave problem, it presents the proposition as one that ought to be adopted solely on the basis of the advantages of that proposition to what is currently being done. Although this pattern can work for any audience attitude, it works best when the audience agrees either that there is a problem that must be solved or, if no particular problem is at issue, that the proposition is superior to its competitors. For example, when people elect to eat out, they have a variety of choices, so a speech advocating Le Petit France Restaurant would emphasize its advantages over its competition. A comparative advantages approach to the school tax proposition would look like this:

comparative advantages pattern
an organization that places all the emphasis on the superiority of the proposed course of action

Proposition: I want my audience to vote in favor of the school tax levy on the November ballot.

I. Income from a tax levy will enable schools to raise the standards of their programs. (advantage 1)

II. Income from a tax levy will enable schools to hire better teachers. (advantage 2)

III. Income from a tax levy will enable schools to better the educational environment. (advantage 3)

In a speech using the comparative advantages pattern, the logic of the organization that shows the relationship between the reasons and the speech goal may be stated as follows: When reasons are presented that show a proposal is a significant improvement over what is being done, then the proposal should be adopted.

Criteria Satisfaction Pattern

criteria satisfaction pattern *an indirect organization that seeks audience agreement on criteria that should be considered when evaluating a particular proposition and then shows how the proposition satisfies those criteria*

The **criteria satisfaction pattern** is an indirect pattern that seeks audience agreement on criteria that should be considered when evaluating a particular proposition and then shows how the proposition satisfies those criteria. When you encounter audiences that are opposed to your propositions, you need a pattern of organization that will not aggravate their hostility. The criteria satisfaction pattern is likely to work because it focuses on developing a "yes" response to criteria before you introduce the proposition and reasons. A criteria satisfaction organization for the school tax proposition would look like this:

Proposition: I want my audience to vote in favor of the school tax levy on the November ballot.

I. We all want good schools. (a community value)

    A. Good schools have programs that prepare our youth to function in society. (one criterion of good schools)

    B. Good schools are those with the best teachers available. (a second criterion of good schools)

II. Passage of the school tax levy will guarantee good schools.

    A. Passage will enable us to increase the quality of vital programs. (satisfaction of one criterion)

    B. Passage will enable us to hire and keep the best teachers. (satisfaction of the second criterion)

In a speech using the criteria satisfaction pattern, the logic of the organization showing the relationship between the reasons and the speech goal may be stated as follows: When a proposal meets a set of agreed-on criteria, it should be adopted.

Motivational Pattern

motivational pattern *an organization that combines problem solving and motivation—it follows a problem solution pattern but includes required steps designed to heighten the motivational effect of the organization*

The **motivational pattern,** the final one we will consider, combines problem solving and motivation—it follows a problem solution pattern but includes required steps designed to heighten the motivational effect of the organization. Much of the thinking behind motivational patterns is credited to Allan Monroe, a professor at Purdue University. Motivational patterns usually include a five-step, unified sequence that replaces the normal introduction–body–conclusion model: (1) an attention step, (2) a need step that fully explains the nature of the problem, (3) a satisfaction step that explains how the proposal solves the problem in a satisfactory manner, (4) a visualization step that provides a personal application of the proposal, and (5) an action appeal step that emphasizes the specific direction listener action should take. A motivational pattern for the school tax proposition would look like this:

Selecting an Organization

Select a pattern of organization for your speech. Justify your selection on the basis of your audience analysis.

Proposition: I want my audience to vote in favor of the school tax levy on the November ballot.

I. Comparisons of worldwide test scores in math and science have refocused our attention on education. (attention)

II. The shortage of money is resulting in cost-saving measures that compromise our ability to teach basic academic subjects well. (need, statement of problem)

III. The proposed increase is large enough to solve those problems in ways that allow for increased emphasis on academic need areas. (satisfaction, how the proposal solves the problem)

IV. Think of the contribution you will be making not only to the education of your future children but also to efforts to return our educational system to the world level it once held. (visualization of personal application)

V. Here are "Vote Yes" buttons that you can wear to show you are willing to support this much-needed tax levy. (action appeal showing specific direction)

Because motivational patterns are variations of problem solution patterns, the logic of the organization is much the same: When the current means are not solving the problem, a new solution that does solve the problem should be adopted.

Using Emotion to Motivate

Principle 5 You are more likely to motivate audience members when you arouse their emotions.

Motivation—"forces acting on or within an organism to initiate and direct behavior"[4]—is often a result of using emotional language. Motivation, to a large extent, is based on what Aristotle called *pathos*, or emotional appeal.

Emotions, such as anger, fear, surprise, and joy, are subjective experiences triggered by actions or words that are accompanied by bodily arousal and by overt behavior.[5] Since effective persuasive speech development entails both logical and emotional elements that act interdependently, we need to look for good reasons and for support that will, if properly phrased, arouse these emotions.

As you work on your speeches, you will want to determine the emotions that you want to arouse, the kinds of information necessary to arouse those emotions, and how the information can be phrased for maximum effect. Let's consider each of these.

motivation   *forces acting on or within an organism to initiate and direct behavior*

emotions   *subjective experiences triggered by actions or words that are accompanied by bodily arousal and by overt behavior*

1. What emotions do you want your audience to experience as you make your point? The emotions you want to arouse will differ from speech to speech. For instance, in a speech calling for more humane treatment of the elderly, you may decide that you want your listeners to feel sadness, anger, grief, caring, or perhaps, guilt. In contrast, in a speech designed to get the audience to attend your school's production of a musical, you may want your listeners to feel joy, excitement, or enthusiasm.

2. What information do you have that could be used to stimulate those emotions? For the speech on the elderly, suppose you have determined that you want your listeners to feel sadness about the treatment of people in nursing homes. Your information might include data from interviews with elderly individuals showing that their only talk of the future is the inevitability of death; accounts of social workers saying that many old people live totally in the past and are reluctant to talk about or even think about the future; or information showing that many nursing homes do very little to give their clients anything to look forward to.

3. Keeping ethical considerations in mind, how can you phrase your information to elicit those emotions? How well you motivate is likely to depend on how well you phrase your information.

For instance, for the speech on the elderly you might be considering saying:

> Currently, elderly people are alienated from society. A high percentage live in nursing homes, live on small fixed incomes, and exist out of the mainstream of society.

But with just the addition of a question and language that creates more vivid pictures, you could make this statement much more emotionally powerful:

> Currently, elderly people are alienated from society that they worked their entire lives to support. What happens to elderly people in America? They become the forgotten segment of society. They are often relegated to "old people's homes" so that they can live out their lives and die without being "a bother" to their sons and daughters. Because they must exist on relatively small fixed incomes, they are confined to a life that for many means separation from the very society they helped to create.

You're likely to find that some of your best opportunities for using meaningful emotional appeal occur in the introduction and conclusion of your speech. Notice how emotional appeals heighten the power of the following introduction and conclusion in a student speech on euthanasia.[6] The student began her speech as follows:

> Let's pretend for a moment. Suppose that on the upper right-hand corner of your desk there is a button. You have the power by pushing that button to quickly and painlessly end the life of one you love: your brother or father. This loved one has terminal cancer and will be confined to a hospital for his remaining days. Would you push the button now? His condition worsens. He is in constant pain, and he is hooked up to a life-support machine. He first requests, but as the pain increases he pleads for you to help. Now would you push that button? Each day you watch him deteriorate until he reaches a point where he cannot talk, he cannot see, he cannot hear—he is only alive by that machine. Now would you push that button?

After giving reasons for changing our laws on euthanasia, she concluded her speech as follows:

> I ask again, how long could you take walking into that hospital room and looking at your brother or father in a coma, knowing he would rather be allowed to die a natural death than be kept alive in such a degrading manner? I've crossed that doorstep—I've gone into that hospital room, and let me tell you, it's hell. I think it's time we reconsider our laws concerning euthanasia. Don't you?

Regardless of your beliefs about the subject of euthanasia, you would be likely to experience sadness as you empathize with her feelings.

In the next chapter, we will take a more detailed look at motivation, incentives, and basic needs.

For the speech at the end of this chapter, Elizabeth Helphinstine thought that one of the best ways to get the audience to respond emotionally was to use some of her own and her family's experiences to dramatize the dangers of the sun's rays.

TECHNOLOGY tips

A way to pretest the strength of the arguments you have developed for your speech is to post them on an electronic bulletin board and see how others respond to your ideas. Be sure to doublecheck the accuracy of information or feedback you receive from those who respond.

Developing Your Credibility

Principle 6   You are more likely to persuade your listeners when they have faith in your credibility.

Credibility is as important, if not even more so, in persuasive speaking as in informative speaking. Almost all studies confirm that speaker credibility has a major effect on audience belief and attitude.[7] In earlier chapters, we outlined the nature of credibility, showing that you will be perceived as a credible speaker if audiences perceive you as knowledgeable, trustworthy, and personable.

Jacques M. Chenet/Corbis

Credibility is important in persuasive speaking. Colin Powell built his credibility through his personal integrity and demonstration of character. The audience's perception of your trustworthiness results from their assessment of your character and your apparent motives for presenting the information.

Presenting the Speech Convincingly

Principle 7   You are more likely to persuade an audience if you develop an effective oral presentation style.

Previous chapters have addressed characteristics of presentation that you must develop to increase your effectiveness, including the importance of practicing your speech until your presentation (language and delivery) enhances it. Although this section is short, you must not forget that it is through your presentation that your listeners "see" your speech.

Considering Gender and Cultural Differences

So far in this chapter, we have discussed reasoning, appealing to emotions, and building credibility—three forms of proof that Aristotle, who wrote the first comprehensive treatment of persuasive speaking, called *logos*, *pathos*, and *ethos*. A legitimate question is whether women and people of other cultures use and appreciate these same forms, which are based on male speaking in a predominantly Eurocentric culture. The answer is that in all cultures, male and female public speakers use the same means of persuasion; however, women and people from other cultures may *emphasize* each of these means differently. Whereas U.S. male culture relies on good reasons supported with factual information and expert opinion, other cultural groups may put more emphasis on credibility of the speaker or emotional arousal and expressiveness.[8]

So, how should you proceed? Again, the advice of Aristotle in his *Rhetoric* is useful to any speaker. When he discussed adapting to audiences, he pointed out that if an audience was truly homogeneous, then a speaker would want to use forms of proof, references, and examples that would relate to their particular experience. But when an audience is heterogeneous, then a speaker would find it most useful to speak to what he called "the golden mean"—that is, a composite that covered the majority of that audience.

FOCUS ON skills

Persuasive Speaking

1. Prepare a 5- to 8-minute speech in which you affect audience belief or move your audience to action. An outline is required.

2. As an addendum to the outline, you may wish to write a persuasive speech plan for adapting to your specific audience that includes:

   a. How your goal adapts to whether your prevailing audience attitude is in favor, no opinion, or opposed.

   b. What reasons you will use, and how the organizational pattern you have selected is appropriate to your topic and audience.

   c. How you will establish your credibility with this audience.

   d. How you will motivate your audience by appealing to their emotions.

Evaluating Speeches

For one or more of the speeches you hear during a round of persuasive speeches, complete the Persuasive Speech Evaluation Checklist and then write a two- to five-paragraph evaluation of the speech. See the sample outline, speech, and analysis that follow.

SPEECH EVALUATION checklist

Persuasive Speech

Check all items that were accomplished effectively.

Primary Criteria

_____ **1.** Was the specific goal designed to affect a belief or move to action?

_____ **2.** Did the speaker present clearly stated reasons?

_____ **3.** Did the speaker use facts and expert opinions to support these reasons?

_____ **4.** Was the organizational pattern appropriate for the type of goal and assumed attitude of the audience?

_____ **5.** Did the speaker use emotional language to motivate the audience?

_____ **6.** Did the speaker's use of material meet ethical standards?

_____ **7.** Was the speaker effective in establishing his or her credibility on this topic?

General Criteria

_____ **1.** Was the specific goal clear?

_____ **2.** Was the introduction effective?

_____ **3.** Were the main points clear?

_____ **4.** Was the conclusion effective?

_____ **5.** Was the language clear, vivid, emphatic, appropriate?

_____ **6.** Was the speech delivered enthusiastically, with vocal expressiveness, fluently, spontaneously, and directly?

Evaluate the speech as (check one):
_____ excellent, _____ good, _____ average, _____ fair, _____ poor.
Use the information from your checklist to support your evaluation.

S A M P L E   speech

Limiting Exposure to the Sun[9]

Outline

Specific Goal: I want my audience to limit their exposure to the harmful rays of the sun.

Introduction

I. How many of you have friends who spent spring break at the beach?

II. They probably did not come back and tell you about the jump start they got on premature aging of their skin or getting a head start on skin cancer.

III. You should limit your exposure to the sun because it causes premature aging and skin cancer, and because it is so easy to do.

Thesis Statement: Although exposure to the sun causes premature aging and skin cancer, it is easy to prevent premature aging and to lower the risk of skin cancer.

Body

I. Exposure to the sun causes premature aging.

    A. Sun damage occurs during your first 18 years.

    B. The sun causes premature aging regardless of skin type.

    C. Sun damage occurs with as little as 20 minutes of exposure twice a week.

(But premature aging is minor compared to the chances of skin cancer.)

II. Exposure to the sun causes skin cancer.

    A. More than 600,000 people will get skin cancer this year.

        1. All people are susceptible to skin cancer.

        2. Some people are at higher risk than others.

    B. Skin cancer is a major killer.

        1. Skin cancer is the number one killer of women ages 26–32.

        2. The number of women dying of skin cancer is higher than the next four leading diseases combined.

(The problem is great, but the cure is relatively easy.)

III. It is easy to prevent premature aging and lower the risk of skin cancer.

    A. Limiting your hours in the sun is the number one way.

    B. But if you want to be in the sun, take necessary precautions.

        1. Wear a T-shirt.

        2. Wear a hat.

        3. Wear sunglasses.

        4. Use sunblock.

Conclusion

I. Limiting your exposure to the sun will reduce premature aging and skin cancer.

II. Preventive measure can lengthen your life.

Sources

Balkan, Jodi. "Practicing Safe Sun." *New Woman*, May 1993, pp. 118–121.

"Everything You Thought You Knew About Sun Protection . . . But Didn't." *Glamour*, May 1994, pp. 216–223.

Farr, Louise. "Sunny & Safe." *Self*, May 1994, pp. 112–118.

Shapiro, Anna. "Taking Cover." *Vogue*, June 1995, 194–196.
"Sunscreens: Everything New Under the Sun." *Consumer Reports*, July 1994,
    pp. 73–75.

Speech Plan

1. Audience attitude toward goal. During my preparation, I found that my audience was fairly apathetic about the sun and its harmful effects. I will attempt to build a positive attitude by making my information relevant to their lives.

2. Organization. I have organized my speech into three reasons, the first two showing the problem and the final one showing how easy it is to solve the problem. I will attempt to use transitions between points.

3. Credibility. I plan to build credibility by relating my own personal history of "sun worship." I will tell the audience about my grandmother's death from skin cancer. I will make reference to several sets of statistics from the American Cancer Society as well as from the American Association of Dermatology.

4. Motivation. I will try to motivate them by making safe sun easy for them. I will tell them that by limiting their exposure to the sun they can not only save their skin, but also their lives.

Thinking Critically: Speech and Analysis

Read the following speech aloud. Then, analyze it in terms of the primary criteria in the Persuasive Speech Evaluation Checklist: goal, reasons, support, organization, motivation, credibility, and ethics.

Speech

How many of you have friends who spent spring break anywhere where it was fun in the sun on the beach? What did your friends come back and tell you the most about? What were they most excited about? Did they tell you about the jump start they got on premature aging of their skin? Or the head start on skin cancer? Probably not. My goal in this speech is to tell you three reasons why you should limit your exposure to the sun.

Let's start with the first reason. The most common effect of the sun is premature aging of the skin. All of us are young, and we think, "Uh, I'm only 19, 21, 24, I don't have to worry about premature aging. That happens later in life." Not so. According to *The American Journal of Public Health*, 78 percent of all premature aging happens before the age of 18. Now we've all seen people who lie out by the pool all day and they think, I'll never look like them. Well, I've got news for you. This damage happened steadily over a number of years starting with their childhood. Now when I read that statistic about 78 percent of all premature aging happening before the age of 18, that scared me. Because I remember as a little girl, my parents would send me off to summer camp every day without any sun protection. Not that they didn't care, but they really didn't know any better. So now, my sun damage clock is ticking every minute I'm out in the sun, adding another dose of aging to my skin. Many of my friends think that because they're African American or have naturally dark skin that they're exempt from the problem. And I thought the same way. But the sun doesn't discriminate—I don't care what nationality you are, what race you are, every one of you [pointing to each person in class] can be a victim.

Now you might be saying, I agree with you on your first point, but I'll take my chances on aging. Well if my first point didn't convince you, my next point should make you scared for your life.

Analysis

Elizabeth uses a series of questions to get audience attention.

Here she previews her procedure.

Her first reason is stated as a complete sentence.

Good direct audience adaptation: "all of us" and "we think."

Good use of startling statistics to keep focus on relevance to this aged audience.

Also notice use of personal pronouns.

Good use of experience that not only personalizes information but also begins to develop emotional appeal.

Excellent transition that also gives an emotional jolt.

Second problem reason is stated as a complete sentence.

Notice, she not only presents statistical support, but she also relates information directly to the audience.

"Well, you may say," adapts by anticipating audience comment. Another personal anecdote that continues to reinforce the strong emotional appeal of the speech.

Now that she's finished her two problem reasons, she lays the groundwork for the solution. Good adaptation to words of a previous speaker.

Here we get the idea that she is going to be talking about how we can prevent skin damage and lower the risks of getting cancer. Third reason is a complete sentence that emphasizes practicality of preventive measures. So far speech has been quite heavy—here she begins to take a more lighthearted approach.

Good use of humor. By poking fun at herself she makes her point that vanity is less important than safety. Reference to Jason's hat is another example of direct adaptation.

Notice that each one of these measures is "easy," just as she had said earlier.

Here she adapts to a prospective audience question. Nice touch. She begins her conclusion by reviewing the reasons. Her final sentence neatly reinforces the point of her speech. Throughout the speech Elizabeth blends logical information and emotional appeal quite well. This is a good persuasive speech that follows the problem solution pattern.

My second point is that the sun causes skin cancer and, in many cases, death. According to the American Cancer Society, over 600,000 people this year alone in the U.S. will get skin cancer. Moreover, it's the number one killer of women ages 24 to 32. That's women like me and women like your sisters and your girlfriends. Well, you may say, but people with cancerous moles can go to their doctor and get them removed within an hour. But that's not true for everyone. When I was a little girl, my grandmother Helphinstine was the most vibrant dynamic woman you would ever want to meet. She had a husband and five children. She would get her chores done, and then grab her tin of Crisco and go lie out in the yard for a couple of hours every day—she lived to tan. She died when I was seven. She died from a cancerous melanoma, a cancerous mole, that couldn't be removed—the cancer couldn't be stopped—it killed her.

I can't do anything about your vanity, but I can do something about your ignorance. Just by being here today, you now know the facts about skin aging and skin cancer. Aging and cancer are not something to be taken lightly—but there is something we all can do about it. The other day Bryan told us about his mother's breast cancer. One of the lines in his speech struck a chord with me. He said, "My mother didn't do anything wrong, she couldn't prevent it, she didn't smoke, there was nothing she could do." But unlike that instance, there is something you can do to prevent skin cancer. According to the Academy of Dermatology, three-fourths of all skin damage can be prevented. Prevention cuts down on aging and cuts down on cancer. If you're cutting down on cancer, of course you're cutting down on that chance of death.

My third point is that prevention is easy. Now I want to tell you about what I do on my fun in the sun days. In this beach bag are a few things you can use to prevent premature aging and skin cancer. The first thing I pull out is a T-shirt. This is your basic T-shirt—it doesn't matter what it has on it or what color it is. A T-shirt has an SPF (a sun protection factor) of 15. This means that with it on you could stay out in the sun for 15 hours before you'd have the effects of 1 hour in the sun without it.

The next thing I pull out is my handy-dandy shark's hat. Now I'm not a real babe in this hat—not many women look good in a hat like this—but because it covers my head and has a full inch brim, according to this month's *Self* magazine, it cuts down on skin damage by at least 10 percent. Any hat will help—you can wear a hat like Jason has back there. Not only would it protect his face, but he could turn it around backwards and protect his neck.

Next I pull out my nifty sunglasses. Make sure yours have UV protection—ultraviolet protection for your eyes.

Finally, I pull out my sunblock. This one is a 35 sunblock—this means you'd have to be in the sun for 35 hours to get the same effect as 1 hour without any protection. Sunblock ranges from 2 all the way up to 45—so you can pick your level of protection.

Now you might say, "Elizabeth, how can you stand up here and tell us to stay out of the sun when you're standing up there with a complete tan. That's my secret. My tan came from this bottle. Because I'm still dedicated to having a tan, I put this on every day. Looks fairly natural, huh?

In conclusion, I've told you the sun causes aging, the sun causes cancer, and that prevention is easy. I hope that now that you have heard these three points, you will limit your time in the sun and when you are in the sun, you'll take action. So, the next time you see a person who has a great natural tan, realize that a great tan contributes to skin damage and may very well be the tan that kills. ■

Christie had promised to give a speech in support of her good friend Maryanne for student body president. The problem was that although Maryanne was a good friend, Christie didn't really believe that she was qualified for the office. Still, she thought, when a friend is in need, you help her.

She had good support for her reasons that Maryanne is a high energy person and that she is honest. But what Maryanne wanted her to stress was her job qualifications. Although Maryanne had held an office of class vice president in 11th grade, she hadn't really been involved in any leadership roles in college.

What Christie thought she would do is talk about what Maryanne had done in high school and act as if it related to college experience. She was careful so that at no time did she really say that she was talking about college experience, but she worded the material in a way that left that impression. When she finished, she said, "Well, that's the best I can do," and she began practicing the speech.

1. Was Christie's behavior ethical?
2. What might she have done to avoid any question of unethical behavior?

Summary

Persuasive speeches are designed to establish or change a belief or motivate an audience to act. The principles governing persuasive speeches are similar to those presented for informative speeches, as are the steps of speech preparation.

First, write a clear persuasive speech goal, or proposition, stating what you want your audience to believe or do.

Second, analyze your audience's interest and knowledge levels and attitude toward your goal.

Third, build the body of the speech with good reasons—statements that answer why the proposition is justified. Support reasons with facts and expert opinions.

Fourth, create an organization for the speech that suits your goal and your analysis of the audience. Five organizational patterns for persuasive speeches are statement of logical reasons, problem solution, comparative advantages, criteria satisfaction, and motivational.

Fifth, motivate your audience by reworking language to appeal to the emotions, especially in your introduction and conclusion.

Sixth, use your credibility advantageously. Especially in persuasive speaking, one of the most important ways of building credibility is to behave in an ethical manner.

Seventh, deliver the speech convincingly. Good delivery is especially important in persuasive speaking.

There is nothing to be afraid of if you believe and know that the cause for which you stand is right.

Martin Luther King, Jr., Speech, Savannah, Georgia, January 1, 1961

David Young-Wolff/PhotoEdit

Practicing Persuasive Speaking Skills

"Kelly, I hear that you're looking at a really neat internship with a political organization for next term."

"Well, in some ways it looks really good, but in other ways it's kind of scary."

"What do you mean?"

"The good news is that it gives me experience working with people in a real political campaign. But they want a person who can provide some ideas for various speech situations."

"That sounds great."

"It is in a way, but I'm concerned about my own preparation. Not only do they want someone who understands persuasion—you know, the whole ethos, logos, pathos bit—but also they want someone who knows something about argument."

"I don't know, Kelly, you seem to argue with people quite a lot!"

"Come on—I mean knowing refutation and rebuttal as well as just preparing speeches."

As our chapter opening suggests, effective speakers are skilled in all aspects of persuasion. The first section of this chapter, Reasoning with Audiences, probes more deeply into forming logical arguments. The second section, Motivating Audiences, provides a broader theoretical look at motivation and suggests lines of development that can increase the likelihood of audiences' acting favorably. The third section of this chapter, Refuting Persuasive Claims, provides a speaker with the information necessary to analyze and then counter ill-conceived or unwarranted proposals.

Reasoning with Audiences

You'll recall from the previous chapter that in public speaking, reasoning with an audience means presenting reasons and evidence in support of a speech goal. We call units of reasons and evidence **arguments.**

In this section, we examine the formulation of sound arguments. The section concludes with a speech assignment and an example of a speech (with outline and speech plan) designed to illustrate reasoning with audiences.

argument *a reason and its supporting evidence*

Essentials of Reasoning

reasoning *the process of drawing inferences from factual information*

arguing *the process of proving a proposition with factual information*

In real-life situations, the word **reasoning** refers to the process of drawing inferences (conclusions) from factual information and **arguing,** the process of proving a proposition with reasons and evidence. Thus, when we observe that our friend's car is "missing" at slow speeds and stalling at stoplights, we can *reason* (draw the inference) that the car needs a tune-up. Likewise, when we talk with our friend, we can *argue* (prove to him) that the car needs a tune-up, because it is "missing" at slow speeds and stalling at stoplights.

Whether you reason by drawing conclusions from information or argue by supporting conclusions with information, you need a method of analyzing the soundness of the reasoning or arguing that you are involved in. The essentials of argument (reasoning) are the claim, the data, and the reasoning process.

claim *the proposition or conclusion to be proven*

Claim   The **claim** is simply the statement of what you want the audience to believe. We may call the claim a speech goal (or proposition), conclusion, or inference to be proven. In our example, the claim is "The car needs a tune-up."

data *reasons and evidence (facts, opinions, observations, evidence, assumptions, or assertions) that support a claim or proposition*

Data   From our discussion in the previous chapter, we know that we support a claim—perhaps the goal of our speech—with reasons and evidence. **Data** is a word that means all support, including both reasons and/or evidence (facts, opinions, observations, assumptions, or assertions). In the car example, the data are two reasons, "missing at slow speeds" and "stalling at lights," along with any supporting information.

We can put our example in speech outline form as follows:

Specific Goal: I want the audience to believe that the car needs a tune-up.

I.   The car misses at slow speeds.

  (evidence to support the reason)

II.   The car stalls at lights.

  (evidence to support the reason)

Now we turn to a method for determining the quality of the reasoning shown in this example.

Reasoning Process   The **reasoning process** is the conscious or subconscious thinking that connects the data (reasons and evidence) to the claim (speech goal or proposition). The reasoning process can be verbalized with a sentence that explains the nature of the leap from data to claim. The sentence we create to verbalize the reasoning process is called a **warrant**.[1] For instance, a person who argues (makes the claim that) "the car needs a tune-up" on the basis of "missing" and "stalling at lights" may verbalize the reasoning process with the warrant "Missing at slow speeds and stalling at lights are common indications or signs that the car needs a tune-up."

> **reasoning process**   *the conscious or subconscious thinking that leads from the data to the claim*

> **warrant**   *a sentence created to verbalize the reasoning process*

The reasoning process statement, then, indicates how you connected the claim and the data. Although the actual statement of the reasoning process may not be included in an oral argument, speakers need to verbalize the reasoning process (give a warrant) in order to analyze or test the soundness of their reasoning. Later we will identify the questions to ask in order to weigh the strength of the warrant (reasoning process).

Using **C** for claim, **D** for data (reason and evidence), and **W** for warrant or reasoning process—a form of analysis first articulated by the philosopher rhetorician Stephen Toulmin[2]—we can write the reasoning for our example in outline form as follows:

C   (Specific Goal) I want the owner to believe that the car needs a tune-up.

D   **I.** The engine misses at slow speeds.
         (plus evidence in support)

    II. The car stalls at lights.
         (plus evidence in support)

W   (Missing and stalling are major indicators—signs—of the need for a tune-up.)

CORBIS/BETTMANN

Sound reasoning is essential to persuasive speakers like consumer advocate Ralph Nader, who know that their evidence and reasoning will be closely scrutinized in public debate.

The warrant is written in parentheses because it is implied rather than actually stated.

Types of Arguments

Although an oral argument always includes a claim and data (reasons and/or evidence), there are many different types of relationships between data and claim. Because they are used so frequently, the following six relationships, or types of argument, are the ones you are most likely to encounter and to use in your persuasive speeches.

arguing from example *supporting a claim with one or more individual examples*

Arguing from Example When you **argue from example,** you support a claim with one or more individual examples. Because you are likely to discover numerous examples in your research for nearly any topic, you are likely to use arguing from example quite frequently. The form for an argument from example is as follows:

C Claim

D Example I
Example II
Etc.

Suppose you are considering supporting Juanita Martinez for president of the senior class. Your claim is that Juanita is electable. In examining her record to find support for this claim, you find several examples of her previous victories. She was elected treasurer of her high school junior class, chairperson of her church youth group, and president of her college sorority. Each of these three is an example that gives support to the claim. How are the claim and examples related? We could say "What was true in several instances is true (or will be true) in general or in other instances."

Let's look at this argument in speech analysis form:

C Juanita Martinez is electable.

D Juanita has won previous elections.

    A. Juanita won the election for treasurer of her high school junior class.

    B. Juanita won the election for chairperson of her church youth group.

    C. Juanita won the election for president of her sorority.

W (Because Juanita Martinez was elected to previous offices, she is electable for this office.)

To test the strength of an argument from example, ask the following questions.

1. Are enough examples cited? Are three elections (junior class treasurer, youth group chairperson, and sorority president) enough examples? Because the instances cited should represent most to all possibilities, enough must be cited to satisfy the listeners that the instances are not isolated or hand-picked.

2. Are the examples typical? Are the three examples typical of all of her campaigns for office? Typical means that the examples cited must be similar to or representative of most or all within the category. If examples are not typical, they do not support the generalization. For instance, if these three successes came in very small organizations, they would not be typical of all organizations.

If the three examples are not typical, then you could question the logic of the argument on that basis.

3. Are negative examples accounted for? In looking at material, we may find one or more exceptions to the generalization. If the exceptions are minor or infrequent, then they do not necessarily invalidate the generalization. For instance, Juanita may have run for chairperson of the chess club but was defeated. That one failure does not necessarily invalidate the generalization. If, however, the exceptions prove to be more than rare or isolated instances, the validity of the generalization is open to serious question. For instance, if you found that Juanita had run for office twelve times and was successful on only the three occasions cited, then the generalization would be fallacious. If you believe that negative examples were not accounted for, then you could question the logic of the argument on that basis.

Arguing from Analogy   When you **argue from analogy,** you support a claim with a reason supported by a single example that is significantly similar to the subject of the claim. Suppose that you wanted to claim that Northwest High should conduct a lottery to raise enough money to buy band uniforms. You could support the claim with a single analogous example: Country Day, a school that is significantly similar to Northwest, conducted a lottery and raised enough money to purchase uniforms for its entire band. The form for arguing from analogy looks like this:

arguing from analogy   *supporting a claim with a single example that is significantly similar to the subject of the claim*

C   Northwest High should conduct a lottery to raise money for band uniforms.

D   Country Day, which is very similar to Northwest High, raised money through a lottery.

W   (What worked at a very similar school will work at Northwest High.)

Let us return to the claim that Juanita is electable for president of the senior class. If you discover that Juanita has essentially the same characteristics as Paula Jefferson, who was elected president two years ago (both are very bright, both have a great deal of drive, and both have track records of successful campaigns), then you can use the single example of Paula to form a reason "Juanita has the same characteristics as Paula Jefferson, who was elected two years ago."

The general warrant for reasoning from analogy can be stated as follows: What was true in one similar case is true (or will be true) in general or in this particular case.

Now let's look at this argument in outline form:

C   Juanita Martinez is electable.

D   Juanita has the same characteristics as Paula Jefferson, who was elected two years ago.

   A.   Juanita and Paula are both very bright.

   B.   Juanita and Paula both have a great deal of drive.

   C.   Juanita and Paula both have track records of successful campaigns.

W   (What was true for Paula will be true for Juanita, who has similar characteristics.)

So, the claim is supported by an analogous example; then support is offered to validate the analogy.

To test the strength of an argument from analogy, ask the following questions.

1. Are the subjects being compared similar in every important way? Are Paula and Juanita similar in intelligence, drive, and track records in elected offices? If subjects do not have significant similarities, then they are not comparable. If the subjects being compared are not similar in important ways, then you can question the reasoning on that basis.

2. Are any of the ways that the subjects are dissimilar important to the outcome? Is Juanita's dissimilarity in sorority affiliation a factor? Is her dissimilarity in religion a factor? If dissimilarities exist that outweigh the subjects' similarities, then conclusions drawn from the comparisons may be invalid. If the ways that the subjects are dissimilar have not been considered, then you can question the reasoning on that basis.

arguing from causation *supporting a claim with one or more examples that come before and are related to the claim*

Arguing from Causation   When you **argue from causation,** you support a claim with one or more examples that have a special connection to the claim. Reasoning from causation says that one or more examples cited always (or at least usually) cause a predictable effect or set of effects. For instance, you could develop reasoning based on the causal relationship between mortgage interest rates and home sales: "Home sales are bound to increase during the next three months, because mortgage interest rates have dropped markedly recently."

The general warrant for arguments from cause can be stated as follows: If an event came before another event and is associated with that event, then we can say that it is the cause of the event. Let's look at this type of argument in outline form:

C   Home sales will increase.

D   Mortgage interest rates have dropped.

W   (Lower interest rates generally lead to higher home sales.)

In analyzing Juanita's election campaign, you might discover that (1) she has campaigned intelligently and (2) she has won the endorsement of key campus organizations. If these two items can be seen as causes for victory, then you can form the reason that Juanita has engaged in procedures that result in campaign victory, thus supporting the claim that she is electable. The argument would look like this:

C   Juanita Martinez will be elected.

D   **A.**   Juanita has campaigned intelligently.

    B.   Juanita has key endorsements.

W   (Intelligent campaigning and getting key endorsements come before and are related to electoral victory.)

To test the strength of an argument from causation, ask the following questions.

1. Are the data alone sufficient cause to bring about the stated effect? Are intelligent campaigning and key endorsements important enough to result in winning elections? If the data are truly important, it means that if the data were eliminated, then the effect would be eliminated as well. If the effect can occur without the data, then you can question the causal relationship.

2. Do other data accompanying the cited data cause the effect? Are other factors (such as luck, drive, friends) more important in determining whether a person wins an election? If the accompanying data appear equally or more important in bringing about the effect, then you can question the causal relationship between the data cited and the conclusion. If you believe that other data caused the effect, then you can question the reasoning on that basis.

3. Is the relationship between cause and effect consistent? Do intelligent campaigning and key endorsements always (or usually) yield electoral victories? If there are times when the effect has not followed the cause, then you can question whether a causal relationship exists. If you believe that the relationship between the cause and effect is not consistent, then you can question the reasoning on that basis.

Arguing from Sign   When you **argue from sign,** you support a claim with one or more examples that act as indicators of the subject of the claim. When certain events, characteristics, or situations always or usually accompany something, those events, characteristics, or situations are signs. For instance, your doctor may argue that you have had an allergic reaction because you have hives and are running a slight fever.

arguing from sign   *supporting a claim with one or more examples that act as indicators of the subject of the claim*

The general warrant for reasoning from sign can be stated as follows: When instances usually or always accompanying a specific situation occur, then that specific situation is occurring (or will occur). Thus, the rationale for the allergy argument might be stated as follows: Hives and a slight fever are indicators (signs) of an allergic reaction.

Let's look at this argument in outline form:

C   You have had an allergic reaction.

D   **A.**   You have hives.

B.   You have a slight fever.

W   (Hives and a slight fever are signs of an allergic reaction.)

Signs are often confused with causes; but signs are indicators, or effects, not causes. A rash and fever don't cause an allergic reaction; they are indications, or effects, of a reaction.

If in analyzing Juanita's campaign, you notice that Juanita has more campaign posters than all other candidates combined and that a greater number of students from all segments of the campus are wearing "Juanita for President" buttons, you may reason "Juanita's campaign has the key signs of an election victory."

A speech outline using this sign argument would look like this:

C   Juanita Martinez will be elected.

D   **A.**   Juanita has more campaign posters than all other candidates combined.

B.   A greater number of students are wearing her campaign buttons.

W   (The presence of a greater number of campaign posters and buttons than the opponents have is a sign/indicator of victory.)

To test the strength of an argument from sign, ask the following questions.

1. Do the signs cited always or usually indicate the conclusion drawn? Do large numbers of posters and campaign buttons always (or usually) indicate election victory? If the data can occur independently of the conclusion, then they are not necessarily indicators. If the data cited do not usually indicate the conclusion, then you can question the reasoning on that basis.

2. Are sufficient signs present? Are campaign posters and buttons enough to indicate a victory? Events or situations are often indicated by several signs. If enough signs are not present, then the conclusion may not follow. If there are insufficient signs, then you can question the reasoning on that basis.

3. Are contradictory signs in evidence? Are posters being torn down in great numbers? If signs usually indicating different conclusions are present, then the stated conclusion may not be valid. If you believe that contradictory signs are evident, then you can question the reasoning on that basis.

arguing from definition *supporting a claim with one or more characteristics that are primary criteria of an event*

Arguing from Definition When you **argue from definition,** you support a claim with one or more examples that usually characterize and define the subject of the claim. For instance, you may wish to argue that a movie is of Academy Award caliber on the basis of its outstanding plot, superior acting, and excellence in direction. The general warrant for an argument from definition is if characteristics are primary criteria of an event, then they define that event. Thus, the warrant for this argument is that excellence in plot, acting, and directing are primary criteria that define Academy Award caliber.

If, in analyzing Juanita's campaign, you notice that Juanita uses good judgment, that her goals are in the best interests of the group, and that she is decisive, you may argue that "Juanita is a leader." In outline form, the argument would look like this:

C Juanita is a leader.

D **A.** Juanita shows good judgment.

    B. Juanita's goals are in the best interests of the group.

    C. Juanita is decisive.

W (Good judgment, consideration of group interests, and decisiveness are key characteristics in the definition of leadership.)

To test the strength of an argument from definition, ask the following questions.

1. Are the characteristics mentioned the most important ones in determining the definition? Are judgment, consideration of group interests, and decisiveness the important criteria for measuring leadership? If other criteria are considered to be more important, then the reasoning is questionable.

2. Are all important aspects of the definition included in the statement of the characteristics? For example, even if the three criteria mentioned are important, are other criteria, such as drive, even more important? If a more important criterion is not mentioned, then the reasoning may be questionable.

3. Are those characteristics best described by some other term? For instance, are the three criteria mentioned normally more true of followership than leadership? If the characteristics or criteria are most often associated with another word, then the reasoning may be questionable.

arguing from authority *supporting a claim with one or more expert opinions*

Arguing from Authority When you **argue from authority,** you support a claim with one or more expert opinions. Reasoning from authority says that one or more expert opinions are enough to establish the claim. For instance, you could claim that the United States has to be more conservation conscious based on waste management authority Gina Gordan's statement that "We have been a throwaway society—we simply have to change our ways." The warrant for this argument might be stated as follows: If an authority on waste disposal favors limiting throwaway items, it should be done. In outline form then, the argument would look like this:

C The United States has to be more conservation conscious.

D Statement of waste management authority: "We have been a throwaway society—we simply have to change our ways."

W (Expert opinion supports the claim.)

If, in analyzing Juanita's campaign, you notice that an influential editorial writer for the school paper predicts her election, then you form the reason "Juanita is supported by a campus opinion leader." In outline form, the reasoning would look like this:

C Juanita will be elected.

D An influential editorial writer for the school paper has said, "Because Juanita Martinez is the best-qualified candidate, she is sure to get elected president of the senior class."

W (If an authority predicts a candidate's election, it is likely to occur.)

To test the strength of an argument from authority, ask the following questions.

1. Is the source of the testimony a recognized authority? For instance, is an editorial writer for the school paper an authority on predicting senior class elections?

2. Is the opinion supported by other authorities? The more authorities that support an idea, the stronger the support is. If you find other authorities that disagree with the claim, then you should question the claim on that basis.

Combining Arguments A speech usually contains several reasons. For a speech with the goal "I want my audience to believe that Juanita is electable," you might draw together three of the reasons we've looked at that you believe provide sound support. Suppose you selected the following:

I. Juanita has run successful campaigns in the past.

   A. Juanita was successful in her campaign for treasurer of her high school class.

   B. Juanita was successful in her campaign for chairperson of her church youth group.

   C. Juanita was successful in her campaign for president of her sorority.

II. Juanita has engaged in procedures that result in campaign victory.

   A. Juanita has campaigned intelligently.

   B. Juanita has key endorsements.

III. Juanita is a strong leader.

   A. Juanita shows good judgment.

   B. Juanita always considers the best interests of the group.

   C. Juanita is decisive.

We have considered warrants for each of these individual arguments. Now you need to consider the warrant for the overall argument. What relationship do all three of these subarguments have with the overall argument? That is, what do running successful campaigns in the past, being engaged in procedures that result in victory, and being a strong leader have to do with whether she is

TECHNOLOGY tips

Personal stories can have emotional impact and make arguments more persuasive. Television news magazines like "20-20" and "60 Minutes" are a good source of these stories. Transcripts for segments are usually available from the show and can often be requested through the network Web site. Check out www.ABC.com or www.CBS.com.

electable? You might write the warrant as "Running successful campaigns in the past, being engaged in procedures that result in victory, and being a strong leader are all signs of electability." Now you can test the soundness of the overall argument by using the tests of sign argument listed earlier.

Avoiding Fallacies of Reasoning   When you think that you have finished constructing reasons, you need to take a minute to make sure that you haven't been guilty of any of the following four common fallacies.

1. Hasty generalization. Because the instances cited should represent most to all possibilities, enough must be cited to satisfy the listeners that the instances are not isolated or hand-picked. A very common fallacy of reasoning, **hasty generalization,** means presenting a generalization (perhaps a reason) that is either not supported with evidence or perhaps supported with only one weak example.

hasty generalization   *presenting a reason or other generalization supported by a single weak example or none at all*

FOCUS ON skills

Evaluating Arguments

For each of the following examples, write the claim that the speaker has made, write a warrant explaining the link between the data and the claim, and identify the reasoning process (example, analogy, causation, sign, definition, or authority). The first one has been done for you, as an example of how to proceed.

I see that Ohio has stiffened its penalties for drunk driving and has begun applying them uniformly. I don't think there is any doubt that we are going to see instances of drunk driving dropping in Ohio.

> **Claim**   The number of instances of drunk driving in Ohio will drop.
>
> **Warrant**   Stiff penalties and uniform application will result in lower numbers of drunk drivers. (causation)

Now write the claim and warrant for each of the following:

1. Attacks against teachers are becoming more severe. In New York, a teacher required hospitalization after being beaten by a gang. In Chicago, a teacher resigned after being terrorized by midnight phone calls and threats against his family.

   > **Claim**
   >
   > **Warrant**

2. If you have been watching indicators lately, you'll notice that interest rates have been creeping upward again. During the past two years, interest rates were flat. For each of the past four months, however, we have seen increasingly higher interest rates. Also, according to an article in *Time,* people are keeping more of their money in savings accounts. I hate to say this, but it seems that we are heading for another recession.

   > **Claim**
   >
   > **Warrant**

3. I don't think there is any doubt that we will have bumper corn and wheat crops this year. In each of the past several months, rainfall has been plentiful—average or above for each month. In addition, we haven't had any wild fluctuations in temperature. For the most part, temperatures have been near normal.

   > **Claim**
   >
   > **Warrant**

A Speech of Reasons

Prepare a 4- to 7-minute speech in which the focus or force of your persuasion rests on the presentation and development of two to four reasons. An outline is required.

1. The speech goal may be to affect a belief or to move to action. Thus, the emphasis in this assignment is not on the type of proposition, but on the means of supporting it.

2. The emphasis of this speech is to show that you can present strong arguments in support of your goal. Each main point should be a reason that is supported with good evidence. Select your reasons on the basis of soundness of argument and potential impact on the intended audience.

3. For this assignment, the main points of your outline are likely to follow a statement of logical reasons, problem solution, or comparative advantages pattern.

4. As an addendum to the outline, you may wish to write a persuasive plan for adapting the speech to your specific audience. For this assignment, the plan should have short sections in which you discuss:

   a. How you will get, build, and maintain audience interest in your topic.

   b. How much background information you need to present in order to prepare the audience to understand your reasons.

   c. Why you organize your reasons as you do.

   d. How you will establish your credibility with this audience.

2. False cause. False cause means attributing causation to an event that is not related to, or does not produce, the effect. It is human nature to look for causes for events, but identifying something that happened or existed before the event or at the time of the event and labeling it as the cause is often a fallacy. Think of the people who blame loss of money, sickness, and problems at work on black cats that ran in front of them, or mirrors that broke, or ladders they walked under. We recognize these as false cause superstitions.

false cause *attributing causation to an event that is not related to, or does not produce, the effect*

3. Appeal to authority. When an argument from authority relies on testimony from a person who is not an authority on the issue, the result is a fallacy known as **appeal to authority.** For instance, advertisers are well aware that because the public idolizes athletes, movie stars, and television performers, people are likely to accept their word on subjects they may know little about. But when a celebrity tries to get the viewer to purchase a car based on the celebrity's supposed "expert" knowledge, the argument is a fallacy.

appeal to authority *relying on the testimony of someone who is not an expert on the issue at hand*

4. Ad hominem argument. An **ad hominem argument** is an attack on the person making the argument rather than on the argument itself. Literally, *ad hominem* means "to the man." For instance, if Michael Jordan presented the argument that athletics are important to the development of the total person, the reply "Great, all we need is some jock justifying his own existence" would be an example of an ad hominem argument.

ad hominem argument *an attack on the person making the argument rather than on the argument itself*

Such a personal attack is often made as a smokescreen to cover a lack of good reasons and evidence. Ad hominem name-calling is used to try to encourage the audience to ignore a lack of evidence, and it is often used in political campaigns. Make no mistake, ridicule, name-calling, and other personal attacks are at times highly successful, but they almost always are fallacious.

Critiquing Speeches

Write a critique of one or more of the speeches given to meet this assignment. Because the focus of this assignment is on reasoning, use the Speech of Reasons Evaluation Checklist.

SPEECH EVALUATION **checklist**

Speech of Reasons

Check all items that were accomplished effectively.

Primary Criteria

_____ **1.** Was the specific goal designed to affect a belief or move to action?

_____ **2.** Did the speaker present clearly stated reasons?

_____ **3.** Did each reason directly support the specific goal?

_____ **4.** Was each reason important to the audience's acceptance of the goal?

_____ **5.** Did the speaker use facts and expert opinions to support these reasons?

_____ **6.** Was the evidence for the reasons well documented?

General Criteria

_____ **1.** Was the specific goal clear?

_____ **2.** Was the introduction effective?

_____ **3.** Were the main points clear?

_____ **4.** Was the conclusion effective?

_____ **5.** Was the language clear, vivid, emphatic, and appropriate?

_____ **6.** Was the speech delivered enthusiastically, with vocal expressiveness, fluently, spontaneously, and directly?

Evaluate the speech as (check one):

_____excellent, _____good, _____average, _____fair, _____poor.

Use the information from this checklist to support your evaluation.

SAMPLE **speech**

Volunteering at a Soup Kitchen[3]

Outline

Specific Goal: I want my audience to volunteer to work at a soup kitchen.

Introduction

I. Imagine not knowing where your next meal is coming from.

II. For many people in Cincinnati, this is a tragic reality.

Thesis Statement: You should volunteer to work at one of Cincinnati's soup kitchens because volunteering meets an important need, takes little time, is easy on the pocketbook, and provides great satisfaction.

Body

I. Volunteering at an Over the Rhine soup kitchen meets an important need.

   A. Volunteers are essential to the running of nonprofit organizations.

   B. Running Over the Rhine soup kitchens requires 10,000 volunteer hours a year.

(You can help to meet this need relatively easily.)

II. Volunteering at an Over the Rhine soup kitchen takes very little time.

   A. Volunteering will cost you a couple of hours at most.

   B. Think of this time as a much deserved break from your studies in order to help someone very much in need.

(But some of you might be wondering whether getting there will cost you money you don't have.)

III. Volunteering at a soup kitchen costs you little if any money.

   A. Since Over the Rhine is in close proximity to campus, transportation costs are low.

      1. You can get to two major soup kitchens by bus for around a dollar round-trip.

      2. Perhaps you can go with two or three other people by car.

   B. Actually you can get to a soup kitchen at no cost to you.

      1. Most kitchens are willing to provide transportation.

      2. Virgil Bolden (Over the Rhine director) says, "I'll get you here."

(So you can see that volunteering doesn't require a lot of time and is easy on the pocketbook. Now let's see what the act of volunteering does for you.)

IV. Volunteering at the soup kitchen will make you feel good about yourself.

   A. Many people volunteer regularly because of the values they see for themselves.

   B. My experience verifies the feelings of satisfaction from volunteering.

      1. You'll see the satisfaction it brings to others.

      2. You'll feel good about yourself taking the time to give.

Conclusion

 I. With the rising number of people who are homeless and hungry in Cincinnati, we cannot expect that their needs will be met if we don't do something about it.

II. I implore you to give just a few hours of your time serving others at a soup kitchen—it's not too much to ask.

Sources

Experience: Volunteered at Over the Rhine soup kitchen three times.
Interview: Pastor Henry Zorn, LCR 11/29/98.

Interview: Kerri Hughes, LPN, RN, Christ Hospital, 11/26/98.
Internet: Walnut Hills/Over the Rhine Soup Kitchens. Nov. 1998.
     Available:angelfire.com/biz2/whotr
Internet: The Total Living Center Ministries, Inc. Nov. 1998.
     Available:totalliv.com/soup_kitchens.htm
Van Biema, David. "Can Charity Fill the Gap?" *Time*, December 4, 1995, pp.
     44–53.

Plan for Adapting to Audience

Audience Analysis: My audience ranges in age from late teens to mid-20s. They are all college students of varying majors and classes.

   1. Creating and maintaining interest. I plan to begin the speech by getting my audience to envision the pain of not knowing where the next meal is coming from.

   2. Background knowledge. I do not believe the information I will present is difficult to understand. Through the speech I will give the necessary information to allow class to get involved.

   3. Organization. I have organized my speech following a statement of reasons pattern. All four of my main points are complete sentences that give an advantage for volunteering time.

   4. Building credibility. I plan to build credibility by sharing my personal experience in working at a soup kitchen.

Thinking Critically: Speech and Analysis

Read the following speech aloud. Then, analyze it in terms of the primary criteria in the Speech of Reasons Evaluation Checklist: goal, reasons, support, relevance, and credibility.

Analysis

Michelle opens her speech by getting the audience to envision an experience. This gets the audience involved right at the beginning. Here she previews her reasons.

Her first reason establishes the importance of considering volunteering. Good use of quotations.

Second reason meets the perceived objection, "I don't have time." She supports her point with a quotation and then builds on it by showing a kind of reward for the student.

Speech

Imagine for a moment that you have not eaten for three days. Your minimum wage earnings barely covered this month's rent. It's the end of the month, and you're wondering where your next meal is going to come from. It's unpleasant to think about, but for many people in Cincinnati, this is a tragic reality.

   But you can help. I would propose that you should volunteer at a soup kitchen. It meets an important need, it requires a small margin of your time, it requires less than a dollar, and it provides great satisfaction.

   Volunteering at a soup kitchen meets an important need. Both the Walnut Hills and Over the Rhine soup kitchen directors agree that "Volunteers are essential to the success of this nonprofit, need-based organization." In fact, according to Executive Director Rev. Bokenkotter, "Because nearly 100,000 meals are prepared yearly to be served at the two soup kitchen locations, an average of 10,000 volunteer hours are required." So we see the need is great, but you can help meet that need relatively easily.

   Volunteering at a soup kitchen requires very little time. Mary Ellen Kajawa, Walnut Hills director, explains that "Volunteers spend from two to three hours there preparing and serving meals to people who are homeless, working poor, and of low income." Think of it, for just two hours or so of your time, an amount that gives you a much deserved break from your studies, you can help make or serve a meal to someone very much in need at the soup kitchen. Pastor Henry Zorn, at Lutheran Church of the Resurrection, reinforces the idea that college students make ideal volunteers for this type of outreach ministry since their schedules tend to be flexible. This brings me to my next point: money.

Volunteering at the soup kitchen requires a dollar or less of our own money. Most of us live on or near campus, and the Over the Rhine area is in close proximity. Well, you might ask, "What is the dollar for?" It's for the cost of the bus or gas money. When I go, I go with members from my church. So it is conceivable that no money is necessary. If you sincerely wish to serve at the soup kitchen, but don't have transportation, give Virgil Bolden, the Over the Rhine director, a call, because he says, "I'll get you here." So there you have it—if coming up with a dollar was a consideration before, it should not be one now!

Volunteering at the soup kitchen provides great satisfaction. When was the last time you did something for someone without expecting anything in return? As for myself, it's been a long time. It's easy to get wrapped up in the everyday life and everything that goes on with that. We forget how privileged we are and how much we take for granted. We don't usually have to worry about where our next meal is coming from. According to Pastor Don Bartow, founder of the Total Living Center Ministries, "The biggest influx of needy people has been in the last year; we give away over 600 bags of groceries a month." Kerri Hughes, a nurse who works at Christ Hospital and has been volunteering every other month at the Over the Rhine soup kitchen for five years says, "I look forward to working at the soup kitchen. I am reminded when I see those peoples' faces of the many things I take for granted and how fortunate I am. I am so glad I am able to help people in need." My own experiences at volunteering validate her observation. I find tremendous satisfaction in helping others.

From personal experience, I can guarantee you that if you go—if you're able to spend a dollar and the two hours it takes to serve these people at the soup kitchen—you will receive the benefits from it. You will receive satisfaction from helping someone. With the vast number of people who are homeless and hungry in Cincinnati, you cannot expect that this need can be met without our doing something about it. I implore you to at least consider devoting one dollar and two hours of your time to serve meals to the hungry at the soup kitchen. It's not too much to ask. ∎

Also notice use of personal pronouns.

Now she focuses on a second important possible objection. A clear reason that is supported with specific information. Then she shows that perhaps volunteering can be done with no cost! Another good use of quotation to verify the assertion.

Her final reason, and perhaps the strongest motivator, emphasizes the satisfaction of achieving the primary goal—helping people.

Good use of volunteer quotation.

Notice how Michelle reinforces the value with her own experiences.

Blending in her own experience, she reviews key reasons. She then prods the audience not only to recognize the need, but to do something about it.

Excellent final two sentences. This is a good speech of reasons that is well organized and well supported.

Motivating Audiences

Reasoning provides a solid logical base for persuasion and a sound rationale for changing an audience's attitude; motivation brings an audience to action. In the previous chapter, we defined *motivation* as "forces acting on or within an organism to initiate and direct behavior,"[4] and we discussed motivating by using language to arouse emotions. In this section, we take a broader theoretical

CORBIS/Gary Nolan

When Bill Gates talks about using Microsoft® products, he is likely to give his audience incentives to motivate their behavior.

perspective, considering two strategies for motivating audiences: incentive theory and needs theory. The section concludes with a speech assignment that enables you to practice motivational strategies and a sample speech (with outline) that illustrates how to motivate an audience.

Incentive Theory: Cost/Reward Ratios

People are more likely to act when the speech goal presents incentives that create a favorable cost/reward ratio.

An **incentive** is "a goal objective that motivates."[5] Thus, if you can earn money by turning in cans and bottles to a recycling center, then you might see earning money as an incentive to recycle. Incentives work best when they are seen as meaningful. Thus, earning money may be a meaningful incentive for someone short of cash, but not necessarily meaningful for someone who has money or who doesn't care about earning small amounts of money.

People are more likely to regard incentives as meaningful if they present a favorable **cost/reward ratio**—that is, if the reward for a behavior exceeds the cost of that behavior.[6] **Rewards** are economic gain, good feelings, prestige, or other positive outcomes. **Costs** are units of expenditure such as time, energy, money, or other negative outcomes.

According to Thibaut and Kelley, the originators of incentive theory, each of us seeks situations in which our behavior will yield us rewards in excess of the costs; or, conversely, each of us will continue our present behavior unless we are shown that either lower costs or higher rewards will come from changing a particular behavior. Consider an example. Suppose that you are asking your audience to give money to a charity. The money you are asking them to give is a negative outcome—a cost. However, giving money can be shown to be rewarding: Audience members may feel civic-minded, responsible, or helpful as a result of giving. If you can show in the speech that those rewards outweigh the cost, then you increase the likelihood of the audience's giving.

incentive   a goal objective that motivates

cost/reward ratio   cost of a behavior relative to the reward it brings

rewards   economic gain, good feelings, prestige, or other positive outcomes

costs   units of expenditure such as time, energy, money, or other negative outcomes

Strategies based on this theory are easy for most people to understand because the theory is so easily supported by commonsense observations. To make this theory work to your advantage, you must understand the cost/reward ratios in relation to the specific topic and your particular audience. Suppose that you are, in fact, trying to motivate the audience to give money to a charity. If you ask people to give a dollar, you won't have to show a great reward because the cost is not great; if you ask people to give ten dollars or more, you'll have to show greater rewards because the cost is higher. Thus, the higher the perceived cost, the harder you will work to achieve your goal.

In your speech, then, you must achieve one of the following:

1. Show that the time, energy, or money investment is small.

2. Show that the benefits in good feelings, prestige, economic gain, or other possible rewards are high.

The speech at the end of this section is an excellent example of the use of this strategy.

Basic Needs Theory

People are more likely to act when the proposition satisfies a strong but unmet need.

Cognitive motivation theories account for the persistent motive within individuals to become competent in coping with their environment.[7] One of the most popular of these theories, and one that is easily adapted to persuasive speaking, is the **basic needs theory** of the humanistic psychologist Abraham Maslow. His theory suggests that people are more likely to take action when a speaker's appeal satisfies a strong, unmet need in audience members.

Maslow devised a **hierarchy of needs** that is particularly useful in providing a framework for needs analysis. He divided basic human needs into five categories (see Figure 14.1) arranged in a hierarchy that begins with the most fundamental needs: (1) physiological needs, including food, drink, and life-sustaining temperature; (2) safety needs, including security and simple self-preservation; (3) belongingness and love needs, including the need to identify with friends, loved ones, and family; (4) esteem needs, including the quest for material goods, recognition, and power or influence; and (5) self-actualization needs, including the need to develop one's self to realize one's full potential.[8] By placing these needs in a hierarchy, Maslow suggested that one set of needs must be met or satisfied before the next higher set of needs emerges. In theory, then, a person will not be motivated to meet an esteem need of gaining recognition until basic physiological, safety, and belongingness needs have been met.

What is the value of this analysis to you as a speaker?

1. It suggests the kinds of needs you may want to appeal to in your speeches.

2. It allows you to understand why a line of development will work on one audience and fail with another. For instance, in difficult economic times, people are more concerned with physiological and safety needs, and so will be less responsive to appeals to affiliation and altruism. Thus, in recessionary times, fund-raisers for the arts experience far more resistance to giving than they do during economic upswings.

3. It alerts you to the need for analysis. When your proposition conflicts with a felt need, you have to be prepared with a strong alternative in

basic needs theory *people are more likely to take action when a speaker's appeal satisfies a strong, unmet need in audience members*

hierarchy of needs *five categories arranged in order of importance: physiological needs, safety needs, belongingness and love needs, esteem needs, self-actualization needs*

FIGURE 14.1 **Maslow's hierarchy of needs**

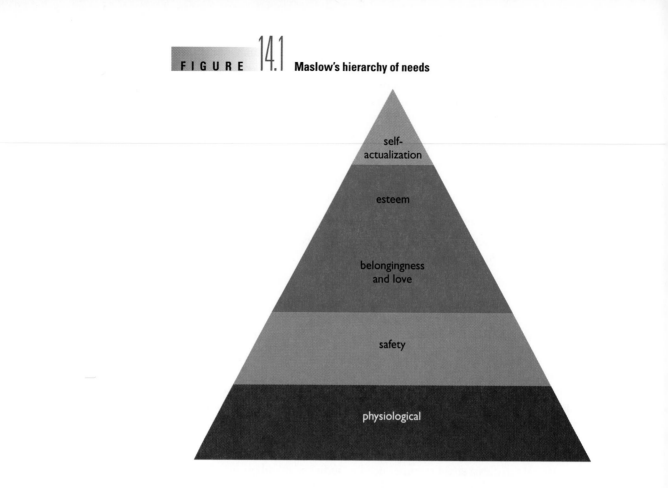

the same category or in a more fundamental category. For instance, if your proposal is going to cost people money (higher taxes), you will have to show how the proposal satisfies a comparable need (perhaps by increasing their security).

Let us make this discussion more specific by looking at just a few powerful motives for action. After you have selected a specific speech goal and have determined reasons for its acceptance, you can try to relate the reasons to basic needs and discover where they may conflict with other motives or other needs.

Wealth   The desire for wealth—the acquisition of money and material goods—is a motive that grows out of an esteem need. For example, those with little money for a car can perhaps be motivated to buy a Ford Escort or a Chevrolet Geo because these cars get good gas mileage and are economical to operate. Those who have a great deal of money can perhaps be motivated to buy a Rolls Royce or a Cadillac because they are prestigious. If your speech goal affects audience wealth or material goods positively, you may want to stress it. On the other hand, if your speech goal requests money, be prepared to cope with an audience's natural resistance. You may be able to appeal to another motive from the same category (esteem) or from a more fundamental category to override the loss of any money the audience will have to give up.

Power Another esteem need is power. For many people, personal worth depends on their power over their own destiny, power over others, and the recognition and prestige that come from the exercise of power. If your proposition allows a person, group, or community to exercise power, it may be worth emphasizing. On the other hand, if your speech takes power away from some or all of your listeners, you will need to provide strong compensation to motivate them.

Conformity Conformity is a major source of motivation for nearly everyone. Conformity grows out of a need for belongingness. People often behave in a given way because a friend, a neighbor, an acquaintance, or a person in the same age bracket behaves that way. Although some people will be more likely to do something if they can be the first to do it or if it makes them appear distinctive, most people feel more secure when they act in ways that conform with others of their kind. The old saying that there is strength in numbers certainly applies to conformity. If you can show that many people similar to the members of your audience favor your plan, that argument may well provide motivation.

Pleasure When people are given a choice of actions, they often pick the one that gives them the greatest pleasure, enjoyment, or happiness. On at least one level, pleasure is a self-actualizing need; however, it also operates as an esteem need. If your speech relates to something that is novel, promises excitement, is fun to do, or offers a challenge, you can probably motivate your audience on that basis.

FOCUS ON SKILLS

Motivating Action

1. Prepare a 5- to 8-minute persuasive speech designed to bring your audience to action. An outline is required.

2. As an addendum to the outline, write a persuasive plan for adapting to your specific audience. For this particular assignment, the plan should have short sections in which you discuss:

   a. How you will get, build, and maintain audience interest in your topic.

   b. How much background information you need to present in order to prepare the audience to understand your speech.

   c. What organizational pattern you will follow. For this speech you are likely to select the pattern (statement of logical reasons, problem solution, comparative advantages, criteria satisfaction, or motivational) that you believe is most likely to increase your chance of motivating this audience.

   d. How you will establish your credibility with this audience.

   e. What overall strategy you will use in motivating your audience to act. You want the audience to believe that the benefits to be gained from the action far outweigh the cost in time, energy, or money invested, or that the specific goal satisfies such basic needs as wealth, power, conformity, or pleasure. You might also want to identify the emotions that you want to arouse in your audience and determine the places in your speech where you are going to focus your emotional appeals.

Speech of Motivation

Check all items that were accomplished effectively.

Primary Criteria

_____ **1.** Did the speech goal call for a specific audience action?

_____ **2.** Were the reasons stated clearly and vividly?

_____ **3.** Were the reasons directed to the needs of this audience?

_____ **4.** Did the speaker use facts and expert opinions to support these reasons?

_____ **5.** Was the speaker effective in establishing his or her credibility on this topic?

_____ **6.** Did the speaker lead the audience to believe that the benefits to be gained from the action far outweigh the cost in time, energy, or money invested; or

_____ **7.** Did the speaker lead the audience to believe that the specific goal satisfies such basic needs as wealth, power, conformity, or pleasure?

_____ **8.** Was the speaker ethical in handling material?

General Criteria

_____ **1.** Was the specific goal clear?

_____ **2.** Was the introduction effective?

_____ **3.** Were the main points clear?

_____ **4.** Was the conclusion effective?

_____ **5.** Was the language clear, vivid, emphatic, and appropriate?

_____ **6.** Was the speech delivered enthusiastically, with vocal expressiveness, fluently, spontaneously, and directly?

Evaluate the speech as (check one):

_____excellent, _____good, _____average, _____fair, _____poor.

Use the information from this checklist to support your evaluation.

These are only four possible motives for action growing out of basic audience needs. Sex appeal, responsibility, justice, and many others operate within each of us. If you discover that you are not relating your material to basic audience needs, then you probably need to revise your procedure.

But knowing which needs an audience has and appealing to those needs are two different things. To maximize your effectiveness, you must understand how to trigger these needs.

What happens when your specific goal does not meet a specific audience need? Either you can change the wording of your goal so that it is in tune with

FOCUS ON skills

Critiquing Speeches

Write a critique of one or more of the motivational speeches given to meet this assignment. Outline the speech. As you outline, answer the questions in the Motivational Speech Evaluation Checklist.

audience needs, or you can work to create or uncover an audience need that the specific goal will meet. For instance, if you are giving a speech intended to motivate the audience to go to dinner at Le Parisien (a very expensive restaurant), your goal may meet a need to eat out occasionally, but it is in opposition to most people's need to eat for a reasonable price. For this speech to be effective, you must either change the specific goal to recommend a more modest restaurant or arouse some needs that would be met by going to Le Parisien.

In planning strategy in terms of basic needs, ask yourself the following:

1. What needs does this audience have at this time?

2. How can I develop my reasons so that they relate to the dominant needs of this audience?

SAMPLE speech

Notes to Neighbors[9]

Outline

Specific Goal: I want the audience to sign up for the American Cancer Society's Notes to Neighbors.

Introduction

   I. I bet all of you know that cancer is a leading cause of death.

  II. And I know from talking with you that many of you know the helpless feeling of dealing with a person with cancer.

 III. But there's a very easy way that you can help.

Thesis Statement: I want all of you to sign up for the Notes to Neighbors program because the demand for donations is tremendous and Notes to Neighbors is a realistic way for students to contribute in the fight against cancer.

Body

   I. The American Cancer Society is only able to meet a small amount of the demand for private research funding.

   A. Of the more than 2,000 applications for research grants, the American Cancer Society was only able to fund 491 of them.

   B. This means that there are more willing researchers than there is money available to fund the research.

   1. Our efforts through Notes to Neighbors would help increase the amount of money available for researchers.

   2. The more research that is done, the closer we get to a cure that may stop the suffering.

  II. Notes to Neighbors is an easy, realistic way for students to contribute to the fight against cancer.

   A. Notes to Neighbors costs the volunteer a maximum of a five-dollar book of stamps.

   1. I know that there are times when I've only had five dollars to get through the rest of the week.

    2. Last year I persuaded my boss to donate five dollars for my book of stamps so that helping didn't really cost me anything.

B. The Notes to Neighbors program takes a maximum of two hours, once a year, to complete.

    1. I know all of our time is precious.

    2. Last year I was able to address my envelopes in only 45 minutes.

    3. Moreover, I was able to accomplish the task in my spare time at work.

Conclusion

I. So we see that research is necessary and the Notes to Neighbors program is easy to complete.

II. But if I still have not convinced you, let me ask how many of you have actually taken care of someone with cancer?

    A. Let me tell you about my experience.

    B. Isn't it worth the small amount of money and time that might reduce that half a million people who now die of cancer?

    C. Remember those people are somebody's children, mothers, father, or siblings—won't you help?

Sources

American Cancer Society website, http://www.cancer.org/   See progress Newsletter, Fall, 1998, Funding

Ohio Department of Health website, http://www.odh.state.oh.us/   See "Data and Statistics" then "Cancer Incidence"

Personal experience: Last spring I participated in the Notes to Neighbors campaign.

Telephone interview: Cincinnati Chapter of American Cancer Society

Plan for Adapting to Audience

Audience Analysis: My audience ranges in age from late teens to mid-20s. They are all college students of varying majors and classes.

    1. Creating and maintaining interest. I plan to begin the speech by getting my audience to see the extent of the problem. Throughout the speech, I will rely on personal experiences to maintain interest. And wherever possible, I will try to identify with audience experience.

    2. Background knowledge. I do not believe the information I will present is difficult to understand. Early in the speech, I will outline what participating in Notes to Neighbors requires.

    3. Organization. I have organized my speech following a motivational pattern. I will get attention in the introduction. I will show the nature of the problem as well as show that student participation is an easy way of helping solve the problem. Then I will help the class visualize the nature of the problem—this will serve to motivate them to follow through with their volunteering time.

    4. Building credibility. I plan to build credibility primarily by sharing my experiences in working with the program.

5. Motivation. During my preparation, I found that my audience was sympathetic with the needs of supporting cancer research. So, I am focusing on motivating them to act. Not only will I show that the requirements of participation are easy to meet, but also that spending the little time and money will do so much.

Thinking Critically: Speech and Analysis

Read the following speech aloud. Then, analyze it in terms of the primary criteria in the Motivational Speech Evaluation Checklist: goal, reasons, support, credibility, motivation, and ethics.

Speech

Cancer is a leading cause of death. Nationally it kills over half a million people a year. In Ohio, according to the Ohio Department of Health, more than 25,000 people have cancer. And in Hamilton County, where a lot of us work and live and go to school, over 2,000 people have cancer.

Now, I know from asking that a lot of you have said that you know someone that had or now has cancer. And so I think you know how I feel. It's a strange feeling, it's a very helpless feeling watching someone you love suffer from cancer. And I've discovered something that helps me fight this feeling, and that's volunteering for the American Cancer Society's fund-raising program called Notes to Neighbors.

This program asks its volunteers to address and mail form letters asking for donations for people in their own area, and they also provide the addresses and forms and lists for these letters. All the volunteer has to do is send out the notes, receive the donations, and then send the total donations to the American Cancer Society. I wish you'd all sign up for Notes to Neighbors because the demand for donations is tremendous. And doing this for neighbors is a really great way to fight against cancer.

Why should you participate in this program? First, because the American Cancer Society is able to meet only a small amount of the demand for private research funding. Of 2,225 applications for grants (these are private grants, mind you), only 491 were able to be funded by the American Cancer Society. That's only 21 percent. Another 231 (about 11 percent) of the applications were accepted, but they weren't funded because the Society ran out of money—so again, only 21 percent got funded. And of the total 2,225 applicants, 1,503 were rejected—a great many of these because of lack of money. So, that's 79 percent of all proposals, a great many of which were worthy, didn't get funded. What this means is that there are more willing researchers to do the work than there is money that the American Cancer Society has to give. What I want you to do is help with Notes to Neighbors in order to increase the amount of money the Cancer Society has to give to researchers, thereby moving along the fight against cancer.

Notes to Neighbors is an excellent way for you to participate because it is an easy and realistic way for you to contribute to the fight against cancer. The dollar cost for participating in the Notes to Neighbors program for one person is really only the cost of one book of stamps. All you have to do is buy one five-dollar book of stamps to participate in this program. Now I know as students we really don't have a lot of money to throw around—there have been weeks when I had only five dollars to eat on all week. And I know everyone has gone

Analysis

Dana uses a series of statistics to get audience attention.

Here she identifies with the audience.

Dana states the name of the program and briefly states what people have to do.

Dana makes her initial appeal to her audience.

Her first reason focuses on the problem—lack of money for research. Good use of statistics to show how few of the proposals got funded.

She shows that researchers are ready and able—they just need money to do the work.

Dana's second reason shows that students can participate for little or no real monetary cost. Good use of reiteration. Here she identifies with students' hesitancy to commit themselves. But then she uses her own experience to show that the monetary problem can be overcome.

Dana's third reason also focuses on
the ease of completing the task.
Again, she shows the ability to
identify with student concerns—
lack of time.
Another excellent use of personal
experience to show how any of us
can make the time.

through this at least once. So you might be saying, "I can't even afford five dollars!" But there are ways of getting around this cost. If you want to do it, you can do it. There are ways. For instance, last year when I did this, I asked my boss at work to donate a book of stamps so that I could complete this program, and he did—so it really cost me nothing. And I bet you can think of a way, too.

In addition to costing only a few dollars at most, Notes to Neighbors takes you only two hours, once a year, to complete. That's only two hours! And that's at a maximum. I know all of you work, because I've asked, and obviously we're all here at school, so I know your time is precious. Most days you don't have a lot of time to contribute to volunteer work because you're here trying to get an education. Last year when I got my envelopes, it only took me only 45 minutes. Moreover, I was able to do this in my spare time while I was at work. Let me explain. You see, I work as a waitress at a restaurant—and when I was waiting for people to come in, I used that time that I ordinarily spent just waiting to write my addresses on the forms. Now everybody has some time during nearly every day where you're waiting, whether it be at your job, at school, or whatever. I'm talking about times when you're not really doing anything. My example was at work waiting for people to come into the restaurant. I'm sure you have times just like mine. By using those times it doesn't cut into your free time. You're not actually taking time away from work or your social life to do this—but you're still helping people.

She reviews the points that the program costs little in the way of money or time. But then, she recognizes that people may still not be motivated to follow through. To provide motivation, she returns again to her own experience. Here Dana vividly shows what cancer can do to people.

Now, I hope I've made this pretty clear that the money and the time it will take to do this is really inconsequential to those of us who really don't have a lot of spare time or money to give. But if I haven't convinced you that this program is easy to do or that it's important to do, I want to ask you a couple of questions. How many of you have taken care of someone who has cancer? How many of you have seen the agony of cancer firsthand? For those of you who haven't, I want to tell you a little bit of what it's like.

My father was diagnosed with brain cancer two years ago this January. He went directly into the hospital a week later for a couple of rounds of radiation and chemotherapy. Since then, I've watched him go from 190 pounds to weighing less than I do—that's more than 70 pounds gone. The problem is, he's not able to eat, and this is due to a lot of the damage done by the radiation to his rib muscles. His salivary glands are destroyed—there's swelling in his throat, and he's not able to eat solid foods. He's had to drink Ensure for every meal everyday for two years. Also, the swelling in his throat has closed his windpipe completely, so they had to do a tracheotomy to relieve the swelling so he can breath and not suffocate. My father is 57 years old, and in the last two years he hasn't been able to work because of his illness. Last week he was forced out of his business that took him 15 years to build. And now he's living on disability— and wasting away in front of the television.

Dana now relates her experience to the entire audience. Throughout the speech, Dana blends logical information and emotional appeal quite well. This is a good persuasive speech that follows the motivational pattern.

What I want you to understand is that the half a million people who die a year from cancer belong to other people—they belong to mothers, daughters, siblings, and fathers. This disease can be cured, but it will take research to find the cures. Please help. Please sign up for Notes to Neighbors to help the American Cancer Society fund that research that is so necessary. ■

Refuting Persuasive Claims

When you are confronted with a speech that makes a claim, you can accept it, reject it, or perhaps suspend judgment. If you reject the speech, you can sit quietly and fume, or you can take issue with the speaker who made the claim. The goal of this section is to give you the expertise to evaluate arguments critically and to refute those that you believe are faulty or not in the best interests of the audience. **Refutation** is the process of proving that an argument or series of arguments, or the conclusion drawn from that argument or those arguments, is false, erroneous, or at least doubtful.

In this section, we consider the steps involved in refuting arguments. The section concludes with a speech assignment that enables you to put refutation into practice, along with a sample refutation speech.

refutation *the process of proving that an argument or series of arguments, or the conclusion drawn from that argument or those arguments, is false, erroneous, or at least doubtful*

Outline What Your Opponent Says and Your Reaction

Divide a piece of paper in half vertically, and outline your opponent's speech in one column. Use the other column to note your refutation of each point. Figure 14.2 illustrates notes on one point of the speaker's argument. Notice that the specific goal is written in full, the main point is written as a complete sentence as nearly as possible to the actual words used, and the subpoints include enough words to reflect the content. Accurate notes will help you avoid distorting what your opponent actually said.

FIGURE 14.2 Notes recorded by opponent while listening to advocate's speech

Outline of Argument	Comments
Specific Goal: To prove that students should purchase insurance while they are young.	
1. Buying insurance while you are young provides systematic, compulsory savings.	True, but are these necessarily beneficial?
A. Each due period you get a notice—banks, etc., don't provide service.	True, but what if you miss a payment?
B. Once money is invested, it is saved—there's no deposit and withdrawal with insurance.	True, but what if you need money? You can borrow, but you have to pay interest on your own money! Cash settlement results in loss of money benefits.

In the comments column, sketch your thoughts related to each point made. Thoughts will come to mind as you outline. If you sketch your reactions as you listen, you will be in a much better position to respond.

Plan Your Procedure

At this stage, you will have a reasonably accurate account of all your opponent has said. Now, how will you reply? You can base your refutation on your opponent's evidence or reasoning.

Evaluating Evidence   If your opponent presented little or no evidence, then think of what you will say to show that lack of evidence.

Although you can occasionally find reasons that are unsupported, it's more likely that your opponent has given support. In this case, you can question the quality of the material.

For every bit of evidence that is presented, ask the following questions:

1. Is the evidence fact or opinion?
2. Where does the evidence come from?
3. Is the evidence recent?
4. Is the evidence relevant?

If you are satisfied with the quality of the evidence in an argument, then you can move to testing the reasoning.

Evaluating the Reasoning (Warrants)   Although attacks on evidence are sometimes effective means of refutation, the most convincing form of refutation is the attack on the reasoning from the evidence. Even if all the facts are true, the conclusion fails if the reasoning is unsound.

FOCUS ON skills

Outlining Arguments

The following is an abbreviated written version of a speech argument. In the space below, outline the argument. After you have completed your outline, compare what you've written with Figure 14.3.

Public schools have been criticized during the past few years, but the results of some schools in the city show that public schools are capable of high levels of achievement. Park Hills, a public school on the west side, is an excellent example. Three years ago, Park Hills raised its standards in all academic courses. It forced its students to work much harder to achieve good grades. According to an article in the June 26 issue of the *Post,* this year Park Hills had three merit scholars, more than any year in its history. Moreover, student SAT scores were up 20 points from student scores just three years ago. Linden, a public school on the east side, is another example. Four years ago, Linden began increasing homework assignments and now requires two hours per evening of homework as well as three major papers a year of all students. According to that same *Post* article, this year Linden had 85 percent of its graduating class accepted to college, up 30 percent from four years ago.

FIGURE 14.3 Outline of a speech argument

I. **Public schools are capable of high levels of achievement.**
   A. Park Hills
      1. Raised standards in all courses
      2. Forced students to work harder for grades
      3. Three merit scholars (more than ever)
      4. SAT scores up 20 points in three years
   B. Linden
      1. Two hours of homework per night
      2. Three papers a year of all students
      3. 85% of graduates accepted to college (up 30% in four years)

As we saw earlier in this chapter, each argument presented in a persuasive speech is composed of claims or propositions and data (reasons and evidence). To refute another's reasoning, first identify arguments by example, analogy, causation, sign, definition, or authority; then ask the questions relevant to each type of reasoning (see pages 282–287) and consider possible fallacies (see pages 288–289) to find the weaknesses of the arguments and attack them directly.

Bob Daemmrich/Stock, Boston/PNI

The better you anticipate your opponent's arguments, the more effective you'll be in refuting them.

Organize and Present Your Refutation

Once you have decided on the line or lines of attack you will take, organize your refutation. Although you do not have as long to consider exactly what you will say, your refutation must be organized nearly as well as your planned speeches. If you think of refutation as units of argument, each organized by following four definite steps, you can prepare and present refutation effectively.

1. State the argument you are going to refute clearly and concisely.

2. State what you will prove; tell your listeners how you plan to proceed so that they can follow your thinking.

3. Present the reasons and data completely and with documentation (a brief reference to source).

4. Draw a conclusion; do not rely on the audience to draw the proper conclusion for themselves. Never go on to another reason/argument before you have drawn your conclusion.

To illustrate this method, let us examine a short unit of refutation directed to the first argument presented in Figure 14.2. In the following abbreviated statement, notice how the four steps of refutation (stating the argument, stating what you will prove, presenting proof, and drawing a conclusion) are incorporated:

1. Mr. Jackson has said that buying insurance provides systematic, compulsory savings.

2. His assumption is that systematic, compulsory saving is a benefit of buying insurance while you are young. But I believe just the opposite is true; I believe that it has at least two serious disadvantages.

3. First, the system is so compulsory that if you miss a payment you stand to lose your entire savings and all benefits. Most insurance contracts include a clause giving you a 30-day grace period, after which the policy is canceled (evidence). Second, if you need money desperately, you have to take a loan against your policy. The end result of such a loan is that you have to pay interest in order to borrow your own money (evidence).

4. From this analysis, I think you can see that this systematic, compulsory saving is more disadvantageous than advantageous for people who are trying to save money.

INFOTRAC COLLEGE EDITION

Investigating the preparation of legal arguments can give you some good insight into improving your persuasive speaking skills. Using InfoTrac College Edition, use "arguments, legal" as your Search Guide topic. Choose two or three articles to read about opening and closing arguments.

FOCUS ON skills

Refuting Arguments

Work with a classmate to select a debatable topic and to phrase a speech goal that establishes or changes a belief—for example, "The United States should establish mandatory, periodic drug tests for all military personnel" or "The United States should withdraw all troops from Eastern Europe." Clear the wording with your instructor. Phrase the specific goal so that the first speaker (you or your classmate) is in favor of the proposal. The first speaker then will give a 3- to 6-minute persuasive speech presenting at least three arguments for the proposal. The second speaker will give a 3- to 6-minute speech opposing the specific arguments presented by the first speaker.

Supporting and Refuting: Two Sides of a Debate

The following two speeches are presented to illustrate a debate format, with one supporting a speech goal and the second refuting the arguments presented in the first speech.[10]

Instead of analyzing the first speech on the basis of its effectiveness as a speech, analyze it as if you were to give the speech of refutation, like the analysis below. That is, consider its strengths and weaknesses, but do so in a context of how you would develop your refutation. After you have determined a strategy for refuting the speech, read the analysis.

SAMPLE

Speech in Favor of Prohibiting the Use of Lie Detector Tests

Lie detector or polygraph tests used either to screen job applicants or to uncover thefts by employees have become a big business. Hundreds of thousands are given each year, and the number is steadily rising. What I propose to you today is that employers should be prohibited from administering lie detector tests to their employees either as a condition of employment or as a condition

Analysis

The negative speaker should outline as clearly as possible the key affirmative points.

Special care should be taken to write affirmative reasons accurately.

Accuracy of tests is critically important. Is there confirmation for this estimate? If so, accept it, work around it, or both. If not, correct it. A decision on how to deal with "misleading" will depend on development.

These two examples are highly emotional and may be persuasive. But: (1) Only two examples have been given. Nothing has been presented to show that the examples are representative. (2) The examples do not necessarily indicate a problem with the mechanics of testing.

Assuming that testers are relatively incompetent, how does this information affect the negative case? Can this be either admitted or ignored? If not, how can it be refuted?

Reemphasis of importance of level of accuracy.

Can instances of abuse be admitted without concluding that tests should be abolished? How?

This material demonstrates a threat of government intervention. But has government intervened? Has government determined what constitutes "invasion of privacy"?

Strong emotional appeal in this summary. How can the effect of this be countered?

of maintaining their job. I support this proposition for two reasons. First, despite technological improvement in equipment, the accuracy of results is open to question; and second, even if the tests are accurate, use of lie detector tests is an invasion of privacy.

First, let's consider their accuracy. Lie detector tests just have not proved to be very accurate. According to Senator Birch Bayh, tests are only 70 percent accurate. And equally important, even the results of this 70 percent can be misleading. Let's look at two examples of the kinds of harm that come from these misleading results.

One case involves a young girl named Linda Boycose. She was at the time of the incident a bookkeeper for Kresge's. One day she reported $1.50 missing from the previous day's receipts. A few weeks later, the store's security man gave her a lie detector test. He first used the equipment with all its intimidating wiring, and then he used persuasion to get information. He accused her of deceiving him and actually stealing the money. After this test, Boycose was so upset she quit her job—she then spent the next two years indulging in Valium at an almost suicidal level. A Detroit jury found Boycose's story so convincing that it ordered the department store chain to award her $100,000. Now, almost six years later, she is still afraid to handle the bookkeeping at the doctor's office she manages.

The next example is of a supermarket clerk in Los Angeles. She was fired after an emotional response to the question "Have you ever given discount groceries to your mother?" It was later discovered that her mother had been dead for five years, thus showing that her response was clearly an emotional one.

Much of the inaccuracy of the tests has to do with the examiner's competence. Jerry Wall, a Los Angeles tester, said that out of an estimated 3,000 U.S. examiners, only 50 are competent. Some polygraph operators tell an interviewee that he or she has lied at one point even if the person has not, just to see how the person will handle the stress. This strategy can destroy a person's poise, leading to inaccuracies. With these examples of stress situations and inefficient examiners, the facts point to the inaccuracy of polygraph test results.

My second reason for abolishing the use of these tests is that they are an invasion of privacy. Examiners can and do ask job applicants about such things as sexual habits and how often they change their underwear. The supposed purpose of lie detector tests is to determine whether an employee is stealing. These irrelevant questions are an invasion of privacy, and not a way to indicate whether someone is breaking the law.

Excesses are such that the federal government has been conducting hearings on misuse. Congress is considering ways to curtail their use.

That they are an invasion of privacy seems to be admitted by the companies that use them. Employers are afraid to reveal too much information from tests because they have a fear of being sued. Because of an examiner's prying questions on an employee's background, and because government has shown such concern about the continued use of polygraphs, we can conclude that they are an invasion of privacy.

In conclusion, let me ask you how, as an employee, you would feel taking such a test. You'd probably feel nervous and reluctant to take the test. Couldn't you see yourself stating something that would be misconstrued, not because of the truth but because of your nervousness? Also, how would you feel about having to answer very personal and intimate questions about yourself in order to get a job?

Because lie detector tests are inaccurate and an invasion of privacy, I believe their use should be prohibited. ■

In the speech of refutation, we would expect the speaker to say something about the two reasons that were presented in the first speech. In your analysis, look to see how the groundwork for refutation is laid; then look for the use of the four-step method of refutation.

SAMPLE **speech**

Speech of Refutation: Using Lie Detector Tests

My opponent has stated that the use of lie detector tests by employers should be abolished. I strongly disagree; I believe employers have to use these tests.

Before examining the two reasons she presented, I'd like to take a look at why more than 20 percent of the nation's largest businesses feel a need to use these tests and why the number is growing each year. Employers use lie detector tests to help curb employee theft. According to the National Retail Merchants Association, employees steal as much as $40 billion of goods each year. Moreover, the figure increases markedly each year. The average merchant doesn't recognize that he loses more to employees than to outsiders—50 to 70 percent of theft losses go to employees, not to shoplifters. This use of lie detector tests is a necessity to curb this internal theft.

Now, I do not believe that my opponent ever tried to show that there is not a problem that lie detector testing solves; nor did she try to show that lie detector testing doesn't help to deter internal theft. Notice that the two reasons she presented are both about abuses. Let's take a closer look at those two reasons.

First, my opponent said that the accuracy of results is open to question; in contrast, I would argue that these tests are remarkably accurate. She mentioned that Senator Bayh reported a 70-percent level of accuracy. Yet the literature on these tests as reported by Ty Kelley, vice president of government affairs of the National Association of Chain Drug Stores, argues that the level is around 90 percent, not 70 percent.

She went on to give two examples of people who were intimidated and/or became emotional and upset when subjected to the test. And on this basis she calls for them to be abolished. I would agree that some people do become emotional, but this is hardly reason for stopping their use. Unless she can show a real problem among many people taking the test, I think we'll have to go along with the need for the tests.

If these tests are so inaccurate, why are one-fifth of the nation's largest companies using them? According to an article in *Business Week*, "Business Buys the Lie Detector," more and more businesses each year see a necessity for using the tests because they deter crime. These tests are now being used by nearly every type of company—banks, businesses, drug stores, as well as retail department stores.

Analysis

Good opening. Speaker has clearly stated her position.
Speaker has clearly laid the groundwork for her negative position. This material establishes a need for some measures to be taken against theft. It shows that tests are not being used without good reason.

This represents further clarification of what affirmative has done and what negative proposes to do. It helps to place the affirmative attack in proper perspective.
Good direct attack on level of accuracy. Notice that she states opponent's point, states her position on the point, and then presents the evidence. But why are Kelley's figures better than Bayh's? The speaker needs to show us with a concluding statement of refutation.
Good job of debating the conclusion to be drawn from the examples. Still, I would like to have heard her make a closer examination of the examples themselves.
That businesses use the tests does not prove that businesses are convinced they are accurate. Need more factual data here.

This is a further attempt to put the affirmative argument into proper perspective. Judge's ruling gives strong support to her position.

Good line of argument. Any attempt at refuting alleged abuses would be damaging to the negative position.

Here the speaker does a nice job of bringing emphasis back to the need for the tests.
This is a good speech of refutation. It illustrates the importance of showing the negative position before launching into refutation; it illustrates good form for refutation; it provides several approaches to refutation.

Her second reason for why the tests should be abolished is that they are an invasion of privacy. I believe, with Mr. Kelley, whom I quoted earlier, that there must be some sort of balance maintained between an individual's right to privacy and an employer's right to protect his property. In Illinois, for instance, a state judge ruled that examiners could ask prying questions—there has yet to be any official ruling that the use is "an invasion of privacy."

My opponent used the example of asking questions about sexual habits and change of underwear. In that regard, I agree with her. I think that a person is probably pretty sick who is asking these kinds of questions—and I think these abuses should be checked. But asking questions to screen out thieves, junkies, liars, alcoholics, and psychotics is necessary. For instance, an Atlanta nursing home uses polygraph tests to screen out potentially sadistic and disturbed nurses and orderlies. Is this an invasion of privacy? I don't think so.

It is obvious to me that some type of lie detector test is needed. Too much theft has gone on, and something must be done to curtail this. I say that lie detector tests are the answer. First, they are accurate. Companies have been using them for a long time, and more and more companies are starting to use them. And second, it is only an invasion of privacy when the wrong types of questions are asked. I agree that these abuses should be curbed, but not by doing away with the tests. Employers cannot do away with these tests and control theft; the benefits far outweigh the risks. ■

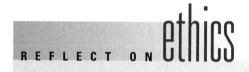

REFLECT ON ethics

Alexandro, a student who had worked full time for three years before returning to college for his sophomore year, had decided that for his final speech he would motivate the members of his class to donate money to the Downtown Food Bank. He was excited about this topic because he had begun volunteering for the Food Bank during those last three years and had seen firsthand the face of hunger in this community.

He planned to support his speech with three reasons: (1) that an increasing number of people in the community needed food; (2) that government agencies were unable to provide sufficient help; and (3) that a high percentage of every donated dollar at the food bank went into food. As he researched these points, he discovered that the number of families who were in need in the community had not really risen in the past two years and that government sponsorship of the Food Bank had increased. Then, when he examined the Food Bank's financial statements, he discovered that only 68 percent of every dollar donated was actually spent on food. Faced with this evidence, he just didn't think his reasons and evidence were very strong.

Yet, because of his experience, he still thought the Food Bank was a cause that deserved financial support, so he decided to focus his entire speech on the heartwarming case of the Hernandez family. Ineligible for government assistance, over the years this family of ten had managed to survive because of the aid they received from the Food Bank. Today, several of the children had graduated from college, and one was a physician working in the barrio. By telling this heart-wrenching story of the struggle to survive, Alexandro thought he would be successful in persuading the class.

Would it be ethical for Alexandro to give his speech in this way? If so, why? If not, what would he need to do to make the speech ethical?

Summary

A speech argument is the product of three essential elements: claim, data, and warrant. A claim is the inference drawn or the inference to be proven. Data constitute the reasons and evidence that provide the basis for a claim. A warrant is a statement that explains the relationship between the evidence (facts and opinion) and the claim (the reason).

Common forms are arguing by example, analogy, causation, sign, definition, and authority. Test reasoning by asking questions about the warrant for the particular argument.

The catalyst for arousing the imagination, inspiring commitment, and moving people to action is the psychological aspect of persuasion called motivation. Two theories of motivation address issues of incentives and basic needs.

Audiences are more likely to be motivated to act when the speech goal presents incentives that create a favorable cost/reward ratio. Costs are units of expenditure; rewards are the benefits received from a behavior. The goal is to have low costs and high rewards.

Audiences are more likely to act when the proposition satisfies a strong, but unmet, need. To use needs strategy in a speech, the speaker can help the audience identify certain unmet needs and then show how acting on the specific speech goal will fulfill those needs.

Refutation is the process of proving that an argument or series of arguments, or the conclusion drawn from that argument or those arguments, is false, erroneous, or at least doubtful. Refutation can be handled systematically. Take careful notes of what your opponent says, note your reaction to each argument, plan your procedure, and present your refutation following the four-step method.

Ritual is the way we carry the presence of the sacred. Ritual is the spark that must not go out.

Christina Baldwin, *Life's Companion: Journal Writing as a Spiritual Quest,* 1990

Speaking at Special Occasions

It was a warm, beautiful spring day. Thousands of people were overflowing the school Green Place, where temporary stands were set up in honor of the U.S. Senator who had been selected to deliver the school's annual address.

he setting just described is typical of those occasions when dignitaries are called upon to meet the needs of a variety of special occasions.

Some of the speaking you are called on to do will be under circumstances that are best described as ceremonial. In these speeches, whether you give information or persuade, you must meet the conventions of the particular occasion. So, even though the guidelines for speech preparation that we have studied throughout this book will serve you well, you must also be familiar with the needs that these occasions serve.

Although no speech can be given by formula, certain occasions require at least the knowledge of conventions that various speakers observe and that audiences may expect. Because speakers should always use their own imagination to determine how to develop the theme, they should never adhere slavishly to those conventions. Still, you must know the conventions before you can decide whether to deviate from or ignore them entirely.

In addition, you may sometimes be called upon to speak or motivated to speak on the spur of the moment.

This chapter gives the basics of preparing and presenting five common types of special speeches—introductions, presentations, acceptances, welcomings, and tributes—as well as speeches for other special occasions. It concludes with sections on impromptu and manuscript speaking.

Introductions

speech of introduction *speech designed to pave the way for the main speaker*

A **speech of introduction** is designed to pave the way for the main speaker. If you make the introduction in a way that psychologically prepares the audience to listen to the speech, then you have accomplished your purpose.

Procedure

Your listeners want to know who the speaker is, what the person is going to talk about, and why they should listen. Sometime before the speech, consult with the speaker to ask what he or she prefers that you say. Usually, you want the necessary biographical information that will show who the speaker is and why he or she is qualified to talk on the subject. The better known the person is, the less you need to say about him or her. For instance, the introduction of the U.S. president is simply, "Ladies and gentlemen, the president of the United States."

Ordinarily, you want enough information to allow you to talk for at least 2 or 3 minutes. Only on rare occasions should a speech of introduction last longer than 3 or 4 minutes; the audience is assembled to hear the speaker, not the introducer. During the first sentence or two, then, establish the nature of the occasion; in the body of the speech, establish the speaker's credibility. The conclusion usually includes the name of the speaker and the title of the talk.

Considerations

Some special cautions apply when preparing a speech of introduction. First, do not overpraise the speaker. If expectations are too high, the speaker will never be able to live up to them. For instance, an overzealous introducer might be in-

Speech of Introduction

Prepare a 2- to 3-minute speech of introduction. Assume that you are introducing the featured speaker for a specific occasion. Criteria for evaluation include creativity in establishing speaker credibility and presenting the name of the speaker and the speech title.

clined to say, "This man [woman] is undoubtedly one of the greatest speakers around today. You will, I am sure, agree with me that this will be one of the best speeches you've ever heard." Although such an introduction may seem complimentary, it does the speaker a disservice by emphasizing comparison rather than speech content.

A second caution is to be familiar with what you have to say. Audiences question sincerity when introducers have to read their praise. Many of us have been present when an introducer said, "And now, it is my great pleasure to present that noted authority . . ." and then had to look at some notes to recall the name. Finally, get your facts straight. The speaker should not have to spend time correcting your mistakes.

A typical speech of introduction might look like the following:

> Fellow club members, it is my pleasure to introduce Susan Wong, the new president of our finance club. I've worked with Susan for three years and have found her to have a gift for organization, insight into the financial markets, and an interest in aligning our club with financial leaders in our community. Susan, as you may not know, has spent the last two summers working as an intern at Salomon Smith Barney, and has now laid the groundwork for more college internships for club members this summer. She is a finance major, with a minor in international business. Susan is ready to lead our finance club for the next year, and we are lucky to have her. Let's give a warm welcome to our new president, Susan Wong!

Presentations

A **presentation speech** is one that presents an award, a prize, or a gift to an individual or a group. Sometimes, a presentation accompanies a long tribute to an individual. Usually, the speech is a fairly short, formal recognition of an accomplishment.

presentation speech *speech that presents an award, a prize, or a gift to an individual or a group*

Procedure

Your speech usually has two goals: (1) to discuss the nature of the award, including its history, donor, or source, and the conditions under which it is made; and (2) to discuss the recipient's accomplishments. If a competition was held, describe what the person did in the competition. Under other circumstances, discuss how the person has met the criteria for the award.

Obviously, you must learn all you can about the award and about the conditions under which such awards are made. Although the award itself may be a certificate, plaque, or trophy symbolizing an achievement, the contest may have

Speech of Presentation

Prepare a 3- to 5-minute speech in which you present a gift, a plaque, or an award to a member of your class. Criteria for evaluation include showing what the award is for, the criteria for winning, and how the person met the criteria.

a long history and tradition that must be mentioned. Because the audience wants to know what the recipient has done, you must know the criteria that were met. For a competition, this includes the number of contestants and the way the contest was judged. If the person earned the award through years of achievement, know the particulars of that achievement.

Ordinarily, the speech is organized to show what the award is for, gives the criteria for winning or achieving the award, and states how the person won or achieved the award. If the announcement of the recipient's name is meant to be a surprise, what is said should build up to the climax—the naming of the winner.

Considerations

For the speech of presentation, there are only two special considerations: (1) Avoid overpraising; do not explain everything in such superlatives that the presentation lacks sincerity and honesty. (2) If you are going to hand the award to the recipient, be careful to hold the award in your left hand and present it to the recipient's left hand. At the same time, you want to shake the right hand in congratulations. With practice, you will be able to present the award and shake the person's hand smoothly and avoid those embarrassing moments when the recipient does not know what he or she is supposed to do.

Acceptances

acceptance speech *a response to a presentation speech*

An **acceptance speech** is a response to a presentation speech. The purpose of the acceptance speech is to give brief thanks for receiving the award.

Procedure

The speech usually has two parts: (1) a brief thanks to the group, agency, or people responsible for giving the award; and (2) thanks to those who share in the honor if the recipient was aided by others.

Considerations

Unless the acceptance is the lead-in to a major address, the acceptance should be brief. (A politician accepting a gift from the Chamber of Commerce may launch into a speech on government, but the audience will probably be expecting it.) As the Academy Awards program so graphically illustrates, however,

Speech of Acceptance

This assignment can go together with the presentation speech assignment. Prepare a 1- to 2-minute speech of acceptance in response to another speaker's speech of presentation. The criterion for evaluation is how imaginatively you can respond in a brief speech.

when people are honored, the tendency is to give overly long and occasionally inappropriate speeches. The audience expects the recipient to show his or her gratitude to the presenter of the award; it does not expect a major address.

The following is an example of an appropriate speech of acceptance:

> On behalf of our Board of Directors, thank you for this award, the Largest Institutional Benefactor in Second Harvest's 1998 Food Drive. It is an honor to be a part of such a worthwhile cause, and it is really our Board who should be thanking you, Second Harvest, for all the wonderful work you have done over the years. You continue to collect and distribute food to thousands of needful families and individuals, especially to our senior citizens and single mothers. Without your work, many would otherwise go hungry. You are a model of community sharing and caring.
>
> I would also like to thank our company staff—Juanita Alverez, Su Lin, Al Pouzorek, Linda Williams, and Jesus Washington—for their efforts in organizing the collection of food and money to go to Second Harvest. They were tireless in their work, persistent in their company memos and meetings requesting donations, and consistent in their positive and upbeat attitudes throughout the drive! We could not have won this award without them! Let's give them a round of applause, too.
>
> Finally, thank you, Second Harvest, for this honor—and we hope to be back next year to receive it again!

TECHNOLOGY *tips*

Watch an awards presentation on television (Academy Awards, MTV Awards, or the like). Evaluate the acceptance speeches to see how many meet the description of an acceptance speech as a "brief thanks" to the people responsible for giving the award, plus thanks to other people who helped them achieve the award.

Stephane Cardinale/Sygma

When accepting an award, show your gratitude for receiving the award and be brief.

Welcomings

welcoming speech *speech that expresses pleasure for the presence of a person or an organization*

A **welcoming speech** is one that expresses pleasure for the presence of a person or an organization. In a way, the speech of welcome is a double speech of introduction. You introduce the newcomer to the organization or city, and you introduce the organization to the newcomer.

Procedure

You must be familiar with both the person or organization you are welcoming and the situation to which you are welcoming the person. It is surprising how little many members of organizations, citizens of a community, and students at a college or university really know about their organization or community. Although you may not have the knowledge on the tip of your tongue, it is inexcusable not to find the material you need to give an appropriate speech. Likewise, you want accurate information about the person or organization you are introducing. Although the speech will be brief, you need accurate and complete information from which to draw.

After expressing pleasure in welcoming the person or organization, give a little information about your guest and about the place or organization to which he or she is being welcomed. Usually the conclusion is a brief statement of your hope for a pleasant and profitable visit.

Considerations

Again, the special caution is to make sure the speech is brief and honest. Welcoming guests does not require you to gush about them or their accomplishments. The speech of welcome should be an informative speech of praise.

speech of tribute *speech that praises someone's accomplishments*

Tributes

A **speech of tribute** is one that praises someone's accomplishments. The occasion may be, for example, a birthday, the taking of an office, retirement, or death. A formal speech of tribute given in memory of a deceased person is called a *eulogy*.

Procedure

The key to an effective tribute is sincerity. Although you want the praise to be apparent, you do not want to overdo it.

You must have in-depth biographical information about your subject. Audiences are interested primarily in new information and specifics that characterize

your assertions, so you must have a mastery of much detail. Focus on the person's laudable characteristics and accomplishments. It is especially noteworthy if you find that the person has had to overcome a special hardship or meet a particularly trying condition. All in all, be prepared to make a sound positive appraisal.

One way to organize a speech of tribute is by focusing on the subject's accomplishments. How detailed you make the speech will depend on whether the person is well known. If the person is well known, be more general in your analysis. If the person is little known, provide many more details so that the audience can see the reasons for the praise. In the case of distinctly prominent individuals, you may be able to show their influence on history.

Considerations

Remember, however, that no one is perfect. Although you need not stress a person's less glowing characteristics or failures, some allusion to this kind of information may make the person's positive features even more meaningful. Probably the most important guide is for you to keep your objectivity. Excessive praise is far worse than understatement. Try to give the person his or her due, honestly and sincerely.

Other Ceremonial Occasions

Other occasions that call for ceremonial speeches are graduations, conferences or conventions, and holidays or events.

Nearly every educational institution includes a **commencement address**—a speech presented by a major political, business, or social figure, or a prominent alumnus/a—in its graduation ceremonies. The goals of most commencement speeches are to praise members of the graduating class and to inspire them in their future work. Although in some instances, the commencement speech is a platform for a major figure to make a major policy statement, the best commencement speeches are ones that the graduating class can identify with.

Most major organizations schedule a **keynote address** near the beginning of their conferences or conventions. Most of us are familiar with the keynote addresses presented at the national Democratic and Republican Party Conventions. The word itself gives us insight into the primary goal of the speech: to present a *keynote* intended to inspire participants in their work. Some keynotes, like those at national political conventions, are given as much or even more for the benefit of the television or radio audience. In these cases, the goal is to inspire listeners to support the particular political party and its candidates for office. Although there are no set guidelines for a keynote speech, the goal is to inspire—to generate enthusiasm among participants and those watching television or listening to the radio.

INFOTRAC COLLEGE EDITION

Using InfoTrac College Edition, conduct a search in the Subject Guide using "tributes" as the keyword. Locate and read the speech President Clinton gave when dedicating the Roosevelt Memorial in May 1997. This is an excellent example of a speech of tribute.

commencement address *a speech presented by a major political, business, or social figure, or a prominent alumnus/a, during graduation ceremonies*

keynote address *a speech presented near the beginning of an organization's conference or convention that is designed to inspire participants in their work*

David Young-Wolff/PhotoEdit

Special occasions such as weddings, birthdays, and retirements call for speeches and toasts. A short, well-prepared speech given with sincerity and sensitivity to the setting and occasion can make the celebration more meaningful and memorable for everyone concerned.

Commemorative addresses are presented to celebrate national holidays or anniversaries of important dates or events. Thus, Memorial Day, the Fourth of July, and Labor Day evoke countless speeches across the United States. Likewise, we hear speeches commemorating the 10th, 25th, or 50th anniversary of significant events such as D-Day, integration of schools, or the founding of organizations. The goals of such speeches often include reminding the audience of the background for the particular holiday, date, or event and then, ultimately, drawing some conclusion about its significance that inspires the audience.

commemorative addresses
speeches that are presented to celebrate national holidays or anniversaries of important dates or events

Impromptu Speeches

Up until this point, we've been operating under the assumption that you are aware that you will be called upon to speak, and thus have time to prepare. But occasionally, your speaking will be **impromptu,** on the spur of the moment. Whether you have attended a meeting and suddenly feel the urge to make a statement, or a reporter corners you and asks you for a statement, you still need to speak with confidence and make sense.

In short, any speech uses all the action steps and guidelines for effective speaking that we have considered except preparing visual aids and practicing. Let's reconsider these steps in terms of impromptu speaking.

impromptu speech *speech given on the spur of the moment*

FOCUS ON skills

Impromptu Speech

Topics   The best topics for impromptu speeches are those that each of you in class will be able to talk about without going beyond your own knowledge and experience. Your instructor will have words and phrases on 3-by-5-inch cards, such as "Uses of Computers," "The Ideal Mate," or "Sex on Television."

Procedure   At the beginning of the round, a student (usually a volunteer) draws three topics, selects one, and begins preparation. The first person in the round has 3 minutes to prepare. The second person in the round draws three cards just before the first person begins talking. The second person (and each subsequent speaker) also has 3 minutes. If the previous speech takes less than 3 minutes, the class uses the time to make comments about the speeches.

1. Determine a goal. Even on the spur of the moment, you should be able to articulate a specific goal. For instance, if you're motivated to speak at a social organization meeting at which the topic of raising dues is being considered, you will quickly think, "I want the organization to support the increase in dues." At the same time, you'll remind yourself of the nature of this organization.

2. Gather material. Although for a formal speech this may involve spending hours at the library, for this impromptu occasion you take a few seconds to call up information that you know. Perhaps you'll rely on observation or your own experience—in any event, impromptu or not, you still need good information to support your views. Perhaps you'll think about some really good ideas that members of the organization had that couldn't be implemented for lack of money.

3. Organize the material. For an impromptu speech, you have to consider common organizational patterns. A persuasive speech requires reasons and evidence. What are the one or two reasons that come to mind in support of the goal to increase dues? From your experience, one reason might be that the money is needed to fund creative programs. Perhaps your experience also suggests that dues haven't been raised for several years. As an introduction, you might just tell the group what you will cover. Yet even in the nanoseconds you have before you actually begin speaking, an idea may come to you. For the conclusion, you may just summarize your reasons and make an appeal.

4. Adapt material to the audience. Time prevents a careful survey of materials and how you can use them. Still, if you keep the audience in mind, ideas for adapting will come to you as you speak. You should certainly be able to use personal pronouns and rhetorical questions—and you should be able to relate any example, illustration, or story to the specific audience.

5. Select the wording. Again, you don't have time to really consider composition. But you can remind yourself to be clear and vivid where possible.

How do you get better at impromptu speaking? Through practice. Don't back away from opportunities to speak. And in the privacy of your own quarters, you might actually talk for a minute or two about a subject that is near to you. We all fantasize about what we might say if we were called upon. Instead of fantasizing, do it.

Manuscript Speech

Prepare a 4- to 6-minute manuscript speech (your professor will indicate the kind of speech by purpose or occasion). Criteria for evaluation will include clarity, vividness, emphasis, and appropriateness.

Manuscript Speeches

Throughout this book, we have been emphasizing extemporaneous speaking. Nevertheless, you may be called upon to give a manuscript speech on a ceremonial occasion when the precise wording of the speech is critical. A **manuscript speech** is one that is written out completely and then read aloud.

manuscript speech *speech that is written out completely and then read aloud*

The final draft of your manuscript should be extremely well worded. You will want to show all that you have learned about making ideas clear, vivid, and appropriate. In your preparation, you should proceed as if you were giving an extemporaneous speech. Then record what you would ordinarily consider your final speech practice. Type the manuscript from your recorded practice, and work on polishing the language. This procedure will ensure that you are working from an oral style rather than from a written essay style.

After the manuscript has been completely written, practice using it effectively. You want to be sufficiently familiar with the material so that you do not have to focus your full attention on the manuscript as you read. Go over the manuscript at least three times in these final stages of practice. You will discover that even when you are reading, you can have some eye contact with your audience. By watching audience reaction, you will know when and if to deviate from the manuscript.

So that the manuscript will be of maximum value to you, I suggest the following tips for preparing it.

1. The manuscript should be typed, preferably on a computer or on a typewriter that has print that is pica-sized or larger. Whatever size type you use, it is wise to double—or even triple—space the manuscript.

   This practice sentence, a nice size for reading, is 14 point.

2. For words that you have difficulty pronouncing, use phonetic spelling, accents, or diacritics to help your pronunciation.

3. Make marks that will help you determine pauses, places of special emphasis, or where to slow down or speed up. Also make sure that the last sentence on each page is completed on that page to prevent any unintended pauses.

4. Number the pages boldly to keep them in their proper order. You may also find it valuable to bend the corner of each page slightly to help you turn pages easily.

5. Make sure to double-check that there will be a lectern or speaker's stand on which the manuscript can be placed.

As Ken and Chet were talking about the Young Leaders of the Community Dinner, Ken looked at Chet and said, "What's the matter, Chet—you really look as if something is bothering you!"

"Well, you know I'm introducing Rick, who's giving a major speech at the dinner. He was asked because he has been so involved in youth activities. He's my friend, and I told him I'd be happy to introduce him. I asked him to give me some information that he'd like me to include. I thought he'd summarize some of the stuff he's done, but instead he wrote out an introduction that includes stuff about him that's largely fiction! When I mentioned this to him, he told me that to make an impression on this audience he'd have to really show that he was worthy of giving this speech. He just doesn't seem to think that what he's done is special enough. I really feel like I'm in a jam, Ken."

"So, he's the one who's giving the speech—he's going to be judged on what he says. You're just giving the introduction he wants you to give. Don't worry about it—nobody's going to pay attention to what you're saying anyway."

But, still, I'm giving the introduction. I'm afraid that I'm going to be the one who gets blamed if people find out that what I've said isn't true."

"I'm telling you—your job is to do what Rick wants. You asked him to give you information and he did."

"I guess you're right—but I'm not going to like doing it."

1. Would Chet be violating ethical principles by giving the opening Rick wants?

2. If so, what should Chet do about it?

Summary

In addition to informative and persuasive speeches, you are likely to have occasion to give speeches of introduction, presentation, acceptance, welcome, and tribute. You may also have occasion to present a commencement address, a keynote speech, or a speech commemorating a particular event or occasion. Moreover, at times you may need to speak impromptu or from a manuscript.

Introductions are speeches that introduce a speaker. A presentation is a speech in which you present an award, a prize, or a gift to an individual or to a group. An acceptance is a response to a speech of presentation. A welcome is a speech that expresses pleasure at the presence of a person or an organization. A tribute is a speech that praises someone's accomplishments.

Commencement speeches are those that praise the graduating class and turn them toward the future. A keynote address, as its title indicates, offers a keynote for a conference or convention. Commemorative speeches celebrate national holidays or anniversaries of important dates.

Impromptu speeches are those that are given on the spur of the moment. Manuscript speeches are written out in full and read.

The genius of a good leader is to leave behind him a situation which common sense, without the grace of genius, can deal with successfully.

Walter Lippman, "Roosevelt Has Gone," April 14, 1945

Leading Problem-Solving Groups

"Chapman, as you know, I'm concerned with the basic skill levels of the people we've been interviewing for jobs in manufacturing. The more I think about it, the more I believe we need to play a more active role in providing adult education that would not only be good for the community, but I think would benefit us in the long run. The reason I called you in here was to see whether you would take leadership in setting up a group whose goal it is to establish an adult literacy program that our company could sponsor. You can select the people you'd like to work with, and I'll give you full support."

ike Norm Chapman, you are likely to be called on to take a leadership role. As much as we may believe that we're up to the task, we are often uncertain exactly how we should go about exercising leadership in group decision making. But public speakers are often called upon to lead groups.

For our purposes, **problem-solving group discussion** is defined as a systematic form of speech in which two or more persons meet face to face and interact orally to accomplish a particular task or to arrive at a solution to a common problem. To lead such groups, you must prepare carefully and understand the responsibilities of both the leader and the group members.

problem-solving group discussion *a systematic form of speech in which two or more persons meet face to face and interact orally to accomplish a particular task or to arrive at a solution to a common problem*

Leadership in Problem-Solving Group Discussion

A problem-solving group discussion will not work well without effective leadership.

Leadership Defined

Leadership may be defined as exerting influence to help a group achieve a goal.[1] Let us explore the two key ideas in this definition.

leadership *exerting influence to help a group achieve a goal*

1. Leadership means exerting influence. Influence is the ability to bring about changes in the attitudes and actions of others. When you influence those in your group, you show them why an idea, a decision, or a means of achieving a goal is superior in such a way that members of the group will follow those ideas of their own free will. Members of your group will continue to be influenced as long as they are convinced that what they have agreed to is right, in their own individual best interest, or in the group's best interest.

2. Leadership results in reaching a goal. In the context of a task or problem-solving discussion, this element of leadership means accomplishing the task or arriving at a solution that tests out to be the best solution available at that time.

Leadership Traits

Leadership traits are individual characteristics that predict an individual's success as a leader. Studies conducted over the years seem to show that the individual traits of ability, sociability, motivation, and communication skills are related to effective leadership. Marvin Shaw, a leading researcher in group studies, found that in the area of ability, leaders exceed average group members in intelligence, scholarship, insight, and verbal facility; with regard to sociability, leaders exceed group members in such things as dependability, activity, cooperativeness, and popularity; regarding motivation, leaders exceed group members in initiative, persistence, and enthusiasm; and, finally, leaders exceed group members in various communication skills.[2]

Although these traits don't guarantee success, people are unlikely to be effective leaders if they do not exhibit at least some of these traits to a greater degree than those whom they are attempting to lead.

leadership traits *individual characteristics that predict an individual's success as a leader*

Leadership Styles

Although there is no one "right" way to lead, different group situations often require different leadership styles. **Leadership styles** are patterns of behavior adopted by group leaders. Thus, you need to understand the various styles of leadership, and which is likely to be more appropriate at a particular time. Even though people will tend to lead a group with a style that reflects their own personality, leaders who want to be effective in all kinds of situations need to learn how to adjust their style to the needs of the situation and the group.

What are the major leadership styles? Most recent studies look at leadership styles as either task-oriented (sometimes called authoritarian) or person-oriented (sometimes called democratic).

The **task-oriented leader** exercises more direct control over the group. Task leaders will determine the statement of the question. They will analyze the problem and decide how the group will proceed to arrive at the solution. They are likely to outline specific tasks for each group member and suggest the roles they desire members to play.

The **person-oriented** or democratic leader may suggest phrasings of the question, suggest procedure, and suggest tasks or roles for individuals. Yet in every facet of the discussion, the person-oriented leader encourages group participation to determine what will actually be done. Everyone feels free to offer suggestions to modify the leader's suggestions. What the group eventually does is determined by the group itself. Person-oriented leaders will listen, encourage, facilitate, clarify, and support. In the final analysis, however, it is the group that decides.

Pioneer work by Ralph White and Ronald Lippitt suggests the following advantages and disadvantages of each style:

1. More work is done under a task-oriented leader than under a person-oriented leader.
2. The least amount of work is done when no leadership exists.

leadership styles *patterns of behavior adopted by group leaders*

task-oriented leader *one who exercises more direct control over the group*

person-oriented leader *one who encourages group participation to determine what will be done*

Bob Daemmrich/Stock, Boston

Every group needs leadership. Whether or not a leader has been appointed or elected, informal leaders often emerge from the ranks of the group on the strength of their leadership traits and skills.

3. Motivation and originality are greater under a person-oriented leader.

4. Task-oriented leadership may create discontent or result in less individual creativity.

5. More friendliness is shown in person-oriented groups.[3]

So, which style is to be preferred? Research by Fred Fiedler suggests that whether a particular leadership style is successful depends on the situation:

1. How good are the leader's interpersonal relations with the group?

2. How clearly defined are the goals and tasks of the group?

3. To what degree does the group accept the leader as having legitimate authority to lead?[4]

Some situations will be favorable to the leader on all dimensions: The leader has good interpersonal relations with the group, the goal is clear, and the group accepts the leader's authority. Some situations will be unfavorable to the leader on all dimensions: The leader has poor interpersonal relations with the group, the goal is unclear, and the group fails to accept the leader's authority. Other situations, of course, are partly favorable or partly unfavorable to the leader on the various dimensions.

Fiedler proposes that task leaders are most effective in favorable or extremely unfavorable situations. In positive situations, where the leader has good interpersonal relations, a clear goal, and group acceptance, the leader can focus entirely on the task. Conversely, in very negative situations, there will be little that the leader can do to improve member perceptions, so the leader may as well storm ahead on the task. Where people-oriented leadership is likely to be most effective is in those moderately good or bad situations where the leader has the most to gain by improving interpersonal relations, clarifying the goal, and building credibility with the group.

Let's consider two specific examples—one of a mostly favorable situation, and one of a moderately unfavorable situation. Suppose you are leading a group of employees who are meeting to determine the recipient of a merit award. If you have good interpersonal relations with the group, if the criteria for determining the award are clearly spelled out, and if the group accepts your authority, you are likely to be highly effective by adopting a task-oriented style of leadership. The group will understand what it is supposed to do and will accept your directions in proceeding to accomplish the task. If, on the other hand, your interpersonal relations with two of the groups other four members has been shaky, the group is not sure how it is supposed to go about making the decision, and at least two members of the group are undecided about your ability to lead, a person-oriented style of leadership is necessary. Before the group can really begin to function with the task, you will need to build your interpersonal relations with at least two members of the group, work with them to clarify the goal, and engage in behaviors that will help build your credibility. So, it isn't a matter of which style is always best; it is a matter of what kinds of circumstances are present.

Are leaders likely to be equally adept at task- and person-oriented styles? Although some are, many people show more skill at one style or the other. Thus, in many groups, even those with a designated leader, more than one person is needed to fulfill all the leadership roles within the group. Nevertheless, throughout this book, we have discussed the kinds of skills that can help you function in either a task- or a people-oriented style.

Leadership Preparation

Whichever style of leadership you use, you are likely to build your credibility with group members if, during group deliberations, you are seen to be exhibiting the following behaviors.

1. Be knowledgeable about the group task. Although the leader is not the primary information giver in a group, group members are more willing to follow when the leader appears to be well informed. The more knowledgeable you are, the better you will be able to analyze individual contributions.

2. Work harder than anyone else in the group. Leadership is often a question of setting an example. When others in the group see a person who is willing to do more than his or her fair share for the good of the group, they are likely to support that person. Of course, such effort can involve personal sacrifice, but the person seeking to lead must be willing to pay the price.

3. Be personally committed to group goals and needs. To gain and maintain leadership takes commitment to the particular task. When you lose that sense of commitment, your leadership may wane and be transferred to others whose enthusiasm is more attuned to a new set of conditions.

4. Be willing to be decisive at key moments in the discussion. When leaders are unsure of themselves or unwilling to make decisions, their groups may ramble aimlessly or become frustrated and short-tempered. Sometimes, leaders must make decisions that will be resented; sometimes, they must decide between competing ideas about courses of action. Any decisions leaders make may cause conflict. Nevertheless, people who are unwilling or unable to be decisive are not going to maintain leadership for long.

5. Interact freely with others in the group. One way to show your potential for leadership is to participate fully in group discussions. This does not mean that you should dominate the group's deliberations, but it does mean sharing your ideas, feelings, and insights concerning both the content of the group's work and, when appropriate, the group process as well. Too often, people sit back silently, thinking, "If only they would call on me for leadership, I would do a really good job." But there is no reason for a group to turn to an unknown quantity. Moreover, by participating fully in the early stages of group work, you can find out whether you are able to influence others before you try to gain leadership.

Gender Differences in Leader Acceptability

A question that has generated considerable research is whether the gender of a leader has any effect on a group's acceptance of leadership. Research suggests that gender does affect group acceptance, but not because women lack the necessary traits or abilities. Negative perceptions are largely a result of sex-role stereotypes and devaluing.

Sex-role stereotypes influence how leaders' behaviors are perceived. A persistent research finding is that the same messages are evaluated differently depending on the source of the message.[5] Thus, whereas some women's behaviors will be considered bossy, dominating, and emotional, men exhibiting essentially the same behaviors will be judged as responsible, as offering high-quality contributions, and as showing leadership. So, the problem that women face is not

Nita Winter Photography MCMXCII

One way to show potential for leadership is to participate fully in group discussions.

INFOTRAC COLLEGE EDITION

As this chapter suggests, many factors can affect leadership in group communication. For more information on group interaction and how it is influenced, use InfoTrac College Edition to locate the article "Leadership Status, Gender, Group Size, and Emotion in Face-to-Face Groups" (Hint: Conduct a search using "leadership" as your keyword in the Subject Guide).

that they don't possess or exhibit leadership characteristics, but that their efforts to show leadership are misperceived.

Moreover, sex-role stereotypes lead to devaluing cooperative and supportive behaviors that many women use quite skillfully. As Sally Helgesen points out, many female leaders are successful *because* they respond to people and their problems with flexibility and *because* they are able to break down barriers between people at all levels of the organization.[6]

As a result of male bias and devaluing of female skills, some women get discouraged in seeking leadership roles. But changes in perception are occurring as the notion of "effective" leadership changes. Thus, as women continue to show their competence, they will be selected as leaders more often. As Jurma and Wright have pointed out, research studies have shown that men and women are equally capable of leading task-oriented groups.[7] Patricia Andrews supports this conclusion, noting that it is more important to consider the unique character of a group and the skills of the person serving as leader than the sex of the leader. She goes on to show that a complex interplay of factors (including how much power the leader has) influences effectiveness more than gender does.[8]

Understanding Problem Solving

To prepare to lead problem-solving groups, you need to understand the problem-solving process. This process includes stating the problem, analyzing it, suggesting possible solutions, and laying the groundwork for selecting the best solution.

State the Goal of Discussion as a Question

Because the goal of discussion is to stimulate group thinking, the discussion problem is stated as a question of policy. Whereas **questions of fact** are concerned with the truth or falsity of an assertion and **questions of value** are concerned with subjective judgments of quality, **questions of policy** involve deciding whether a future action should be taken.

The question is phrased to arrive at a solution or to test a tentative solution to a problem or a felt need. "What should we do to lower the campus crime rate?" seeks a solution that would best solve the problem of campus crime. "Should the university give equal amounts of money to men's and women's athletics?" provides a tentative solution to the problem of how to achieve equity in financial support of athletics. The inclusion of the word *should* emphasizes consideration of a specific plan of action.

An appropriate question for group discussion (1) considers only one subject, (2) is impartially worded, and (3) uses words that can be defined objectively. The question "Should the university offer more classes on diversity and allow students to take more classes pass/fail?" is inappropriate because it includes two different questions. The question "Should the university simplify its ridiculous class registration system?" is neither impartial nor definable.

questions of fact *seeking the truth or falsity of an assertion*

questions of value *making subjective judgments of quality*

questions of policy *judging whether a future action should be taken*

Ask Questions That Analyze the Problem

Analysis means determining the nature of the problem: its size, its causes, the forces that create or sustain it, and the criteria for evaluating solutions.

Questions that analyze the problem are necessary because, when left to their own devices, groups tend to move directly to a discussion of possible solutions. For instance, if your goal is to determine "What should be done to solve the problem of thefts of library books?" the group may want to start by immediately listing possible solutions. But a solution or a plan can work only if it solves the problem at hand. Before you can shape a plan, you must determine what obstacles the solution must overcome or eliminate, as well as whom your plan must satisfy. Before you begin to suggest solutions, you need to determine that the following questions about the problem have been answered:

1. What is its size and scope?
   a. What are its symptoms? (What can we identify that shows something is wrong or needs to be changed?)
   b. What are its causes? (What forces created it, sustain it, or otherwise keep it from being solved?)
2. What criteria should be used to test the solution? Specifically, what checks must the solution meet to best solve this problem? Must the plan eliminate the symptoms, be implemented within present resources, and so on?

Suggest Possible Solutions

Most problems have many possible solutions. At this stage, you need only suggest a few solutions so that you will be able to help the group get started during the discussion.

How do you suggest solutions? One way is for you or the group to brainstorm. You'll recall from our discussion of selecting topics in Chapter 4 that

brainstorming is an uncritical, nonevaluative process of generating associated ideas. Using this free association method, group members state ideas in random order as they come to mind until a long list is compiled. In a good 10- to 15-minute brainstorming session, you may think of several possible solutions by yourself. Depending on the nature of the topic, a group may develop 10, 20, or more possibilities in a relatively short time. Other possible solutions come from reading, interviews with authorities, or observations.

If your goal is phrased as a yes/no question, suggesting solutions is simplified. For instance, the question "Should financial support for women's sports be increased?" has only two possible answers.

Lay the Groundwork for Selecting the Best Solution

At this stage, you don't select a solution—this will be done during discussion. But you must understand how you will proceed during the discussion to arrive at the best solution. If the group has analyzed the problem carefully and listed several potential solutions, then the final step is simply to match each proposed solution against the criteria. For instance, if you have determined that hiring more patrols, putting in closed-circuit TV, and locking outside doors after 9 P.M. are three possible solutions to the problem of increased crime in dorms, then you can begin to measure each against the criteria. The solution that satisfies the most criteria, or the one that meets several criteria most effectively, would be the best selection.

Figure 16.1 outlines the problem-solving method for a group discussion on the question of what should be done to equalize opportunities for women on campus. If leaders take the time to prepare such an outline, they are in a much better position to lead the group through the steps. Notice that the outline doesn't give any information or determine any answers—but it does provide a reasonable framework for a discussion. It also lays the groundwork for planning the agenda, a responsibility of task leaders that is discussed in the following section.

Task Responsibilities of the Leader

Group leadership carries two major responsibilities: task and maintenance. Thus, when we analyze a discussion, we look first to see how and whether the group solved the problem; second, we look to see how well the group members worked together and whether they liked, respected, and understood one another.

The task responsibility involves those activities that contribute directly to meeting the group's goal. In most groups, there are at least four major identifiable task responsibilities: planning the agenda, asking appropriate questions, keeping the group on the topic, and summarizing.

Plan the Agenda

As leader, your first responsibility is to plan the agenda. An **agenda** is an outline of what needs to be accomplished during the meeting. In a problem-solving discussion, the agenda should include the question being considered,

FIGURE 16.1 Preparation for a problem-solving group discussion

Question: What should be done to equalize social, athletic, and political opportunities for women on campus? (Assume that the group has agreed on this wording.)

Analysis

I. What is the size and scope of the problem?

   A. How many women are there on campus?

   B. What is the ratio of females to males on campus?

   C. What opportunities are currently available to women?

      1. What social organizations are available? What is the ratio of women to men who belong?

      2. Are women involved in political organizations on campus? To what extent?

      3. What athletic opportunities are open to women? Are they intramural or intercollegiate?

II. What are the causes of the problem?

   A. Do women feel discriminated against?

   B. Does the institution discriminate?

   C. Do societal norms inhibit women's participation?

   D. Do certain groups discriminate against women?

III. What criteria should be used to test solutions?

   A. Will women favor the solution?

   B. Will it cope with discrimination if discrimination does exist?

   C. Will it be enforceable?

   D. Will it comply with Title IX?

Possible Solutions

Should a Women's Center be created?

Should a special interest seat on all major committees be reserved for women?

Should women's and men's athletic teams be combined?

Etc.

(To be completed during discussion.)

questions related to analysis of the problem, suggested solutions, and selecting a solution. You may prepare the agenda alone or in consultation with the group. When possible, the agenda should be in the hands of the group several days before the meeting. You cannot expect group members to prepare if they do not have an agenda beforehand. When a group proceeds without an agenda, discussion is often haphazard, frustrating, and unproductive.

Figure 16.2 shows a well-planned agenda for a group discussion on the questions equalizing opportunities for women on campus. Notice how the agenda is based on the outline presented in Figure 16.1.

Ask Appropriate Questions

Perhaps one of the most effective leadership tools is asking appropriate questions. You need to know when to ask questions, and you need to know the kinds of questions to ask.

March 1, 1999
To: Athletic Committee
Fr: Angela Freeman
Re: Agenda for discussion
Date: March 8, 1999
Place: Boardroom, Shoemaker Center
Time: 3:00 P.M. (Please be prompt.)

Please come prepared to discuss the following questions. Be sure to bring specific information you can contribute to the discussion of questions 1 through 4. We will consider question 5 on the basis of our resolution of the other questions.

Question: What should be done to equalize social, athletic, and political opportunities for women on campus? (Assume that the group has agreed on this wording.)

Agenda
1. What is the size and scope of the problem?
2. What are the causes of the problem?
3. What criteria should be used to test solutions?
4. What are possible solutions?
5. What is the best solution?

Try to refrain from asking yes-or-no questions. Whether a person answers yes or no, you must either ask another question to draw the members out or change the subject. Two effective types of questions are those that call for supporting information and completely open-ended questions that give members complete freedom of response. For instance, rather than asking John whether he has had any professors who were particularly good lecturers, you could ask, "John, what are some of the characteristics that made your favorite lecturers particularly effective?"

When to ask questions is particularly important. Although we could list 15 to 20 circumstances, let us focus on five purposes of questioning.

1. To encourage the sharing of information. Sharing information and opinion constitutes about 50 percent of what is done in a group, because without information (and well-considered opinions) the group will not have the necessary material from which to draw its conclusions. Effective leaders encourage all members of the group to share their information and opinions. For instance, "To begin with, we need to determine the size and the scope of the problem. Let's start by asking, 'How many women are there on campus?'" or "Okay, we seem to have a pretty good grasp of the nature of the problem, but we haven't looked at any causes yet. What are some of the causes?"

2. To probe for supporting information. For instance, on a question of source, you might ask, "Where did you get that information, Jack?" To develop a point, you might ask, "What do we have that corroborates the point?" To test the strength of a point, you might ask, "Does that statement represent the thinking of the group?"

3. To focus discussion. For instance, "Are you saying that the instances of marijuana leading to hard-drug use don't indicate a direct causal relationship?"

or, to what has just been said, "How does that information relate to the point that Kerisha just made?" or, to ask about an issue or an agenda item, "In what way does this information relate to whether or not marijuana is a health hazard?"

4. To deal with interpersonal problems that develop. For instance, "Ted, I've heard you make some strong statements on this point. Would you care to share them with us?" or, if people seem to be attacking Khalif rather than the information he presented, "Do we have any information that either supports or counters the information Khalif presented?"

5. To consider the reasoning involved in the discussion. Effective leaders probe the contributions of group members to determine whether information is accurate, typical, consistent, and otherwise valid. Suppose a group member reports that according to Paul Stewart, who oversees subscriptions to cable television, the number of new subscriptions dropped last month. The effective leader might ask such questions as "How many new subscriptions has the company been averaging each month over the past year? In how many months were the new subscriptions below the average for the year? for last year? Has this drop been consistent?"

Effective leaders examine the reasoning of various participants. They make such statements as "Enrique, you're generalizing from only one instance. Can you give us some others?" "Wait a minute, after symptoms, we have to take a look at causes." "I think we're passing this possible solution too lightly. There are still questions about it that we haven't answered."

Keep the Group on Track

Whether the group is meeting once or is ongoing, almost invariably some remarks tend to sidetrack the group from the central point or issue.

When the group has strayed, effective leaders make statements like "I'm enjoying this, but I can't quite see what it has to do with resolving the issue," or "Let's see, aren't we still trying to find out whether these are the only criteria that we should be considering?" or "Say, time is getting away from us and we've only considered two possible solutions. Aren't there some more?"

Summarize Frequently

If left to its own devices, a group will discuss a point for a while, then move on to another before a conclusion is drawn. A good problem-solving discussion group will move in an orderly manner toward intermediate conclusions that are represented by summary statements seeking group consensus. For instance, if a group is considering "What should be done to lower the crime rate on campus?" you will need numerous summaries.

When the group seems to have finished with each of the major parts of the discussion (symptoms of the problem, major causes, possible solutions, preferred solution) briefly summarize and state the conclusion that you believe the group is supporting.

The following phrases can be used as a prelude to a summary/conclusion:

"I think most of us are stating the same points. Are we really in agreement that . . . ?" (State the conclusion.)

"We've been discussing this for a while, and I think I sense an agreement. Let me state it, and then we'll see whether it does summarize the group's feelings." (State the conclusion.)

"Now we're getting into another area. Let's make sure that we are really agreed on the point we've just finished." (State the conclusion.)

"Are we ready to summarize our feelings on this point?" (State the conclusion.)

Maintenance Responsibilities of the Leader

The maintenance responsibility involves those activities that contribute to how well group members handle the way they talk about their tasks, the nature of the interaction, and dealing with the feelings of the group. In effective decision-making groups, the leader will establish a good working climate, reward members for their contributions, give everyone an opportunity to speak, and deal with cultural diversity.

Establish a Good Working Climate

Before the group begins talking, you need to set up a comfortable physical environment that will encourage interaction. You are in charge of such physical matters as heat, light, and seating. Make sure the room is at a comfortable temperature, that the room is well lit, and most important, that the seating arrangement will help lead to spirited interaction.

The ideal seating arrangement is a circle. Everyone can see everyone else, and at least physically, everyone has equal status. If the meeting place does not have a round table, you may be better off with either no table or an arrangement of tables to make a square at which the members can come close to the circle arrangement.

TECHNOLOGY tips

Sometimes it is difficult for people who need to meet to come together face to face, so teleconferences have become common. In a voice-only teleconference, it is important for each person to identify herself or himself prior to speaking.

Reward Members for Valuable Contributions

People participating in groups are likely to feel better about their participation when their thoughts and feelings are recognized. Effective leaders help to provide this recognition by acknowledging and rewarding people nonverbally or verbally. Rewarding is done with such nonverbal clues as a smile, a nod, or a vigorous head shake and with such verbal statements as "Good point, Ming," "I really like that idea, Nikki," "It's obvious you've really done your homework, Janelle," and "That's one of the best ideas we've had today, Drew."

Give Everyone an Equal Opportunity to Speak

As leader, you must direct the flow of discussion to ensure that everyone has an equal opportunity to speak. To do so, you must hold those who tend to dominate in check and encourage reluctant members to contribute.

Bob Daemmrich/Stock, Boston

Effective group leaders set up a comfortable physical environment that will encourage interaction. The ideal seating arrangement approximates a circle, so that people can see each other and interact directly.

Often, apparently reluctant speakers want to talk but cannot get the floor. As leader, you can solve this problem by clearing the road for them. For example, Mary may give visual and verbal clues of her desire to speak; she may move to the edge of her seat, she may look as if she wants to talk, or she may even start to say something but pull back when a more aggressive speaker breaks in. To pave the way for her, you might say, "Just a second, Jim, I think Mary has something she wants to say here."

A second method of drawing out reluctant speakers is to phrase a question that requires an opinion rather than a fact. For instance, "Mary, what do

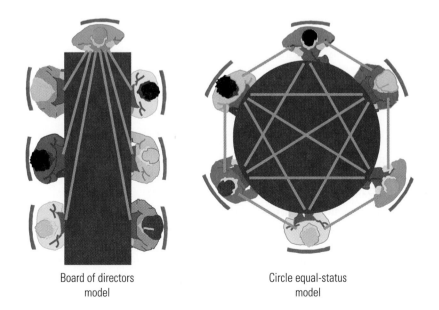

Board of directors
model

Circle equal-status
model

Effects of seating arrangements on group interactions. The board of directors model tends to inhibit interaction; communication emanates from the head of the table. A circle arrangement encourages maximum interaction among group members.

you think of the validity of this approach to combating crime?" is much better than "Mary, do you have any additional statistics?" Not only is it specific, but also it requires more than a yes-or-no answer. Furthermore, such an opinion question will not embarrass Mary if she has no factual material to contribute.

Tactful handling of shy or reluctant persons can pay big dividends. You may get some information that would not have been brought out in any other way; moreover, when Mary contributes a few times, it builds her self-confidence, which in turn makes it easier for her to respond later when she has more to say. Of course, there are times when some members do not have anything worth saying because they simply are not prepared. Under such circumstances, it is best to leave them alone.

As a leader, you must also use tact with overzealous speakers. Remember that talkative Jim may be talkative because he has done his homework—he may have more information than any other member of the group. If you turn him off, the group may suffer immensely. After he has finished talking, try statements such as "Jim, that's a very valuable bit of material; let's see whether we can get some reactions from other members of the group on this issue." Notice that a statement of this kind does not stop him; it suggests that he should hold off for a while.

Participants who are difficult to deal with are those who must be heard regardless of whether they have anything to say. If subtle reminders are ineffective with these individuals, you may have to say, "Jim, I know you want to talk, but you're just not giving anyone else a chance. Would you wait until we've heard everyone else on this point?" Of course, the person who may be the most difficult of all to control is the leader. Leaders often engage in little dialogues with each member of the group. They sometimes exercise so much control that participants believe they can talk only in response to the leader.

Three common patterns of group communication are illustrated in Figure 16.3; the lines represent the flow of discussion among the eight participants. Pattern A represents a leader-dominated group. The lack of interaction often leads to a rigid, formal, and usually poor discussion. Pattern B represents a more spontaneous group. Because three people dominate and two are not heard, however, conclusions will not represent group thinking. Pattern C represents something close to the ideal: a great deal of spontaneity, total group representation, and—theoretically at least—the greatest possibility for reliable conclusions.

Deal with Cultural Diversity

As John Brilhart and Gloria Galanes point out, every group discussion is "intercultural to some extent."[9] Thus, it is important for a leader to recognize and accept differences within the group.

Most Americans see groups as comprised of individuals who, working hard enough together, can make changes. Thus, we see things from an individualistic rather than a collectivist worldview. According to Gudykinst and Kim, individualistic cultures promote self-realization for their members; collectivist cultures require that individuals fit into the group.[10] How might such differences in views affect a group and its work? From a collectivist point of view, the group is comprised of members that sacrifice for the good of the group. When

FIGURE 16.3 Patterns of group discussion

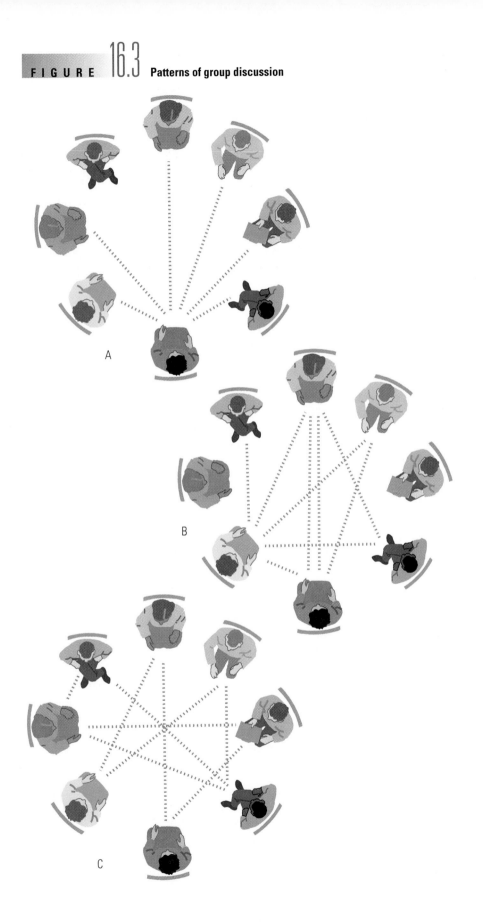

a group does well, all members are praised; if a member stands out from the group, the group may feel an obligation to force the individual to conform. Such a view differs from the individualistic point of view, which sees a group as comprised of individuals and considers it appropriate to praise an individual for his or her contribution to the group effort. Moreover, from an individualistic perspective, it is important to stand out.

To deal with such differences, Brilhart and Galanes suggest that before drawing inferences about group members when their behavior appears to be generally different, ask yourself whether you could be observing a cultural difference and if so, try to adapt to different cultural practices.[11] Since this book is written from an individualist perspective, your task may prove to be even more difficult when you as a leader hold a collectivist perspective. Before a group with major cultural differences can work effectively, it is important for all members to recognize such differences and be willing to try to work through them.

When the Group Goes Public

Although most of your group problem solving will be done in private, without the presence of an onlooking or participating audience, occasionally your group will be called on to go public. At times, this means conducting your deliberations in public; at other times, it means presenting your group's conclusions to another group. In a public discussion, the group is discussing to provide information for the listening audience as much as analyzing or solving a problem. As such, public discussions have much in common with traditional public speaking. Two common forms of public discussion are the symposium and the panel discussion.

Symposium

symposium *a discussion in which a limited number of participants (usually three to five) present individual speeches of approximately the same length dealing with the same subject*

A **symposium** is a discussion in which a limited number of participants (usually three to five) present individual speeches of approximately the same length dealing with the same subject. After delivering their planned speeches, the participants in the symposium may discuss their reactions with one another or respond to questions from the audience.

Despite the potential for interaction, a symposium is often characterized by long, sometimes unrelated speeches. Moreover, the part designated for questions is often shortened or deleted because "our time is about up." Thus, a symposium often omits the interaction necessary for a good discussion. If the participants keep their prepared speeches short enough so that at least half of the available time can be spent on real interaction, a symposium can be interesting and stimulating.

A good symposium that meets the goals of discussion is much more difficult to present than it appears; as a public-speaking assignment, however, the symposium may be beneficial. Rather than solving a problem, a symposium is more effective in shedding light on or explaining various aspects of a problem.

Leading Group Discussion

Divide into groups of about four to six. Each group should be given a question for discussion. Each group then has approximately 30 to 40 minutes of class time for discussion. Each person in the group should have the opportunity to lead the discussion for about 5 minutes. Sample questions for discussion include the following:

What should be done to improve parking (advising, registration) on campus?

What should be done to increase participation in intramural athletics (student government, student activities) on campus?

After the discussion, students can use the group leadership checklist to evaluate one another's performance.

Group Leadership Checklist

For each of the following points, rate the group leader's performance as 1, excellent; 2, good; 3, average; 4, fair; or 5, poor.

	1	2	3	4	5
Task					
Has an agenda	___	___	___	___	___
Promotes systematic problem solving	___	___	___	___	___
Asks good questions	___	___	___	___	___
Keeps the group on the topic	___	___	___	___	___
Summarizes decisions	___	___	___	___	___
Maintenance					
Creates a good working atmosphere	___	___	___	___	___
Rewards members for their contributions	___	___	___	___	___
Encourages balanced participation	___	___	___	___	___
Deals with cultural diversity	___	___	___	___	___

Write an analysis of the person's group leadership (two to five paragraphs) based on this checklist.

Panel Discussion

A **panel discussion** is one in which several participants (usually four to eight) discuss a topic spontaneously, under the direction of a leader and following a planned agenda. After the formal discussion, the audience is often encouraged to question the participants. So that the discussion can be seen and heard by the audience, the group is seated in a semicircle, with the chairperson in the middle to get a good view of both audience and panelists. Because the discussion is for an audience, the panelists are obliged to make good use of traditional public speaking skills. And because a panel discussion encourages spontaneity and interaction, it can be stimulating for both audience and participants. The panel works as a form of problem-solving discussion.

panel discussion *discussion in which several participants (usually four to eight) discuss a topic spontaneously, under the direction of a leader and following a planned agenda*

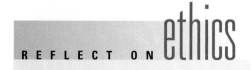
Presentation of Conclusions

More often than not, after a group has finished its deliberations, the leader is asked to state the group's conclusions in a report or public presentation. The spokesperson for the group reviews the group's goal, discusses the analysis of the problem, mentions potential solutions, gives a summary of strengths and weaknesses of each solution, and then presents the group's conclusion.

Summary

Problem-solving group discussion is defined as a systematic form of speech in which two or more persons meet face to face and interact orally to accomplish a particular task or to arrive at a solution to a common problem.

Leadership may be defined as exerting influence to help a group achieve a goal. Although groups often have an appointed leader, in many groups a single person emerges to become the leader. Leaders often show traits of ability, sociability, motivation, and communication skills. Leaders are likely to assume either a task-oriented (authoritarian) or a person-oriented (democratic) style. Either style can be effective, depending on the nature of the task and the group.

The problem-solving process includes stating the problem as a question, analyzing it, suggesting possible solutions, and selecting the best solution. Preparing an outline of relevant questions helps prepare you to lead the discussion.

The leader has both task and maintenance responsibilities. Task responsibilities include planning the agenda, asking appropriate questions, keeping the group on track, and summarizing frequently. Maintenance responsibilities include establishing a good working climate, rewarding members for their contributions, giving everyone an equal opportunity to speak, and dealing with cultural diversity.

Two common forms of public discussion are the symposium and the panel discussion.

Appendix: Sample Speeches

All the sample speeches included in the main text were given by students. The speeches cited in this appendix illustrate how contemporary speakers have met the challenge of effective speaking. First are two speeches printed in their entirety. Each of them contains enough examples of the successful application of basic principles to make them worthy of attention. Your goal is not to copy what these speakers have done, but to read and analyze them in order to better test the value of what you are planning to do in your own speeches. Then follow ten titles of additional speeches you can access through InfoTrac College Edition.

Service: Life Beyond Self[1]

A speech by Geneva B. Johnson, retired President, CEO, Family Service of America, delivered to a Case Western University Convocation in Cleveland, Ohio, on August 27, 1998. Since this is a ceremonial speech, she begins by recognizing those who helped prepare her to function effectively in her field. Then she moves into her three main points in support of the importance of service. Some of the features to look for are her clarity of organization, excellent use of quotations, and most of all, her support of the importance of a life of service.

President Pytte, distinguished faculty, officers, students who will be recognized here for community service, and other students, it is an honor to be a part of this year's convocation. I am humbled by the presentation that I will receive [the President's Distinguished Alumni Award], and I accept it on behalf of my family, who continue to nourish and sustain me. I also accept it with appreciation to the Mandel School of Applied Social Sciences, which prepared me to function effectively and successfully in my chosen field. I was also privileged to serve as the former chairman of the Mandel Center for Nonprofit Organizations, a most unique center in our United States, with a secretariat composed of the deans of the School of Law, the School of [Management], and the [Mandel] School of Applied Social Sciences. I am indebted to Case Western Reserve University for these many experiences, and I'm proud to be an alumna.

My presentation will be on "Service: Life Beyond Self," and I will consider the following areas:

- First, our American heritage of service
- Second, the need for personal commitment and involvement in our society
- Finally, the challenge to live life beyond self

"Man is the only animal that laughs and weeps, for he is the only creature that is struck with the difference between what things are and what they ought to be."

First, our American heritage of service: One of the values we profess in America is we believe in commitments and loyalties beyond self. In a community or nation that includes individuals of diverse religious faiths and non-faiths, diverse politics and personal philosophies, there are bound to be disagreements as to the substance of such commitments. The point is that we do not believe a life lived for self alone is worthy of admiration. John Gardner points out that "all true religion is a path out of the quicksand of self-preoccupation and self-worship. Other such paths are commitments to one's family, to the community and to the betterment of the human condition."

Few observers have penetrated so deeply into the inner workings of American society than Alexis de Tocqueville. Even today, 163 years after the publication of his *Democracy in America*, most of his insights retain a relevance for contemporary society. De Tocqueville pointed out, the danger that faces democratic government is the passivity of the populace; the tendency for individuals to abandon their personal responsibility for social action. Because the voluntary sector provides the opportunity for personal involvement, it becomes the cement that binds our society together. Helping those least able to help themselves also illustrates De Tocqueville's observations that self-interest and volunteerism go hand in hand. "Americans," he said, "show how an enlightened regard for themselves constantly prompts them to assist one another and inclines them willingly to sacrifice a portion of their time and property to the welfare of the state."

Americans continue to take pride in this civic spirit and heritage as expressed in their philanthropic giving and their habits of volunteerism. Deeply rooted in our varied pasts as well as reflecting our religious values, and the constitutional convictions of our first amendments, these traditions of generosity have spawned an outstanding diverse set of institutions. They range from private schools and colleges and universities, to immigrant self-help groups, community-based organizations, policy think tanks, hospitals, museums and symphony orchestras, to grass roots movements, church-based social initiatives, medical charities, disaster relief organizations, foundations and federated fund raising groups—in other words, there is a group or organization to blend with your skills and interests and thereby enabling you to volunteer and make a difference. We can list the important substantive problems faced by our country and the world that cry out for amelioration if not solutions. That list includes problems such as: growing income inequity, deep-seated poverty, educational quality and accessibility to it, health and access to health care and domestic and transnational issues of the environment. We can also identify socially important areas that deserve strengthening, such as increasing access to and participation in arts and culture and integrating a diverse population made even more diverse as a consequence of demographic changes and immigration. And we can identify particular social institutions and networks that need to be bolstered, such as families, communities and civil society.

I have briefly described our American heritage based on the value of service and the state of our society with its myriad problems. This leads me to my second area: the need for personal commitment in our society. In the movie version of the *Wizard of Oz*, the Tin Woodsman joins Dorothy's Emerald City odyssey in hopes that the mighty wizard will give him a heart. His wish comes true when the wizard pronounces him a philanthropist, which he defines as "a doer of good deeds for the good of others."

The wizard's definition of philanthropy certainly works on this side of the rainbow, but not his powers. Here, no one appoints philanthropists. We chose the responsibility for ourselves. As surely as the future will bring new needs and new opportunities, it will also bring the need for new "philanthropists"—new doers of good deeds for the good of others.

We all, at whatever level (whether we're students, faculty, administration and a community person like myself), live with the reality of increasing change. We cannot prevent it, we can only hope to channel it in such a way as to preserve values and other essential continuances. We need to look for opportunities to engage ourselves in activities outside the classrooms and outside the campus and outside our homes to activities inside the community—activities that will enable us to test our judgments in action and perhaps to lead, to strengthen motivation for public service. For students, it can extend your capacity to relate to unfamiliar constituencies, to provide experiences to build self-confidence and self-reliance. Different experiences yield different benefits, but one would hope that any well conceived out-of-class experience would provide you one or more of the following:

• An opportunity to test your judgment under pressure, in the face of opposition and swiftly changing circumstances

• An opportunity to exercise responsibility and perhaps to try out one or another skill required for leadership

• An opportunity to sharpen and test your intuitive gifts and to judge their impact on others

• An opportunity for exposure to new "constituencies," and exposure to the untidy world where decisions must be made on inadequate information, where the soundest argument doesn't always win, where problems do not get fully solved or, if they are solved, they surface as a new problem in another form

We all need boundary-crossing experiences to find our way into unfamiliar culture; and to honor that culture's sensitivities and to develop empathy for its values and assumptions. For faculty and administrative staff—we haven't left you out—there is an urgent need to have your skills, knowledge and expertise to make a difference in rebuilding communities. The community and its organizations need you to cross boundaries and to make a difference and an impact in rebuilding community and assisting organizations to make a difference in people's lives. The health of our society is indivisible. When we allow social ills to spread through any segment of the community, the whole society suffers. The task of rebuilding community and assisting organizations poses challenges worthy of the best that is in us. I am aware of the tremendous contribution that Case Western Reserve University has made to Greater Cleveland. You have provided that dynamic thrust that our society has always had in the past and we don't want to face the danger of losing it.

Amitai Etzioni said, "No social, political, economic or moral order can survive [without personal involvement]. Some measure of caring, sharing, and being our brothers' and sisters' keepers is essential if we are not all to fall back on an even more alienated, deteriorated and unsafe community." So our responsibility as seasoned, responsible and competent adults and students is clear—

we've got to give of ourselves to rebuild the community and assist organizations to increase their effectiveness in making a difference in people's lives.

And now my final area: the challenge to live beyond self—and in the words of Henry VIII to one of his wives . . . "I won't keep you long."

Sometimes we are reluctant to become involved because we're not sure it will make a difference. I'm reminded of a cartoon in the *New Yorker* magazine: I want you to picture a bunch of wolves baying at a bright full moon in the sky. They are all in a full circle howling like crazy, except for one wolf. He turns to the wolf next to him and asks, "Do you think we are having an impact?"

Be confident that you can make an impact, that you can make a difference. Don't get overwhelmed. In Marion Wright Edelman's book, *The Measure of Our Success*, which is a letter to her children, she says, "Sometimes when I get frantic about all I have to do and spin my wheels, I try to recall Carlyle's advice, which is: 'Our main business is not to see what lies dimly at a distance, but to do what lies clearly at hand.'" Remember, she continues, "that sometimes it's important to lose for things that matter and that many fruits of your labor will not become manifest for many, many years. And do not think that you have to make big waves in order to contribute."

John Gardner, on the subject of responsibility, says, "Both aspects of myself are important—the part that is determined by my background, and the part that is mine to shape. Out of the first part, the behavior that links me with my species, my genetic line, my religious or cultural traditions, comes the deep identities that gives me a sense of oneness with something larger, and makes me feel at home in the universe. That part says to me: 'You are living a moment in the drama of human life on this earth. The great themes of birth and death, of love, sorrow, and suffering replay themselves through you. Don't imagine that you are unique or that your struggles are the turning point in the great train of events. Let the ancient drama go on, and take strength from your time-honored part in it.' But the other part of me, that part that is mine to command says, 'You can play your part well or badly. Play it well.'"

Arthur Ashe said, "Remember to achieve greatness, start where you are, use what you have, do what you can."

If we believe in living life beyond self, then we must not become servants of what is, but rather we must be shapers of what might be.

In Henry Emerson Fosdick's 1920 book on *The Meaning of Service*, he uses the analogy from the holy land—rivers that run parallel to human life.

The Sea of Galilee and the Dead Sea are made of the same water. It flows down, clear and cool, from the heights of Harmon to the roots of the cedars of Lebanon. The Sea of Galilee makes beauty of it, for the Sea of Galilee has an outlet—it gets to give. It gathers in its riches that it may pour them out again to fertilize the Jordan plain—but the Dead Sea, with the same water, makes a horror. For the Dead Sea has no outlet—"it gets to keep." Notice especially the phrase "it gets to give." "It is when you give of yourself that you truly give" (Kahlil Gibran).

I will not presume to tell you which direction you should go to live life beyond self, but I would advise you, however, not to follow Yogi Berra's suggestion of, "When you get to the fork in the road, take it." Rather, I would advise you to think on the words of Ralph Waldo Emerson, who challenges us when he advises, "Do not go where the path may be. Go instead where there is no path, and leave a trail." And I would say, it's not the miles you've come that count—it's the journey that you have yet to travel.

We humans have shown ourselves capable of nobility, of kindness, and of generosity. We must draw on our strength from those who exhibit the best that is in them. And, let us remember, "to everything there is a season, and a time to every purpose under the heaven." And if this be not your season, it will come. At least, let them say of you in the future—you cared enough to do the very best. This was the time you planned to serve; this was your seed time for reform. And remember—"Man is the only animal that laughs and weeps, for he is the only creature that is struck with the difference between what things are, and what they ought to be."

Peace be with you. ■

Careers in International Business: Five Ideas or Principles[2]

A speech by William E. Franklin, President, Franklin International, LTD, given at the Japan Business Association and International Business Society, Columbia University, April 8, 1998. After beginning with information that adapts well to his specific audience, he moves into the goal of his speech, a discussion of five ideas or principles about careers. Some of the features to look for are clarity of main points, excellence of audience adaptation throughout the speech, clear and vivid development of main points, and powerful conclusion.

I have been asked to lead a discussion today about careers in international business. I am honored and pleased to do so. Thank you for coming. There is a Japanese proverb that says "Rongo yomi no rongo shirazu" . . . just because you read Confucius does not necessarily mean you understand what he says. Just because I have worked and studied in Asia the past 25 years does not mean I understand everything about Asia. In fact, I spend more time studying about Asia today than when I first moved to Tokyo in 1973. So I would like to have this be a dialogue, more than a lecture, a sharing of experiences and ideas.

After I accepted your invitation I read the report on rankings of business schools and learned Columbia was awarded an overall ranking of 99%. And also, not unimportant, you rank number one in placement success with a median starting salary of $88,000 . . . a higher starting salary than graduates of any other business school in the world. With that kind of success perhaps you should be leading the discussion, with me in the audience. I really do want to hear your ideas, your questions . . . your comments, business questions, personal questions . . . anything that is on your mind.

I recently saw some demographic information which may help to bring perspective to your opportunities and responsibilities, some perspective on your place or role in the world.

If we shrink the world's 5.7 billion population to a village of 100 people . . . with all existing human ratios remaining the same, here is the resulting profile.

Of these 100 people 57 are Asian, 21 European, 14 from North and South America and 8 from Africa.

51 female, 49 male

80 live in sub-standard housing

70 cannot read

Half suffer from malnutrition

75 have never made a phone call

Less than one is on the Internet

Half the entire village's wealth would be in the hands of 6 people

Only one of the hundred has a college education

You are in a very elite group of only 1% who have a college education. But you are even more elite and distinctive because you will soon graduate from what many consider to be the number one Graduate School of Business. The dictionary definition of elite is "the choice part" . . . "a powerful minority group." Whether you realize it or not the fact is that you are the choice part . . . and you have the power of education and knowledge.

Of course that does not guarantee you a good life . . . having that degree does not guarantee you anything. Your graduation will merely be the beginning of a new phase of learning in your life. I personally think the most valuable thing you can learn in any university is to develop your own personal method of learning so you can be a good student the rest of your life.

But being part of this very elite group does give you the potential for power and wealth . . . probably much more than you now realize. Many of you will be important global business leaders . . . some of you will be important government leaders. You will have far more power than you now realize . . . power to enhance the quality of your personal life . . . power to help others in the world who are less fortunate than yourself. It's not too early to begin thinking seriously about your personal values . . . and how you will use your power.

Now why do I talk about all that? Well, you don't have very much uncertainty about finding a job and I would imagine most of you have given a lot of thought to selecting a challenging career.

Your larger question will be "how will you create a rich and rewarding and balanced life?" There are two things to aim for in life. One, to get what you want in life and two to enjoy it. Only the wisest of women and men achieve the second.

I will share with you five ideas or principles about careers, and about life because it is difficult to have a full discussion about your lifetime career without talking about your total life.

FIRST POINT . . . Learn from other cultures. Let me read a quote from a speech by an American . . . see if you can guess who said this. "We have a favorable balance of trade. But if you think you can maintain that balance just by sending salesmen to Japan and China as you would to Montana or Chicago, you are mistaken. You must send people to live there to learn the culture, to learn the language, to learn the way of doing business there." John Wheeler said that in his inaugural speech as the first President of the United States Chamber of Commerce in 1912.

Sometimes we are very diligent in learning about other cultures . . . but to be good leaders we want to learn from other cultures. The other day I was looking at some speeches I made eight or nine years ago . . . attempting to persuade skeptical American audiences that American business and American ideas were not finished . . . and that Asia was not going to take over the world. You may remember how pessimistic everyone was about America then.

Now in 1998, with America's current up cycle and Asia's economic problems, there is a temptation to totally flip-flop and say, only the America way is the right way . . . and reject all Asian values.

As future global leaders, I ask you to think about the possibility that a more rewarding approach is to learn from each other . . . and try to adopt and adapt the best from each culture.

Isis Berlin said "the great human delusion is monism . . . the proposition that there is a single, final solution . . . the ultimate over-arching truth." Sometimes Americans are so passionate about our ideals that we want the whole world to accept our ideals . . . and we feel some obligation to have all countries adopt our form of democracy . . . now. To accept our concept of human rights . . . now. To accept our rule of law . . . now. I think most Americans do this out of a sense of good purpose . . . but when we think that our ideals and institutions are the one best way for all cultures we automatically forgo the possibility of learning that other social and economic systems may have equal validity.

On my first trip to China almost 20 years ago, as part of a government delegation, I had the opportunity to meet Mr. Deng Xiao Peng. After the official government discussions he turned to me and said, "I understand your company has expertise in tree growing and in utilization of the forest resource. Our country needs to improve both . . . Will you help us?" We then met with the Minister of Forestry and that led to us becoming the principal forestry advisor to the PRC during the early 1980s. Mr. Deng said "it does not matter whether the cat is black or white as long as it helps to improve our country" . . . he was open to ideas from other cultures.

One time my friend, Mogi-san, was attempting to explain Japanese business philosophy to us. He said "you Americans always talk about fairness, arms length business transactions, objectivity, no favor to friends . . . very detailed contracts" all words that are pleasing to the ears of most American business women and men. He went on to say, "if we think that is a very cold way to do business we wouldn't want to do business that way. We want to do business with friends."

And later many American companies learned that in order to have a total quality system we needed to adopt some Japanese ideas with respect to customer and supplier relationships. Which, by the way, many Japanese tell me they learned a lot about from Dr. Frederic Demming. We learned from each other.

There is a Zen saying . . . "in a beginner's mind there are many possibilities, in the expert's mind, there are none." I have observed in myself that I am a much better leader when I think of myself as a student of Asia than when I think of myself as an expert on Asia.

To be a good international leader it is not enough just to study other cultures. We need to learn from other cultures.

SECOND POINT. And closely related to the first point. This may sound contradictory to the first point, but it is not. We need to be very conscious of our personal values . . . personal values as defined by our behavior . . . not just what we say . . . but how we spend our time each day. Write them down so you can look at them . . . and update as you get new insights. Be aware you are forming habits today, good habits and bad habits, that you may have the rest of your life.

When you are selecting a company to join do some research to see if the company's values are consistent with your personal values. This is important. You will not do your best work with an organization and people whose values are incompatible with your values.

When I was at another university recently a student asked me "what's the biggest mistake you ever made?" My first response was that I had made so many it would be difficult to say which is the biggest. But later, after I had an opportunity to reflect, I said to this student "the biggest mistake I ever made was anytime I compromised my personal values."

And it usually does not happen in big ways with big issues . . . my values get compromised in small ways for small gains or no gains. One time I was offered a bribe of $1,000,000 on a project in southeast Asia. That was a no brainer; it is easy for anyone to decide what to do in a circumstance that is that black and white. But on a daily basis the choices are always in the gray areas where it is not so clear and the decision may seem so unimportant. But the cost for small compromises in your values is cumulative . . . and it can be a big cost to your effectiveness as a leader . . . a big cost to your total being. One needs to be vigilant every moment to see that doesn't happen.

I heard John Wayne say once ". . . perversion and corruption masquerade as ambiguity. I don't like ambiguity. I don't trust ambiguity." I don't like ambiguity either, but ambiguity is part of reality for an international leader. Your day to day life will not be so black and white as we like to see in John Wayne's movies. Always seek clarity, but learn to live with complexity and ambiguity.

And it is my observation that individuals who have strong personal values have the most freedom and ability and perspective to learn from other cultures. This is even more important in Asia. There is a generalization that Japanese business leaders are selected based on their character, American business leaders selected for their competence. I believe that is changing . . . the integrity and character of an American business leader is more important than it may have been at one time . . . and Japanese are giving more weight to competence.

When I moved back to my home country last year I saw a survey that says a majority of Americans think a businessman will do anything for money. A politician will do anything for a vote. A journalist will do anything for a story. That simply is not true.

Be true to your personal values. That will be your greatest strength.

THIRD POINT. Leadership. Take any opportunity to experience leadership. It is helpful to study leadership, and study other great leaders. But you only learn leadership by experiencing leadership. You only learn leadership by being a leader. You learn leadership by leading a study project, by being secretary of the camera club, by having a part time job, by introducing a speaker.

There will always be temporary shortages of certain technical skills but the law of supply and demand will correct that imbalance. But I have never been in any organization that had enough proven leadership.

Some say leaders are made. Some say leaders are born. It is really not too important whether leaders are made or born . . . because all of us have leadership potential that is never discovered . . . or discovered late in life. I'm talking about leaders who bring about win-win solutions. It's been my experience whether it be trade negotiations or internal corporate competition, only win-win solutions last.

The opening of the Japan building products market is an example of a win-win outcome. I will relate it to you briefly because it has some applicability to trade negotiations in general.

Twenty years ago Japan's residential building codes included many restrictive materials based specifications. Wood was excluded from many uses. Working cooperatively, the North American and Japanese industry and government groups asked the Japanese regulatory agencies to consider using scientific tests to move from materials-based specifications to performance-based specifications. Wood would be required to pass the same fire and earthquake tests as steel, concrete or any other building material . . . but not be prohibited just because it is wood.

After a very long process the regulations were modified to be more performance based. Because leaders in Japan and North America took a win-win approach there is a true win-win outcome. Japanese producers have more business. Foreign suppliers have more business. Wood housing boomed in Japan.

And, most important, the Japanese people are the big winners with high quality, lower cost, safe wood homes. During the Kobe earthquake 2 × 4 wood frame homes proved to be the safest of all. In the 21st century effective leaders will be win-win leaders.

When you have different job opportunities ask yourself which job will give me the best opportunity to experience leadership. When you are starting out with your career many times the worst place to work is the corporate headquarters . . . because a young person has so little opportunity to experience leadership. You are usually better off to take any job in the field where you have measurable accountability for the results of an operation, no matter how small.

Don't confuse being close to leaders at the corporate headquarters with leading. Don't confuse having proximity to power with actually having power. Experience leadership.

FOURTH POINT. Persevere. Johann Goethe, the German philosopher said "in the realm of ideas everything depends on enthusiasm . . . in the real world all rests on perseverance." I heard Paul Newman being interviewed recently. He was asked what makes the difference . . . "why do some actors become very successful and some do not . . . is it luck, is it timing, is it connections . . . or, in the end, doesn't talent rule out?" His response was "no . . . the most important element for an actor to succeed is tenacity."

Nothing will be more important to your getting what you want than perseverance . . . many times making that one final effort when you feel mentally and physically exhausted will be just enough to put you across the finish line.

When you join your new organization you will see many things that need to be changed. I don't know about universities but in corporations you are going to find many people are opposed to change, they will persuasively deny it's necessary. There's a line in a Grateful Dead song, "Denial ain't just a river in Egypt."

Many years ago I heard Jack Welsh being quizzed about how he was bringing about change at GE. He said "change has no constituency." Don't confuse what I said about win-win solutions with waiting until you get consensus before implementing needed changes . . . it will be a long wait. Don't expect applause for making change at least not while you are doing it. Expect failure, rejection and humiliation sometimes.

I keep something on my desk that says "growth involves confusion and pain, moving from the comfortable known to the uncomfortable unknown." Most of us do not welcome confusion and pain . . . even when it is necessary and beneficial for us. You will need perseverance to bring about change.

There is a Zen saying "before enlightenment chop wood, carry water . . . after enlightenment . . . chop wood, carry water." An effective international leader does a lot of chopping wood and carrying water.

Perseverance.

And finally Network. Network. Network. If the U.S. is characterized as a market economy then Japan might be called a network system. And that is true to some degree in many Asian countries. In any culture that is influenced more by rule of man rather than rule of law, networking is not an optional part of doing business . . . it's a requirement for successful business. In many Asian countries it is more customary to do business with friends. And traditional Chinese take it even one step further . . . the business is most often a family business.

Many of us talk about when China adopts the rule of law . . . as if that is inevitable and imminent. Many Chinese do not feel the rule of law is a necessary aspect of the human condition. Confucius said laws are too inflexible to handle all the diversity of human experiences. Chinese say they prefer to trust people, not laws.

Akio Morita, the co-founder of Sony, a fine man and a global thinker long before most of us . . . was being questioned at a dinner one day about the closed Japan market. Finally Morita-san said "well, technically the Japan market is open, it's just that sometimes the door is so small that it's hard for you big guys to get in." His good humor got him off the hook that day but there was as much truth as humor in what he said. The system is designed to do business the Japanese way. Networking is not something you do in your spare time, it's an essential part of business.

To summarize

FIRST IDEA. Learn from other cultures.

SECOND. Be true to your personal values. You will learn that success, on the whole, success depends more on character than either intellect or luck.

THIRD IDEA. Take any opportunity to experience leadership. Leadership must be experienced to be learned.

FOURTH. In the realm of ideas everything depends on enthusiasm, in the real world all rests on perseverance.

AND FINALLY. Network. Network. Network.

Baron Charles Montesquieu said a couple hundred years ago, "Commerce is the best cure for prejudice, peace is the natural effect of trade." If that was true in the 18th century it will be even more true in the 21st century. Trade and investment bring more than just money and goods, they bring ideas. As 21st century leaders you have great opportunity to help us all to overcome prejudice and bring about understanding and peace for all people. I have great confidence that is what you will do. ∎

Other Speeches

You can learn a great deal from reading contemporary speeches presented by a variety of speakers in many settings. I suggest beginning with the following two speeches:

Baker, William F. "The Lost Promise of Television." *Vital Speeches*, September 1, 1998, pp. 684–689.

Heimbold, Charles A. "Attributes and Formation of Good Leaders: Success Is Doing Things Right." *Vital Speeches*, January 1, 1999, pp. 179–184.

I suggest these two because in both cases the content is provocative and the ideas are well presented. To access these and the following speeches, using InfoTrac College Edition, click on PowerTrac. Press on Keyword and drag down to Title. Then enter the title, such as "The lost promise of television." For further suggestions, I offer the following:

Brownback, Sam. "Free Speech: Lyrics, Liberty and License." *Vital Speeches*, May 15, 1998, pp. 454–456.

Conroy, William R. "Never Give Up: The Power of Perseverance." *Vital Speeches*, October 15, 1998, pp. 29–31.

Corlett, Candace. "Shattering the Stereotypes of the 50+ Shopper." *Vital Speeches*, May 15, 1998, pp. 478–480.

Fraser, Edie. "Salute to Women for our Economic Success: And Just You Wait for the New Millennium." *Vital Speeches*, July 15, 1998, pp. 598–600.

Kors, Alan Charles. "Morality on Today's College Campuses: The Assault upon Liberty and Dignity." *Vital Speeches*, August 1, 1998, pp. 633–637.

Lamm, Richard. "Unexamined Assumptions: Destiny, Political Institutions, Democracy and Population." *Vital Speeches*, September 15, 1998, pp. 712–714.

MacCluggage, Reid. "Edit More Skeptically: Question, Question, Question." *Vital Speeches*, December 15, 1998, pp. 141–143.

Sommers, Christina Hoff. "Are We Living in a Moral Stoneage? Teaching the Literary Classics." *Vital Speeches*, May 15, 1998, pp. 475–478.

Notes

Chapter 1

1. Dan B. Curtis, Jerry L. Winsor, and Ronald D. Stephens, "National Preferences in Business and Communication Education," *Communication Education* 38 (January 1989): 11.

2. *The Wall Street Journal*, Tuesday, December 29, 1998, p. A1.

3. *Statistical Abstract of the United States*, 1997, p. 14.

4. Allan Carpenter, *Facts about Cities*, 2d ed. (New York: H. W. Wilson, 1996).

5. Edith R. Horner, ed. *Almanac of the 50 States: Basic Data Profiles with Comparative Tables* (Palo Alto, CA: Information Publications, 1998).

6. William B. Gudykunst, *Bridging Differences: Effective Intergroup Communication* (Newbury Park, CA: Sage, 1991), p. 44.

7. Peter Andersen, "Explaining Intercultural Differences in Nonverbal Communication," in Larry A. Samovar and Richard E. Porter, eds., *Intercultural Communication: A Reader*, 7th ed. (Belmont, CA: Wadsworth, 1994), p. 229.

8. Richard L. Johannesen, *Ethics in Human Communication*, 3d ed. (Prospect Heights, IL: Waveland Press, 1990), p. 1.

9. Patricia Edmunds, "America's Escalating Honesty Crisis," *USA Weekend* (October 16–18, 1998): 14–15.

10. Carl Wellman, *Morals and Ethics*, 2d ed. (Englewood Cliffs, NJ: Prentice-Hall, 1988), p. 305.

11. M. S. Pritchard, *On Becoming Responsible* (Lawrence: University of Kansas Press, 1991), p. 39.

12. Brian Spitzberg, "A Model of Intercultural Communication Competence," in Larry A. Samovar and Richard E. Porter, eds., *Intercultural Communication: A Reader*, 8th ed. (Belmont, CA: Wadsworth, 1997), p. 379.

13. Gerald M. Phillips, *Communication Incompetencies: A Theory of Training Oral Performance Behavior* (Carbondale: Southern Illinois University Press, 1991).

Chapter 2

1. Gerald Phillips, "Rhetoritherapy versus the Medical Model: Dealing with Reticence," *Communication Education* 26 (1977): 37.

2. *Ibid.*

3. Theodore Clevenger, Jr., "A Synthesis of Experimental Research in Stage Fright," *Quarterly Journal of Speech* 45 (April 1959): 136.

4. Gerald Phillips, *Communication Incompetencies: A Theory of Training Oral*

Performance Behavior (Carbondale: Southern Illinois University Press, 1991), p. 6.

5. Kathleen Ellis, "Apprehension, Self-Perceived Competency, and Teacher Immediacy in the Laboratory-Supported Public Speaking Course: Trends and Relationships," *Communication Education* 44 (January 1995): 73.

6. Heidi M. Rose, Andrew S. Rancer, and Kenneth C. Crannell, "The Impact of Basic Courses in Oral Interpretation and Public Speaking on Communication Apprehension," *Communication Reports* 6 (Winter 1993): 58.

7. Joe Ayres and Theodore S. Hopf, "The Long-Term Effect of Visualization in the Classroom: A Brief Research Report," *Communication Education* 39 (January 1990): 77.

8. Phil Scott, "Mind of a Champion," *Natural Health* 27 (Jan.–Feb. 1997): 99.

9. Joe Ayres, Tim Hopf, and Debbie M. Ayres, "An Examination of Whether Imaging Ability Enhances the Effectiveness of an Intervention Designed to Reduce Speech Anxiety, *Communication Education* 43 (July 1994): 256.

10. Virginia P. Richmond and James C. McCroskey, *Communication: Apprehension, Avoidance, and Effectiveness*, 2d ed. (Scottsdale, AZ: Gorsuch Scarisbrick, 1989), pp. 94–101.

11. Virginia P. Richmond and James C. McCroskey, *Communication: Apprehension, Avoidance, and Effectiveness*, 4th ed. (Scottsdale, AZ: Gorsuch Scarisbrick, 1995), p. 98.

12. *Ibid.*, p. 102.

13. Delivered in speech class, University of Cincinnati. Used with permission of Andy Gilgoff.

Chapter 3

1. Andrew Wolvin and Carolyn Gwynn Coakley, *Listening*, 4th ed. (Dubuque, IA: Brown & Benchmark, 1996), p. 69.

2. Michael Purdy, "What Is Listening?" in Michael Purdy and Deborah Borisoff, eds., *Listening in Everyday Life: A Personal and Professional Approach*, 2d ed. (New York: University Press of America, 1997), p. 4.

3. Lyman K. Steil, Larry L. Barker, and Kittie W. Watson, *Effective Listening* (Reading, MA: Addison-Wesley, 1983), p. 51. See also C. Day, "How Do You Rate as a Listener?" *Industry Week* 205 (April 28, 1980): 30–35; and R. W. Rasberry, "Are Your Students Listening? A Method for Putting Listening Instruction into the Business Communication Course," *Proceedings*, Southwest American Business Communication Association Spring Conference (1980): 215.

4. Joan Gorham, "The Relationship Between Verbal Teacher Immediacy Behaviors and Student Learning," *Communication Education* 37 (1988): 51.

5. Wolvin and Coakley, *Listening*, p. 239.

Chapter 5

1. R. B. Rubin, A. M. Rubin, and L. J. Piele, *Communication Research: Strategies and Sources*, 4th ed. (Belmont, CA: Wadsworth, 1996).

2. Joanna Zakalik, ed., and Sara Burak, assoc. ed., *Gale Guide to Internet Databases* (Belmont, CA: Gale Research, 1995).

3. John A. Courtright and Elizabeth M. Perse, *Communicating Online: A Guide to the Internet* (Mountain View, CA: Mayfield, 1998), pp. 106–108.

4. Craig T. Tengler and Frederic M. Jablin, "Effects of Question Type, Orientation, and Sequencing in the Employment Screening Interview," *Communication Monographs* 50 (1983): 261.

5. Shirley Biagi, *Interviews That Work: A Practical Guide for Journalists*, 2d ed. (Belmont, CA: Wadsworth, 1992), p. 94.

6. John Ahladas, "Global Warming," *Vital Speeches* (April 1, 1989): 382.

7. Donald Baeder, "Chemical Wastes," *Vital Speeches* (June 1, 1980): 497.

8. William E. Franklin, "Careers in International Business: Five Ideas or Principles," *Vital Speeches* (September 15, 1998): 719.

9. Randall Tobias, "In Today Walks Tomorrow: Shaping the Future of Telecommunication," *Vital Speeches* (February 15, 1993): 273.

10. Steven Trachtenberg, "Five Ways in Which Thinking Is Dangerous," *Vital Speeches* (August 15, 1986): 653.

11. G. Michael Durst, "The Manager as a Developer," *Vital Speeches* (March 1, 1989): 309–310.

12. Catherine Ahles, "The Dynamics of Discovery: Creating Your Own Opportunities," *Vital Speeches* (March 15, 1993): 352.

13. C. Charles Bahr, "Sick Companies Don't Have to Die," *Vital Speeches* (September 1, 1988): 685.

Chapter 7

1. Wendy Liebermann, "How America Shops," *Vital Speeches*, July 15, 1998, p. 595.

2. Earnest W. Deavenport, "Walking the High Wire: Balancing Stakeholder Interests," *Vital Speeches*, November 15, 1995, p. 49.

3. Dana G. Mead, "Courage to Grow: Preparing for a New Commercial Century," *Vital Speeches*, May 15, 1998, p. 465.

4. David Boaz, "Liberty vs. Power: The Eternal Struggle." *Vital Speeches*, September 1, 1998, p. 698.

5. Nancy W. Dickey, "Packing My Bag for the Road Ahead: Everyone's Access to Medicine," *Vital Speeches*, September 15, 1998, p. 717.

6. Edward E. Crutchfield, Jr., "Profitable Banking in the 1980's," *Vital Speeches*, June 15, 1980, p. 537.

7. William E. Franklin, "Careers in International Business: Five Ideas or Principles," *Vital Speeches*, September 15, 1998, p. 721.

8. Richard Lamm, "Unexamined Assumptions: Destiny, Political Institutions, Democracy and Population," *Vital Speeches*, September 15, 1998, p. 714.

Chapter 9

1. Michael E. Patterson, Donald F. Danscreau, and Dianna Newbern, "Effects of Communication Aids on Cooperative Teaching," *Journal of Educational Psychology* 84 (1992), 453–461.

2. Barbara Tversky, "Memory for Pictures, Maps, Environments, and Graphs," in David G. Payne and Frederick G. Conrad, eds., *Intersections in Basic and Applied Memory Research* (Mahwah, NJ: Laurence Erlbaum, 1997), pp. 257–277.

3. Joe Ayres, "Using Visual Aids to Reduce Speech Anxiety," *Communication Research Reports*, June–December 1991, 73–79.

Chapter 10

1. Richard Weaver, "Language Is Sermonic," in James L. Golden, Goodwin F. Berquist, and William E. Coleman, eds., *The Rhetoric of Western Thought*, 6th ed. (Dubuque, IA: Kendall/Hunt, 1997), p. 178.

2. C. K. Ogden and I. A. Richards, *The Meaning of Meaning* (London: Kegan, Paul, Trench, Trubner, 1923).

3. M. L. Hecht, M. J. Collier, and S. A. Ribeau, *African American Communication: Ethnic Identity and Cultural Interpretation* (Newbury Park, CA: Sage, 1993), p. 84.

4. W. B. Gudykunst and Y. Matsumoto, "Cross-cultural Variability of Communication in Personal Relationships," in W. B. Gudykunst, S. Ting-Toomey, and T. Nishida, eds., *Communication in Personal Relationships Across Cultures* (Thousand Oaks, CA: Sage, 1996), p. 21.

5. G. Hofstede, *Cultures and Organizations: Software of the Mind* (New York: McGraw-Hill, 1991), p. 67.

6. D. Levine, *The Flight from Ambiguity* (Chicago: University of Chicago Press, 1985), p. 28.

7. Beverly Chiodo, "Choose Wisely," *Vital Speeches*, November 1, 1987, 42.

8. For instance, in his analysis of language, Walter Nash discusses more than 20 figures of syntax and semantics. Walter Nash, *Rhetoric: The Wit of Persuasion* (Cambridge, MA: Basil Blackwell, 1989), pp. 112–129.

9. Robert H. Schertz, "Deregulation: After the Airlines, Is Trucking Next?" *Vital Speeches*, November 1, 1977, 40.

10. Carl Wayne Hensley, "Speak with Style and Watch the Impact: Make Things Happen," *Vital Speeches*, September 1, 1995, 703.

11. Gerry Sikorski, "Will and Vision," *Vital Speeches*, August 1, 1986, 615.

12. Reed E. Hundt, "Serving Kids and the Community: Do We Want TV to Help or Hurt Children?" *Vital Speeches*, September 1, 1995, 675.

13. Ronald W. Roskens, "Webs of Sand," *Vital Speeches*, February 1, 1986, 233.

14. James N. Sites, "Chemophobia," *Vital Speeches*, December 15, 1980, 154.

15. Sheridan Baker, *The Complete Stylist and Handbook* (New York: Thomas Y. Crowell, 1966), pp. 73–74.

Chapter 11

1. Judee K. Burgoon, Deborah A. Coker, and Ray A. Coker, "Communicative Effects of Gaze Behavior: A Test of Two Contrasting Explanations," *Human Communication Research* 12 (1986): 495–524.

2. K. E. Menzel and L. J. Carrell, "The Relationship between Preparation and Performance in Public Speaking," *Communication Education* 43 (1994): 23.

3. Delivered in speech class, University of Cincinnati. Used with permission of Roxanne Butler.

Chapter 12

1. H. J. Eysenck, "The Measurement of Creativity," in M. A. Boden, ed., *Dimensions of Creativity* (Cambridge, MA: MIT Press, 1994), p. 200.

2. Carol Koehler, "Mending the Body by Lending an Ear: The Healing Power of Listening." *Vital Speeches*, June 15, 1998, 543–544.

3. Delivered in speech class, University of Cincinnati. Used with permission of Jennifer Howell Streyle.

4. Delivered in speech class, University of Cincinnati. Used with permission of Doug Jaclin.

5. Richard Weaver, "Language Is Sermonic," in R. L. Johanannesen, R. Strickland, and R. T. Eubanks, eds., *Language Is Sermonic* (Baton Rouge: Louisiana State University Press, 1970), p. 212.

6. Delivered in speech class, University of Cincinnati. Used with permission of Wendy Finkleman.

Chapter 13

1. Richard Weaver, "Language Is Sermonic," in James L. Golden, Goodwin F. Berquist, and William E. Coleman, eds., *The Rhetoric of Western Thought*, 6th ed. (Dubuque, IA: Kendall Hunt, 1997), p. 178.

2. Richard E. Petty and Cacioppo, *Attitudes and Persuasion: Classic and Contemporary Approaches* (Boulder, CO: Westview, 1996), p. 7.

3. Kay Deaux, Francis C. Dane, and Lawrence S. Wrightsman, *Social Psychology in the '90s*, 6th ed. (Pacific Grove, CA: Brooks/Cole, 1993), p. 19.

4. Herbert L. Petri, *Motivation: Theory, Research, and Applications*, 4th ed. (Belmont, CA: Wadsworth, 1996), p. 3.

5. Wayne Weiten, *Themes and Variations* (Pacific Grove, CA: Brooks/Cole, 1995), p. 711.

6. Betsy Burke, speech on euthanasia delivered in speech class, University of Cincinnati. Portions used with permission of Betsy Burke.

7. Kenneth E. Anderson and Theodore Clevenger, Jr., "A Summary of Experimental Research in Ethos," *Speech Monographs* 30 (1963): 59–78.

8. See particularly Glen Fisher, "International Negotiation," in Larry A. Samovar and Richard E. Porter, eds., *Intercultural Communication: A Reader*, 5th ed. (Belmont, CA: Wadsworth, 1988), pp. 192–200; Devorah A. Lieberman, "Ethnocognitivism, Problem Solving, and Hemisphericity," in Larry A. Samovar and Richard E. Porter, eds., *Intercultural Communication: A Reader*, 7th ed. (Belmont, CA: Wadsworth, 1995), pp. 178–193; and Robert A. Friday, "Contrasts in Discussion Behaviors of German and American Managers," in Larry A. Samovar and Richard E. Porter, eds., *Intercultural Communication: A Reader*, 7th ed. (Belmont, CA: Wadsworth, 1995), pp. 274–285.

9. Delivered in speech class, University of Cincinnati. Used with permission of Elizabeth Helphinstine.

Chapter 14

1. Stephen Toulmin, *The Uses of Argument* (Cambridge: Cambridge University Press, 1958).

2. *Ibid.*

3. Delivered in speech class, University of Cincinnati. Used with permission of Michelle E. Wudke.

4. Herbert L. Petri, *Motivation: Theory, Research, and Applications*, 4th ed. (Belmont, CA: Wadsworth, 1996), p. 3.

5. *Ibid.*, p. 185.

6. John W. Thibaut and Harold H. Kelley, *The Social Psychology of Groups* (New York: Wiley, 1959), p. 10.

7. Petri, *Motivation*, p. 316.

8. Abraham H. Maslow, *Motivation and Personality* (New York: Harper & Row, 1954), pp. 80–92.

9. Delivered in speech class, University of Cincinnati. Used with permission of Dana Bowers.

10. The following two speeches are based on a debate between Sheila Kohler and Martha Feinberg presented at the University of Cincinnati, and are used here with their permission.

Chapter 16

1. See Bernard M. Bass, *Bass and Stogdill's Handbook of Leadership: Theory, Research, and Managerial Applications*, 3d ed. (New York: Free Press, 1990), pp. 19–20.

2. Marvin E. Shaw, *Group Dynamics: The Psychology of Small Group Behavior*, 3d ed. (New York: McGraw-Hill, 1981), p. 325.

3. Ralph White and Ronald Lippitt, "Leader Behavior and Member Reaction in Three 'Social Climates,'" in Dorwin Cartwright and Alvin Zander, eds., *Group Dynamics*, 3d ed. (New York: Harper & Row, 1968), p. 334. The point that groups are largely unproductive under laissez-faire leadership is reinforced by Bass, *Handbook of Leadership*, p. 559.

4. Fred E. Fiedler, *A Theory of Leadership Effectiveness* (New York: McGraw-Hill, 1967).

5. Dore Butler and Florence L. Geis, "Nonverbal Affect Responses to Male and Female Leaders: Implications for Leadership Evaluations," *Journal of Personality and Social Psychology* 58 (1990): 54.

6. Sally Helgesen, *The Female Advantage: Woman's Ways of Leadership* (New York: Doubleday, 1990).

7. William E. Jurma and Beverly C. Wright, "Follower Reactions to Male and Female Leaders Who Maintain or Lose Reward Power," *Small Group Research* 21 (1990): 110.

8. Patricia H. Andrews, "Sex and Gender Differences in Group Communication: Impact on the Facilitation Process," *Small Group Research* 23 (1992): 90.

9. John K. Brilhart and Gloria J. Galanes, *Effective Group Discussion*, 8th ed. (Madison, WI: Brown & Benchmark, 1995), p. 107.

10. William B. Gudykunst and Young Yun Kim, *Communicating with Strangers: An Approach to Intercultural Communication*, 2d ed. (New York: McGraw-Hill, 1992), pp. 42–43.

11. Brilhart and Galanes, *Effective Group Discussion*, p. 107.

Appendix

1. Geneva B. Johnson, "Service: Life Beyond Self," *Vital Speeches*, October 1, 1998, pp. 766–768. Reprinted by permission of *Vital Speeches* and Geneva B. Johnson.

2. William E. Franklin, "Careers in International Business: Five Ideas or Principles," *Vital Speeches*, September 15, 1998, pp. 719–722. Reprinted by permission of *Vital Speeches* and William E. Franklin, President, Franklin International, Ltd.

Glossary

abbreviated outline speaker's outline of key sentences, phrases, and words

accent the inflection, tone, and speech habits typical of the natives of a particular country, region, state, or city

acceptance speech a response to a presentation speech

acronym a word formed from initial letters of each of the successive parts of a compound term, a common word made up of the first letters of objects or concepts, or a sentence made up of words whose initial letters signal something else

active listening behaviors specific behaviors that turn a speech into a kind of dialogue

adaptation relating a speech to audience interests and needs

agenda an outline of the topics that need to be covered at a meeting

analyzing speeches determining the quality of the speech material—how truthful, authentic, or believable you judge the information to be—and the speaker's skill in communicating content, organization, language, visual aids, and delivery

anecdotes brief, often amusing stories

antonyms words that have opposite meanings

appeal to authority relying on the testimony of someone who is not an expert on the issue at hand

appeal type of conclusion that describes the behavior you want your listeners to follow

arguing the process of proving a proposition with factual information

arguing from analogy supporting a claim with a single example that is significantly similar to the subject of the claim

arguing from authority supporting a claim with one or more expert opinions

arguing from causation supporting a claim with one or more examples that come before and are related to the claim

arguing from definition supporting a claim with one or more characteristics that are primary criteria of an event

arguing from example supporting a claim with one or more individual examples

arguing from sign supporting a claim with one or more examples that act as indicators of the subject of the claim

argument a reason and its supporting evidence

articulation the shaping of speech sounds into recognizable oral symbols that combine to produce a word

association the tendency of one thought to stimulate recall of another, similar thought

attending the perceptual process of selecting specific stimuli from the countless stimuli reaching the senses

attitude a general or enduring positive or negative feeling about some person, object, or issue; usually expressed as an opinion

audience adaptation the active process of relating your speech material directly to your specific audience

audience analysis the study of the specific audience for a speech

bar graph a diagram that uses vertical or horizontal bars to show relationships between two or more variables at the same time or at various times on one or more dimensions

basic needs theory people are more likely to take action when a speaker's appeal satisfies a strong, unmet need in audience members

behavior an action related to or resulting from an attitude or a belief

behavioral nervousness physically displaying characteristics of nervousness

belief the cognitive, or mental, aspect of an attitude

brainstorming an uncritical, nonevaluative process of generating associated ideas

browser a device that serves as a kind of directory for accessing documents on the World Wide Web

channel both the route traveled by the message and the means of transportation

chart graphic representation that presents information in an easily interpreted format

chronological following an order that moves from first to last

chunking the reorganizing process of grouping like ideas

claim the proposition or conclusion to be proven

clear (main points) wording that is likely to call up the same images in the minds of all audience members

closed questions narrow-focus questions, ranging from those that require yes or no to those that require only a short answer

cognitive nervousness thinking about how nervous you're likely to be

cognitive restructuring a form of treatment for reducing nervousness that helps people to identify the illogical beliefs they hold and provides individualized instruction in formulating more appropriate beliefs

commemorative addresses speeches that are presented to celebrate national holidays or anniversaries of important dates or events

commencement address a speech presented by a major political, business, or social figure, or a prominent alumnus/a, during graduation ceremonies

common ground awareness that the speaker and audience share the same or similar information, feelings, and experiences

comparative advantages pattern an organization that places all the emphasis on the superiority of the proposed course of action

competence the impression that communication behavior is appropriate and effective

concrete words words that appeal to the senses or conjure up a picture

connotation the feelings or evaluations associated with a word

context the interrelated conditions of communication

context the surrounding verbal elements that help determine the specific meaning of a word

conversational quality a style of presentation that sounds like conversation to your listeners

cost-reward ratio cost of a behavior relative to the reward it brings

costs units of expenditure such as time, energy, money, or other negative outcomes

creativity a person's capacity to produce new or original ideas and insights

credibility the level of trust that an audience has or will have in the speaker

credible being seen by an audience as having knowledge and expertise, being trustworthy, and having an engaging personality

criteria satisfaction pattern an indirect organization that seeks audience agreement on criteria that should be considered when evaluating a particular proposition and then shows how the proposition satisfies those criteria

critical thinking an analytical and evaluative process using logic or reasoning to present information in a way that is likely to provide understanding, change a belief, or uncover problems in another person's informative or persuasive message

culture systems of knowledge shared by a relatively large group of people

data reasons and evidence (facts, opinions, observations, evidence, assumptions, or assertions) that support a claim or proposition

decoding the process of transforming messages back into ideas and feelings

demonstration going through a hands-on process in front of the audience

denotation direct, explicit meaning of a word; dictionary definition

determining effectiveness evaluating the extent to which a speaker has achieved his or her specific goal

diversity differences between and among people

electronic database information stored so that it can be retrieved from a computer terminal

emotions subjective experiences triggered by actions or words that are accompanied by bodily arousal and by overt behavior

encoding the process of transforming ideas and feelings into words, sounds, and actions

enthusiasm the excitement or passion about a topic

ethical issues focus on degrees of rightness and wrongness in human behavior

etymology the derivation or history of a particular word

examples specific instances that illustrate or explain a general factual statement

expert opinions interpretations and judgments made by authorities in a particular subject area

expository speech a general informative speech that seeks to convey understanding of an idea and that requires outside source material to give the speech depth

extemporaneous a speech that is carefully prepared and practiced, but with the exact wording determined at the time of utterance

extemporaneous speaking giving a speech that is researched, outlined, and practiced until the ideas of the speech are firmly in mind, but varying the wording from practice to practice and in the actual delivery

external noises the sights, sounds, and other stimuli that draw people's attention away from intended meaning

eye contact looking at various groups of people in all parts of an audience throughout a speech

facial expression eye and mouth movement

factual statements statements that can be verified

false cause attributing causation to an event that is not related to, or does not produce, the effect

feedback verbal and/or nonverbal responses to messages

flipchart large pad of paper

mounted on an easel, used for visual displays

fluent devoid of hesitations and vocal interferences

follow-up questions questions designed to pursue the answers given to primary questions

general goal the type of speech you are intending to give—entertaining, informing, or persuading

gestures movements of hands, arms, and fingers

graph a diagram that compares information

hasty generalization presenting a reason or other generalization supported by a single weak example or none at all

hierarchy of needs five categories arranged in order of importance: physiological needs, safety needs, belongingness and love needs, esteem needs, self-actualization needs

historical setting previous communication episodes

impromptu speech speech given on the spur of the moment

incentive a goal objective that motivates

intellectually stimulating information that is new to audience members and/or meets deep-seated needs to know

internal noises the thoughts and feelings that interfere with meaning

internal transitions words and phrases that link parts of a sentence in ways that help people see the relationships of the parts

internet an international electronic network of networks

interviewing the skillful asking and answering of questions

keynote address a speech presented near the beginning of an organization's conference or convention that is designed to inspire participants in their work

knowledge and expertise qualifications or capability—a track record

LCD liquid crystal display panel that sits on top of an overhead projector for displaying electronic visuals

leadership exerting influence to help a group achieve a goal

leadership styles patterns of behavior adopted by group leaders

leadership traits individual characteristics that predict an individual's success as a leader

leading questions questions phrased in a way that suggests the interviewer has a preferred answer

learning the speech understanding the ideas of the speech, but having the freedom to word the ideas differently each time

line graph a diagram that uses connected points to indicate changes in one or more variables over time

listening the process of receiving, attending to, and assigning meaning to aural and visual stimuli

logical reasons order organizing the main points of a speech with statements that indicate why the audience should believe something or behave in a particular way

main points complete-sentence representations of the ideas used in the thesis statement

manuscript speech speech that is written out completely and then read aloud

map pictorial representation of a territory

marking adding gender, race, age, or other designations unnecessarily to a general word

meaningful (main points) wording that is informative

message ideas and feelings presented to an audience through words, sound, and actions symbols that are selected and organized by the speaker and interpreted by members of the audience

metaphor like a simile, but instead of a direct comparison using *like* or *as*, builds a direct identification between the objects being compared

mnemonics memory aids

monotone a voice in which the pitch, volume, and rate remain constant, with no word, idea, or sentence differing significantly from any other

motivation forces acting on or within an organism to initiate and direct behavior

motivational pattern an organization that combines problem solving and motivation—it follows a problem solution pattern but includes required steps designed to heighten the motivational effect of the organization

movement motion of the entire body

narratives tales, accounts, personal experiences, or lengthier stories

nervousness a state of fear or anxiety about public speaking interaction

neutral questions questions phrased without direction from the interviewer

noise any stimulus that gets in the way of sharing meaning

open questions broad-based questions that ask the interviewee to provide whatever information he or she wishes

opinion verbal expression of a belief or attitude

oral style language that is instantly intelligible to the ear

organizational chart symbols and connecting lines used to diagram a complicated system or procedure

overhead transparencies acetate sheets projected onto a screen via an overhead projector

panel discussion discussion in which several participants (usually four to eight) discuss a topic spontaneously, under the direction of a leader and following a planned agenda

parallel (main points) wording that follows the same structural pattern, often using the same introductory words

paraphrase a statement in your own words of the meaning you have assigned to a message

personal pronouns pronouns referring directly to the person speaking, spoken to, or spoken about

personality the impression you make on your audience based on such traits as enthusiasm, friendliness, warmth, and a ready smile

personalize relate information to specific audience references

person-oriented leader one who encourages group participation to determine what will be done

persuasive speaking a process in which a speaker presents a message intended to affect beliefs or move an audience to act

physical setting the location, time of day, light, temperature, distance between communicators, and seating arrangements

pie graph a circular diagram that shows the relationship among parts of a single unit

pitch the highness or lowness of your voice

placement and sequencing constructing a list of items in such a way that the most important item comes last

plagiarism to steal and pass off the ideas and words of another as one's own, or to use a created production without crediting the source

poise assurance of manner

posture the position or bearing of the body that gives further evidence of poise

precise words words that most accurately or correctly capture the sense of what we are saying

presentation speech speech that presents an award, a prize, or a gift to an individual or a group

primary questions questions the interviewer plans ahead of time, serving as the main points for the interview outline

problem solution pattern an organization that first clarifies the nature of the problem, then proposes a solution and shows why it is the best one

problem-solving group discussion a systematic form of speech in which two or more persons meet face to face and interact orally to accomplish a particular task or to arrive at a solution to a common problem

process explanation telling how to do something, how to make something, or how something works

pronunciation the form and accent of various syllables of a word

proposition a persuasive speech goal

proximity a relationship to one's personal space

psychological setting the manner in which people perceive both themselves and those with whom they communicate

quality the tone, timbre, or sound of your voice

questions of fact concerned with the truth or falsity of an assertion

questions of policy judging whether a future action should be taken

questions of value making subjective judgments of quality

rate the speed at which you talk

reasoning the process of drawing inferences from factual information

reasoning process the conscious or subconscious thinking that leads from the data to the claim

reasons statements that tell why a proposition is justified

refutation the process of proving that an argument or series of arguments, or the conclusion drawn from that argument or those arguments, is false, erroneous, or at least doubtful

rehearsing practicing the presentation of a speech aloud

relevance the personal value that

people find in information when it relates to their needs and interests

repetition   saying the same words again

restatement   echoing the same idea in different words

retaining   storing information in memory and using techniques that will help you identify and recall that information

rewards   economic gain, good feelings, prestige, or other positive outcomes

rhetoric   the study of public speaking, often equated with persuasion

rhetorical questions   questions phrased to stimulate a mental response rather than an actual spoken response on the part of the audience

search engines   programs that help you locate information that is available on the World Wide Web

section transitions   complete sentences that link major sections of a speech

semantic noises   alternate meanings aroused by a speaker's symbols

serious   having physical, economic, or psychological impact

server or service provider   an agency that provides the necessary software for you to interface with electronic systems

setting   the location and occasion for a speech

simile   a direct comparison of dissimilar things

skimming   a method of rapidly going through a work to determine what is covered and how

slide   mounted transparency that can be projected individually

space order   organizing the main points of a speech by following a spatial or geographic progression

speaking appropriately   using language that adapts to the needs, interests, knowledge, and attitudes of the listener, and avoiding language that alienates

specific goal   a complete sentence that specifies the exact response the speaker wants from the audience

specific words   words that clarify meaning by narrowing what is understood from a general category to a particular group within that category

speech goal   what you want your listeners to know, believe, or do

speech notes   a word or phrase outline, plus hard-to-remember information such as quotations and statistics

speech of introduction   speech designed to pave the way for the main speaker

speech of tribute   speech that praises someone's accomplishments

speech plan   a written strategy for determining how you will use common ground, develop and maintain interest, ensure understanding, and cope with potential negative reactions to you as a speaker and/or your topic or goal

spontaneity   being so responsive to your ideas that the speech seems as fresh as a lively conversation, even though it has been well practiced

statement of logical reasons   a straightforward organization in which you present the best-supported reasons you can find, with your second strongest reason first and strongest reason last

statistics   numerical facts

stereotyping   assigning characteristics to people solely on the basis of their class or category

subject   a broad area of knowledge, such as the stock market, cognitive psychology, baseball, or the Middle East

survey   means of gathering information directly from people, often using a questionnaire

symposium   a discussion in which a limited number of participants (usually three to five) present individual speeches of approximately the same length dealing with the same subject

synonyms   words that have the same or nearly the same meanings

systematic desensitization   a form of treatment for reducing nervousness that involves using relaxation techniques while exposing people to the stimulus they fear

task-oriented leader   one who exercises more direct control over the group

thesis statement   a sentence that outlines the specific elements of the speech supporting the goal statement

timely   relating to now

time order (chronological order) organizing the main points of a speech as a sequence of ideas or events, focusing on what comes first, second, third, and so on

topic   some specific aspect of a subject

topic order   organizing the main points of a speech by categories or divisions of a subject

topical   following an order of headings

transitions   words, phrases, and sentences that show relationships between and among ideas, words, phrases, or sentences

trustworthiness   both character and apparent motives for speaking

understanding   the ability to decode a message by correctly assigning a meaning to it

URL   Uniform Resource Locator— the path name or "address" of any document on the World Wide Web

verbal clutter   use of extraneous words, unnecessary repetition of words, repetitious modifiers, and empty adjectives

visual aid   a form of speech development that allows the audience to see as well as hear information

visualization   a technique for reducing nervousness that involves developing a mental strategy and picturing yourself implementing that strategy successfully

vital information   information the audience perceives as a matter of life or death

vivid   full of life, vigorous, bright, intense

vocal expressiveness   vocal contrasts in pitch, volume, rate, and quality that affect the meaning audiences get from the sentences you present

volume   the loudness of the tone you make

warrant   a sentence created to verbalize the reasoning process

welcoming speech   speech that expresses pleasure for the presence of a person or an organization

word chart   a summary, list, or outline

Index

Page numbers in bold indicate definitions. Page numbers in italics indicate figures, checklists, or other special material.